FROM ABYSSINIAN TO ZION

COLUMBIA UNIVERSITY PRESS
New York

CONTEMPORARY PHOTOGRAPHS
by David W. Dunlap

HISTORICAL IMAGES
from the New-York Historical Society and other sources

FROM ABYSSINIAN TO ZION

A Guide to

Manhattan's

Houses of Worship

DAVID W. DUNLAP

Published in collaboration with the New-York Historical Society.
The author gratefully acknowledges assistance from
Furthermore, the publication program of the J. M. Kaplan
Fund, toward the costs of publishing this book.

COLUMBIA UNIVERSITY PRESS
Publishers Since 1893
New York   Chichester, West Sussex
Copyright © 2004 David W. Dunlap
Photographs not otherwise credited copyright © 2004 David W. Dunlap
Maps copyright © 2004 John Papasian

Eighty-eight entries appeared originally in different form in *Glory in Gotham: Manhattan's Houses of Worship* by David W. Dunlap and Joseph J. Vecchione, a City & Company guide published in 2001, and have been modified for use in this work with the permission of Joseph J. Vecchione and City & Company. In addition, fifty-nine photographs appeared in *Glory in Gotham*.

Library of Congress Cataloging-in-Publication Data
Dunlap, David W.
From Abyssinian to Zion : a guide to Manhattan's houses of worship / David W. Dunlap; contemporary photographs by David W. Dunlap; historical images from the New-York Historical Society and other sources.
    p. cm.
    Includes bibliographical references and index.
    ISBN 0-231-12542-9 (cloth: alk. paper)
    ISBN 0-231-12543-7 (pbk: alk. paper)
    1. Religious institutions—New York (State)—New York. 2. Church architecture—New York (State)—New York. 3. Manhattan (New York, N.Y.)—Religion. I. Title.
BL2527.N7D855 2004
200′.25′7471—dc22
  ⊜

Columbia University Press books are printed on permanent and durable acid-free paper.
Printed in the United States of America
Designed by Teresa Bonner
c 10 9 8 7 6 5 4 3 2 1
p 10 9 8 7 6 5 4 3 2 1

For Scott

CONTENTS

THE COMPLETE

FOREWORD

David W. Dunlap has proved more effectively than
even Henry Codman Potter, Stephen S. Wise, Adam
Clayton Powell Jr., Norman Vincent Peale, Felix Adler,
Paul Moore Jr., John Cardinal O'Connor, and Reverend Ike ever managed to do that New York is not a
godless city. Each of these people held sway over one
house of worship. Dunlap gives us more than a thousand, and in so doing he makes it clear that religious
buildings are as much a part of the fabric of New York
as brownstones. In *From Abyssinian to Zion: A Guide
to Manhattan's Houses of Worship*, Dunlap has done
what I would have thought to be impossible: he has
documented a wide swath of New York's social, cultural, and architectural history by viewing it through the
lens of a single building type. This book is organized
in the form of an encyclopedia, with alphabetical
entries of churches, synagogues, temples, and mosques
both past and present. The buildings are not organized
geographically, presumably to make certain that no
one treats this volume as nothing more than a guide-
book, and they are not organized chronologically, so it
cannot be confused with a conventional history. The
effect of reading *From Abyssinian to Zion*, however, is
to feel as though you have experienced both the best
aspects of a guidebook, since Dunlap whisks you all
around Manhattan, and the most appealing qualities
of a history, since he moves back and forth easily across
time.

This book is an extraordinary piece of research, but it also represents a conceptual leap, since who would have guessed that so much of the story of New York could be told through this one kind of building, an architectural category that never has been as closely identified with the city as skyscrapers or bridges or train stations or parks. While a great number of religious buildings are official city landmarks, few of them are in the category of those iconic structures that are emblematic of New York—St. Patrick's Cathedral, perhaps, or the Cathedral Church of St. John the Divine or Trinity Church and St. Paul's Chapel in lower Manhattan. The most important thing about *From Abyssinian to Zion* is to remind us not only how much more there is in the category of religious buildings than the famous ones and how prevalent they are in the cityscape, but also how deeply connected they are to the development of New York as a city.

This is a book about religious buildings, not about religion, and it is resolutely ecumenical. There are Buddhist temples and Islamic mosques as well as synagogues and churches of every imaginable Christian denomination. Dunlap has included even the Temple of Dendur, the Egyptian temple that was reconstructed under glass in the Sackler Wing of the Metropolitan Museum of Art. And why not? This book has no particular point of view about religious structures other than to imply that they are basically good things to have around. Dunlap is more interested in architectural and urban history than in ecclesiastical, and, like every good architectural historian, he knows that buildings are not inert objects, but mirrors of the world that created them and forces that are capable of acting on other eras, often with great power. Dunlap thinks a great deal about the effects of time, and if his book has any message, it is that buildings constructed for religious purposes are a vital part of the architectural legacy of Manhattan, that many of them have been lost, and that more of them are in danger of disappearing. We do not build churches, synagogues, and temples in the quantity that we once did; indeed, as *From Abyssinian to Zion* makes strikingly clear, relatively few houses of worship were constructed in the past generation, or even in the past half century. Of the religious buildings that survive, many are not used for worship any longer, which disturbs Dunlap far less than it might trouble a writer with a different sensibility. He is right, of course. Better to have a church function as a theater or community center than to have it disappear to make way for an office building. Dunlap helps us understand that the building that remains, even if its use has changed, is still a vehicle to display the passion of its builders and, in so doing, becomes a way of enriching the city and affecting the lives of those who come in contact with it.

Passion, of course, is the key. Every one of these buildings was created out of a deep reservoir of emotion, even if it is not always immediately visible in the final product, and that alone distinguishes these structures from so much of the commercial architecture of New York. Almost every religious building in Manhattan is worthy of a story and an affectionate description. Once, in New York as in cities all over the world, church spires were the defining elements on the skyline—Richard Upjohn's Trinity Church was the tallest structure in Manhattan from 1846 until the towers of the Brooklyn Bridge rose in the 1870s, and it was not for years more that a commercial building would surpass the bridge. For most of the nineteenth century, churches dominated the cityscape, and not only because of their height. They were also the buildings that offered drama, excitement, energy, and bedazzlement to a populace that, at least in those years, had relatively little in terms of a generous public realm.

As I read this book, I began to think that Dunlap knows all there is to be known about religious buildings in New York. But he wears his knowledge lightly and writes with warmth, grace, and wit. Who else could tell the story of the Church of the Strangers, which migrated from Mercer Street to West 57th Street, in terms of the movement of transients around New York? Or the history of the Little Church Around the Corner as a kind of mini-morality play? I suspect that every reader will find in this book favorite passages to treasure. Dunlap describes one of my favorite churches, St. Vincent Ferrer by Bertram Grosvenor Goodhue, by saying that "an ancient architectural vernacular is swept into the industrial age with piston-like buttresses, not unlike a great ecclesiastical locomotive." And on the Meeting House of the New York Society for Ethical Culture: "There are few sanctuaries as starkly imposing as this enormous cube...with massive walls facing Central Park like sheer cliffs of Indiana limestone. The paradox is that it was built by a humanistic movement known for its spirit of openness and welcome." Or the Eldridge Street Synagogue, which Dunlap describes as "a poignant mix of ruin and revival."

It is not only the makers of these religious buildings who have managed to communicate their passion. It is also David W. Dunlap himself, and we are all the richer for the way his love of New York shines through these pages.

Paul Goldberger

PREFACE

From Abyssinian to Zion: A Guide to Manhattan's Houses of Worship is heir to a tradition going back a century and a half, to Jonathan Greenleaf 's *History of the Churches, of All Denominations, in the City of New York, from the First Settlement to the Year 1846*. The next important survey was the "Shrines of Worship" chapter in *King's Handbook of New York City*, compiled by Moses King in 1893. The magnificent, six-volume *Iconography of Manhattan Island, 1498–1909*, by Isaac Newton Phelps Stokes, published from 1915 to 1928, gave detailed histories of nearly 200 churches and synagogues. In the late 1930s and early 1940s, the Historical Records Survey of the Works Progress Administration meticulously inventoried nearly 800 congregations. There are also dozens of denominational albums (John Gilmary Shea's *Catholic Churches of New York City* of 1878 being the most superb example) and congregational histories (foremost among them being the six-volume *History of the Parish of Trinity Church in the City of New York*, published from 1898 to 1962). A lesser known treasure is the Herman N. Liberman Photograph Collection at the New-York Historical Society. Liberman, a stockbroker, set out in 1966 to photograph every single house of worship he could find in Manhattan. Seven years later, he had produced four albums with 889 prints, depicting everything from St. Patrick's Cathedral to the Little Widow's Mite Baptist Church on West 135th Street. And Edward F. Bergman's *Spiritual Traveler: New York City* leads a recent crop of guidebooks to the city's sacred sites, which also includes Terri Cook's *Sacred Havens: A Guide to Manhattan's Spiritual Places* and Cynthia Hickman's *Harlem Churches at the End of the Twentieth Century: An Illustrated Guide.*

From Abyssinian to Zion was the idea of Joseph J. Vecchione, a friend and colleague at the *New York Times.* I wrote the first draft in 1991 to fulfill a 16-year incomplete on my senior paper in architectural history. Joe and I used that as the basis for our project, which split into two books, the first being *Glory in Gotham: Manhattan's Houses of Worship*, which complements its publisher's 50 Best and 100 Best series.

Unlike *Glory in Gotham*, which highlights 105 extant buildings, *From Abyssinian to Zion* describes 1,079 structures of architectural interest, 654 from the present and 425 from the past.

Frankly, I am biased toward the classic and the eccentric. My favorite building in New York is St. Paul's Chapel, because its civic utility has run from the bright day of George Washington's inauguration to the dark days of Ground Zero. And I think that the most perfectly beautiful house of worship in Manhattan— even though it is now an apartment building—is the Village Presbyterian Church. But I wish that I had been around to see the Church of the Holy Zebra, the Church of the Homely Oilcloth, and their mad Victorian kin.

"Architectural interest" can mean arresting modesty or surpassing plainness. However, it does not typically mean storefront or parlorfront sanctuaries with only a sign over the door to distinguish them. No disrespect is intended to these vital congregations. Rather, this book is more concerned with civic presence than religious function.

Because institutions move so frequently and buildings change hands so often, I thought that the most cohesive organizing thread would be the congregations themselves. They are arranged alphabetically by the first word of their proper names. The Church of the Holy Apostles is therefore not under *C*, but *H*. Similarly, Congregation Rodeph Sholom is not under *C*, but *R*.

In Hebrew transliterations, I tried to follow the spelling preferred by the congregations rather than impose a uniform orthography. This results in a few anomalies, such as Congregation Ansche Chesed appearing before Congregation Anshe

Baranove, thanks to the *c* in the first Ansche. English-language versions of congregational names are often subject to different interpretations. For example, one source will render Zedek as Righteousness; another, as Justice. I tried to be guided by congregational preferences, when they are known.

Hispanic Protestant churches are listed under their Spanish names. For consistency's sake, however, all the ethnic or national churches in the Roman Catholic archdiocese appear as entries under their English names, though the Spanish equivalent is often noted when it is in common use in a given parish: Encarnación, Nuestra Señora de la Guadalupe, San Judas, Santa Isabel, Santísimo Redentor.

When names are identical, alphabetization turns on denomination, even if it is not part of the title. Thus the Episcopal Church of the Holy Trinity precedes the Roman Catholic Church of the Holy Trinity. For congregations with distinct formal and popular names, I tried to honor the institutions' preference, expressed in signage, literature, and Web sites. Therefore, the Little Church Around the Corner shows up under *L*, not under *T* for Church of the Transfiguration. I also tried to hew to current congregational preference when a name has been rendered or spelled inconsistently over time or by different sources.

Buildings that have served several congregations or purposes appear most often under the name of their latest or last religious occupant. For instance, the Westside Theater, built as the Second German Baptist Church, is found under Rauschenbusch Memorial United Church of Christ, which it was most recently.

The cross-references are not comprehensive but are intended principally to help the contemporary reader with alternative names that either are now in use or have been in recent decades: Actors Studio, Carlebach Shul, Holy Communion, Limelight, Spanish and Portuguese Synagogue, Westside Theater, and so on.

Entries for merged parishes like Calvary and St. George's typically include the histories of all the preceding constituent bodies. Congregations that have spun off, as did numerous inner-city mission churches, are treated separately from their forebears.

Fixing the date for a congregation's origin can be tricky. Is it when the founders first met to discuss the possibility? Or when they adopted the name of their institution? Or when they incorporated? When they broke away from an older group? Or when the predecessor group began? Some of the dates in *From Abyssinian to Zion* may differ from those in other accounts, but they generally reflect the current usage of the congregations in question.

Equally vexing is the date of buildings. Sources vary widely. Some count construction as beginning with excavation; others, with the laying of the cornerstone. Some consider buildings complete when they are structurally enclosed, when they are partly used for the first time (numerous Catholic parishes have worshiped in basement sanctuaries while waiting for the main church upstairs to be finished), when they are entirely in use, when they are dedicated, or when they are consecrated. *From Abyssinian to Zion* generally offers a range of dates to indicate the span of time over which the house of worship was under way. Often, that begins with the year that the plan was filed, as recorded in the *Record and Guide Quarterly*, a real-estate publication. When the development period extended over parts of two successive years, a slash is used: 1967/1968.

Some denominations have changed names over time. What is now the United Methodist Church was once the Methodist Episcopal Church. Today's Episcopal Church was yesterday's Protestant Episcopal Church. The Collegiate churches were once more commonly referred to as Reformed Dutch. And the notion of Conservative and Reform Judaism is largely a product of the later nineteenth century. I have updated the names of existing congregations, like Broadway Temple United Methodist Church, but left alone historic names, like Asbury Methodist Episcopal Church.

Sometimes, what changes is not the name of the house of worship, but the street on which it sits. Among the major thoroughfares with double or triple identities are Sixth Avenue, also known as Avenue of the Americas below Central Park and as Lenox Avenue or Malcolm X Boulevard above; Seventh Avenue, called Adam Clayton Powell Jr. Boulevard above 110th Street; Eighth Avenue, which becomes Frederick Douglass Boulevard after its 51-block run as Central Park West; and St. Nicholas Avenue, also known as Juan Pablo Duarte Boulevard. Any and all of these names appear in the text, depending largely on chronological context. (It does not make much sense to say that Temple Israel was built on Malcolm X Boulevard.) One exception—with no offense intended to the memory of the greatest American clergyman of the twentieth century—is that 125th Street is always referred to as such, not as Dr. Martin Luther King Jr. Boulevard.

To follow the congregations' journeys over time, I relied on city directories published in the mid-nineteenth century by John Doggett Jr.; in the late nineteenth and early twentieth centuries by the Trow Directory, Printing and Bookbinding Company; in the early twentieth century by the *New York World*; and in the mid- to late twentieth century by the New York Telephone Company, especially the so-called criss-cross directories, which give listings by address rather than name.

In October 2002, I sent a 12-question survey to 399 houses of worship, primarily smaller, newer, poorer, or lesser-known congregations whose stories are not commonly told in New York guidebooks and histories. Fifty-one houses of worship, listed in the bibliography, responded with information about when they formed, where they worshiped, and whom they count among their leading clergy.

Although this book is mainly about architecture, there are many congregations whose stories simply cannot be told without reference to their spiritual leaders, from the incandescently liberal John Haynes Holmes to the immovably conservative John J. O'Connor. I confess a prejudice that will be evident anyway to the careful reader. I am more interested in the activists—since they seem to express the spirit of New York—than in the shepherds, vital as their pastoral role has been.

The Rosetta stone to all this information is the map key. Each of the 1,079 buildings has its own key number, corresponding to 24 neighborhood maps from [A] in lower Manhattan to [X] in Inwood and Marble Hill. A boldface key means that the building still stands. A lightface key means that it is gone. In the text, key numbers beginning with a [●] signify buildings that are extant. Those ending with a [☆] are in historic districts that have been created by the New York City Landmarks Preservation Commission, while those with a [★] are individually designated landmarks.

With a title like *From Abyssinian to Zion*, this book carries a special obligation to uptown Manhattan. About one-third of all the buildings described are north of 96th Street. The longest single entry (apart from Trinity Church, which takes in 10 chapels) is the Islamic Cultural Center, which I believe is the most important new house of worship to have been constructed in Manhattan in the second half of the twentieth century.

Even the longest entry is not very long, however. Squeezing more than 1,000 buildings into fewer than 300 pages has required a great deal of painful truncation and omission. In the process, errors have also undoubtedly crept into the text. This is by way of apologizing in advance to individual congregations, whose disappointment I anticipate since their stories are so much richer than these brief summaries can possibly intimate. It is also to invite corrections and suggestions.

Far from being the last word, *From Abyssinian to Zion* is meant to be an introduction—a window into a splendid architectural, artistic, cultural, spiritual, and social legacy, an image of its physical form and a record of the lives that have shaped it. It comes at a moment when the sacred cityscape, like New York itself, has never seemed more precious.

David W. Dunlap
New York, October 2003

ACKNOWLEDGMENTS

If you already have thumbed through this book and found yourself wondering how one person did all this—the answer is: he didn't. He couldn't possibly have. *From Abyssinian to Zion: A Guide to Manhattan's Houses of Worship* was a collaborative effort from the outset. I am pleased to acknowledge the many people who have helped shape this work, even if their names are not on the cover.

Joseph J. Vecchione heads the list because the book was his idea in 1990. We worked together on the project for more than a decade and had the satisfaction of seeing a shorter version published in 2001 as *Glory in Gotham: Manhattan's Houses of Worship*. He and Helene Silver of City & Company also allowed me to borrow liberally in this book from *Glory in Gotham*, and I thank them both.

Paul Gunther and Betsy Gotbaum of the New-York Historical Society come next because of their enormous enthusiasm for this project in its embryonic phase. Not only did they make the abundant resources of the society available on the most generous terms, but they also introduced us to Columbia University Press.

John L. Michel and William B. Strachan of the press were extraordinarily supportive as they committed to undertake a book of considerable complexity. Irene Pavitt brought a sharp eye for detail, a great knowledge of New York City, and a love of language to the daunting task of editing the manuscript. Fred Leise compiled the scrupulous index. Linda Secondari and Teresa Bonner designed the book, working graciously with a persnickety author. And Jeanie Lu helped prepare the manuscript for production.

Joan K. Davidson, president of Furthermore, the publication program of the J. M. Kaplan Fund, made possible several key features of the book, including the specially commissioned neighborhood maps and the purchase of more than 200 archival photographic prints. And there is no mentioning Furthermore without thanking Ann Birckmayer, the program associate.

John Papasian is responsible for the handsome and richly detailed maps, handling a most challenging and taxing assignment with artistry and good humor.

Paul Goldberger took a chance twenty-five years ago on a fledgling photographer to illustrate his guidebook, *The City Observed: New York, a Guide to the Architecture of Manhattan.* So in a very real sense, he launched the career that culminates in this volume, which he has ushered into the world with a heartening and thoughtful foreword.

Professor Vincent Scully and Dean Christa Dove permitted me to submit the first draft of this manuscript in 1991 to satisfy a 16-year-old obligation to finish my senior paper at Yale College (History of Art 91B).

Laurie Marcus of the Karpfinger Agency guided me skillfully to a contract. Barney M. Karpfinger has kept me as a client for a quarter of a century despite earnings that have rarely exceeded dozens of dollars. Andrew Alpern offered invaluable advice on copyright matters.

Christopher Gray, who writes the "Streetscapes" column in the *New York Times* Real Estate section, and his associate, Suzanne Braley, are virtually co-authors of this book. They helped me track down hundreds of architectural attributions that—I believe it is safe to say—never have been published in any architectural guide. Christopher opened the shelves and filing cabinets of his Office for Metropolitan History to me. He and Suzanne then dug in to find the information that eluded my research efforts.

Yeshaya Metal, the public service librarian/reference librarian of the YIVO Institute for Jewish Research at the Center for Jewish History, not only transliterated the names of nearly 100 congregations but helped put them into religious and historical context.

Anthony DePalma of the *New York Times* and Miriam Rodriguez DePalma of School 15 in Clifton, New Jersey, helped translate the names of almost 50 Spanish-speaking congregations and helped me understand the origins and significance of those names (and why some defied translation). The book benefited tremendously from discerning and enormously knowledgeable vetting. These readers contributed keen insights and steered me clear of many potential errors:

Michael Henry Adams, the author of *Harlem, Lost and Found: An Architectural and Social History, 1765–1915*, and guest curator of "Harlem Lost and Found" at the Museum of the City of New York.

Edward F. Bergman, professor of geography at Lehman College and the author of *The Spiritual Traveler: New York City: The Guide to Sacred Spaces and Peaceful Places*, which set a new standard for such guides.

Mary Beth Betts, the director of research at the New York City Landmarks Preservation Commission, who also helped the book in its earliest stages when she was at the New-York Historical Society.

Jeffrey S. Gurock, the Libby M. Klaperman Professor of Jewish History at Yeshiva University and the author of *When Harlem Was Jewish, 1870–1930*, and *American Jewish Orthodoxy in Historical Perspective*.

Michael J. Leahy, the real-estate editor of the *New York Times*, to whom I am further indebted for the broad latitude he has given me to pursue this book and the many opportunities he has given to me to write articles that have furthered my knowledge of the subject.

Because their comments and counsel informed *Glory in Gotham*, which is the nucleus for *From Abyssinian to Zion*, it is appropriate to acknowledge the first readers, too: Robert Braham, Laura M. Chmielewski, William G. Connolly, Andrew Scott Dolkart, Holly Kaye, Ken M. Lustbader, the Rev. Richard R. McKeon, Rosalie R. Radomsky, the Right Rev. Catherine S. Roskam, Mervyn Rothstein, Stephen Wagley, and Darren Walker.

Assistance and support has also come from Michael Amato, Mark Bernstein, the Rev. Canon George W. Brandt Jr., Miron Chu, Msgr. Eugene V. Clark, Barbara Cohen, Roy Finamore, Ilyse Fink, Doris Goddard, the Rev. David Johnson, Kathy Jolowicz, Lora Korbut, the Rev. Peter Laarman, Myrna Manners, Michael A. McCarthy, Patricia A. McCormack, the Rev. T. Kenjitsu Nakagaki, Dr. Abdel-Rahman Osman, Fred Otero, Bishop James P. Roberts Jr., Sam Roberts, Jeff Roth, the Rev. Dr. Byron E. Shafer, Tim Stone, Judith Stonehill, Edgar Tafel, Scott Trotter, Daniel J. Wakin, Maxine West, and Craig R. Whitney.

Especially helpful at the New-York Historical Society were Diana Arecco, Glenn Castellano, Joseph Ditta, Holly Hinman, Marybeth Kavanagh, Valerie Komor, Dale Neighbors, and Julie Viggiano.

Although the society furnished the great majority of archival illustrations, I am indebted to those who helped me round out the historical images: Kenneth R. Cobb of the New York City Municipal Archives, Barbara Cohen of New York Bound, the Rev. Dr. Charles A. Curtis of Mount Olivet Baptist Church, Christopher Gray, Hilda Rodriguez of the Metropolitan Museum of Art, and the Rev. Milind Sojwal and Paul Johnson of All Angels' Church.

Modernage Custom Digital Imaging Labs has made the prints for all four of the books I've illustrated since 1979 and continues to keep alive the art and craft of silver-based photography. Besides the printers and darkroom staff, I am indebted to Lainey C. Friedlander and Margaret Mood.

In October 2002, I sent a questionnaire to 399 congregations. Fifty-one responded. I am, of course, grateful to all those who took the time to fill out the form, but especially appreciate those who put extra effort into writing or furnishing detailed congregational histories: the Rev. Walter C. Barton Jr., the Rev. Getulio Cruz Jr., the Rev. Steed V. Davidson, Justine M. Gidicsin, the Rev. Paul A. Grauls, Rana D. Hobson, Dorothy Eaton Jones, the Rev. A. Eric Joseph, Ernest Logan, the Rev. Angel V. Ortiz, Dr. Paul Radensky, the Rev. Carlos R. Reyes, Linda Reynolds, the Rev. Rafael Rivera-Rosa, the Rev. Dr. Thomas L. Robinson, Diana Rossero, Rabbi Reuven Siegel, the Rev. Graciano Torres, Luisa Vega-Williams, the Rev. Carl L. Washington Jr., and the Rev. J. David Waugh.

At my side throughout the last nine years of this project, Scott L. Bane also influenced the book profoundly with an exacting line-by-line editing that helped me refocus many entries to make them livelier, clearer, and more approachable. For nearly a decade, Scott has shared my thrill of discovery, never begrudged the time we spent apart, and encouraged me at every dispiriting moment—and there were more than a few—to keep believing.

NEIGHBORHOOD MAPS

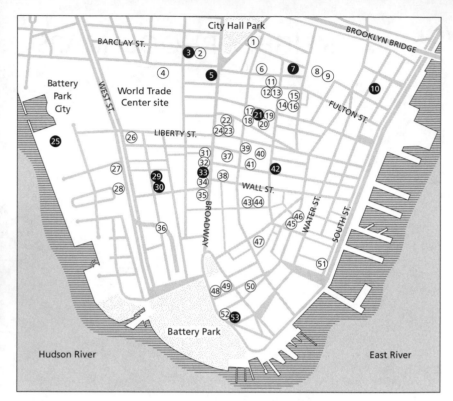

A1 **Brick Meeting,** Beekman St., pp. 30–31

A2 **St. Peter's Church,** 22 Barclay St., p. 242

A3 **St. Peter's Church,** 22 Barclay St., p. 242

A4 **St. Christopher's Chapel,** 209 Fulton St., p. 278

A5 **St. Paul's Chapel,** Broadway, pp. 279–280

A6 **Christ Church,** 49 Ann St., pp. 42–43

A7 **Wall Street Synagogue,** 47 Beekman St., p. 290

A8 **St. George's Chapel,** Beekman St., pp. 36–37

A9 **St. George's Church,** Beekman St., pp. 36–37

A10 **Seaport Chapel,** 241 Water St., pp. 254–255

A11 **North Reformed Dutch Church,** William St., p. 159

A12 **First Moravian Church,** 106 Fulton St., p. 76

A13 **First Moravian Church,** 106 Fulton St., p. 76

A14 **Rigging Loft Methodist Meeting Place,** 120 William St., p. 183

A15 **First Baptist Church,** 35 Gold St., p. 73

A16 **First Baptist Church,** 35 Gold St., p. 73

A17 **German Reformed Church,** 64 Nassau St., pp. 72–73

A18 **German Reformed Church,** 64 Nassau St., pp. 72–73

A19 **Wesley Chapel,** 44 John St., pp. 118–119

A20 **John Street Church,** 44 John St., pp. 118–119

A21 **John Street Church,** 44 John St., pp. 118–119

A22 **Friends Meeting House,** Liberty Pl., pp. 70–71

A23 **Friends Meeting House,** Liberty St., pp. 70–71

A24 **Friends Meeting House,** Liberty St., pp. 70–71

A25 **St. Joseph's Chapel,** 385 South End Ave., p. 242

A26 **St. Nicholas Greek Orthodox Church,** 155 Cedar St., p. 233

A27 **Bethel Ship *John Wesley*,** Carlisle St., p. 26

A28 **Bethel Ship *John Wesley*,** Rector St., p. 26

A29 **True Buddha Diamond Temple,** 105 Washington St., p. 281

A30 **St. George Chapel,** 103 Washington St., p. 205

A31 **Trinity Church,** Broadway, pp. 276–280

A32 **Trinity Church,** Broadway, pp. 276–280

A33 **Trinity Church,** Broadway, pp. 276–280

A34 **Trinity Lutheran Church,** Broadway, p. 229

A35 **Grace Church,** Broadway, pp. 88–89

A36 St. Joseph Maronite Church, 57 Washington St., p. 220

A37 Scotch Presbyterian Church, Cedar St., p. 256

A38 First Presbyterian Church, 10 Wall St., pp. 76–77

A39 Middle Reformed Dutch Church, Nassau St., p. 145

A40 Cedar Street Presbyterian Church, Cedar St., p. 71

A41 Église Française du St.-Esprit, 18 Pine St., pp. 202–203

A42 Church of Our Lady of Victory, 60 William St., p. 168

A43 South Reformed Dutch Church, Exchange Pl., p. 264

A44 South Reformed Dutch Church, Exchange Pl., p. 264

A45 Congregation Shearith Israel, 20 S. William St., pp. 260–261

A46 Congregation Shearith Israel, 20 S. William St., pp. 260–261

A47 Église Française du St.-Esprit, Marketfield St., pp. 202–203

A48 King's Chapel, Fort Amsterdam, pp. 124–125

A49 King's Chapel, Fort James, pp. 124–125

A50 Reformed Dutch Church, 39 Pearl St., p. 181

A51 Seamen's Church Institute, 25 South St., pp. 254–255

A52 Seamen's Church Institute, 15 State St., pp. 254–255

A53 Church of Our Lady of the Rosary, 7 State St., p. 167

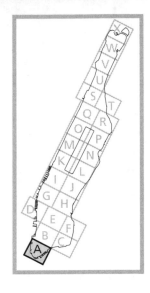

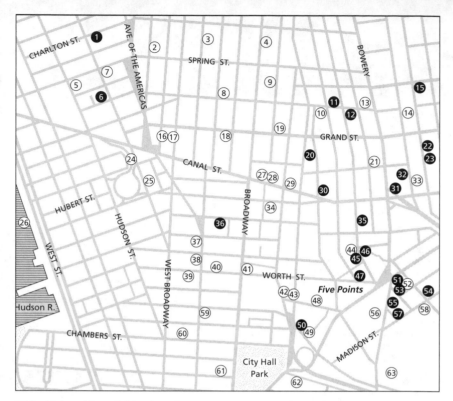

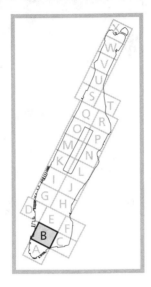

B29 First Colored Presbyterian Church, Lafayette St., p. 262

B30 Church of the Most Precious Blood, 113 Baxter St., p. 148

B31 Mahayana Buddhist Temple, 133 Canal St., p. 136

B32 Grace Faith Church, 65 Chrystie St., p. 89

B33 Congregation Emanu-El, 56 Chrystie St., p. 62

B34 Evangelical Lutheran Church of St. Matthew, Walker St., p. 229

B35 Eastern States Buddhist Temple of America, 64 Mott St., p. 59

B36 Civic Center Synagogue, 49 White St., p. 47

B37 Église Française du St.-Esprit, Church St., pp. 202–203

B38 Mother A.M.E. Zion Church, Church St., pp. 148–149

B39 Abyssinian Baptist Church, 44 Worth St., p. 6

B40 Christ Church, 79 Worth St., pp. 42–43

B41 Broadway Tabernacle, Broadway, p. 33

B42 St. Philip's Church, Centre St., pp. 242–243

B43 St. Philip's Church, Centre St., pp. 242–243

B44 Zion Episcopal Church, 25 Mott St., p. 230

B45 Church of the Transfiguration, 25 Mott St., p. 275

B46 First Chinese Baptist Church, 21 Pell St., p. 73

B47 True Light Lutheran Church, 195 Worth St., p. 281

B48 Zion Baptist Church, 488 Pearl St., p. 297

B49 Church of St. Andrew, 27 Duane St., p. 190

B50 Church of St. Andrew, 27 Duane St., p. 190

B51 Trans World Buddhist Association Buddha Virtue Temple, 7 E. Broadway, p. 274

B52 Oliver Street Baptist Church, 12 Oliver St., pp. 140–141

B53 Mariners' Temple Baptist Church, 3 Henry St., pp. 140–141

B54 Chinese United Methodist Church, 69 Madison St.,p. 42

B55 Congregation Shearith Israel Cemetery, St. James Pl., pp. 260–261

B56 Church of St. Joachim, 22 Roosevelt St., p. 213

B57 St. James Church, 32 James St., pp. 210–211

B58 Mariners' Church, 46 Catherine St., p. 140

B59 Duane Street Presbyterian Church, Duane St., p. 71

B60 First Congregational Church, Chambers St., p. 12

B61 Fourth Universalist Society, Murray St., p. 81

B62 Christ Church, Frankfort St., p. 229

B63 Mariners' Church, 73 Roosevelt St., p. 140

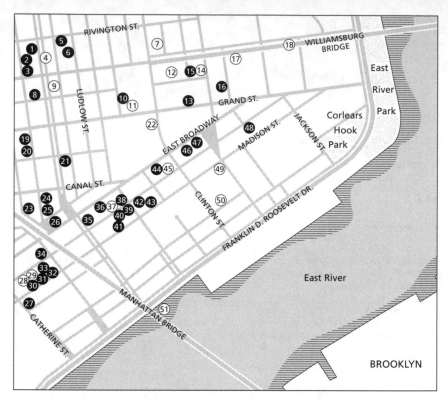

C1 Church of Grace to Fujianese, 133 Allen St., p. 89

C2 Templo Pentecostal Mar de Galilea, 166 Eldridge St., p. 139

C3 New York Chinese Alliance Church, 162 Eldridge St., p. 158

C4 Congregation Tiffereth Israel, 126 Allen St., p. 273

C5 First Roumanian-American Congregation, 89 Rivington St., p. 78

C6 Congregation Kadisha Anshei Podolsk, 121 Ludlow St., p. 122

C7 Congregation Beth Haknesseth Mogen Avraham, 87 Attorney St., p. 22

C8 Congregation Kehila Kedosha Janina, 280 Broome St., p. 122

C9 Second Universalist Church, 97 Orchard St., p. 257

C10 Congregation Beth Hamedrash Hagodol, 60 Norfolk St., p. 22

C11 Emanuel Baptist Church, 47 Suffolk St., p. 63

C12 Congregation Mogen Abram, 50 Attorney St., p. 146

C13 Church of St. Mary, 440 Grand St., p. 227

C14 Seventh Presbyterian Church, 142 Broome St., p. 258

C15 Downtown Talmud Torah Synagogue, 142 Broome St., p. 56

C16 Bialystoker Synagogue, 7 Bialystoker Pl., p. 27

C17 Church of St. Mary, Sheriff St., p. 227

C18 Church of St. Rose, 34 Cannon St., p. 243

C19 Lincoln Memorial A.M.E. Church, 87 Eldridge St., p. 130

C20 Bethel Chinese Assembly of God Church, 77 Eldridge St., p. 25

C21 First Roumanian-American Congregation, 70 Hester St., p. 78

C22 Congregation Thilom Anshei Wishkowe, 169 Clinton St., pp. 262–263

C23 St. Barbara Greek Orthodox Church, 27 Forsyth St., p. 194

C24 Pu Chao Temple, 20 Eldridge St., p. 177

C25 Eldridge Street Synagogue, 12 Eldridge St., pp. 60–61

C26 East Dhyana Temple, 83 Division St., p. 58

C27 Church of St. Joseph, 5 Monroe St., p. 219

C28 Congregation Shaare Zedek, 38 Henry St., p. 260

C29 Congregation Shaare Zedek, 40 Henry St., p. 260

C30 Chinese Evangel Mission Church, 97 Madison St., p. 42

Chinatown, Lower East Side

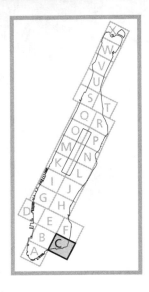

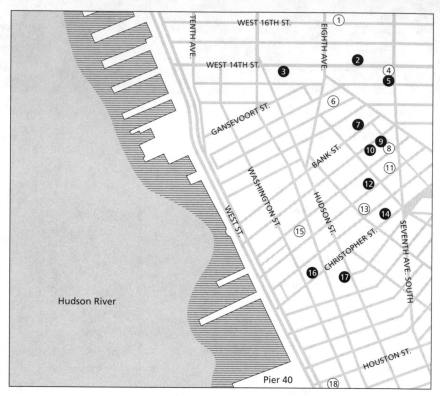

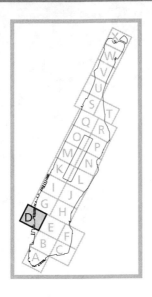

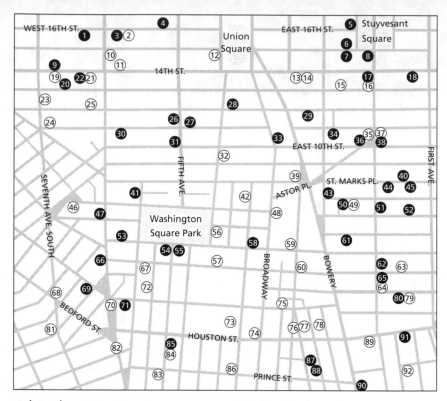

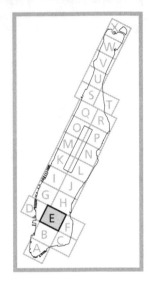

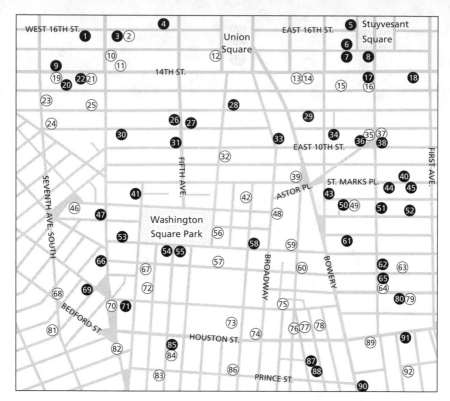

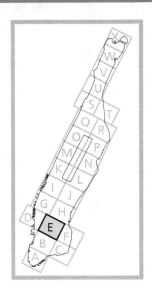

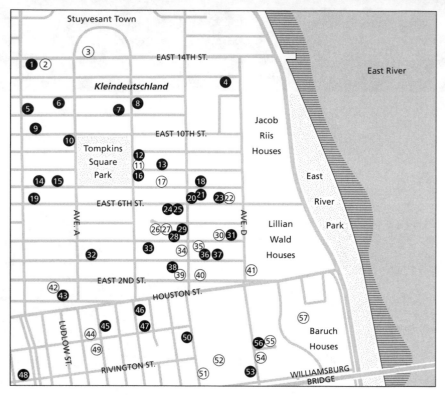

Stuyvesant Town

EAST 14TH ST.

East River

Kleindeutschland

Jacob
Riis
Houses

EAST 10TH ST.

Tompkins
Square
Park

East
River
Park

EAST 6TH ST.

AVE. A

AVE. D

Lillian
Wald
Houses

EAST 2ND ST.

HOUSTON ST.

Baruch
Houses

LUDLOW ST.

RIVINGTON ST.

WILLIAMSBURG
BRIDGE

F1 Church of the Immaculate Conception, 406 E. 14th St., p. 110

F2 Church of St. Stephen of Hungary, 420 E. 14th St., p. 245

F3 Church of the Immaculate Conception, 505 E. 14th St., p. 110

F4 Church of St. Emeric, 740 E. 13th St., p. 202

F5 Madina Masjid, 401 E. 11th St., p. 134

F6 Church of Mary Help of Christians, 436 E. 12th St., p. 141

F7 Father's Heart Ministry Center, 543 E. 11th St., p. 70

F8 Iglesia de Dios Pentecostal Elim, 185 Avenue B, p. 61

F9 Tenth Street Church of Christ, 257 E. 10th St., p. 271

F10 St. Nicholas of Myra Orthodox Church, 288 E. 10th St., p. 234

F11 Trinity Lower East Side Lutheran Parish, 139 Avenue B, p. 280

F12 Trinity Lower East Side Lutheran Parish, 602 E. 9th St., p. 280

F13 Congregation B'nai Moses Joseph Anshei Zawichost and Zosmer, 317 E. 8th St., p. 30

F14 Church of St. Stanislaus Bishop and Martyr, 101 E. 7th St., p. 245

F15 St. Mary's American Orthodox Greek Catholic Church, 121 E. 7th St., p. 227

F16 Church of St. Brigid, 119 Avenue B, pp. 196–197

F17 Congregation B'nai Rappaport Anshe Dombrowa, 207 E. 7th St., p. 30

F18 Iglesia Cristiana Misionera, 247 E. 7th St., p. 51

F19 Congregation Adas Yisroel Anshe Mezeritz, 415 E. 6th St., p. 7

F20 Iglesia Pentecostal Sarepta, 701 E. 6th St., p. 254

F21 Congregation Beth Hamedrash Hagodol Anshe Ungarn, 242 E. 7th St., p. 22

F22 Emmanuel Presbyterian Church, 737 E. 6th St., p. 63

F23 Emmanuel Presbyterian Church, 737 E. 6th St., p. 63

F24 Iglesia de Dios, 636 E. 6th St., p. 55

F25 Congregation Ahawath Yeshurun Shara Torah, 638 E. 6th St., p. 8

F26 Congregation Kolbuszower Teitelbaum Chevra Banai, 622 E. 5th St., p. 126

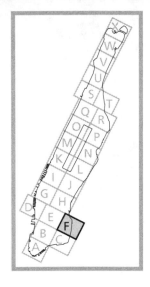

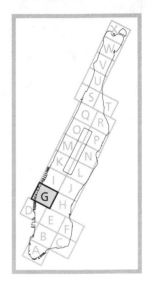

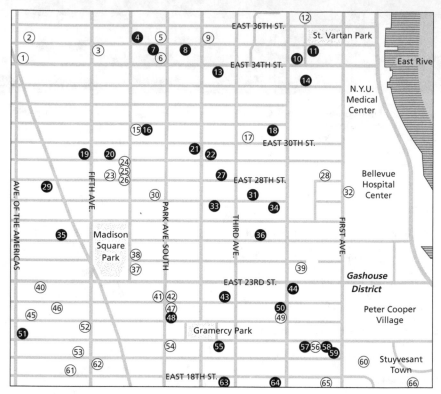

EAST 36TH ST. ⑫

St. Vartan Park

② ④ ⑤ ⑨

③ ⑦ ⑧

① ⑥

EAST 34TH ST. ⑩ ⑪

East Rive

⑬

EAST 34TH ST.

⑭

N.Y.U.
Medical
Center

⑮⑯ ⑱

⑰ **EAST 30TH ST.**

⑲ ⑳ ㉑ ㉒

㉔

FIFTH AVE.

㉓ ㉕

㉖

㉗ **EAST 28TH ST.** ㉘

㉙ ㉜

Bellevue
Hospital
Center

AVE. OF THE AMERICAS

㉚ ㉛

PARK AVE. SOUTH

㉝ ㉞

THIRD AVE.

㉟ ㊱

FIRST AVE.

Madison
Square
Park ㊳

㊲

㊴ ㊴

EAST 23RD ST. ㊹

Gashouse
District

㊺ ㊻ ㊸

㊺ ㊼ ㊾

㊿

㊽

Peter Cooper
Village

㊿ ㊾

Gramercy Park

㊶

㋀

㊾ ㊿

㊿ ㊾ ㊿

㊿

Stuyvesant
Town

㊶ ㊲

EAST 18TH ST. ㊻ ㊽ ㊿ ㊿

H1 Broadway Tabernacle, 582 Sixth Ave., p. 33

H2 St. Mark's Methodist Episcopal Church, 65 W. 35th St., p. 226

H3 Christ Church, E. 35th St., pp. 42–43

H4 Church of the Incarnation, 209 Madison Ave., p. 111

H5 Church of the Covenant, 20 Park Ave., p. 51

H6 Community Church of New York, Park Ave., pp. 48–49

H7 Community Church of New York, 40 E. 35th St., pp. 48–49

H8 New Church, 112 E. 35th St., p. 156

H9 Church of the Epiphany, 257 Lexington Ave., p. 65

H10 St. Vartan Armenian Cathedral, 620 Second Ave., pp. 248–249

H11 St. Gregory the Illuminator Church, 314 E. 35th St., p. 207

H12 Church of St. Gabriel, 310 E. 37th St., p. 205

H13 Armenian Evangelical Church, 152 E. 34th St., p. 16

H14 Church of the Sacred Hearts of Jesus and Mary, 307 E. 33rd St., p. 252

H15 Madison Avenue Baptist Church, 133 Madison Ave., pp. 134–135

H16 Madison Avenue Baptist Church, 30 E. 31st St., pp. 134–135

H17 Adams-Parkhurst Presbyterian Church, 211 E. 30th St., p. 7

H18 Church of the Good Shepherd, 238 E. 31st St., p. 85

H19 Marble Collegiate Church, 1 W. 29th St., p. 140

H20 Little Church Around the Corner, 1 E. 29th St., p. 131

H21 First Moravian Church, 154 Lexington Ave., p. 76

H22 Congregation Talmud Torah Adereth El, 135 E. 29th St., p. 270

H23 Church of St. Leo, 11 E. 28th St., p. 221

H24 Rutgers Presbyterian Church, 90 Madison Ave., p. 186

H25 Rutgers Presbyterian Church, 90 Madison Ave., p. 186

H26 Church of the Atonement, 80 Madison Ave., p. 18

H27 Church of Our Lady of the Scapular–St. Stephen, 149 E. 28th St., p. 168

H28 Church of Our Lady of the Scapular of Mount Carmel, 341 E. 28th St., p. 168

H29 Church of the Disciples of Christ, 28 W. 28th St., p. 56

H30 Église Française du St.-Esprit, 45 E. 27th St., pp. 202–203

H31 St. Illuminator's Armenian Apostolic Cathedral, 221 E. 27th St., p. 209

H32 Chapel of Christ the Consoler, E. 26th St., p. 45

H33 First Swedish Baptist Church, 138 E. 27th St., p. 276

H34 First Christian Church of the Valley, 234 E. 27th St., p. 74

H35 St. Sava Serbian Orthodox Cathedral, 15 W. 25th St., p. 244

H36 Ninth Church of Christ, Scientist, 223 E. 25th St., p. 159

H37 Madison Square Presbyterian Church, 7 Madison Ave., p. 136

H38 Madison Square Presbyterian Church, 11 Madison Ave., p. 136

H39 Church of St. Sebastian, 312 E. 24th St., p. 244

H40 Calvary Baptist Church, 50 W. 23rd St., p. 37

H41 Fourth Avenue Presbyterian Church, 286 Park Ave. S., p. 32

H42 St. Paul's Methodist Episcopal Church, Park Ave. S., p. 237

H43 Evangelical Lutheran Church of Gustavus Adolphus, 149 E. 22nd St., p. 93

H44 East End Temple, 300 E. 23rd St., p. 58

H45 Holy Trinity Lutheran Church, 47 W. 21st St., p. 105

H46 Église Française du St.-Esprit, 30 W. 22nd St., pp. 202–203

H47 Calvary Church, 273 Park Ave. S., pp. 36–37

H48 Calvary Church, 273 Park Ave. S., pp. 36–37

H49 Church of the Epiphany, 373 Second Ave., p. 65

H50 Church of the Epiphany, 373 Second Ave., p. 65

H51 Church of the Holy Communion, 47 W. 20th St., pp. 36–37

H52 South Reformed Dutch Church, Fifth Ave., p. 264

H53 Congregation Shearith Israel, 5 W. 19th St., pp. 260–261

H54 All Souls Church, 249 Park Ave. S., p. 12

H55 Brotherhood Synagogue, 28 Gramercy Park S., p. 34

H56 Holy Trinity Slovak Lutheran Church, 332 E. 20th St., p. 105

H57 Holy Trinity Slovak Lutheran Church, 332 E. 20th St., p. 105

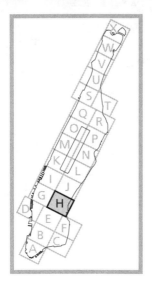

H58 Congregation Zichron Moshe, 342 E. 20th St., p. 297

H59 Christ Lutheran Church, 355 E. 19th St., p. 44

H60 Christ Lutheran Church, 406 E. 19th St., p. 44

H61 St. Ann's Church for the Deaf, 7 W. 18th St., p. 192

H62 Fifth Avenue Presbyterian Church, Fifth Ave., p. 71

H63 Greek Orthodox Church of St. John the Baptist, 143 E. 17th St., p. 216

H64 East End Temple, 245 E. 17th St., p. 58

H65 Hedding Methodist Episcopal Church, 337 E. 17th St., p. 97

H66 Church of St. Mary Magdalene, 529 E. 17th St., p. 228

WEST 55TH ST.

De Witt Clinton Park

WEST 53RD ST.

WEST 49TH ST.

Hudson River

TWELFTH AVE.

TENTH AVE.

EIGHTH AVE.

BROADWAY

WEST 45TH ST.

Times Square

WEST 42ND ST.

DYRE AVE.

Port Authority Bus Terminal

WEST 38TH ST.

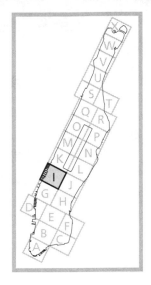

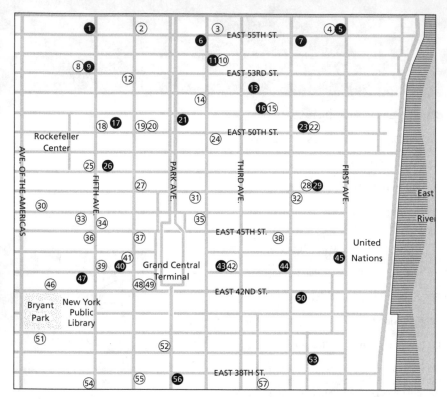

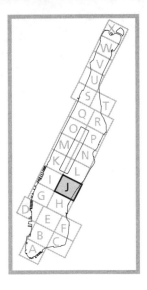

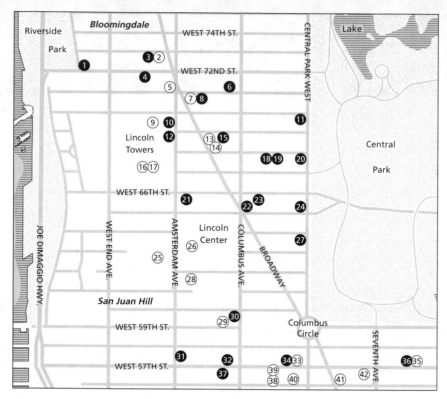

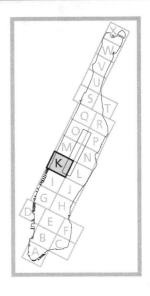

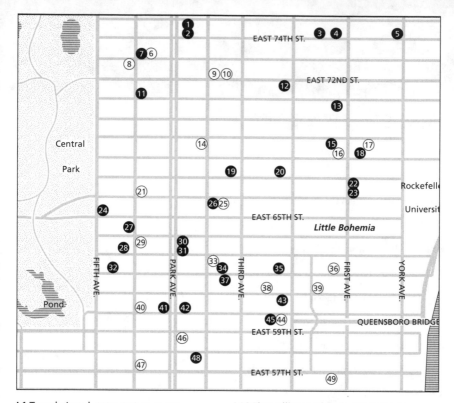

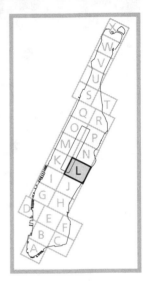

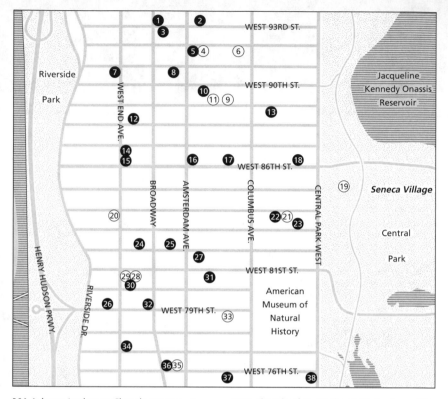

M1 Advent Lutheran Church, 2504 Broadway, p. 8

M2 Iglesia Adventista del Séptimo Día Broadway, 161 W. 93rd St., p. 32

M3 Congregation Shaare Zedek, 212 W. 93rd St., p. 260

M4 Central Baptist Church, 166 W. 92nd St., p. 38

M5 Central Baptist Church, 166 W. 92nd St., pp. 38, 39

M6 Chapel of St. Agnes, 120 W. 92nd St., p. 278

M7 Greek Orthodox Church of the Annunciation, 302 W. 91st St., p. 14

M8 Young Israel of the West Side, 210 W. 91st St., p. 296

M9 Church of St. Gregory the Great, 119 W. 89th St., p. 207

M10 Church of St. Gregory the Great, 144 W. 90th St., p. 207

M11 Mother A.M.E. Zion Church, 127 W. 89th St., pp. 148–149

M12 Congregation B'nai Jeshurun, 257 W. 88th St., p. 29

M13 Romanian Orthodox Church of St. Dumitru, 50 W. 89th St., p. 200

M14 Church of St. Ignatius of Antioch, 552 West End Ave., pp. 208–209

M15 Church of St. Paul and St. Andrew, 540 West End Ave., p. 237

M16 West-Park Presbyterian Church, 539 Amsterdam Ave., p. 293

M17 Jewish Center, 131 W. 86th St., p. 118

M18 Society for the Advancement of Judaism, 15 W. 86th St., p. 263

M19 All Angels' Church, W. 85th St., p. 9

M20 Eighty-fourth Street Presbyterian Church, West End Ave., p. 293

M21 St. Matthew's Church, 26 W. 84th St., p. 230

M22 Church of St. Matthew and St. Timothy, 26 W. 84th St., p. 230

M23 Congregation Rodeph Sholom, 7 W. 83rd St., p. 185

M24 Fourth Church of Christ, Scientist, 251 W. 82nd St., p. 81

M25 Church of the Holy Trinity, 213 W. 82nd St., p. 104

M26 Congregation Kehilath Jacob, 305 W. 79th St., p. 122

M27 Ukrainian Autocephalic Orthodox Church of St. Volodymyr, 160 W. 82nd St., p. 250

M28 All Angels' Church, 428 West End Ave., pp. 8, 9

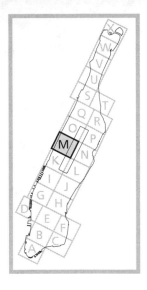

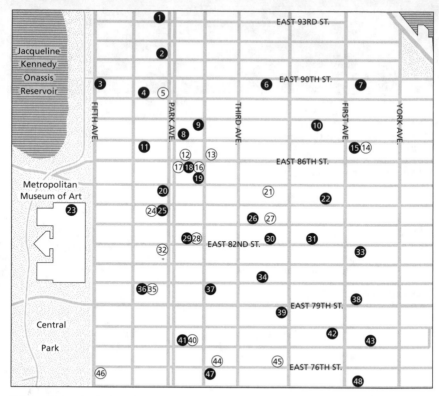

N1 Synodal Cathedral of the Mother of God of the Sign, 75 E. 93rd St., p. 149

N2 Brick Presbyterian Church, 1140 Park Ave., pp. 30–31

N3 Church of the Heavenly Rest, 2 E. 90th St., pp. 96–97

N4 Church of St. Thomas More, 65 E. 89th St., p. 247

N5 Prospect Hill Reformed Church, Park Ave., p. 177

N6 Church of Our Lady of Good Counsel, 230 E. 90th St., p. 164

N7 St. Joseph's Asylum Chapel, 402 E. 90th St., p. 220

N8 Church of the Advent Hope, 111 E. 87th St., p. 7

N9 Immanuel Lutheran Church, 122 E. 88th St., pp. 110–111

N10 Church of the Holy Trinity, 316 E. 88th St., p. 103

N11 Park Avenue Synagogue, 50 E. 87th St., pp. 172–173

N12 Congregation Agudat Yesharim, 115 E. 86th St., pp. 172–173

N13 First Union Presbyterian Church, 145 E. 86th St., pp. 30–31

N14 Church of St. Joseph, E. 87th St., p. 220

N15 Church of St. Joseph, 408 E. 87th St., p. 220

N16 Yorkville Methodist Church, E. 86th St., p. 173

N17 Park Avenue Methodist Episcopal Church, 1031 Park Ave., p. 173

N18 Park Avenue United Methodist Church, 106 E. 86th St., p. 173

N19 Congregation Kehilath Jeshurun, 117 E. 85th St., pp. 122–123

N20 Park Avenue Christian Church, 1010 Park Ave., p. 172

N21 Church of the Redeemer, 230 E. 85th St., p. 181

N22 Zion–St. Mark's Lutheran Church, 339 E. 84th St., p. 297

N23 Temple of Isis at Dendur, 1000 Fifth Ave., p. 55

N24 Church of St. Lawrence O'Toole, E. 84th St., p. 208

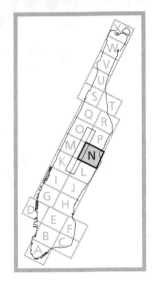

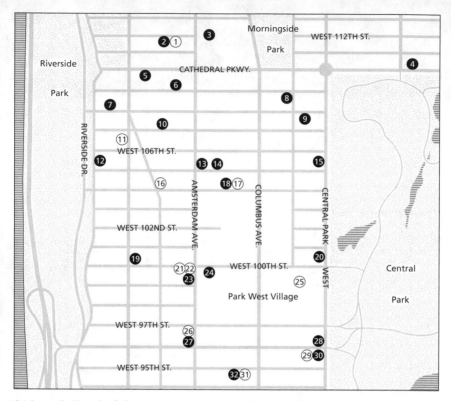

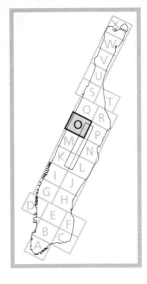

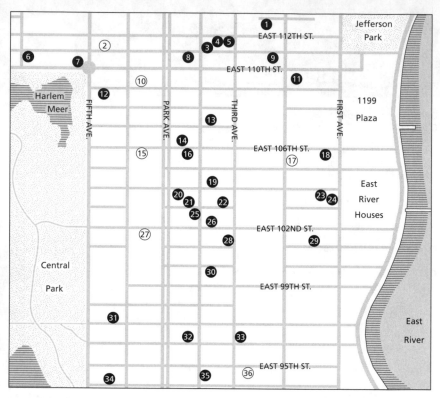

P1 Church of Our Lady Queen of Angels, 228 E. 113th St., p. 169

P2 Iglesia Pentecostal Macedonia, 15 E. 111th St., p. 134

P3 Primera Iglesia Metodista Unida Hispana, 1791 Lexington Ave., p. 176

P4 Christ Apostolic Church of U.S.A., 160 E. 112th St., p. 44

P5 Quinta Iglesia de Dios Pentecostal, 174 E. 112th St., p. 177

P6 Second Canaan Baptist Church, 10 Malcolm X Blvd., p. 255

P7 Iglesia Cristiana la Hermosa, 3 Central Park N., p. 98

P8 Greater Highway Deliverance Temple, 132 E. 111th St., p. 91

P9 Holy Family Mission, 236 E. 111th St., p. 101

P10 Congregation Nachlath Zvi, 65 E. 109th St., p. 156

P11 St. Ann's Roman Catholic Church, 312 E. 110th St., p. 192

P12 St. Edward the Martyr Church, 14 E. 109th St., p. 200

P13 Iglesia ACyM Hispana, 155 E. 107th St., p. 98

P14 Primera Iglesia Evangélica Presbiteriana el Buen Vecino, 115 E. 106th St., p. 34

P15 St. Hedwig's Church, 62 E. 106th St., p. 245

P16 Church of St. Cecilia, 120 E. 106th St., p. 197

P17 Church of St. Cecilia, Second Ave., p. 197

P18 Iglesia Pentecostal Macedonia, 340 E. 106th St., p. 134

P19 Church of the Living Hope, 161 E. 104th St., p. 132

P20 Iglesia Pentecostal Nueva Gethsemani, 112 E. 104th St., p. 160

P21 Iglesia Cristiana Betania, 131 E. 103rd St., p. 21

P22 Thy Will Be Done! Christian Ministries, 165 E. 103rd St., p. 273

P23 Church of St. Lucy, 338 E. 104th St., p. 222

P24 East Ward Missionary Baptist Church, 2011 First Ave., p. 59

P25 Hellenic Orthodox Church of SS. George and Demetrios, 140 E. 103rd St., p. 205

P26 Segunda Iglesia Bautista, 163 E. 102nd St., p. 257

P27 People's Tabernacle, 52 E. 102nd St., p. 174

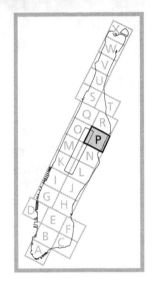

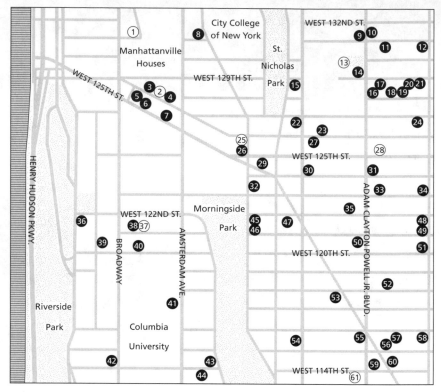

City College of New York

WEST 132ND ST.

Manhattanville Houses

St. Nicholas Park

WEST 129TH ST.

WEST 125TH ST.

HENRY HUDSON PKWY.

WEST 122ND ST.

Morningside Park

WEST 125TH ST.

WEST 120TH ST.

ADAM CLAYTON POWELL JR. BLVD.

BROADWAY

AMSTERDAM AVE.

Riverside Park

Columbia University

WEST 114TH ST.

Q1 Church of the Annunciation, Old Broadway, p. 13

Q2 Church of St. Mary's–Manhattanville, 521 W. 126th St., p. 229

Q3 Church of St. Mary's–Manhattanville, 521 W. 126th St., p. 229

Q4 Templo Bíblico, 503 W. 126th St., p. 271

Q5 Old Broadway Synagogue, 15 Old Broadway, p. 162

Q6 Manhattan Pentecostal Church, 541 W. 125th St., p. 138

Q7 Antioch Baptist Church, 515 W. 125th St., p. 16

Q8 Church of the Annunciation, 80 Convent Ave., p. 13

Q9 Shiloh Baptist Church, 2226 Adam Clayton Powell Jr. Blvd., p. 262

Q10 Williams Institutional C.M.E. Church, 2225 Adam Clayton Powell Jr. Blvd., p. 294

Q11 Friendship Baptist Church, 144 W. 131st St., p. 82

Q12 Downtown Baptist Church, 413 Malcolm X Blvd., p. 56

Q13 Williams Institutional C.M.E. Church, 220 W. 130th St., p. 294

Q14 Salem United Methodist Church, 211 W. 129th St., p. 252

Q15 Jehovah's Witnesses Kingdom Hall, 310 W. 129th St., p. 117

Q16 Metropolitan Baptist Church, 151 W. 128th St., p. 143

Q17 Faith Mission Christian Fellowship, 160 W. 129th St., p. 70

Q18 Glendale Baptist Church, 131 W. 128th St., p. 84

Q19 House of God Church Keith Dominion, 127 W. 128th St., p. 107

Q20 Prophetic Church of God, 130 W. 129th St., p. 177

Q21 Holy Cross African Orthodox Pro-Cathedral, 122 W. 129th St., p. 99

Q22 Greater Zion Hill Baptist Church, 2365 Frederick Douglass Blvd., pp. 92–93

Q23 Trinity A.M.E. Church, 259 W. 126th St., p. 275

Q24 Muhammad's Mosque Number Seven, 106 W. 127th St., p. 154

Q25 Manhattanville Presbyterian Church, 152 Morningside Ave., p. 139

Q26 Church of St. Joseph of the Holy Family, 405 W. 125th St., pp. 220, 221

Q27 Thomas Memorial Wesleyan Methodist Church, 270 W. 126th St., pp. 272, 273

Q28 Kingdom of Father Divine, 152 W. 126th St., p. 124

Q29 LaGree Baptist Church, 362 W. 125th St., p. 128

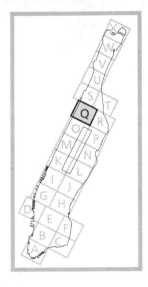

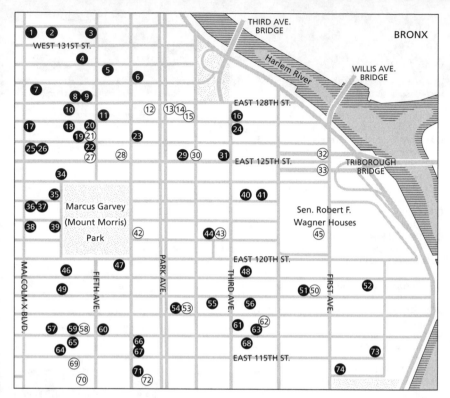

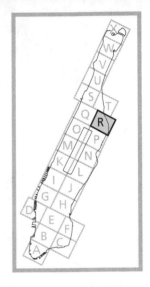

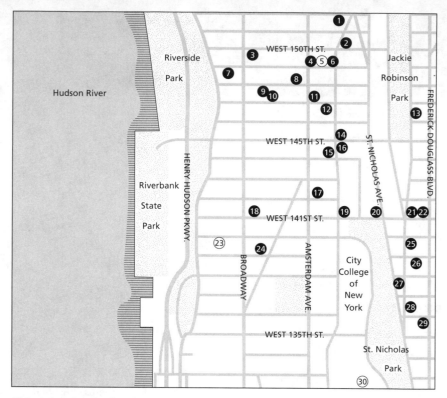

S27 St. Mark's United Methodist Church, 49
Edgecombe Ave., p. 226
S28 New Hope Seventh-Day Adventist
Church, 28 Edgecombe Ave., p. 157
S29 Healing from Heaven Temple, 2535
Frederick Douglass Blvd., p. 96
S30 Manhattanville College of the Sacred
Heart Chapel, Convent Ave., p. 139

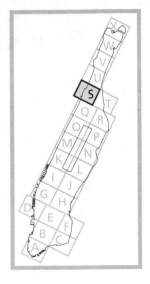

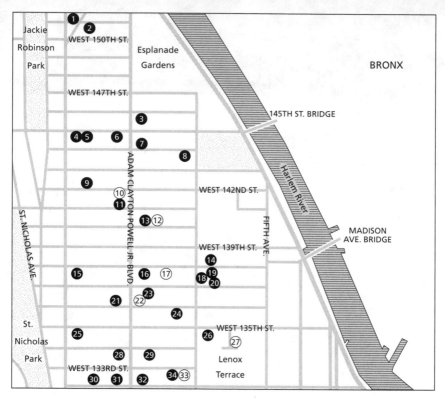

T1 St. Matthew's Baptist Church, 43 Macombs Pl., p. 230

T2 Church of the Resurrection, 276 W. 151st St., p. 183

T3 Greater Hood Memorial A.M.E. Zion Church, 160 W. 146th St., p. 91

T4 St. Paul's Community Church, 256 W. 145th St., p. 239

T5 Union Baptist Church, 240 W. 145th St., p. 284

T6 Church of God, 220 W. 145th St., p. 85

T7 St. Thomas the Apostle Liberal Catholic Church, 147 W. 144th St., p. 248

T8 New Mount Calvary Baptist Church, 102 W. 144th St., p. 157

T9 Mount Calvary Baptist Church, 231 W. 142nd St., p. 149

T10 Church of St. Charles Borromeo, W. 142nd St., p. 198

T11 Church of St. Charles Borromeo, 211 W. 141st St., p. 198

T12 Little Mount Zion Baptist Church, 171 W. 140th St., p. 157

T13 New Mount Zion Baptist Church, 171 W. 140th St., p. 157

T14 Church of St. Mark the Evangelist, 65 W. 138th St., p. 225

T15 Victory Tabernacle Seventh-Day Christian Church, 252 W. 138th St., p. 287

T16 Abyssinian Baptist Church, 132 W. 138th St., p. 6

T17 Metropolitan Baptist Tabernacle, 120 W. 138th St., p. 143

T18 Salvation Army Harlem Temple, 540 Malcolm X Blvd., p. 253

T19 Union Congregational Church, 60 W. 138th St., p. 284

T20 Rendall Memorial Presbyterian Church, 59 W. 137th St., p. 182

T21 Beulah Wesleyan Methodist Church, 221 W. 136th St., p. 27

T22 Mother A.M.E. Zion Church, 151 W. 136th St., pp. 148–149

T23 Mother A.M.E. Zion Church, 146 W. 137th St., pp. 148–149

T24 Way of the Cross Tabernacle of Christ, 126 W. 136th St., p. 291

T25 Faithful Workers Christ of God Church, 264 W. 135th St., p. 70

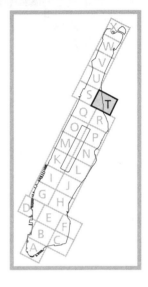

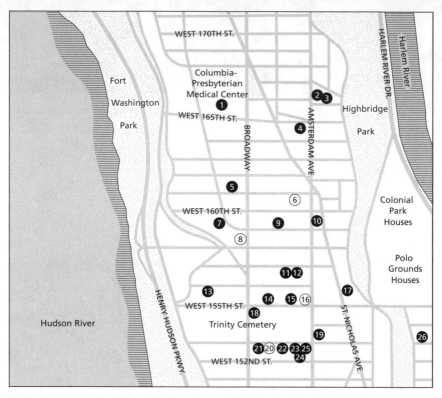

U1 Pauline A. Hartford Memorial Chapel, W. 168th St., p. 174

U2 Iglesia Pentecostal Padre, Hijo y Espíritu Santo, 2141 Amsterdam Ave., p. 172

U3 Templo Bíblico Capilla Evangélica, 461 W. 166th St., p. 271

U4 Church of St. Rose of Lima, 510 W. 165th St., p. 243

U5 Jehovah's Witnesses Kingdom Hall, 609 W. 161st St., p. 117

U6 Washington Heights Congregation, 510 W. 161st St., p. 290

U7 Paradise Baptist Church, 23 Fort Washington Ave., p. 172

U8 Church of the Intercession, 3801 Broadway, p. 112

U9 Little Mount Zion Pentecostal Church, 535 W. 159th St., p. 132

U10 Church on the Hill A.M.E. Zion, 975 St. Nicholas Ave., pp. 46–47

U11 New Covenant Holiness Church, 512 W. 157th St., p. 157

U12 Iglesia Adventista del Séptimo Día Fort Washington, 502 W. 157th St., p. 80

U13 Church of Our Lady of Esperanza, 624 W. 156th St., p. 163

U14 North Presbyterian Church, 529 W. 155th St., p. 159

U15 Greater File Chapel Baptist Church, 505 W. 155th St., p. 91

U16 Washington Heights Presbyterian Church, 1920 Amsterdam Ave., pp. 290–291

U17 Bethel Holy Church of Mount Sinai, 922 St. Nicholas Ave., p. 26

U18 Church of the Intercession, 550 W. 155th St., p. 112

U19 Congregational Church of God, 1889 Amsterdam Ave., p. 50

U20 Washington Heights German Evangelical Lutheran Church, 542 W. 153rd St., pp. 280–281

U21 Trinity Lutheran Church, 542 W. 153rd St., pp. 280–281

U22 Holy Fathers Russian Orthodox Church, 524 W. 153rd St., p. 101

U23 Church of St. Catherine of Genoa, 500 W. 153rd St., p. 197

U24 Move of God Cathedral, 501 W. 152nd St., p. 154

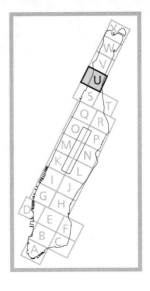

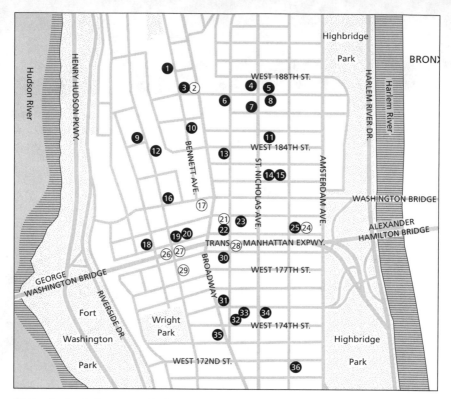

V1 Our Saviour's Atonement Lutheran Church, 178 Bennett Ave., p. 170

V2 Church of St. Elizabeth, 4381 Broadway, p. 201

V3 Congregation Mount Sinai Anshe Emeth, 4381 Broadway, p. 153

V4 SS. Anargyroi Greek Orthodox Church, 1547 St. Nicholas Ave., p. 189

V5 Iglesia de Dios Pentecostal Amor, Poder y Gracia, 563 W. 187th St., p. 13

V6 Church of St. Elizabeth, 268 Wadsworth Ave., p. 201

V7 Iglesia Presbiteriana Fort George, 1525 St. Nicholas Ave., p. 79

V8 Holy Cross Armenian Apostolic Church, 580 W. 187th St., p. 99

V9 Hebrew Tabernacle of Washington Heights, 551 Fort Washington Ave., p. 97

V10 Congregation K'hal Adath Jeshurun, 85 Bennett Ave., p. 123

V11 Congregation Gates of Israel, 560 W. 185th St., p. 84

V12 Fort Tryon Jewish Center, 524 Fort Washington Ave., p. 79

V13 Wadsworth Avenue Baptist Church, 210 Wadsworth Ave., p. 290

V14 Congregation Beth Hillel of Washington Heights, 571 W. 182nd St., p. 23

V15 Prince of Peace Universal Tabernacle Spiritual Church, 557 W. 182nd St., pp. 176, 177

V16 Fort Washington Collegiate Church, 470 Fort Washington Ave., p. 80

V17 Holyrood Church, 4255 Broadway, pp. 106–107

V18 Washington Heights Congregation, 815 W. 179th St., p. 290

V19 Holyrood Church, 715 W. 179th St., pp. 106–107

V20 Congregation Shaare Hatikvah Ahavath Torah v'Tikvoh Chadoshoh, 711 W. 179th St., p. 259

V21 Washington Heights Hellenic Church of St. Spyridon, 124 Wadsworth Ave., pp. 244–245

V22 Washington Heights Hellenic Church of St. Spyridon, 124 Wadsworth Ave., pp. 244–245

V23 Iglesia Congregación Mita, 612 W. 180th St., p. 49

V24 Church of Our Saviour, 525 W. 179th St., p. 170

V25 Iglesia Pentecostal de Washington Heights, 281 Audubon Ave., p. 290
V26 Chelsea Methodist Episcopal Church, Fort Washington Ave., pp. 32–33
V27 Fourth Church of Christ, Scientist, 410 Fort Washington Ave., p. 81
V28 Congregation Mount Sinai Anshe Emeth, 109 Wadsworth Ave., p. 153
V29 Congregation Nodah bi Yehuda, 392 Fort Washington Ave., p. 159
V30 Primera Iglesia Bautista Hispana de Manhattan, 96 Wadsworth Ave., p. 176
V31 United Palace, 4140 Broadway, p. 286
V32 Iglesia Presbiteriana Fort Washington Heights, 21 Wadsworth Ave., p. 80
V33 Congregation Beth Hamedrash Hagodol of Washington Heights, 610 W. 175th St., p. 22
V34 Church of the Incarnation, 1290 St. Nicholas Ave., p. 111
V35 Broadway Temple United Methodist Church, 4111 Broadway, pp. 32–33
V36 Iglesia el Camino, 141 Audubon Ave., p. 37

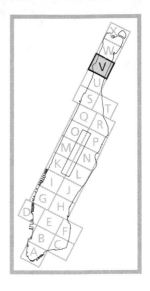

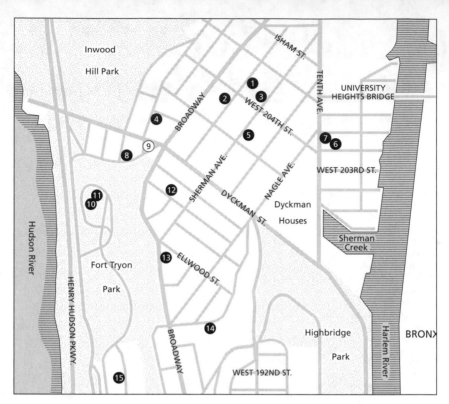

W

Fort George, Fort Tryon, Inwood

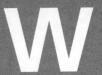

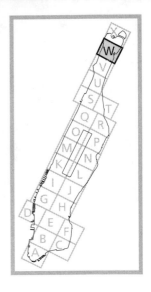

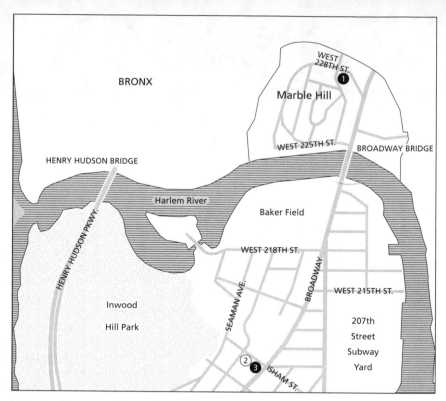

X1 St. Stephen's United Methodist Church,
144 W. 228th St., p. 246
X2 Good Shepherd Roman Catholic Church,
Cooper St., p. 86
X3 Good Shepherd Roman Catholic Church,
4967 Broadway, p. 86

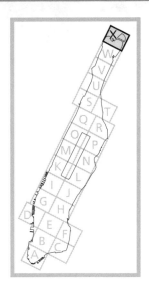

INTRODUCTION

Manhattan being Manhattan, there was a decent inn here before there was a good church. But it was the city's secularity, paradoxically, that quickly made it a fertile religious ground, as the British governor reported in 1678: "There are Religions of all sorts, one Church of England, several Presbiterians and Independents, Quakers, and Anabaptists of severall sects, some Jews." Because New York's leaders most prized commercial success, rather than religious orthodoxy, some degree of tolerance was almost always assured. Why expel people who could help in the broader goal of making the town prosperous?

Not until after the Revolution, however, when Roman Catholics were allowed to build their first church, did the sacred cityscape began to take real form. At first, almost every New York church came in a single barn-like model. Some were festooned with ornament or topped by elaborate steeples, but at heart they were simple meeting halls.[1] As trade increased with Europe and inland America in the early nineteenth century and the city's wealth grew, so did its taste and pretension. Meeting halls became lovely

---

1. Meeting halls that survive are St. Paul's Chapel, Church of the Transfiguration, Bialystoker Synagogue, First Chinese Presbyterian Church, St. Augustine's Episcopal Church, St. John's Evangelical Lutheran Church, and St. Mark's Church in-the-Bowery.

Greek temples.[2] This Arcadian period gave way in the 1830s and 1840s to the more complex Gothic Revival, fueled in part by a ritualistic movement among Episcopalians, who were then the predominant church builders.[3] Apart from liturgical overtones, Gothic architecture had a deeply Romantic appeal and was embraced not only by Catholics and some Protestants, but even by the German Jews who built the city's first grand synagogue.[4] It did not take long for this sensory overload to spawn a reaction, expressed by the more straightforward Romanesque Revival of the 1850s.[5]

After the Civil War, it is impossible to chart a cohesive stylistic trend. Jews seeking architectural roots turned to the "Oriental" style of Moorish Spain.[6] Romanesque architecture grew more rugged.[7] Gothic turned prickly and spiky, though these multicolored exercises in Victorian exuberance had an unusually short life span, perhaps because they were so provocative.[8] Punctuating this symphony were distinctly ethnic strains.[9]

The most important development in sacred architecture in the late nineteenth and early twentieth centuries was the evolution of the multipurpose educational, recreational, and welfare center, in which the sanctuary was only one of many facilities. Competing for the young, the unchurched, the unschooled, and the poor, con-

2. Extant Greek Revival temples are the second St. Peter's Church, Mariners' Temple Baptist Church, St. James Church, Village Presbyterian Church, Church of St. Joseph, Community Synagogue, St. Illuminator's Armenian Apostolic Cathedral, and West Forty-fourth Street United Presbyterian Church.

3. Early Gothic Revival buildings for the Episcopal Church include Trinity Church, Church of the Ascension, Grace Church, St. Peter's Church, and Church of the Holy Communion.

4. Originally built for Congregation Anshe Chesed, the synagogue was later home to Congregation Anshe Slonim.

5. Early Romanesque Revival sanctuaries include St. George's Church, Marble Collegiate Church, First Moravian Church, and Church of Our Lady of the Scapular–St. Stephen.

6. Moorish elements were piled on at Eldridge Street Synagogue, Central Synagogue, Congregation Emanu-El, Park East Synagogue, and Congregation Beth El.

7. Inspired by Henry Hobson Richardson, this later Romanesque Revival influenced St. James Lutheran Church, Chapel of St. Agnes, West-Park Presbyterian Church, St. Martin's Episcopal Church, and St. Luke's Church.

8. The wildest and wooliest included St. Augustine's Chapel, All Souls Church (nicknamed Church of the Holy Zebra), First Reformed Episcopal Church, Collegiate Church of St. Nicholas, West Presbyterian Church, and Church of the Holy Trinity (or Homely Oilcloth), all of which are gone.

9. Among the earliest buildings with ethnic elements are First Hungarian Reformed Church, Trinity Baptist Church, and St. Nicholas Russian Orthodox Cathedral.

gregations created an extraordinary social-service infrastructure.[10] The thinking seemed to be: win adherents in the kitchen, gymnasium, swimming pool, library, or sewing circle, and you might have a chance to woo them to your pews—and your collection plate.

At the same time, steeples were ceding their place in the skyline to office towers. New York's loftiest Gothic pinnacle of the twentieth century was the "Cathedral of Commerce," as the Rev. S. Parkes Cadman called the Woolworth Building of 1913. No church could match it, but some congregations dipped into commercial real estate by turning over their properties to developers who constructed Skyscraper Churches, with sanctuaries at the base and apartments, hotels, or offices above.[11]

Skyscraper Churches were built by congregations that wanted to stay put. But most groups were on the move in the late nineteenth and early twentieth centuries, following the restless population. In fact, about half the existing houses of worship in Manhattan serve a different congregation, religion, or purpose today than they did when constructed. Some of the most distinctive churches in Harlem and Washington Heights, for example, started as theaters or synagogues.[12] Elsewhere, you can find a Buddhist temple that began as an Orthodox shul, an Orthodox shul that was established as a Christian Science meetinghouse, a Reformed Dutch church that now serves Chinese Presbyterians, a Trinity

---

10. Some of the more noteworthy are Broome Street Tabernacle, Labor Temple, Church of the Immaculate Conception, St. Nicholas of Myra Orthodox Church, De Witt Reformed Church, Christ Presbyterian Church, Broadway United Church of Christ, Central Presbyterian Church, Jewish Center, Church of the Holy Trinity, Congregation Ansche Chesed, and Riverside Church. The Broadway Temple United Methodist Church, had it been built as planned, would have been the towering epitome of this type.

11. Some Skyscraper Churches are Madison Avenue Baptist Church, First Reformed Episcopal Church, Church of the Strangers, Calvary Baptist Church, Manhattan Congregational Church, and Second Presbyterian Church. St. Peter's Church, next to the Citigroup Center, is a more ambitious and successful freestanding expression of the phenomenon.

12. Former theaters include Williams Institutional C.M.E. Church, LaGree Baptist Church, First Corinthian Baptist Church, Canaan Baptist Church of Christ, Church of the Lord Jesus Christ of the Apostolic Faith, New Covenant Temple, Childs Memorial Temple Church of God in Christ, St. Paul's Community Church, Union Baptist Church, Paradise Baptist Church, and United Palace. Churches that were once synagogues are Christ Apostolic Church of U.S.A., Mount Olivet Baptist Church, Mount Neboh Baptist Church, Bethel Way of the Cross Church of Christ, Baptist Temple Church, City Tabernacle of Seventh-Day Adventists, Gospel Missionary Baptist Church, and Jehovah's Witnesses Kingdom Hall on West 161st Street.

chapel that has long been the Serbian Orthodox Cathedral, and a Presbyterian mission to the Italians that was acquired by a Puerto Rican Pentecostal flock.[13]

Obviously, houses of worship are markers of urban development. They speak of New York's turbulent history and commanding artistry, its astonishing wealth and appalling poverty, and those civic and spiritual aspirations that sometimes transcend its celebrated materialism. They offer—even to those who are not at all religious—oases of beauty, dignity, grace, and calm that are so necessary and welcome in the urban maelstrom, particularly in these perilous days. They confer identity to the neighborhoods and nameless little "villages" that compose the metropolis, serving as homeless shelters through the dawn, day-care centers in the morning, soup kitchens at lunchtime, classrooms in the afternoon, concert halls in the evening, and, at night, meeting places for Alcoholics Anonymous, Weight Watchers, or the local community board.

They are also in crisis. As small congregations struggle to maintain large and aging physical plants, agonizing over whether scarce dollars should go toward mission or mortar, the sacred cityscape is diminishing. Since 1970, some 40 noteworthy churches and synagogues have been demolished, destroyed by fire, or lost to terrorism.[14] Some have been replaced, but many have simply disappeared.

It is about time, therefore, for a group portrait.

---

13. They are, respectively, Sung Tak Buddhist Association, Hebrew Tabernacle of Washington Heights, First Chinese Presbyterian Church, St. Sava Serbian Orthodox Cathedral, and Iglesia Pentecostal Macedonia.

14. Sanctuaries destroyed by fire or demolished were Church of St. Alphonsus Liguori, Congregation Beth Haknesseth Mogen Avraham, Congregation Mogen Abram, St. John's in the Village, St. Mary's Catholic Church of the Byzantine Rite, St. George Ukrainian Catholic Church, Congregation Kochob Jacob Anshe Kamenitz de Lite, Church of the Nativity, Church of Our Lady of Loreto, Trinity Lower East Side Lutheran Parish, Congregation B'nai Rappaport Anshe Dombrowa, Emmanuel Presbyterian Church, Congregation Kolbuszower Teitelbaum Chevra Banai, Congregation Anshe Baranove, East Side Tabernacle, St. Eleftherios Greek Orthodox Church, Church of St. Leo, Church of Our Lady of the Scapular of Mount Carmel, Church of St. Sebastian, Knox Memorial Chapel, Church of St. John the Evangelist, St. Peter's Church, Sutton Place Synagogue, Church of St. Agnes, Christ Church, Broadway United Church of Christ, First Alliance Church, Evangelical Bethesda Church, Church of Our Lady of Perpetual Help, All Angels' Church, Mount Neboh Synagogue, Congregation Or Zarua, Seventh Church of Christ, Scientist, Grace United Methodist Church, Cathedral of the Good Shepherd, Kings Chapel of the Apostolic Faith, Christ the Savior Orthodox Church, Greater Emanuel Baptist Church, and Congregation Nodah bi Yehuda. St. Nicholas Greek Orthodox Church was crushed on September 11, 2001. And the fate of the Church of St. Brigid, West-Park Presbyterian Church, and the Church of St. Thomas the Apostle are in the balance.

A

Abyssinian Baptist Church **[E46]**

Abyssinian Baptist Church **[I50]**

Abyssinian Baptist Church **[T16]**

Abyssinian Baptist Church. They were only looking for a place to worship. Several traders from Abyssinia—now Ethiopia—came to the First Baptist Church on Gold Street one Sunday in 1808. They were ushered to the slave loft. "Wealthy, educated world travelers, proud human beings, with a well-defined philosophy of religion that matched that of anyone in that auditorium, they resented this and walked out in protest," the Rev. Adam Clayton Powell Jr. wrote. Eighteen black members of First Baptist joined their boycott, forming the nucleus of Abyssinian Baptist Church, founded in 1809.

They worshiped first at 44 Anthony Street [B39], as Worth Street was called, moving in 1856 to 166 Waverly Place [E46], when Greenwich Village was an African-American hub. This little building once stood on Christopher Street, but had been moved in its entirety in 1826 by the Second Reformed Presbyterian Church. Abyssinian followed the black population uptown in 1902, moving to 242 West 40th Street [I50], the former Fourth German Mission Reformed Dutch Church. Membership swelled after the Rev. Adam Clayton Powell Sr. began preaching in a tent next to Marcus Garvey's Liberty Hall in Harlem. The new Abyssinian was built on the same block in 1922/1923, at 132 West 138th Street [●T16★], since renamed Odell M. Clark Place after an Abyssinian deacon. The amphitheater-style church was designed by Charles W. Bolton & Son in Tudor Gothic style. There were some 13,000 members in the 1930s, when Abyssinian was described as the largest and most influential black church in New York, and the world's largest Baptist church.

Much of its influence was owed to the younger Powell, a charismatic maverick who assumed the pulpit in 1937 and, in 1944, became the first African-American elected to the House of Representatives from New York State. Upper Seventh Avenue was renamed in his honor. He was followed by the Rev. Samuel DeWitt Proctor and the Rev. Calvin O. Butts III, who established the Abyssinian Development Corporation, which has played a leading role in the recent redevelopment of Harlem.

Actors' Chapel. *See* St. Malachy's Church

Actors Studio. *See* West Forty-fourth Street United Presbyterian Church

Actors' Temple. *See* Ezrath Israel, Congregation

Adams-Parkhurst Presbyterian Church. This Victorian Gothic castle by J. Cleveland Cady was built in 1875 at 211 East 30th Street [H17] as the Memorial Chapel of the Madison Square Presbyterian Church, later renamed to honor two pastors of Madison Square: the Rev. William Adams and the Rev. Charles Henry Parkhurst. The Armenian Evangelical Church and radio station WLIB shared the building over time. Adams-Parkhurst merged in 1965 with the Church of the Covenant, and the sanctuary was razed. A 10-story apartment building now stands on the site.

Adams-Parkhurst Presbyterian Church [H17]

Adas Yisroel Anshe Mezeritz, Congregation. Unlike most nearby synagogues, this exquisite sanctuary at 415 East 6th Street [●F19] is marvelously preserved. It was altered in 1910 from a three-story dwelling by Hermann Horenburger. It is nearly identical to the contemporary Congregation Kolbuszower Teitelbaum Chevra Banai. Adas Yisroel Anshe Mezeritz (Community of Israel, People of Mezeritz) was founded in 1892 and named for a town in Poland that was once a center of Jewish learning. The Orthodox group remains here to this day.

Congregation Adas Yisroel Anshe Mezeritz [F19]

Adoration, Chapel of the. The Cenacle of St. Regis, at 628 West 140th Street [S23], a Roman Catholic retreat for women and children, was built in 1901 to designs by W. E. Bosworth and W. C. Chase. A large chapel stood on the bucolic grounds, which were used until 1952.

Advent Hope, Church of the. At home in German Yorkville, at 111 East 87th Street [●N8], is the HAUS DER ADVENT HOFFNUNG, as it says over the entryway, a Seventh-Day Adventist church. Plans for the Church of the Advent Hope were filed in 1955 by the architect Alfred B. Heiser.

Church of the Advent Hope [N8]

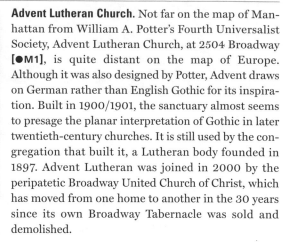

Advent Lutheran Church [M1]

Advent Lutheran Church. Not far on the map of Manhattan from William A. Potter's Fourth Universalist Society, Advent Lutheran Church, at 2504 Broadway [●M1], is quite distant on the map of Europe. Although it was also designed by Potter, Advent draws on German rather than English Gothic for its inspiration. Built in 1900/1901, the sanctuary almost seems to presage the planar interpretation of Gothic in later twentieth-century churches. It is still used by the congregation that built it, a Lutheran body founded in 1897. Advent Lutheran was joined in 2000 by the peripatetic Broadway United Church of Christ, which has moved from one home to another in the 30 years since its own Broadway Tabernacle was sold and demolished.

Agudas Anshei Mamod Ubeis Vead Lachachomim, Congregation. *See* Chung Te Buddhist Association

Agudat Yesharim, Congregation. *See* Park Avenue Synagogue

Congregation Agudath Achim M'Krakau [F51]

Agudath Achim M'Krakau, Congregation. Originally built as a parochial school in 1855, 54 Pitt Street [F51] later served Congregations Brith Sholem, Kochob Jacob Anshe Kamenitz de Lite, Poel Zedek Anshe Ileya, and Agudath Achim M'Krakau. This congregation from Poland, founded in 1867, moved to 525 West 147th Street [●S10], now Bethel Holy Church of Deliverance.

Ahavath Acheim Anshe Ungarn, Congregation. Congregation Ohab Zedek's first synagogue, built in 1881 at 70 Columbia Street [F54], was later used by the Hungarian congregation Ahavath Acheim Anshe Ungarn.

Ahawath Chesed Shaar Hashomayim, Congregation. *See* Central Synagogue

All Angels' Church [M28]

Ahawath Yeshurun Shara Torah, Congregation. The name of Congregation Ahawath Yeshurun Shara Torah (Love of Israel, Gates of the Torah) is still visible at 638 East 6th Street [●F25], which is now the Sixth Street Community Center.

All Angels' Church. In the community of Seneca Village, in the middle of what would become Central Park, All Angels' Episcopal parish was organized in 1846. Its first wooden church, described by the Rev. Thomas McClure Peters as a place "in which white and black and all intermediate shades worshiped harmoniously together," was consecrated in 1849 and stood approximately on the line of West 85th Street [M19]. Property condemnation for the new park closed this church in 1856. A new sanctuary was opened two years later at 428 West End Avenue [M28]. In 1873, the Rev. Charles F. Hoffman was called as rector. Heir to a large fortune, he offered to pay for the cost of a new church on the same site [M29]. Built from 1888 to 1890 and designed by Samuel B. Snook of J. B. Snook & Sons, this Gothic building was ingeniously oriented on a diagonal bias, creating a 140-foot-long sanctuary on a 100- by 102-foot plot of ground. But the size of All Angels' Church, which seated 1,200, was ultimately a liability for a parish that had only 150 members by 1976. Services and operations were moved into the parish house, at 251 West 80th Street [●M30]—built in 1904 to designs by Henry J. Hardenbergh, architect of the Dakota apartments and Plaza Hotel—and the church was razed in 1979 to make way for a 21-story apartment tower, West River House.

All Angels' Church [M29]

All Nations, Church for. Recalling a bit the work of Frank Furness, that wildly inventive Victorian Gothic architect, this expressive, muscular, ruddy sanctuary at 417 West 57th Street [●K32★] was built for the Catholic Apostolic Church. It is sui generis. And so was the denomination: a group organized in Britain in 1832 around Edward Irving and 12 new apostles in the belief that the Second Coming was imminent. Christ did not return to Earth in 1835, but the movement continued. The New York congregation, organized in 1848, worshiped for three decades at 126 West 16th Street [●E1], now the Église Évangélique Française. Its West 57th Street church was built in 1886/1887 to designs by Francis Hatch Kimball. In 1995, a badly weakened congregation offered its sanctuary to the Lutheran Life's Journey Ministries. The building was rededicated in 1997 as the Church for All Nations.

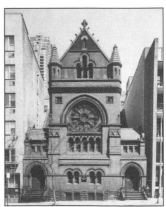

All Angels' Church **[M30]**

Church for All Nations **[K32]**

All Peoples Church (New Dramatists Theater) **[I35]**

All Saints' Church (before renovation) **[L45]**

All Saints' Church (after renovation) **[L45]**

All Peoples Church. St. Matthew's German Lutheran Church filed plans in 1903 for a church at 422 West 44th Street [●I35] by John Boese. The building was subsequently home to the Lutheran Church of the Redeemer and the Lutheran Metropolitan Inner Mission Society, a hive of Lutheran charities, including a child-welfare office, an immigrant ministry, and a seaman's mission. By the mid-1960s, it was All Peoples Church. It is now the New Dramatists Theater.

All Saints' Church. "There is a stirring and emotional Christianity sometimes to be witnessed in cultivated circles and perfumed boudoirs, which weeps plenteously over the hardships and sacrifices of missionary life in far off latitudes, while the ignorant and neglected and the comfortless of its own neighborhood... are suffered remorselessly to live and die in a darkness more dense that that of heathendom." With that charge in 1858 by the Rev. William F. Morgan, the cultivated and perfumed St. Thomas Church began its own Episcopal inner-city mission: St. Thomas Chapel. Its first sanctuary, at 117 Thompson Street [E83], had been built in 1833 as the Second Associate Presbyterian Church and had also been the Church of the Annunciation. After St. Thomas moved uptown, the Greek Revival building became St. Ambrose Church, an Episcopal parish that disbanded in 1903.

A new St. Thomas Chapel was constructed in 1871 at 230 East 60th Street [L44]. The present sanctuary, on the same site [●L45], was built in 1894 to designs by C. E. Miller. By the 1930s, the chapel was more a working-class parish than a slum mission. A remodeling in the 1950s obliterated most details under a smothering coat of stucco. Renamed All Saints', the congregation became an independent body in 1965. In 2002, the church was renovated with a new facade inspired by the Carpenter Gothic of Alexander Jackson Davis and by the Bodleian Library at Oxford. A new rose window by Sylvia Nicolas, depicting the Resurrection of Jesus, was installed. The architect, Samuel G. White of Platt Byard Dovell White, is a great-grandson of Stanford White.

All Saints Church. Out of a neighborhood where many churches are quite modest erupts this effusive Venetian Gothic mountain range. In addition to its sheer size, the Roman Catholic All Saints Church, at 47 East 129th Street [●R6], is notable for wheel windows in the clerestory, patterned brickwork, and a tall bell tower. It is called the St. Patrick's of Harlem, and the historian Michael Henry Adams credits James Renwick Jr. directly with the design of All Saints. His nephew, William W. Renwick, also worked on the church, which was dedicated in 1893. Once Irish, the parish is now predominantly African-American and offers a Nigerian Mass.

All Saints Church **[R6]**

All Saints Ukrainian Orthodox Church. One of several Ukrainian sanctuaries in the neighborhood, the spartan though undeniably ecclesiastical All Saints Ukrainian Orthodox Church, at 206 East 11th Street [●E34], was once the Smyrna, or Welsh, Congregational Church.

All Souls' Church. On the eve of the Civil War, in 1859, All Souls' Episcopal parish was formed. Its first home, built two years later at 139 West 48th Street [I22], later became the First Church of Christ, Scientist. In 1890, All Souls' bought a Romanesque Revival sanctuary by R. H. Robertson, built from 1881 to 1883 as the Episcopal Church of the Holy Spirit, at 775 Madison Avenue [L21]. This building was sold in 1905 to a parishioner who replaced it with a magnificent apartment house, 45 East 66th Street, by Harde & Short. All Souls' then lent its money and name to the struggling Church of the Archangel, at 88 St. Nicholas Avenue. Archangel's first building, by Janes & Leo, had burned down on the eve of opening in 1903. It constructed the present building on the same site [●Q60], also designed by Janes & Leo, in 1908. All Souls' paid the debt, and the parishes merged. In 1932, this was the setting of a dramatic integration fight, when Bishop William T. Manning of the Episcopal diocese forced his way into the locked church—against the wishes of a majority of the white vestrymen—and declared it open "to all the people in the neighborhood who wish to attend its services, without distinction of race or color."

All Saints Ukrainian Orthodox Church **[E34]**

All Souls' Church [L21]

All Souls' Church **[Q60]**

Church of the Divine Unity [B4]

All Souls Church [H54]

All Souls Church **[N37]**

All Souls Church. This Unitarian Universalist body has been known since its founding in 1819 by many names: the First Congregational Church, the Church of the Divine Unity, Dr. Bellows's Church (for the Rev. Henry Whitney Bellows), and even the Church of the Holy Zebra. Early members included Herman Melville, William Cullen Bryant, Peter Cooper of Cooper Union, and Nathaniel Currier of Currier & Ives. The First Congregational Church was built on Chambers Street [B60] in 1820/1821. Its next sanctuary, dedicated in 1845 at 548 Broadway [B4], was called Divine Unity.

What Bellows called All Souls, New Yorkers knew as Holy Zebra or the Beefsteak Church. Its breathtaking facade by Jacob Wrey Mould featured contrasting bands of red and white brickwork and Caen stone. Built from 1853 to 1855, it stood on what is now Park Avenue South, at 249 Fourth Avenue [H54], and influenced Leopold Eidlitz, architect of the Church of the Holy Trinity on Madison Avenue and Temple Emanu-El on East 43rd Street. The loss of All Souls Church, bad enough, was compounded by the banality of the apartment building that took its place.

The present sanctuary, at 1157 Lexington Avenue [●N37], is a neo-Colonial work by Hobart Upjohn, Richard Upjohn's grandson. It opened in 1932. The congregation has been led for more than two decades by the Rev. F. Forrester Church, whose charismatic style is credited with greatly revitalizing this venerable institution.

American Society for Buddhist Studies. Lured to 214 Centre Street [●B20] by the smell of incense, you will see great Buddha figures with neon nimbuses through the windows. The American Society for Buddhist Studies, a Chinese temple, is affiliated with the Ch'an school of Zen Buddhism.

Amity Baptist Church. Friendly as it may sound, this congregation was actually named for a street, Amity, as 3rd Street was once called. Its first sanctuary, designed by Samuel Dunbar in Greek Revival style, was built in 1834 at 33 Amity Street [E57]. The congregation moved in 1867 to a charming clapboard Gothic sanctuary far out in the countryside, at 310 West 54th Street [16], that had been built in 1860 for St. Timothy's Church. The building was later dismantled, shipped to Marlborough-on-Hudson, New York, and rebuilt near the home of the Rev. Leighton Williams, who was the minister from 1887 to 1917.

The new Amity Baptist Church, with a vast herringbone tile dome by Rafael Guastavino, was built on the same site [17] in 1907/1908 to designs by Rossiter & Wright. It was later the Greek Orthodox Church of the Annunciation. Although the church was demolished, some idea of the magnificence of its dome can be had at the Church of the Holy Trinity on West 82nd Street and St. Paul's Chapel at Columbia University, where Guastavino ceilings still soar.

Iglesia de Dios Pentecostal Amor, Poder y Gracia **[V5]**

Amor, Poder y Gracia, Iglesia de Dios Pentecostal. Love, Will, and Grace, a Pentecostal Church of God, was founded in a basement space in 1980. The congregation—which includes Dominicans, Puerto Ricans, Mexicans, Hondurans, and Salvadorans—moved to 563 West 187th Street **[●V5]** in 1992.

Angel Orensanz Foundation Center for the Arts. *See* Anshe Slonim, Congregation

Church of the Annunciation [E19]

Annunciation, Church of the. The first home of this Episcopal parish, founded in 1838, was 117 Thompson Street [E83], a building that had been the Second Associate Presbyterian Church and later became St. Thomas Chapel and St. Ambrose Church. In 1846, the cornerstone was laid for the Gothic Revival Church of the Annunciation at 144 West 14th Street [E19]. The parish lasted for another half century before disbanding.

Church of the Annunciation [Q1]

Annunciation, Church of the. Way out in the country, near Manhattanville College, the Roman Catholic Church of the Annunciation was organized in 1853. Its Gothic sanctuary, on Old Broadway [Q1], was built in 1853/1854. The present sanctuary, at 80 Convent Avenue **[●Q8]**, proto-Modernist in its stripped-down Gothicism, was designed by Elliott Lynch of Lynch & Orchard and was constructed in 1906/1907.

Church of the Annunciation **[Q8]**

First Associate Presbyterian Church
(as a stable) [B18]

Greek Orthodox Church of the
Annunciation **[M7]**

Annunciation, Greek Orthodox Church of the. Both the Greek Orthodox Church of the Annunciation and the sanctuary it now occupies share the birth date of 1892.

The story begins with the Fourth Presbyterian Church, founded in 1785 as the First Associate Presbyterian Church. In 1824, it built a Greek Revival sanctuary at Grand and Mercer Streets [B18] that later became a stable. In 1852, as Fourth Presbyterian, it moved to the nearby Scotch Presbyterian Church [B19]. From there, it moved to West 34th Street [G16] and finally settled in 1892 at 302 West 91st Street [●M7✩], on West End Avenue. Heins & La Farge, the original architects of the Cathedral Church of St. John the Divine, designed this Gothic sanctuary, whose corner clock tower is a welcoming beacon. The Presbyterians sold their sanctuary to the Greek Orthodox parish in 1953.

The Church of the Annunciation—also known by its Greek name, Evangelismos—had once occupied the former Amity Baptist Church, at 310 West 54th Street [I7]. It then moved to 325 West 85th Street. In 1954, it transferred its relics and icons to Fourth Presbyterian, where the parish has been ever since. A restoration campaign has been led by the Rev. James G. Moskovites and prominent parishioners, including John Catsimatidis.

Ansche Chesed, Congregation. Founded in Yorkville in 1876, the German-speaking Congregation Ansche Chesed (People of Mercy) soon moved uptown to Harlem, 160 East 112th Street [●P4], now Christ Apostolic Church of U.S.A. It then built much grander quarters from 1907 to 1909: a twin-towered synagogue at 1883 Seventh Avenue [●Q59], designed by Edward I. Shire. (This building was sold in 1927 and became the Church of Our Lady of the Miraculous Medal. It is now Mount Neboh Baptist Church. There may be only one other sanctuary in Manhattan—St. Ann's Armenian Catholic Cathedral—that has been shared over time by Jews, Roman Catholics, and Protestants.) The current home of the Conservative congregation was also designed by Shire. "The synagogue, which enshrines the sacred book, is the cornerstone of all that is Jewish," said the rabbi, Jacob Kohn, as the cornerstone was laid in 1927 at 251 West 100th Street [●O19].

Congregation Ansche Chesed **[O19]**

Anshe Baranove, Congregation. The Parque de Tranquilidad marks the site, at 316 East 4th Street [F35], of a sanctuary built in 1870. It was the Church of SS. Cyrillus and Methodius, a Bohemian Roman Catholic parish from which emerged Our Lady of Perpetual Help. By the 1890s, it had become a synagogue, used by Congregations B'nai Peyser, Ahavath Sholom, and Anshe Baranove (People of Baranove, Poland), founded in 1885.

Congregation Anshe Baranove [F35]

Anshe Sineer, Congregation. Built in 1856 at 290 Madison Street [C49] as the Olive Branch Baptist Church, this building was later the First German Presbyterian Church and then Congregation Anshe Sineer, or the Sineerer Shul, named after a district in Ukraine. After the synagogue burned in 1972, the congregation merged with the Wilno Shul to form Congregation Senier and Wilno.

Congregation Anshe Sineer [C49]

Anshe Slonim, Congregation. Gothic architecture makes for haunting ruins. And by the early 1980s, that is what had become of this landmark—the oldest existing purpose-built synagogue in New York City—at 172 Norfolk Street [●F45★]. Designed by Alexander Saeltzer, it was constructed in 1850 for Congregation Anshe Chesed (no relation to the current congregation by that name). Although it looked like a church, it was the city's largest synagogue, with room for 700 men on the main floor and 500 women in the gallery. Anshe Chesed, composed primarily of German Jews, merged in 1874 with Congregation Adas Jeshurun to form Congregation Beth El, which later merged into Congregation Emanu-El. This building was used by Congregations Shaari Rachmim, Ohab Zedek, and Anshe Slonim (People of Slonim, Belarus), founded in 1888. Abandoned in 1974, it was acquired by the Spanish sculptor Angel Orensanz and his brother, Al. In 1992, the Angel Orensanz Foundation Center for the Arts was established as a setting for art exhibits, performances, like Mandy Patinkin's *Mamaloshen*, and the wedding of Sarah Jessica Parker and Matthew Broderick. More recently, the oldest synagogue has become home of one of the newest congregations: the Shul of New York, organized in 1997.

Congregation Anshe Slonim (Angel Orensanz Foundation Center for the Arts) **[F45]**

Antioch Baptist Church **[Q7]**

Antioch Baptist Church. Proving the adaptability of buildings and congregations, Antioch Baptist Church, led by the Rev. Alfloyd Alston, occupies a structure at 515 West 125th Street **[●Q7]** that has served as a tire and battery service center and as a supermarket.

Arca de Refugio, Iglesia de Dios Pentecostal. Like a number of uptown congregations, the Ark of Refuge occupies an old theater. The Fox Manhattan, at 213 Manhattan Avenue **[●O8]**, was in business through the 1950s.

Iglesia de Dios Pentecostal
Arca de Refugio **[O8]**

Armenian Evangelical Church. Through the 1880s, the Armenian presence in the United States was minuscule. But after a plan for the extermination of Armenians was put into effect by the Ottoman sultan, the numbers grew. The first services of the Armenian Evangelical Church of New York, under the Rev. H. H. Khazoyan, were conducted in 1896. The congregation shared the Adams-Parkhurst Presbyterian Church, at 211 East 30th Street [H17]. In 1921, the church purchased the former Nineteenth Ward Bank, at 152 East 34th Street **[●H13]**, designed by William Emerson and constructed in 1907. The church sold its air rights in 1985 to the developer of an apartment tower next door, creating an endowment and permitting a renovation.

Armenian Evangelical Church **[H13]**

Armitage Chapel. The turn-of-the-century brick Armitage Chapel, at 743 Tenth Avenue [I16], later became a YWCA lunchroom.

Asambleas de Iglesia Pentecostal de Jesucristo. A great A-frame structure at 220 East 118th Street **[●R56]** was built in 1888 to designs by Henry F. Kilburn as the First German Baptist Church of Harlem, founded in 1874. It has been a Pentecostal church since the 1960s, minus its peaked gable.

Asbury Methodist Episcopal Church. Cynosure of Washington Square Park, this early Gothic Revival sanctuary was built from 1837 to 1840 at 84 Washington Square East [E56] as the Washington Square Reformed Dutch Church, which worshiped in the New York University chapel while its sanctuary was under

Asambleas de Iglesia Pentecostal de
Jesucristo **[R56]**

construction. The design has been attributed to Minard Lafever or James H. Dakin.

In 1876, the sanctuary was acquired by the former Greene Street Methodist Episcopal Church, organized in 1831, and renamed the Asbury Church. (The Rev. Francis Asbury was the first Methodist Episcopal bishop ordained in America.) The congregation merged in 1893 with the Washington Square Methodist Episcopal Church. The sanctuary was demolished in 1895 and replaced with a warehouse that is now used by New York University, drawing the historical circle to a close.

Asbury Methodist Episcopal Church [E56]

Ascension, Church of the. Not long after opening on Fifth Avenue, the Episcopal Church of the Ascension was the setting for the wedding of President John Tyler to the very much younger Julia Gardiner. The mismatched couple was the "laughing-stock of this city," John Quincy Adams said, but Ascension survived with its dignity intact.

Founded in 1827, Ascension occupied a Greek Revival church on Canal Street [B27], built in 1828/1829 and designed by Ithiel Town and Martin E. Thompson. It burned in 1839. Two years later, the parish moved to Fifth Avenue and West 10th Street [●E31✫], a newly fashionable quarter, and into a sanctuary designed by Richard Upjohn. In the 1880s, the chancel was remodeled by Stanford White and received John La Farge's 30- by 35-foot mural *The Ascension of Christ*. Stained glass by La Farge, D. Maitland Armstrong, and the Tiffany Glass and Decorating Company was also added.

Ascension established a mission chapel in 1865. Called the Chapel of the Shepherd's Flock, it evolved into Ascension Memorial Church, at 249 West 43rd Street [I38]. After the stock-market crash of 1929, the Rev. Donald Bradshaw Aldrich opened the doors of the Fifth Avenue sanctuary around the clock as a place of prayer and meditation. By the 1960s, some 30,000 visitors a year availed themselves of the Church of the Open Door, whose illuminated altar was visible to passersby. Ascension is no longer open all day, but it still welcomes the public with everything from musical programs to a food pantry.

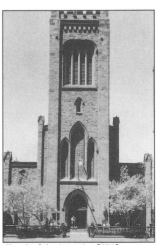

Church of the Ascension **[E31]**

Church of the Ascension **[O10]**

Ascension Memorial Church [I38]

Church of the
Assumption [I18]

Church of the Atonement [H26]

Ascension, Church of the. This bold, rock-faced Romanesque Revival church at 221 West 107th Street [●O10] was designed by Schickel & Ditmars and built in 1896/1897 for the Roman Catholic Church of the Ascension, organized in 1895.

Ascension Memorial Church. The Rev. John Cotton Smith, rector of the Episcopal Church of the Ascension, believed that "only the religion of the helping hand could save large cities." In 1865, he founded the Chapel of the Shepherd's Flock, which evolved into Ascension Memorial Church. Its sanctuary, at 249 West 43rd Street [I38], which came to be called the Little Brick Church in Times Square, was built in 1895. It proudly counted chorus girls among its parishioners.

Assumption, Church of the. While Christ ascended into heaven, Mary was assumed—that is, taken up—according to Roman Catholic belief and doctrine. The German parish commemorating the Assumption of the Blessed Virgin Mary was founded in 1858 and, the next year, built a Romanesque sanctuary at 427 West 49th Street [I18].

Ateris Zwie, Congregation. A large and early synagogue in Harlem, Congregation Ateris Zwie (Crown of Zvi Israel) was at 347 East 121st Street [R45] around the turn of the twentieth century.

Atonement, Church of the. This could be called the Big Church Around the Corner, for it was here that the Rev. William T. Sabine told the friends of the actor George Holland, looking for a place for his funeral: "I believe there is a little church around the corner where they do that sort of thing." The Gothic sanctuary at Madison Avenue and East 28th Street [H26] was built in 1850 as a mission chapel of Grace Church that evolved into the Church of the Incarnation. After that body moved out, the building was taken over by the Church of the Atonement, which merged into Zion Episcopal Church in 1880 following Sabine's departure to join the First Reformed Episcopal Church.

Baptist Tabernacle [E37]

Baptist Tabernacle. The words BAPTIST TABERNACLE can still be seen over a grand doorway at Warren Hall, 168 Second Avenue [●E38], testament to the origins of this 15-story building as a Skyscraper Church, designed by Emery Roth. It occupies the site [E37] of a Gothic sanctuary built in 1850 by the Baptist Tabernacle, founded in 1839. The church, also known as Second Avenue Baptist, shared the block with the New-York Historical Society. The new sanctuary was built from 1928 to 1930 and played a polyglot role in the 1940s, as home to Italian, Polish, and Russian Baptist congregations. It is now an Urban Outfitters store.

Baptist Tabernacle (Urban Outfitters) **[E38]**

Baptist Temple Church. The Baptist Temple Church, at 18 West 116th Street [●R65], gives away its origins on close examination: Stars of David atop the flanking towers. Baptist Temple, a black congregation, was organized in 1899 on West 52nd Street as an offshoot of Mount Olivet Baptist Church, then only two blocks away. Its early home in Harlem was at 11 West 116th Street [R58], before moving to 159 West 132nd Street [●T32], now the New Way Baptist Church. Its present sanctuary was designed by Hedman & Schoen and built in 1906/1907 for Congregation Ohab Zedek, which occupied it until 1926.

Bar Bat, Le. *See* Strangers, Church of the

Bedford Street Methodist Church. If you feel a shiver on the No. 1 or 9 train near Houston Street, it may be because you are riding through the burial ground of the Bedford Street Methodist Church. The congregation, founded in 1805, built and rebuilt at Bedford and Morton Streets [E68]. The last church was constructed in 1866 and used until 1913, when Bedford Street merged into the Metropolitan-Duane United Methodist Church.

Beekman Hill Methodist Church. The delightful Victorian Gothic sanctuary of the Beekman Hill Methodist Church, at 317 East 50th Street [J22], served a congregation that existed from 1860 to 1921. Like Beekman Place, it took its name from the eighteenth-century Beekman family estate.

Baptist Temple Church **[R65]**

Beit Yaakov, Congregation. Manhattan's newest grand sanctuary, completed in 2002, looks as though it were built a century ago. Congregation Beit Yaakov (House of Jacob), founded by the financier Edmond J. Safra and named after his father, commissioned Thierry W. Despont to design a lavish, plutocratic, 60-foot-tall Beaux-Arts synagogue, clad in straw-and-honey Jerusalem limestone, at 11 East 63rd Street [●L28☆]. The main sanctuary sits under a 45-foot-high oak dome.

Betania, Iglesia Cristiana. The small Bethany Christian Church, at 131 East 103rd Street [●P21], is marked simply by an arched parapet.

Congregation Beit Yaakov **[L28]**

Beth Achim, Congregation. See Brotherhood Synagogue

Beth Am, The People's Temple. See Our Saviour's Atonement Lutheran Church

Iglesia Cristiana Betania **[P21]**

Beth El, Congregation. Every bit the House of God, as its name proclaims, Temple Beth El was the last great synagogue to be built before Jewish sacred architecture came to be dominated by the Neoclassical school. Its dome was a commanding presence over Central Park.

The congregation was born in 1874 of a merger between Congregation Anshe Chesed, which had built the synagogue at 172 Norfolk Street that is now the Angel Orensanz Foundation, and Congregation Adas Jeshurun, at 227 West 39th Street, whose synagogue became the Second Reformed Presbyterian Church. At the time of the merger, Anshe Chesed was in a madly Victorian Romanesque synagogue at Lexington Avenue and East 63rd Street [L33], by D. & J. Jardine. This became Temple Beth El.

For Beth El's synagogue at 945 Fifth Avenue [N46], built in 1891, Arnold W. Brunner of Brunner & Tryon mixed Romanesque, Venetian, and Moorish motifs. After Congregation Beth El merged with Congregation Emanu-El in 1927, some architectural elements of this synagogue were moved into Emanu-El's new sanctuary, which has a Beth El Chapel. The East 75th Street synagogue was demolished in 1947.

Congregation Beth El [N46]

Congregation Beth Haknesseth
Mogen Avraham [C7]

Beth Haknesseth Mogen Avraham, Congregation. A lovely Bricklayer Greek Revival temple at 87 Attorney Street [C7] was built in 1845 for the First Methodist Protestant Church and then became the Emanuel A.M.E. Church. At the turn of the twentieth century, it was home to the First Congregation Galiz Duckler Mogen Abraham, named for the Galicia region of Poland and Ukraine and the Polish city of Dukla. In later years, the congregation was known simply as Beth Haknesseth Mogen Avraham (Synagogue of the Shield of Abraham).

Congregation Beth Hamedrash
Hagodol [C10]

Beth Hamedrash Hagodol, Congregation. The twin towers of this Gothic Revival landmark at 60 Norfolk Street [●C10★]—the Great House of Study—are a proud assertion of history in the face of urban renewal. Built in 1850, this was originally the Norfolk Street Baptist Church, forerunner of Riverside Church. The sanctuary was purchased in 1885 by Congregation Beth Hamedrash Hagodol, an Orthodox Russian group founded by Rabbi Abraham Joseph Ash in 1852. When the synagogue was threatened by demolition in 1967, Rabbi Ephraim Oshry, who had maintained Jewish customs, laws, and traditions during the Nazi occupation of Lithuania, secured a landmark designation. In 1997, the central window was blown out in a windstorm, and in 2001, fire destroyed the roof and ceiling.

Congregation Beth
Hamedrash Hagodol
Anshe Ungarn [F21]

Beth Hamedrash Hagodol Anshe Ungarn, Congregation. There are apartment buzzers at the front door, but the exquisite Neoclassical building at 242 East 7th Street [●F21] is unmistakably a synagogue, built in 1905 as Beth Hamedrash Hagodol Anshe Ungarn (Great House of Study of the People of Hungary), a congregation founded in 1883. It was converted to residential use in 1985.

Congregation Beth Hamedrash Hagodol of
Washington Heights [V33]

Beth Hamedrash Hagodol of Washington Heights, Congregation. One of the last surviving uptown synagogues south of the George Washington Bridge is housed in a large Neoclassical sanctuary at 610 West 175th Street [●V33]. Plans were filed in 1925 by Sommerfeld & Sass for Congregation Beth Hamedrash Hagodol, an Orthodox group dating to 1916.

Beth Hamedrash Shaarei Torah, Congregation. A poignant lesson in why it pays to keep your eyes open when walking around the Lower East Side is offered at 80 Forsyth Street [●B22]. This pea-green building might be mistaken for any of its neighbors except for the pointed arches and the Stars of David in the wrought-iron fire escape. Yes, this was a synagogue, for Congregation Beth Hamedrash Shaarei Torah (House of Study Gates of the Law), at the turn of the twentieth century.

Congregation Beth Hamedrash
Shaarei Torah **[B22]**

Beth Hillel of Washington Heights, Congregation. You would not be wrong to mistake this Neoclassical building at 571 West 182nd Street [●V14] for a post office. That is what it was built to be. In 1948, it was acquired by Beth Hillel, an Orthodox congregation founded in 1939 by Jews from Munich. That body existed until 2000, after which the building reverted to secular use.

Beth Israel West Side Jewish Center. An incongruous spiritual presence in the commercial district around Penn Station is the three-story Beth Israel West Side Jewish Center, at 347 West 34th Street [●G4]. The Orthodox congregation was founded in 1890. For a time, it worshiped at 352 West 35th Street [G5], a sanctuary later used by St. Paul Baptist Church. In 1905, it filed plans by John H. Knubel for a synagogue at 252 West 35th Street [G8]. Gronenberg & Leuchtag designed the present sanctuary, which was built in 1924/1925. The synagogue serves the business community and visitors from Israel, South America, and Europe.

Beth Israel West Side Jewish
Center **[G4]**

Beth Simchat Torah, Congregation.
See Holy Apostles, Church of the

Beth Yitzchock, Congregation. This modestly Moderne synagogue at 108 East 1st Street [●F43] was built in 1926 for Congregation Beth Haknesseth Anshe Padheitze (Synagogue of the People of Padheitze, Ukraine). It was later home to Congregations Kochob Jacob Anshe Kamenitz de Lite and Beth Yitzchock (House of Isaac). A large Star of David is still present on the exterior, but the building was converted into a residence.

Congregation Beth Yitzchock **[F43]**

Bethany Baptist Church **[U26]**

Bethany Baptist Church. A sober modern interpretation of the traditional side-tower church stands at 303 West 153rd Street **[●U26]**, home of Bethany Baptist Church, founded in 1932. Plans were filed by Maurice Instrator in 1953. The cornerstone was laid in 1956. Bethany, the village of Lazarus, was visited by Jesus the week before his death and gives its name to several congregations.

Bethany Congregational Church. Bethany Congregational Church originated in 1877 as a mission of the Broadway Tabernacle. Its colorful sanctuary at 455 Tenth Avenue [G1] was dedicated in 1883 and closed in 1928. The building later housed the WPA Federal Theater Project.

Bethany Memorial Reformed Church **[L22]**

Bethany Memorial Reformed Church. Organized in 1898 as a mission of the Madison Avenue Reformed Church, Bethany Memorial Reformed Church, at 400 East 67th Street **[●L22]**, was built in 1910 to designs by Nelson & Van Wagenen. When the Madison Avenue church disbanded in 1917, it gave its property to the Collegiate Reformed Protestant Dutch Church, with the condition that Collegiate support Bethany for 99 years. In the early 1980s, under the Rev. William L. Hanousek, Bethany Memorial began offering lodging to relatives of patients at nearby hospitals, a ministry that eventually brought him into conflict with Collegiate leaders, who hoped to sell the very valuable site for development.

Bethel A.M.E. Church [E72]

Bethel A.M.E. Church. "Taught by the Declaration of Independence, sustained by the Constitution of the United States, this nation can no more resist the advancing tread of the hosts of the oncoming blacks than it can bind the stars or halt the resistless motion of the tide," said the Rev. Reverdy C. Ransom, pastor of the Bethel African Methodist Episcopal Church in the early twentieth century.

Bethel, which means "house of God," was founded in 1819 on Mott Street and then settled on East 2nd Street. In 1862, Bethel bought 214 Sullivan Street [E72], which had been built in 1839 as the Sullivan Street Methodist Episcopal Church. Bethel moved again in 1894 to a pinnacle-framed Gothic Revival

Bethel A.M.E. Church [G31]

sanctuary at 239 West 25th Street [G31], in the notorious Tenderloin district, which Ransom deplored as a "valley of Baca," filled with "moral shipwrecks" and "ravening wolves." Bethel joined the exodus to Harlem in 1912, building a sanctuary at 52 West 132nd Street [●R2], designed by Wengenroth & Matsin. Members have included A. Philip Randolph, founder of the Brotherhood of Sleeping Car Porters, and Roy Wilkins, executive director of the NAACP. It was here in 1917 that Marcus Garvey expounded on his Back-to-Africa movement, shortly before founding the Universal Negro Improvement Association. Bethel still provides a key pulpit for those wishing to reach the Harlem community, as President Bill Clinton did in 1994.

Bethel A.M.E. Church **[R2]**

Bethel Chinese Assembly of God Church. Of all the flourishes added to plain buildings in an effort to signify their religious role, there are few as appealingly modest as the little steeple stuck on top of the two-story box at 77 Eldridge Street [●C20] that is home to the Bethel Chinese Assembly of God Church.

Bethel Chinese Assembly of God Church **[C20]**

Bethel Gospel Assembly. Among the biggest churches in Harlem, by virtue of occupying the former James Fenimore Cooper Junior High School, at 2 East 120th Street [●R47], the Bethel Gospel Assembly also has a large membership and offers many social and spiritual programs. Founded in 1916 by Mae Allison and C. Glover, who were rejected for membership at a white church, Bethel moved from East 101st Street to Bradhurst Avenue to West 131st Street before settling in 1947 in the former Harlem Club, at 34 West 123rd Street [●R36☆]. It was there until the early 1980s, under the Rev. Ezra Nehemiah Williams, when it acquired and renovated this Classical Moderne school, built in 1942, erecting a tall gold cross in the courtyard.

Bethel Gospel Assembly **[R47]**

Bethel Holy Church of Deliverance. Domestically scaled but clearly not a row house—not with those Gothic windows—525 West 147th Street [●S10] was home to Congregation Peni-El (Face of God), which merged in 1927 with Congregation Mount Zion. Its sanctuary was later used by Congregation Agudath Achim M'Krakau and the Mount Zion Tabernacle Christian Mission of Panama.

Bethel Holy Church of Deliverance **[S10]**

Bethel Holy Church of
Mount Sinai **[U17]**

Bethel Ship *John Wesley* [A27]

Bethel Way of the Cross Church of Christ
[R49]

Bethelite Community Baptist
Church **[R36]** at right and Greater
Bethel A.M.E Church **[R37]** at left

Bethel Holy Church of Mount Sinai. The Neoclassical facade gives away the institutional origins of 922 St. Nicholas Avenue **[●U17]**. It was the Washington Heights Free Library, built in 1899. The Bethel Holy Church of Mount Sinai was founded in 1932 by Bishop Ida Robinson and moved here in 1950, after the building had housed the Welsh Congregational Church.

Bethel Ship *John Wesley.* In a waterborne city, perhaps only floating churches could yield "the truant sailor restored to his long-waiting and weeping mother and wife, with money in his pocket and Christ in his heart," as the Bethel Ship *John Wesley* claimed to do. A Methodist Episcopal mission, the Floating Bethel Church was founded in 1845 to minister to Scandinavian and German seamen. It was anchored in the North (Hudson) River at Rector Street [A28], using the remodeled *Henry Leed.* A new ship was dedicated in 1857 and moved to Carlisle Street [A27]. The chapel was closed in 1872, but the ministry continued at Immanuel Swedish Methodist Episcopal Church in Brooklyn.

Bethel Way of the Cross Church of Christ. Squat onion domes, a rose window, horseshoe arches, and scarlet walls enliven 25 West 118th Street **[●R49]**. But closer inspection reveals the real delight: abundant Moorish relief work. This was Congregation Shaare Zedek of Harlem, built in 1900 to designs by Schneider & Herter. After the Harlem group reunited with the downtown Shaare Zedek in 1914, this became the Canaan Baptist Church and then the Bethel Way of the Cross Church of Christ. From here, one can see the former Congregation Ohab Zedek, at 18 West 116th Street, now the Baptist Temple Church.

Bethelite Community Baptist Church. The Harlem Club was the pinnacle of local society in the late nineteenth century, and its clubhouse, at 34 West 123rd Street **[●R36☆]**, reflected that stately position. Built in 1888/1889, it was designed by Lamb & Rich. The club was foreclosed in 1907, and the building has served as

Father Divine's Mansion, the Bethel Gospel Assembly, and the Bethelite Community Baptist Church.

Bethlehem Memorial Presbyterian Church. Both the Little Red School House and Elisabeth Irwin High School occupy buildings originally used by the Bethlehem Memorial Presbyterian Church. The Bethlehem Mission was organized in 1873 by the University Place Presbyterian Church. Bethlehem Chapel, at 196 Bleecker Street [●E71], was dedicated in 1890. It offered lectures, socials, and classes; a library, gymnasium, and bank branch. Memorial House, at 198 Bleecker Street, had a nursery, children's medical clinic, and milk station. Bethlehem Chapel merged in 1931 with the Charlton Street Memorial Church, at 40 Charlton Street [●B1], for which plans were filed in 1911 by Lansing C. Holden. The Bleecker Street properties were acquired by the Little Red School House, and the Charlton Street building houses the affiliated high school, Elisabeth Irwin. Bethlehem Memorial was dissolved in 1959.

Bethlehem Memorial Presbyterian Church (Elisabeth Irwin High School) **[B1]**

Beulah Wesleyan Methodist Church. This Modernist sanctuary at 221 West 136th Street [●T21] is actually the consolidation of three nineteenth-century row houses, renovated by Leon Dunkley in 1965, during the pastorate of the Rev. Neville N. Simmons-Smith. The Beulah Wesleyan Methodist Church was founded in 1914.

Beulah Wesleyan Methodist Church **[T21]**

Bialystoker Synagogue. Plain enough outside, befitting its origins in 1826 as the Willett Street Methodist Church, this sanctuary at 7 Bialystoker Place [●C16★] was lavishly remodeled inside as an Orthodox synagogue, with a richly carved two-story Ark and jewel-box stained-glass windows. It is the oldest building used as a synagogue in New York. Congregation Beth Haknesseth Anshe Bialystok (Synagogue of the People of Bialystok, Poland) was founded in 1878 and acquired the church in 1905. While nearby synagogues were abandoned in the 1970s and 1980s, Bialystoker endured under Rabbi Yitzchok Singer. And in the 1990s, it restored the sanctuary.

Bialystoker Synagogue **[C16]**

Church of the Blessed
Sacrament **[K8]**

Blessed Sacrament, Church of the. The soaring nave, ranks of statuary, tympanum inspired by Raphael, and vast rose window by Clement Heaton are monumental enough to terminate a grand axis. But the Church of the Blessed Sacrament sits at 152 West 71st Street [●K8☆], waiting to surprise or overwhelm passersby. The parish built a brick church on this site [K7] in 1887, by Napoleon Le Brun & Sons. In 1917, Gustave Steinback designed the present sanctuary. The church's valuable Broadway parcel was sold in 1922 to the developers of the Hotel Alamac, which is now an apartment building.

Bloomingdale Reformed Dutch
Church [K13]

Bloomingdale Reformed Dutch Church. In the hamlet of Harsenville, around present-day Lincoln Square, Jacob Harsen and his neighbors founded a church in 1805. They built a stout sanctuary from 1814 to 1816 on the Bloomingdale Road [K13]. It was razed in 1868 so the road could be widened, leaving just enough of the churchyard and burial ground that local goats could find "sacrilegious pasture above the dead." The congregation returned to the site [K14] and built a new church in 1884/1885, by Samuel B. Reed. Because of the lowering of the street grade since the nineteenth century, it is likely that a Food Emporium at Broadway and West 68th Street now occupies the volume of the old graveyard. The last stand of the Bloomingdale Reformed Dutch Church was at 949 West End Avenue [O11], designed in 1905 by Ludlow & Valentine.

Bloomingdale Reformed Dutch
Church [K14]

B'nai Israel, Congregation. See Village Temple

B'nai Israel of Washington Heights, Temple. See Gospel Missionary Baptist Church

B'nai Jacob Anshei Brzezan, Congregation. A hardy survivor, the Orthodox Congregation B'nai Jacob Anshei Brzezan (Sons of Jacob, People of Brzezan, Poland) was founded in 1891. Louis A. Sheinart altered 180 Stanton Street [●F47] in 1913 for its use. It continues to this day, having survived a recent ownership battle between the congregation and Rabbi Joseph Singer, who had kept the Stanton Street Syn-

Congregation B'nai
Jacob Anshei Brzezan
[F47]

agogue going through many lean years, but in the end tried to sell it.

B'nai Jehudah, Congregation. *See* Yorkville Synagogue

B'nai Jeshurun, Congregation. Shearith Israel was once the only synagogue in town. In the early nineteenth century, immigrants from Germany, Poland, Holland, and England worshiped there despite the differences between their Ashkenazic ritual and the Sephardic order of service. When they were rebuffed in their attempt to conduct separate services, they broke away in 1825 to form Congregation B'nai Jeshurun (Sons of Israel). They secured a sanctuary at 119 Elm Street [B29] from the First Colored Presbyterian Church and reconsecrated it in 5587, or 1827.

Congregation B'nai Jeshurun [E73]

The second synagogue, on Greene Street [E73], was built in 1850/1851 in the Perpendicular Gothic style by Field & Correja. The third synagogue, on West 34th Street [G11], where Macy's stands, was constructed in 1864/1865 in the Moorish style. The fourth synagogue, at 746 Madison Avenue [●L27☆], was built in 1884/1885 to designs by Rafael Guastavino and Schwarzmann & Buchman in the style of the West 34th Street sanctuary, using some of its bricks and masonry. Radically altered around 1918, the building still stands, and you can see its bricked-up side windows.

Congregation B'nai Jeshurun [G11]

The present synagogue, at 257 West 88th Street [●M12☆], was built in 1917/1918 and designed by Walter S. Schneider and Henry B. Herts what they called a "Semitic character" to prove that synagogues need not be "servile copies of Mohammedan mosques" or "ape the prevalent styles of Christian churches or Pagan temples." In the 1980s, the synagogue was reinfused with life by Rabbi Marshall T. Meyer, who reached out to young singles, homeless people, Christians, and Muslims. Services had to be moved to the Church of St. Paul and St. Andrew after the ceiling collapsed in 1991. "BJ," now under Rabbis J. Rolando Matalon and Marcelo R. Bronstein, was able to return home five years later but still uses the church, too, as its 3,000 members cannot be accommodated in a sanctuary built for 1,100.

Congregation B'nai Jeshurun **[L27]**

Congregation B'nai Jeshurun **[M12]**

Congregation B'nai Moses Joseph Anshei Zawichost and Zosmer [F13]

B'nai Levi, Chevra. *See* East Fifty-fifth Conservative Synagogue

B'nai Moses Joseph Anshei Zawichost and Zosmer, Congregation. This sanctuary at 317 East 8th Street [●F13] was built for the Orthodox Congregation B'nai Moses Joseph Anshei Zawichost and Zosmer (People of Zavichost, Poland, and Zosmer, Poland), founded in 1908. After years of sitting idle because of declining membership, the shul was taken over in the 1990s by a retired firefighter and a rabbi, who began holding services. But the congregation planned to sell the building for conversion into housing and sued to remove them.

Congregation B'nai Rappaport Anshe Dombrowa [F17]

B'nai Rappaport Anshe Dombrowa, Congregation. Congregation B'nai Rappaport Anshe Dombrowa, founded in 1884, filed plans in 1910 for a synagogue at 207 East 7th Street [F17], designed by Bernstein & Bernstein with strong bands of rustication. It was abandoned in 1975.

Bowery Mission Chapel. No one goes to the Bowery in search of beauty. But it is there to be found, in the Gothic Revival chapel of the Bowery Mission, at 227 Bowery [●E90], where stained-glass windows depict the story of the prodigal son. The mission, founded in 1879, bought this former coffin factory in 1908. The architects Marshall L. and Henry G. Emery remodeled it with a chapel, which President William Howard Taft visited in 1909. From the mission's standpoint, the hope was to induce at least a few of its unhappy charges to accept Jesus as their savior. To ensure this, chapel was a mandatory prelude to social service. "You cannot be fed, flopped, shaved and deloused without first hearing the gospel message," Elmer Bendiner wrote in *The Bowery Man.* "The soup line winds through the chapel." The sanctuary, which doubles as a shelter on the coldest nights, was renovated in 2001 by Diffendale & Kubec.

Bowery Mission Chapel [E90]

Brick Presbyterian Church. Rich in tradition, the Brick Presbyterian Church has never departed far from the architecture—or the building material—of its first Georgian sanctuary, erected while New York was actually ruled by the Georges. The congregation was founded in 1767 as the "uptown" home of the First Presbyterian Church, then on Wall Street. Its building on Beekman Street [A1], which opened in 1768, was first known as the New Church. But soon, the red-brick structure was called the Brick Meeting. Used as a military hospital and prison during the Revolutionary War, Brick was restored to religious service in 1784. It became independent in 1809 and commissioned John McComb Jr. to undertake alterations in 1822. Brick sold this property in 1856, and the *New York Times* built its new office on the spot.

Brick Meeting [A1]

Brick's next site, on Fifth Avenue [J54], had been the suburban villa of Coventry Waddell. The new church opened in 1858, with the old bell in its 250-foot spire. Griffith Thomas was the architect. In 1894, the Church of the Covenant was merged into Brick (but the Covenant name endured—and does to this day—in a sanctuary at 310 East 42nd Street). Brick Church sponsored inner-city mission work, most prominently at Christ Presbyterian Church.

Brick Presbyterian Church [J54]

In 1937, Brick sold its midtown property and bought a lot on the Upper East Side. That year, it joined with the Park Avenue Presbyterian Church, at 1010 Park Avenue [●N20], which had been organized in 1870 as a merger of the Park and Yorkville churches, known as First Union Presbyterian Church when it worshiped at 145 East 86th Street [N13].

The cornerstone for the new Brick Presbyterian Church, at 1140 Park Avenue [●N2☆], was laid in 1938, and the building was dedicated in 1940. "It's not dimmed and kept dark to create the atmosphere of mysticism," Mayor Fiorello H. LaGuardia said. "It's bright, it's lighted, the sunshine comes in." The design, by Lewis Ayres of York & Sawyer, includes the original bell and weather vane. The Chapel of the Reformed Faith, by Adams & Woodbridge, was added in 1952. History is never far here. In the old parish-house garden are two relics found a number of years ago at Christ Church: the cornerstones of the first two Brick Churches.

First Union Presbyterian Church [N13]

Brick Presbyterian Church **[N2]**

Brith Sholem, Congregation. The Hungarian Congregation Brith Sholem filed plans in 1901 for a synagogue at 6 Avenue D [F41], designed by George F. Pelham.

Broadway, Iglesia Adventista del Séptimo Día. This palazzo at 161 West 93rd Street [●M2] by John V. Van Pelt was originally the Nippon Club, founded by Jokichi Takamine, the man responsible for the cherry trees in Washington. It served as a clubhouse from 1912 until the beginning of World War II, when the building was closed and seized by the government. The Seventh-Day Adventist Church bought the structure in 1968.

Iglesia Adventista del Séptimo Día Broadway **[M2]**

Broadway Presbyterian Church. Taking a new name with each move, this church was organized in 1825 as Bleecker Street Presbyterian, with a sanctuary at 65 Bleecker Street [E75] by John McComb Jr. It then moved and became Fourth Avenue Presbyterian, occupying a Romanesque–Gothic sanctuary built in 1854/1855 at 286 Fourth Avenue [H41]. This building was also known as Dr. Crosby's Church after the celebrated Rev. Howard Crosby, founder of the Society for the Prevention of Crime. The church maintained the Hope Chapel, at 339 East 4th Street [F30], from 1893 to 1910. The last stop on the journey uptown was 601 West 114th Street [●Q42], at Broadway, a Collegiate Gothic sanctuary built in 1911/1912. The composition of the Broadway Presbyterian Church is akin to that of the Metropolitan-Duane United Methodist Church, also designed by Louis E. Jallade.

Fourth Avenue Presbyterian Church [H41]

Broadway Temple United Methodist Church. What a church this would have been! The 12-story apartment buildings that flank the modest Broadway Temple United Methodist Church, at 4111 Broadway [●V35], were supposed to have been mere bookend pedestals for a skyscraper with a revolving electric cross rising 725 feet into the sky, an auditorium seating several thousand, a social hall for 1,200, a pool and gymnasium, and more than 400 hotel rooms and apartments. This marvelously mad project was the brainchild of the Rev. Christian F. Reisner, pastor of the Chelsea Methodist Episcopal Church.

Broadway Presbyterian Church **[Q42]**

Chelsea was organized in 1843 and worshiped from 1849 until 1907 at 331 West 30th Street [G22]. In 1907, it moved to Fort Washington Avenue and West 178th Street [V26]. Reisner arrived in 1920 and boosted attendance with such evangelical stunts as the Snow Sermon, delivered in July from a hill of crushed ice. But Chelsea learned in 1923 that its church was doomed by the George Washington Bridge. That was Reisner's cue to undertake a "magnificent advertisement of God's business." Donn Barber designed the building, which Reisner unveiled in 1923. The apartments opened in 1927, followed the next year by the social hall, gymnasium, and bowling alley. But the Depression put an end to the greater scheme. Reisner's successor, the Rev. Allen Claxton, oversaw the construction in 1952 of a three-story sanctuary by Shreve, Lamb & Harmon, architects of the Empire State Building.

Broadway Temple Methodist Episcopal Church (as planned) [V35]

Broadway Temple United Methodist Church **[V35]**

Broadway United Church of Christ. "The Tabernacle inspired me, standing as it does in the midst of that awful Broadway," an English pastor said in 1928. The Broadway Tabernacle was founded by the Rev. Charles Grandison Finney, an architect of America's Second Great Awakening and of the first Tabernacle sanctuary, on lower Broadway [B41], built in 1835/1836. The second church, by Leopold Eidlitz, went up in 1859 at 582 Sixth Avenue [H1]. The last one, built at 1750 Broadway [K41] from 1903 to 1905, was a complex whose many functions were hidden in an overblown ecclesiastical shell by the architect J. Stewart Barney of Barney & Chapman. The crossing tower was a 10-story office and classroom building. In 1969, as the Broadway United Church of Christ, the congregation moved to the Church of St. Paul the Apostle on Columbus Avenue [●K30], perhaps the first time Protestants and Catholics in New York had shared a sanctuary for regular services. It now shares Advent Lutheran Church, at 2504 Broadway [●M1]. Although the Tabernacle on West 56th Street was razed, its presence can still be discerned in the architecture of the Argonaut Building, at Broadway and West 57th Street, whose white Gothic terra-cotta facade was designed to harmonize with the church next door.

Broadway Tabernacle [H1]

Broadway United Church of Christ [K41]

Broome Street Tabernacle [B10]

Brotherhood Synagogue **[H55]**

Primera Iglesia Evangélica Presbiteriana el Buen Vecino **[P14]**

Broome Street Tabernacle. With something of the rude power of the towers of San Gimignano, the Broome Street Tabernacle rose at Centre Market Place [B10], across from Police Headquarters. Designed by J. C. Cady & Company, it was built in 1885 for the New York City Mission Society, with a gymnasium and library that served 24,000 readers a year. The building was razed in 1959.

Brotherhood Synagogue. "The theme of our Synagogue is love, its message is brotherhood, its tool is the Bible, its aim is peace," said Rabbi Irving J. Block in 1954 as he founded Beth Achim (House of Brothers), a Conservative congregation known as the Brotherhood Synagogue.

Until 1973, it shared the Village Presbyterian Church, at 143 West 13th Street [●E20☆]. Then it acquired the Quakers' Twentieth Street Meeting House, at 28 Gramercy Park South [●H55★], designed by King & Kellum and built in 1859/1860. This sanctuary had resulted from an 1828 schism in which the Religious Society of Friends divided into liberal and orthodox branches. The orthodox group built a meetinghouse at 38 Henry Street [C28] and then this structure on Gramercy Park. They were here for almost a century before rejoining the liberal group at the Fifteenth Street Meeting House. James Stewart Polshek designed the renovation for the Brotherhood Synagogue and the Garden of Remembrance outside.

Buen Vecino, Primera Iglesia Evangélica Presbiteriana el. The Good Neighbor Federation Building, at 115 East 106th Street [●P14], was acquired in 1952 by the New York City Mission Society as a home for the 40-year-old First Spanish Church. The new institution was called the Good Neighbor (Buen Vecino) Church and Community House.

Calvario, Iglesia Cristiana el. Calvary Christian Church, at 409 West 47th Street [●123], is a reminder of Clinton's disappearing diversity.

Calvary and St. George's Church. Rather than compete for dwindling resources and prospective parishioners, three nearby Episcopal churches, each a landmark in its own right, merged in 1976 to form Calvary, Holy Communion, and St. George's Church.

St. George's was founded in 1749 as a chapel of Trinity Church. Its sanctuary on Beekman Street [A8] was the site of the first commencement for King's College, now Columbia University. In 1811, St. George's became a freestanding parish. The church burned in 1814 and was rebuilt on the site [A9]. Then it moved to Stuyvesant Square, where from 1846 to 1848 it erected a great Romanesque Revival church, by Leopold Eidlitz and Otto Blesch, at 209 East 16th Street [●E5★]. The Rev. Stephen H. Tyng belonged to the evangelical Low Church and may have chosen a Romanesque design to distinguish his sanctuary from the Gothic of fancy High Church parishes. A fire in 1865 badly weakened the twin steeples, which were taken down in 1889. The funeral in 1913 of J. P. Morgan, a church warden, drew a crowd of 30,000. The church established several mission chapels, including Free Grace, on East 19th Street [H60], and Bread of Life, on East 14th Street [F2]. Under the Rev. Thomas F. Pike, St. George's was one of the first churches in New York to house the homeless, beginning in 1982.

Calvary parish was organized in 1836 in a frame church on Fourth Avenue. This building was removed in 1842 to the present site [H47]. The sanctuary that stands today at 273 Park Avenue South [●H48☆] was designed by James Renwick Jr. and completed in 1848. Under the Rev. Samuel Shoemaker, Calvary Church was a leading center for the Oxford Group movement, from which Alcoholics Anonymous borrowed several key tenets. Both the Calvary and St. George's sanctuaries serve the current parish.

Holy Communion was founded in 1844. Its charming countryside church, at 47 West 20th Street [●H51★], was designed by Richard Upjohn and finished in 1846. Anna C. Rogers built the church in mem-

St. George's Church [A9]

St. George's Church **[E5]**

Calvary Church **[H48]**

ory of her husband, whose dying wish was for a house of God "where rich and poor might meet together." In 1883, the church was the host of the first convocation of black Episcopal clergymen. Deconsecrated after the 1976 merger, the Church of the Holy Communion was turned over to the Odyssey Institute for use as a drug-rehabilitation center. Odyssey sold the building to Peter Gatien, who opened the notorious Limelight disco in 1983 with a party at which Andy Warhol was the host and one guest arrived on a cross. Linked by law-enforcement authorities to widespread drug trafficking, Limelight was closed in 1996. After a brief reprise under Gatien, the club was reopened in 2002 as Estate, with a design by the Desgrippes Gobé Group that sought to reduce the ecclesiastical ambience.

Church of the Holy Communion (Limelight) **[H51]**

Calvary Baptist Church. Perhaps the most spectacular Skyscraper Church, at 123 West 57th Street **[●K36]**, is in the base of the Hotel Salisbury, with a tremendous Tudor Gothic portal inscribed WE PREACH CHRIST CRUCIFIED, RISEN, AND COMING AGAIN.

Calvary was founded in 1847 and built a church in 1854 at 50 West 23rd Street [H40]. It moved to a large red-sandstone Gothic sanctuary, built in 1883/1884, at 123 West 57th Street [K35]. John Rochester Thomas was the architect. Calvary maintained a chapel at 223 West 67th Street [K16] that later served as St. Matthew's Hall for the nearby Roman Catholic church of that name. In 1929, it filed plans for a 16-story church and apartment hotel by Jardine, Hill & Murdock at its West 57th Street site. The developers, Vincent J. Slattery and Morris H. Rothschild, had completed similar projects with the Church of the Strangers and the Second Presbyterian Church. The present Calvary Baptist Church was dedicated in 1931, with a parsonage on the fourteenth floor.

Calvary Baptist Church [K35]

Calvary Baptist Church **[K36]**

Camino, Iglesia el. Built as the Washington Heights United Presbyterian Church in 1894 to designs by Andrew Spence, the sanctuary at 141 Audubon Avenue **[●V36]** has since served as the Fort Washington Adventist Church and the Camino Church, part of the Christian and Missionary Alliance.

Iglesia el Camino **[V36]**

Iglesia Pentecostal Camino
a Damasco **[F28]**

Canaan Baptist Church of
Christ **[Q57]**

Laight Street Baptist Church [B24]

Central Baptist Church [I44]

Camino a Damasco, Iglesia Pentecostal. Since the late nineteeth century, the sanctuary at 289 East 4th Street **[●F28]** has served Congregation B'nai Israel, St. John Nepomucene Church, Congregation Nachlas Zvi, and Road to Damascus Pentecostal Church.

Canaan, Iglesia Cristiana. The tiny, spartan Canaan Christian Church, at 221 West 109th Street **[●O6]**, was designed in 1956 by Don A. Summo.

Canaan Baptist Church of Christ. Don't let the small entrance at 132 West 116th Street **[●Q57]** fool you; there is a huge auditorium in the rear, built in 1911 as Loew's 116th Street Theater, by Henry B. Herts. It is the pulpit of the Rev. Wyatt Tee Walker: housing developer, human-rights activist, author, and one-time aide to the Rev. Martin Luther King Jr., who attended Walker's installation as pastor in 1968. The Canaan Baptist Church of Christ was founded in 1932 as an offshoot of Mount Moriah Baptist Church and led by the Rev. Edward M. Moore. He brought the congregation to this building. Among many important visitors over the years, Canaan has counted Nelson Mandela, who came in 1994 on his first trip to the United States as the president of South Africa.

Carlebach Shul. See Kehilath Jacob, Congregation

Catholic Apostolic Church. See All Nations, Church for

Central Baptist Church. A huge window and tall tower resembling Bell Harry at Canterbury distinguish this church at 166 West 92nd Street **[●M5]**, designed in 1915 by Walter Cook. Central Baptist Church is descended from the Laight Street Baptist Church [B24], founded in 1842, which occupied an exquisite Greco-Italianate structure built in 1825 for a Presbyterian group. The Baptists moved to another striking church at 220 West 42nd Street [I44] in the 1860s and then to the former Riverside Baptist Chapel of 1888 on Amsterdam Avenue [M4], designed by Edelmann & Smith. It constructed the current sanctuary on the same site.

Central Park Baptist Church. Founded in 1855, Central Park Baptist Church was at 235 East 83rd Street [N27] well into the twentieth century.

Central Presbyterian Church. The former Park Avenue Baptist Church is an ecclesiastical complex behind a single Gothic facade at 593 Park Avenue [●L30☆]. Note, for example, that there are two full floors above the main west window. In its skillful manipulation of a medieval style to mask a twentieth-century urban form—church rooms piled up vertically on some of the world's most precious real estate—this structure is kin to Riverside Church. That's fitting, because it was built for the same congregation, once known as Park Avenue Baptist, by the same architects, Allen & Collens, working with Henry C. Pelton. One of the largest carillons in America, a 53-bell suite by Gillett & Johnston of Croydon, England, was given to Park Avenue Baptist by John D. Rockefeller Jr. After the Baptists decamped in 1929 to the new Riverside Church, Central Presbyterian moved in.

Central Baptist Church **[M5]**

Central Presbyterian Church [K42]

The Central Presbyterian Church was organized in 1821 in a schoolroom. Its first proper church, on Broome Street, opened the next year. In 1876, Central was given the Fifth Avenue Presbyterian Church, on East 19th Street, a Victorian Gothic structure by Leopold Eidlitz that had been erected two decades earlier. It moved this entire building to 220 West 57th Street [K42], where Charles Ives was organist and choirmaster. Central also ran the Mizpah Chapel, at 422 West 57th Street [●K37], which is now Trinity Presbyterian Church. Central's next home was another hand-me-down: the Madison Avenue Reformed Church [L47], built from 1869 to 1871 to designs by Ebenezer L. Roberts.

Central Presbyterian Church [L47]

Its current home was built for the Baptists from 1920 to 1922. The architects had to fit the church, parish house, Sunday school, 500-seat Bible Class study hall, and offices on a 7,800-square-foot site. The massing and fenestration are so skillful that it takes a second look to realize that this is much more than a place of traditional worship. All that's missing is the carillon, which the Baptists took with them to Riverside Church.

Central Presbyterian Church **[L30]**

Central Synagogue **[J6]**

Central Synagogue. Using Moorish architecture to proclaim itself vibrantly and exuberantly different from Christian churches, this venerable synagogue at 652 Lexington Avenue **[● J6★]** is notable for its minaret towers, copper globes, bichromatic masonry, and rose window with star tracery, modeled on the Dohany Street Synagogue in Budapest. Inside, it is—if possible—even more exotic, with intricate, scintillating stenciling. Designed by Henry Fernbach and constructed from 1870 to 1872, Central Synagogue is the oldest synagogue building in New York still in use by the same congregation that built it: Ahawath Chesed, founded on Ludlow Street in 1846 by German-speaking Bohemian immigrants, which merged in 1898 with Congregation Shaar Hashomayim, a German group founded in 1839 on Attorney Street. Members have included Senator Jacob K. Javits, Evelyn Lauder, Lewis Rudin, and Laurence A. Tisch.

Under Rabbi Peter J. Rubinstein, a renovation was begun in the 1990s. As work neared completion in 1998, fire blazed through the roof and gutted the sanctuary, though it spared the Ark. "We will take our Torah scrolls, which we have, and we will wander for a period of time, and then in a great triumphant moment, we will return to that building," Rubinstein promised. At High Holy Days that year, services were held in the Seventh Regiment Armory. A $40 million restoration and renovation by Hardy Holzman Pfeiffer Associates was finished in 2001, two days before the attack on New York, when, to the flourish of trumpeting shofars, the Reform congregation returned to its home—now one of the newest synagogues in Manhattan as well as one of the oldest.

Centro María. *See* St. Ambrose, Church of

Chambers Memorial Baptist Church. The strongly Romanesque design of the Chambers Memorial Baptist Church, at 219 East 123rd Street **[●R40]**, shows the hand of Henry F. Kilburn. Originally the Carmel Baptist Church, the sanctuary was built in 1890/1891. The Rev. Adam Chambers, pastor from 1903 to 1921, is remembered in its name.

Charles Street Presbyterian Church. The Carolus apartments, at 31 Charles Street [D11], mark the site of the Greek Revival Charles Street Presbyterian Church, built in 1844 as the Third Associate Presbyterian Church.

Chasam Sopher, Congregation. Even in its modesty, there is an undeniable dignity and grandeur to this Romanesque synagogue at 8 Clinton Street [●F46], Manhattan's second oldest surviving purpose-built synagogue. It was constructed in 1853 as the home of Congregation Rodeph Sholom. After that congregation moved in 1886, the synagogue was acquired by Congregation Czenstochauer Chasam Sopher (Seal of the Scribe) W'Anshei Unterstanester. As the Orthodox group began dwindling, the building was cared for almost single-handedly by Morris Weiser, who had survived the Janowska concentration camp and arrived in this country in 1947. "People say that God saved me from Hitler," he said, "so I could save this shul."

Congregation Chasam Sopher [F46]

Westminster Presbyterian Church [G40]

Chelsea Presbyterian Church. It's a good bet that party boys at the Twirl nightclub have no idea that the large space in the old Carteret Hotel, at 214 West 23rd Street [●G39], was designed as a Skyscraper Church for a venerable congregation. Chelsea Presbyterian was organized in 1834 as the Eighth Avenue Church. After building a sanctuary in 1854 on West 23rd Street [G38], it became the West Twenty-third Street Church. This body merged in 1890 with the Westminster Presbyterian Church, which had built its Greek Revival sanctuary in 1856 at 151 West 22nd Street [G40]. The combined fold was renamed Chelsea Presbyterian Church in 1923. "We are doing that which is going to be done from here to the Pacific Coast," the Rev. T. F. Savage said in 1926 when he announced plans to replace the church with a hotel and sanctuary designed by Emery Roth. This was not to the liking of the *New York Times*, which asked, "Must we visualize a New York in which no spire points heavenward?" After Chelsea left, the space was used by the Vanguard Recording Studio before becoming a nightclub.

Chelsea Presbyterian Church [G38]

Chelsea Presbyterian Church (Twirl) [G39]

Childs Memorial Temple
Church of God in Christ
[S11]

Childs Memorial Temple Church of God in Christ. When Harlem's other churches shut their doors to Malcolm X's funeral, Bishop Alvin A. Childs of the Faith Temple Church of God in Christ opened his. Here the actor Ossie Davis, in his eulogy, bade farewell to "a Prince— our own black shining Prince!—who didn't hesitate to die, because he loved us so." The setting was the former Lido Theater, at 1763 Amsterdam Avenue **[●S11]**, built as a bowling alley and used briefly as a synagogue before being acquired in 1952 by Faith Temple, organized four years earlier by Childs, a tremendously popular evangelist. The church was renamed in his honor in 1974, a year after his death.

Chinese Conservative Baptist Church. At 103 Madison Street **[●C32]**, the Chinese Conservative Baptist Church is one of four Chinese sanctuaries on a single block.

Chinese United Methodist
Church **[B54]**

Chinese Evangel Mission Church. In the central bay of the five-story Chinese Evangel Mission Church, at 97 Madison Street **[●C30]**, is a two-story cross.

Chinese Missionary Baptist Church. The Chinese Missionary Baptist Church, at 136 Henry Street **[●C40]**, was once Congregation Anshe Wolkoviska.

Chinese United Methodist Church. The little Chinese United Methodist Church, at 69 Madison Street **[●B54]**, is descended from the Five Points Mission, named for the notoriously hellish slum nearby. Begun in 1850 by the New-York Ladies' Home Missionary Society of the Methodist Episcopal Church, Five Points began actively proselytizing Chinese-Americans in the late 1870s.

Christ Church [B40]

Christ and St. Stephen's Church. Stand at 120 West 69th Street **[●K15☆]**, close your eyes, and think of the Little Church Around the Corner: picturesquely haphazard, nooks and crannies, a low roofline set far from the street behind trees and shrubbery. Open your eyes, and here it is, the suburban chapel of the Church of the Transfiguration, the oldest sanctuary on the Upper West Side. It was built in 1876 under the Rev. George

Christ Church [H3]

H. Houghton. William H. Day was the architect. The sanctuary was remodeled by J. D. Fouquet and acquired in 1897 by St. Stephen's Episcopal parish, founded in 1805, which began on Broome Street [B14] and spent a quarter century at the old Church of the Advent on West 46th Street [J30], with which it merged. The arrival of St. Stephen's Church at the West 69th Street chapel did not at first please Christ Church, which was at the time only three blocks away, but the two bodies eventually merged.

Christ Church [K5]

The second oldest Episcopal parish in New York, Christ Church was organized in 1793 and first worshiped at 49 Ann Street [A6]. This sanctuary was later used by Christ Roman Catholic Church, precursor to the Transfiguration Roman Catholic parish. (Here is how the circle turns in religious real estate: St. Stephen's broke away from the Zion English Lutheran Church, whose original home on Mott Street is now used by Transfiguration parish, successor to the Roman Catholic church housed in the first sanctuary of Christ Episcopal Church, which is now allied with St. Stephen's.) The parish moved in 1823 to 79 Anthony Street [B40], now Worth Street; in 1854 to 7 West 18th Street [H61], later St. Ann's Church for the Deaf; in 1859 to the former Fifth Avenue Baptist Church, on East 35th Street [H3]; and finally to a Romanesque building by Charles Coolidge Haight on Broadway [K5], built in 1889/1890, with a tower that looked like a Victorian gazebo in the sky.

St. Stephen's Church [J30]

Christ Church sold its Broadway frontage in 1925, and the building lost its gorgeous tower, as it was truncated to accommodate a small commercial structure, the Lester Building, at 2061 Broadway. In the 1970s, Christ and St. Stephen's Churches, depleted by the loss of parishioners displaced by Lincoln Center, joined under the Rev. Joseph Zorawick. Christ parish moved to St. Stephen's home on West 69th Street. The remaining portion of its former sanctuary was used by the Bible Deliverance Evangelical Church before being razed to make way for the Lincoln Park apartments. A ghost image of the nave, in cross section, can be seen on the west wall of the Lester Building, whose cherubic column capitals echo those of the old Christ Church.

Christ and St. Stephen's Church **[K15]**

Christ Apostolic Church of U.S.A. **[P4]**

Madison Avenue Methodist Episcopal Church [L40]

Christ Church, United Methodist **[L41]**

Christ Apostolic Church of U.S.A. Congregation Ansche Chesed worshiped at the turn of the twentieth century in this sanctuary, formerly Moses Montefiore, at 160 East 112th Street **[●P4]**. It was Congregation Tikvath Israel of Harlem as late as the 1980s.

Christ Church, United Methodist. The brightest colors in a house of worship are not always in the windows. At 520 Park Avenue **[●L41]**, they are in the vaults and arches—dazzling mosaics that fracture Manhattan's monochrome and recall the fabulous tiled churches of Ravenna. Unlike most Protestant churches, which are closed between services, Christ Church, United Methodist, is open and well worth visiting.

The congregation was formed by the union of the Madison Avenue and Sixty-first Street Methodist Episcopal Churches. The Madison Avenue group, founded in 1881, built a church on East 60th Street [L40] from 1881 to 1884. Designed by R. H. Robertson, it had a powerful bell tower and an open belvedere framed by round arches. The Sixty-first Street congregation, founded in 1863, was at 229 East 61st Street [L38], a Gothic sanctuary built in 1874/1875, later used by the Église Française du St.-Esprit.

Although Ralph Adams Cram was a master of Gothic, for the Park Avenue sanctuary, finished in 1933, he used a robust Romanesque–Byzantine palette, explaining that the "Protestant congregation was averse to Medieval Catholicism both by inheritance and doctrine." Christ Church was known around the country through the Rev. Ralph Washington Sockman's *National Radio Pulpit*, broadcast on NBC from 1928 to 1962.

Christ Lutheran Church. An anvil served as the first pulpit in 1868 for this German and English church, founded above a blacksmith shop on East 14th Street. In 1882, the Rev. George U. Wenner bought a sanctuary at 406 East 19th Street [H60] that had been the Chapel of Free Grace, built in 1859 by St. George's Episcopal Church. After Stuyvesant Town took over its site, Christ Lutheran Church built its current sanctuary, at 355 East 19th Street **[●H59]**, in 1948. The pared-down Gothic design was by Herbert E. Matz.

Christ Lutheran Church **[H59]**

Christ Presbyterian Church. A social-service complex with a Gothic nave grafted on, almost like a medieval accretion, stands at 336 West 36th Street **[●G6]**. Around this island of repose swirls the chaos of the garment district. Christ Presbyterian Church began as the West Side mission of the Brick Presbyterian Church, completed in 1867 at 228 West 35th Street [G9], a jaunty hybrid of Romanesque and Gothic. The Christ Church Memorial Buildings on West 36th Street, by Parish & Schroeder, were built in 1904/1905 with a great Sunday-school room, bowling alleys, gymnasium, pool room, library, workshop, and kitchen. The complex is now used by the Postgraduate Center for Mental Health, a not-for-profit organization that trains professionals and offers treatment and programs for those unable to afford them, so the buildings continue to serve a human-welfare mission.

Christ Presbyterian Church (Postgraduate Center for Mental Health) **[G6]**

Christ Temple of the Apostolic Faith. Rich in Gothic trimming, 17 West 128th Street **[●R8]** was designed by Louis Giele and built in 1921 for the Missionary Sisters of the Third Order of St. Francis. This building and an adjoining nineteenth-century villa on West 129th Street—notable for the Moorish-style gingerbread porches added in the 1880s—were acquired in 1941 by the Peace Center–Nazareth Mission Church and then in 1979 by Christ Temple of the Apostolic Faith, founded in 1957 by Bishop James I. Clark Sr.

Christ the Consoler, Chapel of. Hospital chapels, which now tend to be tucked away, were once visibly part of a medical campus. The ivy-covered Chapel of Christ the Consoler of 1889, run by the New York Protestant Episcopal City Mission Society, occupied a courtyard of Bellevue Hospital at the foot of East 26th Street [H32] until 1937.

Christ Temple of the Apostolic Faith **[R8]**

Christ the Lord, Chapel of. The Modernist Chapel of Christ the Lord, in the base of the Episcopal Church Center at 815 Second Avenue **[● J44]**, was designed by Adams & Woodbridge and built in 1961. The abstract stained-glass windows were by Gabriel Loire of Chartres.

Chapel of Christ the Lord
[J44]

Christ the Savior Orthodox Church [R42]

Christ the Savior Orthodox Church. There was once a bit of Plymouth Rock in Harlem, embedded in the pulpit of the Pilgrim Congregational Church, at 51 East 121st Street [R42], by Lawrence B. Valk, built in 1882. In 1927, the sanctuary was bought by the three-year-old Christ the Savior Orthodox Church, a Russian congregation. The parish moved in 1970 to a far more modest sanctuary at 340 East 71st Street [●L13], remodeled by Vladimir B. Morosov, where services continue to be offered in Russian and English. North General Hospital took the place of the great uptown church.

Christ the Savior Orthodox Church [L13]

Christian and Missionary Alliance Church. *See First Alliance Church*

Chung Te Buddhist Association. Deco-inspired sanctuaries are few, but 152 Henry Street [●C42], designed in 1945 by Emil Koeppel, clearly shows the Art Moderne influence of the 1930s. It was once the House of Sages, or Congregation Agudas Anshei Mamod Ubeis Vead Lachachomim, where services were held for retired rabbis, who came daily "to pray, meet friends, talk over old times, discourse on points of talmudic law," as Gerard R. Wolfe wrote in *The Synagogues of New York's Lower East Side* in 1978. Not long thereafter, the building was acquired by the Chung Te Buddhist Association, whose sign obscures a Hebrew inscription underneath. The temple is affiliated with the Chinese Pure Land school of Buddhism and associated with the World Buddhist Center, next door at 158 Henry Street. This is not the only synagogue to undergo such a striking transformation. The Kalvarier Shul on Pike Street is now the Sung Tak Buddhist Association.

Chung Te Buddhist Association [C42]

Church on the Hill A.M.E. Zion. The sanctuary at 975 St. Nicholas Avenue [●U10] has a spare, institutional front. But a closer look reveals that the blank bays are metal screens, behind which is the facade of an older and more ornate structure that served as the Republican Club, Commonwealth Hall, Glencoe Athletic Club, and YMHA of Washington Heights. The African Methodist Episcopal Zion Church on the Hill was organized in 1949. This structure was rebuilt and

Church on the Hill A.M.E. Zion [U10]

rededicated in 1970, under the pastorate of the Rev. U. Jackson.

City Tabernacle of Seventh-Day Adventists.

Several of Harlem's synagogues, though long ago converted to Christian use, have been exceptionally well maintained, allowing modern viewers to get a much better sense of that brief period of Jewish life. The City Tabernacle of Seventh-Day Adventists, at 562 West 150th Street [●S3], originally Mount Neboh Synagogue, was built from 1915 to 1917 and designed by Berlinger & Moscowitz to repudiate both Moorish–Romanesque and Neoclassical synagogues, which, because they resembled small bank buildings, suggested "temples of Mammon and not, as they should, temples of God." After 13 years, Mount Neboh moved downtown to the Unity Synagogue, at 130 West 79th Street [M33★], where it remained until going out of existence in 1978. Both Mount Neboh Synagogues were acquired by the Seventh-Day Adventists. The Harlem sanctuary, minus its Decalogue, was rededicated in 1950. Services are still held on Saturdays.

City Tabernacle of Seventh-Day Adventists **[S3]**

Civic Center Synagogue.

A flame is supposed to come to your mind when looking at the bulbous front of this 1969 synagogue by William N. Breger at 49 White Street [●B36☆] in Tribeca. The Civic Center Synagogue, home to Congregation Shaare Zedek (a different group from that on West 93rd Street), may look more like a marble-clad pot-bellied stove, but at least it represents an effort to use a distinctly Modernist vocabulary for a house of worship. And it does have some sublime moments; for instance, the building seems to float overhead as you approach it. Shaare Zedek was founded in 1938 to serve textile workers and civil servants in the neighborhood. Today, it also caters to a residential and artistic population in lower Manhattan. "Traditional Judaism," said Rabbi Jonathan Wilson Glass, "can be a vehicle for anyone's Jewish expression."

Civic Center Synagogue **[B36]**

Cloisters.

See Notre-Dame-du-Bourg, Chapel of, and San Martín, Church of

Commandment Keepers Ethiopian
Hebrew Congregation **[R35]**

Commandment Keepers Ethiopian Hebrew Congregation. Since 1962, this nineteenth-century town house on Mount Morris Park [●R35☆] has been the spiritual home of New York's small black Jewish population. (It was once home to John Dwight of Church & Dwight, makers of Arm & Hammer baking soda.) Commandment Keepers Ethiopian Hebrew Congregation is the successor to the Beth B'nai Abraham Synagogue of Black Jews, at 29 West 131st Street, founded in 1924 by Rabbi Wentworth Arthur Matthew. "We are self-sustained," he said in 1970. "All our members are working. We have no broken families." Following readings from the Torah, with the scroll in his arms, Matthew would lead the men in marching around the synagogue while everyone sang hymns and clapped, followed by shouts of "Hallelujah, Amen" or "Holy God" after he replaced the Torah in the Ark.

Church of the Messiah [E86]

Church of the Messiah
[E48]

Community Church of New York | Metropolitan Synagogue of New York. The last house of worship begun before World War II was built by a leading pacifist, the Rev. John Haynes Holmes. Magoon & Salo designed the brick box at 40 East 35th Street [●H7] in the International Style. It was begun in 1940, but not completed until 1948.

As starkly modern as the church appears to be, the congregation goes well back in New York history as the Second Unitarian Church or Church of the Messiah, founded in 1825. Its first sanctuary, on Mercer Street [E86], by Josiah Brady, was one of the earliest Greek Revival buildings in New York. After it burned, the congregation built at 728 Broadway [E48] in 1839. The dry-goods king A. T. Stewart bought this building in 1865 and turned it into a theater for his protégé, Lucy Rushton. Never successful, it changed hands constantly, inspiring a verse: "You may paint, you may fresco the place as you will / But the scent of church lingers about it still."

Messiah resettled on Park Avenue [H6] in a Victorian Romanesque sanctuary by Carl Pfeiffer built in 1867. Holmes, called to the congregation in 1907, was a founder of the NAACP and the ACLU; an opponent of both world wars (the only ornament on his church is the sculpture *Swords into Plowshares* by Moissaye Marans); and, with Rabbi Stephen S. Wise, the organizer of a committee whose charges of corruption in the administration of Mayor James J. Walker helped pave the way to Walker's downfall. Under Holmes, Messiah broke for several decades with Unitarian leadership and renamed itself the Community Church of New York, to denote its broadly nondenominational outlook. "Just as our radical ideas in theology, psychology and politics break down barriers, smash traditions, and carry on into new realms of thought and life, so the radical ideas of material and plan which have gone into the making of this building defy old practices," Holmes said. "When you look at this church, you behold not a replica of what has been, but a prophecy of what is yet to be." Holmes was succeeded in 1949 by the Rev. Donald Szantho Harrington. The Metropolitan Synagogue of New York held its first service here in 1959.

Community Church of New York [H6]

Community Church of New York **[H7]**

Community Synagogue. Upon no single church in New York has tragedy fallen harder than on St. Mark's Lutheran, at 325 East 6th Street [●**E52**], the heart of Kleindeutschland. Almost 800 of its members perished in the burning of the excursion steamer *General Slocum* in the East River on June 15, 1904. There were 156 hearses in one of the many processions from the church to the Lutheran Cemetery in Queens. (Four blocks away, in Tompkins Square Park, is the Slocum Memorial Fountain, a 9-foot marble stele.) The congregation never really recovered, though it worshiped here until 1940 before merging with Zion Church in Yorkville to form Zion–St. Mark's Lutheran Church. Then this sanctuary became the Community Synagogue, an Orthodox congregation. Named in honor of Rabbi Max D. Raiskin, it sits across from the aromatic Indian restaurant row.

Community Synagogue **[E52]**

Congregación Mita, Iglesia. This Neoclassical structure at 612 West 180th Street [●**V23**] was designed in 1922 by Sommerfeld & Steckler and built as the Temple of the Covenant, a congregation founded in 1913.

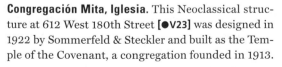

Iglesia Congregación Mita **[V23]**

Congregational Church of God
[U19]

Convent Avenue Baptist Church **[S16]**

Corpus Christi Church **[Q38]**

Congregational Church of God. The Congregational Church of God was built in 1967 at 1889 Amsterdam Avenue [●U19], in the pastorate of the Rev. William Aaron.

Convent Avenue Baptist Church. Wrapped around a Norman tower is a gabled roof scape that makes the Convent Avenue Baptist Church, at 420 West 145th Street [●S16☆], as important an architectural presence as it is a pastoral, historical, and political one. Built from 1897 to 1899 for the Washington Heights Baptist Church, it was designed by Lamb & Rich. Under the Rev. John W. Saunders, the present congregation arrived in 1942. The Rev. Mannie Lee Wilson, the first black Protestant to preach at St. Patrick's Cathedral and the first black clergyman to preach at the White House, was pastor from 1961 to 1982. This is the site of an annual commemoration by the Baptist Ministers Conference of Greater New York of the Rev. Martin Luther King Jr., whose last public appearance in New York was at this church on March 26, 1968, nine days before he was assassinated. He had come to enlist support for his nationwide Poor People's Campaign.

Cornell Memorial Methodist Episcopal Church. The Cornell Memorial Methodist Episcopal Church, at 231 East 76th Street [N45], by D. & J. Jardine, was built in 1883 to serve a congregation founded in 1869.

Cornerstone Center.
See Our Saviour's Atonement Lutheran Church

Corpus Christi Church. Founded in 1897 as a chapel of the Little Church Around the Corner, which had given up an outpost two blocks away, the Episcopal Corpus Christi Church, at 221 West 69th Street [K9], was later the Cathedral of Our Saviour of the Holy Orthodox Church in America.

Corpus Christi Church. After Columbia University moved to Morningside Heights, this Roman Catholic parish was established in 1906. Plans were filed for the first church, at 529 West 121st Street [Q37], by F. A. de Meuron. It was replaced with the present neo-Georgian sanctuary on the same site [●Q38], completed in

1936 and designed by Wilfred E. Anthony. Thomas Merton, author of *The Seven Storey Mountain*, was instructed in Catholicism at Corpus Christi Church.

Covenant, Church of the. There are several delightful country chapels in Manhattan, but none more incongruously situated than the Presbyterian Church of the Covenant, a little Victorian Gothic gem at 310 East 42nd Street [● J50✰], in the heart of midtown.

The first Church of the Covenant, on Park Avenue [H5], was designed by James Renwick Jr. and dedicated in 1865. Its mission school occupied space above a stable on East 40th Street and was headed by the architect J. Cleveland Cady. He designed a new chapel on East 42nd Street, dedicated in 1871, that eventually grew stronger than the mother church. So Memorial Chapel became the Church of the Covenant in 1893, and the old Covenant on Park Avenue was merged into the Brick Presbyterian Church in 1894. A Fellowship Hall was added to the 42nd Street site in 1927, with a half-timbered facade to complement neighboring Tudor City. Long after Covenant was built, the bed of 42nd Street was lowered, which is why the church seems to be standing on a hillock. The congregation of the Adams-Parkhurst Presbyterian Church, also designed by Cady, merged into this body in 1965.

Church of the Covenant [H5]

Church of the Covenant **[J50]**

Cristiana Misionera, Iglesia. The Christian Missionary Church has been a longtime presence at 247 East 7th Street [●F18].

Crossroads, Presbyterian Church of the. *See* Labor Temple

Crossroads Seventh-Day Adventist Church. One of three nearby German churches designed by John Boese, the sanctuary at 410 West 45th Street [●I31] was begun in 1903. The Fourth German Mission Reformed Dutch Church moved here after conveying its West 40th Street sanctuary to Abyssinian Baptist Church. The West 45th Street building has since been the Third Moravian Church (now part of the United Moravian Church) and the Crossroads Seventh-Day Adventist Church, which came here from the former Mount Neboh Synagogue, at 130 West 79th Street [M33★].

Iglesia Cristiana Misionera **[F18]**

Crossroads Seventh-Day Adventist Church **[I31]**

Chapel of the Crucifixion
[I37]

Crucifixion, Chapel of the. John's Pizzeria, at 260 West 44th Street [●I37], is a cradle of the worldwide Christian and Missionary Alliance movement as the former Gospel Tabernacle, a revival house built in 1889/1890 by the Rev. Albert Benjamin Simpson, working with Edelmann & Smith. Simpson organized the congregation in 1883, and it briefly occupied the Northwest Reformed Dutch Church, at 145 West 23rd Street [G34], and the Church of the Disciples, on Madison Avenue [J37]. The Eighth Avenue facade, which dates to 1924, has nothing ecclesiastical except two Gothic doorways. Inside is a large sanctuary under a honey-colored stained-glass skylight. In the 1980s, as part of Covenant House, founded by the Rev. Bruce Ritter to help runaway teenagers, it was the Chapel of the Crucifixion, with a 24- by 30-foot copper relief mural, *Passion on Eighth Avenue*, by Charles Vukovich. In 1997, the room was transformed into John's by the architect Andrew Tesoro and the muralist Douglas Cooper.

Church of the Crucifixion [S5]

Church of the Crucifixion **[S6]**

Crucifixion, Church of the. Corbusier comes to Harlem? Well, no, but the Episcopal Church of the Crucifixion, at 459 West 149th Street [●S6], by Costas Machlouzarides, is as close as anything in Manhattan to Ronchamp. It's terrifically dynamic. Four inclined conical concrete sections—altar, baptistery, chapel, and shrine—converge under an airfoil-shaped roof. Originally on this site [S5] was the Hamilton Grange Reformed Church of 1906 by Bannister & Schell. After that congregation merged with the Fort Washington Collegiate Church in 1937, the building was taken over by Crucifixion, an African-American and Afro-Caribbean Episcopal group founded in 1916 by the Rev. Jedediah Edmead of St. Kitts. His three successors, including the Rev. A. Eric Joseph of Dominica-Antigua, all have come from the Caribbean. The old church burned in 1963 and was replaced in 1967.

Czernowitz-Bukoviner, Congregation. The synagogue of Congregation Czernowitz-Bukoviner, at 224 East 5th Street [●E61], named for a city and region in Ukraine, is now Kraus House, run by the Association for the Help of Retarded Children.

Congregation Darech Amuno **[D12]**

De Witt Reformed Church [F55]

De Witt Reformed Church **[F56]**

Iglesia Adventista del Séptimo Día Delancey **[B15]**

Darech Amuno, Congregation. Congregation Darech Amuno (Way of Faith), organized in 1838, seemed fated to wander: Greene Street, Sixth Avenue, Seventh Avenue, Bleecker Street, West 4th Street. Finally, it dedicated this Neoclassical, yellow-brick sanctuary at 53 Charles Street [●D12☆] in 1917. Designed by Sommerfeld & Steckler, it was an alteration of an older building.

De Witt Reformed Church. A breath of fresh ecclesiastical air from the architect Edgar Tafel, the DeWitt Reformed Church, at 280 Rivington Street [●F56], seems to have been built around a rough-hewn lumber cross. De Witt was developed by the New York City Mission Society, whose object was "to promote morality and religion among the poor and destitute." The first church on this site [F55] was built in 1880/1881 in memory of the Rev. Thomas De Witt, pastor of Marble Collegiate Church. The architect was J. Cleveland Cady. It offered English, German, and Italian services; Chinese Sunday school; and meetings for "Hebrew Christians." It had a library, gymnasium, and rooftop playground. And when people would not come to De Witt, De Witt went to them, holding services in apartments. De Witt rebuilt in 1957/1958 to serve African-Americans, Puerto Ricans, and Russians. The timber cross came from the society's camp in Pawling, New York; some of the bricks came from old buildings nearby, a few from De Witt itself.

Delancey, Iglesia Adventista del Séptimo Día. The entrance is at 126 Forsyth Street [●B15], but Delancey Street is where the action was: storefronts to furnish income to the congregation. J. C. Cady & Company designed this sanctuary in 1890 for the Allen Street Presbyterian Church. Congregation Poel Zedek Anshe Ileya (Righteous-doers of Ileya, Belarus) was here until 1970, when the building was purchased by the Seventh-Day Adventist congregation, under the Rev. Hildebrando Saldía, which traces its origins to 1955. By the 1980s, the pews were filled with Dominicans, Ecuadoreans, Cubans, Puerto Ricans, and, at a separate service, Chinese. On Saturdays—Adventists also celebrate Sabbath on Saturday—babies were being baptized where the Ark once stood. But there was still a Star of David over the door.

Dendur, Temple of Isis at. The only house of worship in Manhattan built during the reign of Caesar Augustus sits on its own serene island in the Sackler Wing of the Metropolitan Museum of Art **[●N23★]**. But the story of the Temple of Dendur is pure tumult from its origins more than 2,000 years ago in the Nubian settlement of Dendur. Doing battle with Abyssinia, Petesi and Pihor, the sons of a local chieftain, were drowned in the Nile. This shrine was built around 15 b.c.e. by order of Emperor Augustus, dedicated to their memory and the goddess Isis. In 577, the temple was converted into a Coptic church. In the early 1960s, as the Aswan High Dam was being built, the rising Nile threatened both Dendur and the temples at Abu Simbel, which were relocated with assistance from the United States. In return, the Egyptian government offered Dendur to America. The Met and the Smithsonian vied for it, as did 22 other institutions, governments, and private groups, including one in Cairo, Illinois. In 1968, 661 crates containing the disassembled temple landed in Brooklyn on a freighter also laden with cheeses, canned tomatoes, and maraschino cherries. Ten years later, the Sackler Wing opened, designed by Kevin Roche John Dinkeloo Associates.

Temple of Isis at Dendur **[N23]**

Dios, Iglesia de. One of the twins of East 6th Street, no. 636 **[●F24]** was designed by Vaux & Radford and built in 1889. Now the Church of God, it was once the United Brethren Mission.

Iglesia de Dios **[F24]**

Disciples, Church of the. Like a domical mountain range, or at least a colony of beehives, this fantastic church on Madison Avenue [J37] was designed by Lawrence B. Valk and built in 1872/1873. The pulpit was occupied by the Rev. George Hughes Hepworth, who counted Ulysses S. Grant in his congregation, and the Rev. John Philip Newman, Grant's spiritual adviser. It also served briefly as the Gospel Tabernacle, under the Rev. Albert Benjamin Simpson. The Church of the Disciples did not last more than two decades.

Church of the Disciples [J37]

Church of the Disciples of Christ
(Everard Baths) **[H29]**

Iglesia Pentecostal el Divino
Maestro **[F38]**

Downtown Baptist Church
[Q12]

Downtown Talmud Torah
Synagogue **[C15]**

Disciples of Christ, Church of the. New York's most enduring and notorious gay bathhouse, the Everard, occupied what was once the Church of the Disciples of Christ, on West 28th Street **[●H29]**. It was built in 1860 as Free Will Baptist and acquired five years later by the Disciples of Christ. James Everard converted it into Turkish, Roman, and Electric Baths in 1888. By 1919, it had become a gay resort. It was still operating in 1977 when a dreadful fire claimed nine lives. The great Romanesque entry arch can still be seen at what is now the Yung Kee Wholesale Center.

The Disciples built a Romanesque church by Charles Mettam at 323 West 56th Street [K40] in 1883. They moved to what is now the Mount Pleasant Baptist Church, at 142 West 81st Street **[●M31☆]**, before crossing over to the East Side, to the Park Avenue Christian Church, at 1010 Park Avenue **[●N20]**, where they have been since 1945.

Divino Maestro, Iglesia Pentecostal el. The sanctuary of the Divine Teacher Pentecostal Church, at 250 East 3rd Street **[●F38]**, was Congregation Beth Haknesseth Anshei Mieletz (Synagogue of the People of Mieletz, Poland), founded in 1888. Plans were filed in 1946 by Robert Teichman.

Downtown Baptist Church. Very much uptown, the Downtown Baptist Church is in a former house at 413 Malcolm X Boulevard **[●Q12]** that was once part of an elegant row designed by Lamb & Rich and built in 1883.

Downtown Talmud Torah Synagogue. The school building at 142 Broome Street **[●C15]** is recognizable by the Decalogue atop the central pavilion as a place of worship as well. Plans were filed in 1957 by David Moed. The Downtown Talmud Torah Synagogue opened in 1959.

Dyckman, Iglesia Adventista del Séptimo Día.
See Inwood Hebrew Congregation

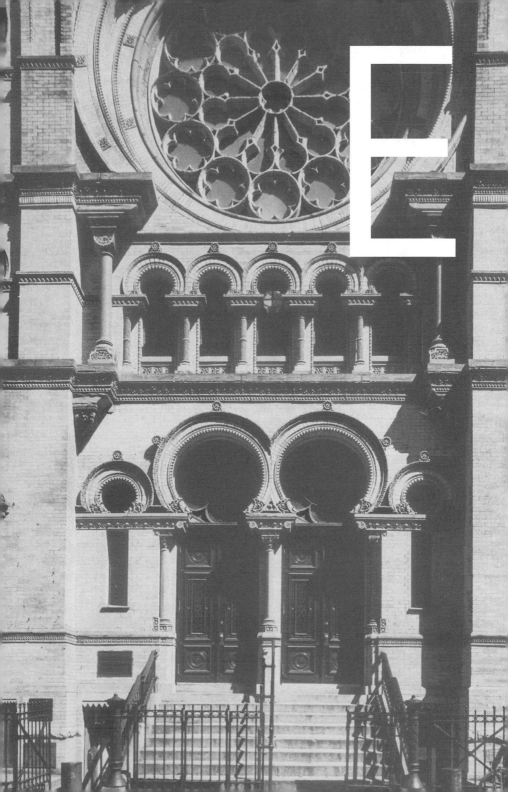

East Dhyana Temple **[C26]**

East Dhyana Temple. The entrance to the East Dhyana Temple, at 83 Division Street **[●C26]**, affiliated with the Ch'an school of Buddhism, is marked by upswept eaves supported on two large columns. The large character over the door that looks like a cross on top and vaguely like a capital *J* on the bottom, separated by a horizontal bar, is the word *szu*, for "Buddhist temple."

East End Temple **[H44]**

East End Temple. To serve families in Peter Cooper Village and Stuyvesant Town, East End Temple, a Reform congregation also known as El Emet (God of Truth), was founded in 1948. In 1957, it purchased a Bank for Savings branch at 300 East 23rd Street **[●H44]** for use as its synagogue. It hoped to get a new synagogue in the redevelopment of that site. Plans were filed in 1985 by Wechsler, Grasso & Menziuso for a 25-story temple and residence, but that project came to naught. The congregation sold the property and moved in 1999 to a temporary home in a former restaurant at East Midtown Plaza on First Avenue. It then renovated a house at 245 East 17th Street **[●H64☆]**, designed by Richard Morris Hunt and built in 1883 for Sidney Webster, Hamilton Fish's son-in-law. The project, by BKSK Architects and LWC Design, includes an entirely new sanctuary, with an Ark truly oriented to magnetic east rather than Manhattan east. East End joins a kind of religious campus around Stuyvesant Square, including St. George's Church, the Fifteenth Street Meeting House, and St. Mary's Catholic Church of the Byzantine Rite.

East End Temple **[H64]**

East Fifty-fifth Conservative Synagogue. A planar Modernist facade of polished stone at 308 East 55th Street **[● J7]**, ornamented with abstract pilasters and a menorah relief, masks the body of the nineteenth-century St. Paul's Methodist Episcopal Church. Chevra B'nai Levi, a Conservative congregation founded in 1906, arrived here in 1916 and has used the building ever since. The remodeling was undertaken in 1966 by George G. Miller.

East Fifty-fifth Conservative Synagogue **[J7]**

East Mount Olive Baptist Church. For decades, East Mount Olive Baptist Church has been at 26 West 128th Street **[●R10]**.

East Side Tabernacle. Beginning in the 1840s, a ministry to Kleindeutschland called the First German Methodist Episcopal Church operated at 254 East 2nd Street [F39]. After First German moved to St. Mark's Place, the Lenox Assembly Hall opened here. In the mid-1980s, the building was used as a club called World, whose habitués included Keith Haring. It was acquired in 1993 by Morningstar Tabernacle and more recently was the East Side Tabernacle before being demolished in 2002.

East Side Tabernacle [F39]

East Ward Missionary Baptist Church. Across from the East River Houses at 2011 First Avenue [●P24], the East Ward Missionary Baptist Church occupies a former branch of the Chase National Bank (whose name is still visible) built in 1925.

East Ward Missionary Baptist Church [P24]

Eastern States Buddhist Temple of America. Founded by James Ying and Jin Yu-Tang, the Eastern States Buddhist Temple of America, affiliated with the Ch'an school, also runs the imposing Mahayana Buddhist Temple on Canal Street. Eastern States occupies a storefront in the Chinese Community Center, at 64 Mott Street [●B35], designed by Ben Ronis in 1959. As headquarters of the quasi-governmental Chinese Consolidated Benevolent Association, this building is essentially Chinatown's city hall. Buddhist statuary, like that pictured at right, fills the temple window.

Eastern States Buddhist Temple of America [B35]

Ebenezer Gospel Tabernacle. Romanesque in feeling though Gothic in detail, this handsomely compact sanctuary at 221 Malcolm X Boulevard [●Q49✰] was built as the Lenox Avenue Unitarian Church from 1889 to 1891. Charles B. Atwood, the architect, also designed the Reliance Building and the Museum of Science and Industry in Chicago. The church was sold in 1919 to Congregation Ukadisha B'nai Israel Mikalwarie (Holy Sons of Israel from Kalwarie, Lithuania), whose 20-year tenancy is recalled by stained-glass Stars of David. It was acquired in 1942 by the Ebenezer Gospel Tabernacle. Under the Rev. Jabez Springer, the church was awarded one of the first grants from the Upper Manhattan Historic Preservation Fund in 2000.

Ebenezer Gospel Tabernacle [Q49]

Iglesia el Edén **[B23]**

Eighteenth Street Methodist
Episcopal Church [G44]

Eighth Church of Christ,
Scientist **[N41]**

Edén, Iglesia el. A big cross marks this small church at 66 Forsyth Street **[●B23]**.

Edmond J. Safra Synagogue. *See* Beit Yaakov, Congregation

Eighteenth Street Methodist Episcopal Church. Built in 1835/1836 on the site of a Methodist cemetery at 309 West 18th Street [G44], the Greek Revival Eighteenth Street Methodist Episcopal Church was designed by William S. Hunt. It was remodeled in 1885 by Howard S. Bush.

Eighth Church of Christ, Scientist. Art Deco goes Georgian at 103 East 77th Street **[●N41]**, an amazing hybrid of styles—the red-brick, steepled meetinghouse embellished with bold modern rectilinear decoration. C. Dale Badgeley was the architect of the Eighth Church of Christ, Scientist, built in 1950/1951 on the site of an earlier sanctuary [N40] occupied by the same group.

El Emet, Congregation. *See* East End Temple

Eldridge Street Synagogue. Extraordinary for its architecture and its historical place as the first great house of worship built by Eastern European Jews in America, the Eldridge Street Synagogue is a poignant mix of ruin and revival as a long-running restoration plays out while a tiny congregation continues an unbroken line of worship going back to 1887.

The origins of Congregation K'hal Adath Jeshurun (Community of the Congregation of Israel) have been traced back to the 1850s and two predecessor congregations, Beth Hamedrash and Holche Josher Wizaner, though it was not organized until 1869, by Romanian Jews, according to the scholar Jeffrey S. Gurock. As its membership swelled with the immigration from Eastern Europe, K'hal Adath Jeshurun built a grand synagogue at 12 Eldridge Street **[●C25★]**. The architects Peter and Francis William Herter used Gothic, Moorish, and Romanesque elements to symbolize Jewish beliefs, holidays, and history. Shortly after the dedication, K'hal Adath Jeshurun merged with Congregation Anshe Lubz (People of Lubz, Poland).

Later, as the size of the congregation dwindled, services were moved to the basement, and the enormous main sanctuary was sealed off in 1933. It was unsealed in 1971 by Gerard R. Wolfe, a professor at New York University. His hair stood on end as he beheld a time capsule of an almost vanished Jewish community. He started Friends of the Eldridge Street Synagogue to rescue the landmark, an effort that was succeeded by the Eldridge Street Project, founded by Roberta Brandes Gratz. In 2001, a ritual bath called a *mikvah* was discovered by an archaeologist excavating a vacant lot behind the synagogue, meaning that this amazing time capsule just keeps opening.

Eldridge Street Synagogue
[C25]

Elim, Iglesia de Dios Pentecostal. This church occupies the former Bijou Theater at 185 Avenue B **[●F8]**.

Elisabeth Irwin High School.
See Bethlehem Memorial Presbyterian Church

Harlem Reformed Dutch Church [R43]

Elmendorf Reformed Church. Dutch roots underlie this handsome survivor at 171 East 121st Street **[●R44]**, across from a one-block remnant of the Boston Road. The Elmendorf Reformed Church was built as a parish house and Sunday school for the First Collegiate Church of Harlem, which began as the Harlem Reformed Dutch Church in 1660. Its first sanctuary was constructed by Jan Gulcke and Nels Matthyssen from 1665 to 1667 on the Great Way, corresponding roughly to East 125th Street [R32], as was the second church [R33], built in 1686/1687 by William Hellaker. In 1825, the congregation erected an Arcadian clapboard sanctuary by Martin E. Thompson on the Boston Road [R43] that it later uprooted and turned 90 degrees, to face East 121st Street.

In 1887, prosperous church members in western Harlem built a new sanctuary, at 101 West 123rd Street **[●Q34☆]**. The parish was unified corporately but divided economically into the richer Second Collegiate Church and the poorer First Collegiate Church. Under the Rev. Joachim Elmendorf, in 1893/1894, First Collegiate built a Neoclassical parish house, by Joseph Ireland. The dual collegiate system was abandoned in 1908, the old church on East 121st Street was razed, and the parish house was rebuilt as the Elmendorf Chapel. It is today the Elmendorf Reformed Church, heir to a Harlem legacy three and a half centuries old.

Harlem Reformed Dutch Church (reoriented) [R43]

Elmendorf Reformed Church **[R44]**

Congregation Emanu-El
[B33]

Congregation Emanu-El [J39]

Congregation Emanu-El **[L24]**

Emanu-El, Congregation. Superlatives abound at Temple Emanu-El: the largest synagogue in the world is home to the largest Reform congregation in the nation and the oldest Reform congregation in the city, founded in 1845 to serve German Jews. Today, it even counts the mayor, Michael R. Bloomberg, among its members.

But Congregation Emanu-El (God Is with Us) began modestly enough, with 33 worshipers in rented space at Grand and Clinton Streets. In 1848, they moved to 56 Chrystie Street [B33], a former Methodist sanctuary built in 1820 that was remodeled by Leopold Eidlitz, who added Stars of David and disguised the round-arched windows with horseshoe-shaped molding. This sanctuary was later used by Congregations Beth Israel Bikur Cholim and Mishkan Israel Anshei Suwalk. Emanu-El's next home was the Twelfth Street Baptist Church, at 120 East 12th Street [●E29], beginning in 1854. This is now St. Ann's Armenian Catholic Cathedral. The congregation moved in 1868 to a grand Moorish sanctuary on Fifth Avenue [J39], by Eidlitz and Henry Fernbach.

In 1927, under the leadership of Louis Marshall, the president of the congregation, Emanu-El merged with Congregation Beth El (House of God) and began constructing the enormous Fifth Avenue synagogue at 1 East 65th Street [●L24☆]. It was designed by Robert D. Kohn, Charles Butler, and Clarence Stein, who described the architecture as "Romanesque as used in the south of Italy under the influence of the Moorish, because it was an expression of the intermingling of Occidental and Oriental thought." A Tiffany window from the old Beth El synagogue was also brought here. The temple opened in 1929. The walls of the soaring, dimly mysterious main sanctuary, which seats 2,500, have vertical strips of glazed tile that thread the space with strands of lambent light. "A building which must be small as compared with the skyscrapers of New York," Stein wrote in 1930, "must secure its dignity through simplicity of form and largeness of scale."

Emanuel A.M.E. Church. Since it was built in 1887 to designs by George G. Jones, this sanctuary at 37 West 119th Street [●R46☆] has been used by the First

Reformed Presbyterian Church; the Lenox Avenue Union Church–Disciples of Christ; and Congregation Mount Zion, which merged with Congregation Peni-El to build the Unity Synagogue. Emanuel African Methodist Episcopal Church, founded in 1914 in San Juan Hill, worshiped at 148 West 62nd Street [K28]. In 1926, under the Rev. Decatur Ward Nichols, it moved to Harlem.

Emanuel A.M.E. Church [R46]

Emanuel Baptist Church. Like the Middle Collegiate Church, Emanuel Baptist Church, built in 1883 at 47 Suffolk Street [C11], by D. & J. Jardine, was later turned into a post office.

Emmanuel, Iglesia Bautista. Kin to the myriad small synagogues nearby is Emmanuel Baptist Church, the former Lemberger Congregation, at 256 East 4th Street [●F33], where the remnant of a Decalogue can be seen in the facade. Plans were filed in 1925 by James J. Millman.

Iglesia Bautista Emmanuel [F33]

Emmanuel Presbyterian Church. Joseph Papp's free presentation of Shakespeare, a phenomenon insepa-rable in the public mind from the Delacorte Theater in Central Park, originated in a little Gothic church at 737 East 6th Street [F22] in 1954.

The congregation was founded in 1852 as a chapel of the University Place Presbyterian Church. The first East 6th Street sanctuary was dedicated in 1874, its ministry directed to Germans. The Sabbath school was at one time the second largest in the nation. After University Place merged into the First Presbyterian Church in 1918, Emmanuel Presbyterian became a church in its own right. Papp, a stage manager for CBS television, organized an actors' workshop in the base-ment in 1953. Audiences first saw the results in "An Evening with Shakespeare and Marlowe." Productions were moved to the East River Park Amphitheater in 1956. In 1970, a new Emmanuel Presbyterian Church on the same site [●F23] was built to designs by Edgar Tafel, who recalled that his orders were: "Make it very simple so if the church doesn't work out we can sell it and turn it into a supermarket."

Emmanuel Presbyterian Church [F22]

Emmanuel Presbyterian Church [F23]

Congregation Emunath Israel
[G37]

Emunath Israel, Congregation. The synagogue next door to the Chelsea Hotel, at 236 West 23rd Street [●G37], was built in the 1860s as the Third Reformed Presbyterian Church. It was remodeled in 1878 by John Correja. Congregation Emunath Israel (Faith of Israel) was founded in 1865 on West 18th Street and moved from Eighth Avenue to West 29th Street before taking over this sanctuary from the Presbyterians in 1920.

Encarnación, Iglesia de la. *See* Incarnation, Church of the

Ephesus Seventh-Day Adventist Church. Harlem's skyline landmark is the slender steeple, at 101 West 123rd Street [●Q34☆], of Ephesus Seventh-Day Adventist Church. This is a cultural landmark, too, as the birthplace in 1968 of the Boys Choir of Harlem. The roots of this sanctuary are common with those of the Elmendorf Reformed Church. Both emerged from the Harlem Reformed Dutch Church, which separated along economic and geographic lines in 1887, when this building was constructed as the Second Collegiate Church of Harlem, to serve the wealthier families living in western Harlem. John Rochester Thomas was the architect. A bell cast in Amsterdam in 1734 for the original Harlem church was brought here. After the Reformed congregation moved downtown in 1929 to become the East Eighty-ninth Street Reformed Church—taking the bell with them—this building was leased and then bought in 1939 by an Adventist congregation formed by the merger of two older black groups. Fire destroyed the interior in 1969 and forced the removal of the upper 20 feet of the spire. It is to be restored through the help of the Upper Manhattan Historic Preservation Fund.

Ephesus Seventh-Day Adventist
Church **[Q34]**

Epiphany, Baptist Church of the. This short-lived Victorian Gothic sanctuary at 723 Madison Avenue [L29] was designed by John E. Terhune and built in 1882 for a Baptist congregation descended from the Fayette Street Church, which was organized in 1791. The Baptist Church of the Epiphany dissolved in 1908, and the building was razed.

Baptist Church of the Epiphany
[L29]

Epiphany, Church of the. In design terms, yes: an epiphany, an intriguingly different way of thinking about nave, chancel, and tower. The Episcopal Church of the Epiphany, at 1393 York Avenue [●L5], is one of a handful of prewar houses of worship proving that imagination and a spirit of adventure are by no means incompatible with sacred architecture.

Epiphany was founded in 1833 as the first church of the New York Protestant Episcopal City Mission Society and was free—that is, without pew rentals—from the outset. Its sanctuary opened in 1834 at 130 Stanton Street [F44]. From 1881 to 1893, it occupied the former St. Alban's Church, built in 1865 on East 47th Street [J31], which later served as Epiphany's Heavenly Rest Chapel. The parish moved into and absorbed the Church of St. John the Baptist, built in 1856 at 257 Lexington Avenue [H9]. When Epiphany decided in 1937 that it was time to move again, Bishop William T. Manning insisted, contrary to the vestry's wishes, that it relocate near the East Side hospitals. Wyeth & King and Eugene W. Mason designed the building, completed in 1939. The tower is actually the chancel, and the alter is flooded with soft light from the clerestory windows. Every Sunday, there is a public service of healing for patients, family, and hospital staff.

Church of the Epiphany [H9]

Church of the Epiphany **[L5]**

Epiphany, Church of the. This Modernist Roman Catholic sanctuary at 373 Second Avenue [●H50] was built from 1965 to 1967, to designs by Belfatto & Pavarini, for a parish founded in 1868. Ambitious and largely successful in its design, it does not wholly compensate for the loss of the original Church of the Epiphany of Our Lord on this site [H49], an exceptionally exuberant Lombard-style structure by Napoleon Le Brun, built in 1869/1870. Five days before Christmas in 1963, it burned down. The new design made no effort to evoke Le Brun, though it used fragments of an original window by Mayer of Munich. Instead, its walls curve gently, and its bell tower stretches heavenward with two walls of unequal height surmounted by a cross. One enters the sanctuary obliquely, parting symbolically from the outside world.

Church of the Epiphany [H49]

Church of the Epiphany **[H50]**

Erste Janalubelska, Congregation. The large synagogue at 82 Lewis Street [F57] was founded in 1893. Congregation Erste Janalubelska took its name from a Polish city.

Erste Lutowisker Shul **[F53]**

Erste Lutowisker Shul. Given its tough surroundings, it is not surprising that the Erste Lutowisker Shul, built in 1956 at 262 Delancey Street [●F53] and also known as the Lithuanian Shul, strikes a defensive posture with its plain brick walls and small windows. The plans were by Joshua Huberland.

Erste Warshawer, Congregation. One of the great synagogues of the Lower East Side, at 60 Rivington Street [●F48], was built in 1903 for Congregation Adath Jeshurun of Jassy, named after Iasi in Moldavia, an old and very substantial Jewish community. The plans were by Stein, Cohen & Roth, owned by the young Emery Roth. There were two galleries, though in its final years, Congregation Erste Warshawer held services in the basement. By 1978, the building was abandoned and being guarded by volunteers from the Synagogue Rescue Project at the Educational Alliance. The Warshawer Shul has since been purchased and converted into a studio. By the removal of certain mullions, the figure in the rose window has been turned from a Star of David into the overlapping leaves of a camera shutter.

Congregation Erste Warshawer **[F48]**

Ethical Culture, Meeting House of the New York Society for. There are few sanctuaries as starkly imposing as this enormous cube at 2 West 64th Street [●K27★], with massive walls facing Central Park like sheer cliffs of Indiana limestone. The paradox is that it was built by a humanistic movement known for its spirit of openness and welcome. Dr. Felix Adler, who immigrated from the Rhineland when his father was called to Temple Emanu-El, founded the Society for Ethical Culture in 1876, placing human capacity, dignity, responsibility, and community at the center of its moral and spiritual quest: "Diversity in the creed; unity in the deed." The society's first permanent structure was not an auditorium but a school by Carrère & Hastings, with Robert D. Kohn as associate architect,

Meeting House of the New York Society for Ethical Culture **[K27]**

that opened in 1904 on Central Park West. The meetinghouse, by Kohn, was built in 1909/1910. The exterior, influenced by the Vienna Secession, is free of any but geometric details. The only representational element is a relief by Estelle Rumbold Kohn, showing the stages of a man's life. "In this house, for which we make the claim that it is holy ground, where men will meet to strive toward the highest, there is no altar and no ark," said E. R. A. Seligman in his dedicatory address. The speaker's platform, he noted, is also subordinated: "The Leader who utters the word is not set up, as in the older religious meeting houses, high above the heads of his hearers, delivering to them a revelation from above." In 2000, the society launched a campaign to renovate its meetinghouse.

Etz Chaim, Congregation.
See Fifth Avenue, Conservative Synagogue of

Congregation Etz Chaim Anshe Wolozin **[C43]**

Etz Chaim Anshe Wolozin, Congregation.
The apartment house at 209 Madison Street [●C43] bears an unmistakable trace of its religious past: the frame of a stained-glass rose window. This was constructed in 1886 as the Madison Street Mission, directly descended from the First Mariners Methodist Episcopal Church, built on Cherry Street [C50] in 1844. The mission ended in 1894. It was later home to Congregation Etz Chaim Anshe Wolozin (Tree of Life, People of Wolozin, Belarus). The building was converted to residential use in 1993.

First Mariners Methodist Episcopal Church [C50]

Evangelical Bethesda Church.
Among small-scale losses of sacred architecture in recent decades, the demolition of the Evangelical Bethesda Church, at 359 East 62nd Street [L36], ranks among the saddest. Designed in 1903 by Robertson & Potter with a fountain-like cascade of compound arches, it was originally the John Hall Memorial Chapel of the Fifth Avenue Presbyterian Church, equipped with a gymnasium, baths, bowling alley, pool, classrooms, and library. After a period as the Evangelical Bethesda Church, the building was used by radio station WBAI in the 1970s, still a center of social activism. It has been replaced by the Beta II apartments.

Evangelical Bethesda Church [L36]

Everard Baths. *See* Disciples of Christ, Church of the

Congregation Ezrath Israel **[124]**

Ezrath Israel, Congregation. This synagogue at 339 West 47th Street [●124], designed in 1922 by Sidney F. Oppenheim, could almost be mistaken in its plainness for an annex to the school next door. But its significance is not architectural. Rather, it is the fact that the Conservative Congregation Ezrath Israel (Help of Israel) began ministering to actors in the 1920s, under Rabbi Bernard Birstein, who reversed a previously discriminatory policy—actors were not even allowed to say kaddish here—and told Sophie Tucker: "I want actors to come to us, to feel welcome for a change." Jack Benny, Milton Berle, Red Buttons, Eddie Cantor, Moe and Curly Howard, Oscar Levant, and Henny Youngman were among the many who responded to that invitation. Indeed, the synagogue is better known as the Actors' Temple.

Faith Mission Christian Fellowship **[Q17]**

Faith Mission Christian Fellowship. A landmark of both the labor and civil-rights movements, the former Imperial Lodge No. 127 of the Improved Benevolent Protective Order of the Elks of the World, at 160 West 129th Street **[●Q17]**, which opened in 1924, was the work of Vertner Woodson Tandy, one of America's leading—and few—black architects. In 1925, A. Philip Randolph convened 500 workers here to form the Brotherhood of Sleeping Car Porters. In the 1930s, it was the home of St. Ambrose Episcopal Church. And the hall was also the scene of one of the grand drag balls chronicled in the 1990 documentary film *Paris Is Burning*. It is now home to the Faith Mission Christian Fellowship, founded in 1986.

Faithful Workers Christ of God Church. The small yellow-brick storefront with Gothic windows at 264 West 135th Street **[●T25]** is home to the Faithful Workers Christ of God Church.

Father's Heart Ministry Center. Finials and pointed windows give away 543 East 11th Street **[●F7]** as a sanctuary. Now the Father's Heart Ministry Center, it was built in 1868 as the Eleventh Street Methodist Chapel, which it remained until 1929.

Father's Heart Ministry Center **[F7]**

Fifteenth Street Meeting House. New York may not seem to be a peaceable, Quaker kind of town, but the Religious Society of Friends has a long history here. In fact, the 1694 meetinghouse in Flushing, Queens, is the oldest existing house of worship in the city. The first meetinghouse in Manhattan was built around 1696 on what is now Liberty Place [A22]; the second [A23] and third [A24], on the same block, faced what is now Liberty Street. In 1819, the Friends built a meetinghouse on Hester Street [B21] that survived into the twentieth century as an office of the Consolidated Gas Company. The orthodox Friends split off in 1828, and the Hicksites, liberal followers of Elias Hicks, eventually moved to 15 Rutherford Place **[●E6★]**, a meetinghouse built in 1861 and credited to the architect Charles T. Bunting. Situated on Stuyvesant Square, the simple structure reflects a form of worship that brooks

Fifteenth Street Meeting House **[E6]**

no ostentation or distraction, that is free of symbols and formal liturgy. Although the Friends were not striving for conventional aesthetic beauty, they created a meetinghouse so pure that it is, indeed, beautiful.

Fifth Avenue, Conservative Synagogue of. After holding services in the Fifth Avenue Hotel, Congregation Etz Chaim (Tree of Life), founded in 1959, moved to 11 East 11th Street [●E27☆], establishing the Conservative Synagogue of Fifth Avenue in a former stable set far from the street behind a deep yard.

Conservative Synagogue of Fifth Avenue **[E27]**

Fifth Avenue Presbyterian Church. A great Victorian gingerbread castle, the Fifth Avenue Presbyterian Church remains every bit the cynosure it was on completion in 1875. Like Old Trinity, it holds its own against skyscraping neighbors. It is the largest Presbyterian sanctuary in Manhattan, with the largest congregation.

Duane Street Presbyterian Church **[B59]**

Founded as the Cedar Street Presbyterian Church in 1808, it occupied a building [A40] by John McComb Jr. The congregation moved to a Greek Revival temple by James H. Dakin on Duane Street [B59] in 1836. Under the Rev. James Waddell Alexander, it moved to Fifth Avenue and 19th Street [H62], a spiky Victorian Gothic structure by Leopold Eidlitz, built in 1851/1852. An outpost at 7 King Street [E82], the Alexander Chapel, was named after the pastor, who worried about "the waste of church energy on the rich, its small operation on the poor." Alexander's brother William was the first president of the Equitable Life Assurance Society, formed by Henry Baldwin Hyde and investors from the Fifth Avenue church. In the later nineteenth century, the church was known informally by the name of the Rev. John Hall. In 1876, the building was given to the Central Presbyterian Church, which moved the structure to 220 West 57th Street [K42].

The new Fifth Avenue Presbyterian, at 7 West 55th Street [● J1], by Carl Pfeiffer, was built from 1873 to 1875 with amphitheater seating. In a 1990 renovation by Swanke Hayden Connell, a 45-foot steeple was restored to the north tower, which had been without one since 1913.

Fifth Avenue Presbyterian Church **[J1]**

Fifth Avenue Synagogue **[L32]**

Fifth Avenue Synagogue. What looks like a small apartment building with cat's-eye windows at 5 East 62nd Street **[●L32☆]** is in fact the work of Percival Goodman, one of the most prolific and influential postwar synagogue architects. Built from 1956 to 1959, the Fifth Avenue Synagogue has a menorah in front but little other evidence of being a house of worship. Those cat's eyes, however, are stained-glass windows by Robert Pinart that illuminate the sanctuary. "My challenge has been to make Orthodoxy elegant and fashionable, and to show that you don't have to live in squalor to be a strictly traditional Jew," said its first rabbi, Dr. Immanuel Jakobovits, who served from 1958 to 1967 and went on to be chief rabbi of the British Commonwealth and the first rabbi to sit in the House of Lords, as Baron Jakobovits.

Fifth Church of Christ, Scientist **[J40]**

Fifth Church of Christ, Scientist. Nestled among temples of commerce is an Ionic colonnade at 9 East 43rd Street **[● J40]** that could easily be a bank but is—and always has been—the Fifth Church of Christ, Scientist. Built in 1920/1921, it was designed by A. D. Pickering as a Skyscraper Church, part of the Canadian Pacific Building. The congregation was incorporated in 1901 and had worshiped in the former Church of St. Mary the Virgin, at 228 West 45th Street [I32].

First Alliance Church [L16]

First Alliance Church. The demolition in recent years of the former First German Reformed Church on St. Catherine's Park, at 351 East 68th Street [L16], was a significant historical loss.

Given world events in the twentieth century, it is not surprising that the story of German New York should have been eclipsed, but it is worth recalling that Germans were among the earliest inhabitants of the city and once accounted for 25 percent of the population. The German Reformed Church was organized in 1758, worshiping first in Hallam's Theatre, at 64 Nassau Street [A17]. A new church on the site [A18] was built in 1765. John Jacob Astor and Baron Friedrich Wilhelm von Steuben belonged to the congregation. (Astor, appropriately, was treasurer.)

In 1861, the church moved to 149 Norfolk Street [F49] and in 1897 to the East 68th Street sanctuary, by Kurtzer & Rohl. The congregation's 150th anniversary was marked here by the gift of a bell from Kaiser Wil-helm II. Sixty years later, in 1968, First German Reformed closed. The First Church of the Christian and Missionary Alliance moved in, after leaving the Gospel Tabernacle, at 260 West 44th Street [●I37], which is now John's Pizzeria. The last service here was in 1999. The church was razed to make way for the Sidney Kimmel Center for Prostate and Urologic Cancers of Memorial Sloan-Kettering. The congregation is remodeling a space at 127 West 26th Street.

First Baptist Church [B13]

First Baptist Church. The First Baptist Church embraces the intersection of Broadway and West 79th Street as though with outstretched arms. Organized in 1745, it built its first sanctuary at 35 Gold Street [A15] in 1759/1760. The pastor, the Rev. John Gano, a chaplain in the Revolutionary War, is said to have baptized George Washington, at the general's request, while in camp at Newburgh. In 1801/1802, a second church was built on Gold Street [A16]. Its inhospitability to a group of African visitors spurred the creation of Abyssinian Baptist Church. The third building, constructed in 1841/1842 at 354 Broome Street [B13], was a powerful early Gothic Revival work, later used by the Evangelical Lutheran Church of St. Matthew. In 1871, First Baptist dedicated a brownstone Gothic church on Park Avenue [J52]. From 1890 to 1893, it built the present church, by George Keister, at 265 West 79th Street [●M32]. The sanctuary was set 45 degrees to the street, just as at All Angels' Church, and was graced with a barrel-vaulted skylight ceiling that was long ago covered up. Those asymmetrical towers are no accident. The four-tier south tower symbolizes Christ as head of the church. Its one-tier companion represents the church on Earth—incomplete until Christ's return. Keister put this theatrical flair to good use. Twenty years after First Baptist, he designed the Apollo Theater on 125th street.

First Baptist Church [J52]

First Baptist Church **[M32]**

First Bethel A.M.E. Church. See Bethel A.M.E. Church

First Chinese Baptist Church. The small First Chinese Baptist Church, at 21 Pell Street [●B46], is marked by the upswept eaves in its entablature.

First Chinese Baptist Church **[B46]**

First Chinese Presbyterian Church **[C34]**

First Christian Church of the Valley **[H34]**

First Church of Christ, Scientist [I22]

First Chinese Presbyterian Church. Several country-style churches in the tough precincts of Chinatown and the Lower East Side are gentle reminders of the rural past. Long before the sanctuary at 61 Henry Street [●C34★] was occupied by the First Chinese Presbyterian Church, it was known as the "Kirk on Rutgers Farm," standing on land donated by Colonel Henry Rutgers, benefactor of the State University of New Jersey and Rutgers Presbyterian Church. Built as the Northeast Reformed Dutch Church from 1817 to 1819, it straddles Georgian and Gothic architecture with pointed-arch windows under a gabled roof. The building was transferred in 1866 to the New York Presbytery and renamed the Church of the Sea and Land, ministering to seamen. As Chinese workers moved to New York in the 1870s and 1880s, the Rev. Huie Kin began a mission on University Place. In 1910, he was named pastor of the new First Chinese Presbyterian Church. From 1951 until 1972, when Sea and Land was dissolved, the Chinese and mariners' congregations shared this building.

First Christian Church of the Valley. Sacred buildings do not get much more spartan than this 1974 brick box for the Assemblies of God at 234 East 27th Street [●H34], by Bernard A. Marson.

First Church of Christ, Scientist. Dispatched from Boston in 1886 by Mary Baker Eddy to sow the seeds of Christian Science in New York, Augusta Emma Stetson organized the First Church of Christ, Scientist, the next year. In 1896, working with William H. Hume & Son, the First Church altered a Romanesque barn at 139 West 48th Street [I22] that was formerly All Souls' Church. From 1901 to 1903, Stetson built an imposing structure at 1 West 96th Street [●O28★] by Carrère & Hastings—a combination steeple-topped New England meetinghouse, Neoclassical temple, and Mannerist work in the style of the British architect Nicholas Hawksmoor. In conceiving a church in New York to rival the Mother Church in Boston, Stetson ran afoul of Eddy. In 1909, she was forced out, though she never left her home next door to the church. On the occasion of the building's centenary, in 2003, it was put up for sale by the congregation, which no longer needed anything like a 2,200-seat sanctuary. Members of the First Church moved in with the Second Church, 28 blocks south on Central Park West [●K20☆].

First Church of the Evangelical Association. The ecclesiastical landscape of the far West Side was shaped in part by John Boese, who designed the Second Church of the Evangelical Association, at 424 West 55th Street [●I2], in 1898. It was later taken over by the First Church of the Evangelical Association, founded in 1839, which moved from 214 West 35th Street [G10]— a case of first following second. Later, as Theater Four, this was where *The Boys in the Band* opened in 1968.

First Church of Christ, Scientist
[O28]

First Church of the
Evangelical Association
(Theater Four) **[I2]**

First Corinthian Baptist Church. Delicious delirium— hooray for Hollywood!—harnessed into spiritual service. The Regent was New York's first deluxe theater built specially for motion pictures, designed by Thomas W. Lamb and constructed in 1912/1913 at 1912 Seventh Avenue [●Q55★], now Adam Clayton Powell Jr. Boulevard. Its theatrical heyday occurred under S. L. Rothapfel, the showman later renowned as Roxy. It remained a theater until 1964, when it was acquired and remodeled by the First Corinthian Baptist Church, a congregation founded in 1933 that had been at 2553 Eighth Avenue.

First Corinthian Baptist Church
[Q55]

First Hungarian Congregation Ohab Zedek.
See Ohab Zedek, Congregation

First Hungarian Reformed Church. Before his name became synonymous with luxury apartment houses and utilitarian office towers, Emery Roth designed the New Yorki Elsö Magyar Református Templom, built in 1915/1916. This charming sanctuary at 344 East 69th Street [●L15] mixes Vienna Secessionist motifs with the vernacular style of Roth's native Hungary. Its 80-foot bell tower soars over low-rise neighbors. The congregation formed in 1895 and worshiped at 121 East 7th Street [●F15], now St. Mary's American Orthodox Greek Catholic Church, before moving to its current home.

First Hungarian Reformed
Church **[L15]**

First Moravian Church [A13]

First Moravian Church **[H21]**

First Moravian Church. Members of the Unitas Fratrum (Unity of the Brethren) Church were called Moravians after a province in what is now the Czech Republic from which they had fled in the eighteenth century. The New York congregation was organized in 1748 and built the First Moravian Church at 106 Fulton Street [A12] in 1751/1752. A new building at the same location [A13] was constructed in 1829. Around 1869, the Moravians moved to 154 Lexington Avenue [●H21], built about 20 years earlier for the Rose Hill Baptist Church, which evolved into the present-day Madison Avenue Baptist Church. Between the Baptists and the Moravians, who still occupy the building, this sanctuary served briefly as the Episcopal Church of the Mediator.

First Presbyterian Church. You are in Greenwich Village, but Trinity Church comes to mind: a deep-brown Gothic Revival tower rising from an improbably expansive and verdant churchyard, framed by highrises, and overlooking a vital thoroughfare. The similarities between Old Trinity and Old First do not end there.

The First Presbyterian Church also began on Wall Street [A38], not long after Trinity, in 1716. Like Trinity, it was the center of a hub-and-spoke system that yielded significant congregations: Brick Presbyterian in 1767; Rutgers Presbyterian in 1798; and Cedar Street Presbyterian, now Fifth Avenue Presbyterian, in 1808. Its sanctuary was built in 1719 and rebuilt in 1748 and 1810. The structure was later shipped to Jersey City and re-erected.

Unlike Trinity, First Presbyterian moved uptown, under the Rev. William Wirt Phillips, when it became clear that lower Manhattan was being taken over by business. The present church was built in 1845/1846 on Fifth Avenue, between 11th and 12th Streets [●E26☆]. The surprisingly ample grounds, ringed by a cast-iron fence, create a beautiful setting for the building, designed by Joseph C. Wells and patterned on the Church of St. Saviour in Bath, England, with a tower modeled on that of Magdalen College, Oxford. The south transept, by McKim, Mead & White, was added in 1893. From that year until 1916, a suite of

First Presbyterian Church [A38]

stained-glass windows was added, by Louis Comfort Tiffany, D. Maitland Armstrong, Charles Lamb, and Francis Lathrop. They were restored in 1988 under the supervision of William Stivale. The church house was added in 1960 by Edgar Tafel, a protégé of Frank Lloyd Wright, who blended Gothic details with the Prairie Style.

Old First merged in 1918 with the Madison Square and University Place Presbyterian Churches. The Rev. Harry Emerson Fosdick caused a storm in 1922 when he asserted that Darwinism was not inconsistent with the Christian faith. He resigned three years later and wound up in the pulpit of Riverside Church.

First Presbyterian Church **[E26]**

First Reformed Episcopal Church. The Reformed Episcopal denomination can be traced in part to the Fifth Avenue Presbyterian Church. Facing criticism for having participated in communion there, Bishop George David Cummins, joined by clergymen and lay members, withdrew from the Episcopal Church to form this new branch in 1874.

In 1876, the young denomination built a madly marvelous Victorian Gothic church at 551 Madison Avenue [J2], designed by James Stroud. In charge was the Rev. William T. Sabine, formerly of the Church of the Atonement. The present home, at 317 East 50th Street [● J23], is a Skyscraper Church, built on land occupied by the Beekman Hill Methodist Church [J22] from 1860 to 1921. In the 1920s, the First Reformed Episcopal Church bought the land and formed the Beekman Hill Apartments Corporation to develop a 12-story apartment house, by George G. Miller, which would pay rent to the parish. The church portion, which opened in 1930, is set apart by Gothic details and the inscription TO TESTIFY THE GOSPEL OF THE GRACE OF GOD.

First Reformed Episcopal Church [J2]

First Reformed Episcopal Church **[J23]**

First Reformed Presbyterian Church. The three blocks bounded by Sixth and Seventh Avenues, West 11th and West 14th Streets, were once a Presbyterian hotbed: four churches in all. At 123 West 12th Street [E25] stood the First Reformed Presbyterian Church, built in 1849 for a congregation founded in 1797.

First Reformed Presbyterian Church [E25]

First Roumanian-American
Congregation **[C21]**

First Roumanian-American
Congregation **[C5]**

First Russian Baptist Church **[N43]**

First Roumanian-American Congregation. Roman, not Romanian, comes to mind, for this building at 89 Rivington Street **[●C5]** looks like those hybrid structures in Rome that bear witness to the accretion of centuries. The sanctuary was built in 1888 as the Allen Street Methodist Episcopal Church, which existed from 1810 to 1902. The building has long been occupied by First Roumanian-American, or Congregation Shaarey Shamoyim (Gates of Heaven), which dates to 1860. Its former synagogue, at 70 Hester Street **[●C21]**, built in 1882, still has the haunting remnant of horseshoe-arched windows. First Roumanian-American is not the only synagogue to call itself the "Cantor's Carnegie Hall," but it makes a good claim, having resonated to the voices of Jan Peerce (Jacob Pincus Perelmuth), Richard Tucker (Reuben Ticker), Moishe Koussevitsky, Moishe Oysher, and Yossele Rosenblatt. The excellence of a cantor was more than a liturgical concern. It had an impact on the financial health of congregations, which depended on the sale of seats at the High Holy Days. Better cantors yielded higher receipts. These days, the small congregation worships in the downstairs social hall.

First Russian Baptist Church. Sweetly diminutive, this mid-nineteenth-century sanctuary at 429 East 77th Street **[●N43]** has reflected the changes in Yorkville, serving over time as the New York Evangelical Mission, the Dingeldein Memorial (German) Church, the Czechoslovak Baptist Church, and the First Russian Baptist Church.

First Sharon Baptist Church. The Rev. Norman Thomas? Reverend? For those who know him as a Socialist leader and perennial Socialist presidential candidate, the idea is startling. But Thomas was a very active Presbyterian minister in the years before 1918, and this Gothic church at 233 East 116th Street **[●R63]** was his pulpit.

Designed by Henry Devoe and built in 1868, it was originally the First United Presbyterian Church of Harlem and then the East Harlem Presbyterian Church. Thomas became the minister in 1911. He directed the American Parish, a federation of churches and agencies serving Italians, Hungarians, Poles, and Russian Jews—a little League of Nations, as he called it. Influenced by the Christian Socialism of the Rev. Walter Rauschenbusch, Thomas said, "I believe that the Christian ethics are impossible in the present order of society, and that every Christian must desire a new social order based on cooperation rather than competition." In 1918, when his pacifism, activism, and Socialism threatened donations to the American Parish, Thomas resigned. In later years, the building served the Hungarian First Presbyterian Church and is now the First Sharon Baptist Church.

First Sharon Baptist Church **[R63]**

First Spanish Baptist Church of Manhattan.
See Primera Iglesia Bautista Hispana de Manhattan

First Spanish United Methodist Church.
See Primera Iglesia Metodista Unida Hispana

First Spanish-Speaking Baptist Church of New York.
See Primera Iglesia Bautista de Habla Española de Nueva York

First Ukrainian Assembly of God **[E43]**

First Ukrainian Assembly of God. Mammon was the first god served at 9 East 7th Street **[●E43★]**, built in 1867 as the Metropolitan Savings Bank, by Carl Pfeiffer. It was purchased by the Ukrainian Assembly of God congregation in 1937.

First Waldensian Church. See Or Zarua, Congregation

Florence and Sol Shenk Synagogue.
See Gates of Israel, Congregation

Iglesia Presbiteriana Fort George **[V7]**

Fort George, Iglesia Presbiteriana. A strikingly traditional sentinel stands amid the modern bustle of Juan Pablo Duarte Boulevard, or St. Nicholas Avenue. The Fort George Presbyterian Church formed in 1918 and worshiped in a frame building on West 185th Street. Plans for the Gothic sanctuary at 1525 St. Nicholas Avenue **[●V7]** were filed in 1925 by Clarence W. Brazer.

Fort Tryon Jewish Center. Home to a Conservative congregation, the Modernist Fort Tryon Jewish Center, across from Bennett Park at 524 Fort Washington Avenue **[●V12]**, was designed in 1950 by N. J. Sapienza.

Fort Tryon Jewish Center **[V12]**

Iglesia Adventista del Séptimo Día
Fort Washington **[U12]**

Fort Washington Collegiate Church **[V16]**

Iglesia Presbiteriana Fort
Washington Heights **[V32]**

Fourteenth Church of Christ,
Scientist **[S18]**

Fort Washington, Iglesia Adventista del Séptimo Día. A fantastic Baroque pastry, this sanctuary at 502 West 157th Street [●U12] was formerly Congregation Ahavath Israel. The Adventist congregation moved here from what is now Iglesia el Camino.

Fort Washington Collegiate Church. Few churches in Manhattan enjoy as picturesque a setting as this snug Country Gothic sanctuary, reached through an iron gate at 470 Fort Washington Avenue [●V16] and along a winding path in a sunken yard. Fort Washington is one of four bodies in the Collegiate Reformed Protestant Dutch Church. (The others are the Marble, Middle, and West End Collegiate Churches.) It was built in 1908/1909 and designed by Nelson & Van Wagenen. The site was regraded and the church reoriented during a disruptive period when streets were rebuilt and the Independent subway tunneled through the neighborhood. In 1916, Fort Washington gained standing as a full Collegiate church, growing further with the merger into it of the Hamilton Grange Reformed Church and the arrival in 1950 of former members of the Harlem Reformed Dutch Church who had been worshiping as the East Eighty-ninth Street Reformed Church.

Fort Washington Heights, Iglesia Presbiteriana. Looking as though it would be at home somewhere in London, this Georgian church at 21 Wadsworth Avenue [●V32] by Thomas Hastings was built in 1913/1914. In massing, though not details, it is similar to Carrère & Hastings's earlier First Church of Christ, Scientist. Originally the Fort Washington Presbyterian Church, the congregation was founded in 1913 and endowed as part of the merger agreement between the West Church (established in 1829) and the Park Church (founded in 1854), at 539 Amsterdam Avenue [●M16]. That is why the dates 1829 and 1854 appear on the cornerstone.

Fort Washington Synagogue.
See Prince of Peace Universal Tabernacle Spiritual Church

Fourteenth Church of Christ, Scientist. In keeping with the avoidance by Christian Science churches of religious iconography, the Fourteenth Church of Christ, Scientist, at 555 West 141st Street [●S18], altered in 1925 from two row houses by Charles F. Winkelman, is an unadorned but handsome institutional structure.

Fourth Church of Christ, Scientist. If you're leafing through this book in the Barnes & Noble at Broadway and 82nd Street, take a look at the south facade on your way out. The gabled pavilion at 251 West 82nd Street [●M24] was the home of the Fourth Church of Christ, Scientist, in the early twentieth century. The congregation then moved to a Neoclassical sanctuary at 410 Fort Washington Avenue [V27], designed in 1913 by Solon Spencer Beman of Chicago, architect of a pavilion at the World's Columbian Exposition that served as a prototype for Christian Science churches. The Washington Heights sanctuary was later a YMHA/YWHA. In 1931/1932, the Fourth Church built an Art Deco temple at 551 Fort Washington Avenue [●V9], now the Hebrew Tabernacle of Washington Heights.

Fourth Universalist Society. Its architectural profile is fifteenth century—an icicle-delicate tower straight out of Magdalen College, Oxford—but its spiritual profile is strictly twentieth century. The Unitarian Universalist Association, formed in 1961 by the Universalists and the Unitarians, calls itself a noncreedal, liberal religion born of Jewish and Christian traditions.

The Fourth Universalist Society in New York was founded in 1838. Its home in the 1840s was a Greco-Egyptian sanctuary on Murray Street [B61], built for the South Reformed Dutch Church. The arrival in 1848 of the Rev. Edwin H. Chapin drew so many churchgoers that new quarters were needed. The congregation took over a sanctuary on Broadway [B4] that had been vacated by the Church of the Divine Unity. Chapin's flock moved in 1866 to a sanctuary on Fifth Avenue [J36], designed by John Correja, and restyled itself the Church of the Divine Paternity. The current church, at 160 Central Park West [●M38☆], was built in 1897/1898 to designs by William A. Potter. Courted by developers in the 1980s for its attractive site, the society instead formed an alliance called SOUL—Save Our Universalist Landmark.

Fourth Church of Christ, Scientist [V27]

Fourth Universalist Society [B61]

Church of the Divine Paternity [J36]

Fourth Universalist Society **[M38]**

Église Baptiste d'Expression
Française **[S21]**

Française, Église Baptiste d'Expression. Defiantly jaunty, the crazy-angled 315 West 141st Street **[●S21]** is a 1992 renovation by Donald D. Fisher and Allan Thaler. The French Baptist Church serves the growing number of French-speaking Haitian refugees and makes a statement of its own, proving that spirit and imagination can render inspiring sacred architecture on a limited budget.

Française, Église Évangélique. Tier upon tier upon tier of arches appear at 126 West 16th Street **[●E1]**, which was, back in the 1860s, the Catholic Apostolic Church, before it moved to West 57th Street. This building was renovated in 1886 by Alfred D. F. Hamlin and has served for more than a century as the French Evangelical Church, a Presbyterian group founded in 1848.

Église Évangélique Française **[E1]**

Friendship Baptist Church. If friendliness can be imputed to architecture, there is something amicable about this stout little sanctuary at 144 West 131st Street **[●Q11]**. Designed by William J. Merritt, it was built in 1883 and served as the Baptist Church of the Redeemer, Congregation Anshe Emeth of West Harlem, and the New York United Sabbath Day Adventist Church. The Friendship Baptist Church was founded in 1900 by the Rev. John I. Mumford. Its pastor at mid-century, the Rev. Thomas Kilgore Jr., was closely associated with the Southern Christian Leadership Conference and was a key organizer of the 1963 March on Washington, addressed so memorably by the Rev. Martin Luther King Jr. Kilgore also headed both the American Baptist and Progressive National Baptist Conventions.

Friendship Baptist Church **[Q11]**

Fuentidueña Chapel. *See San Martín, Church of*

Fur Center Synagogue. You'd expect something in mink, but the Orthodox Fur Center Synagogue, at 230 West 29th Street **[●G24]**, was built in 1964, when spare Modernism was the watchword. The only decorative touch was a mosaic menorah over the entrance. The synagogue closed as the fur industry virtually disappeared. In 1997, the building was acquired by a spiritual movement known as Subud (Susila Budhi Dharma). It is now the Subud Chelsea Center.

Fur Center Synagogue **[G24]**

Congregation Gates of
Israel (Schottenstein
Center) **[V11]**

Glad Tidings Tabernacle
[G14]

Glendale Baptist Church **[Q18]**

Church of God **[T6]**

Garment Center Synagogue. The Orthodox Congregation Knesset Israel (Assembly of Israel) was founded
by Rabbi Yaakov Yosef Friedman in 1930 to serve garment workers. By the early 1960s, it held 15 services
daily over a Seventh Avenue luncheonette. Its current
sanctuary, at 205 West 40th Street [●I46], was designed by William Lescaze and built in 1965. The congregation shares the building with the David Schwartz
Fashion Education Center of the Parsons School of
Design.

Gates of Israel, Congregation. Of the neo-Georgian synagogues, Temple Israel of Washington Heights, at 560
West 185th Street [●V11], is the most imposing. Its
columns support a pediment with a Decalogue over the
words THOU SHALT LOVE THY NEIGHBOR AS THYSELF.
Plans were filed in 1921 by Sommerfeld & Steckler. This
building was later Congregation Gates of Israel, founded in 1931, and is now the Schottenstein Center of
Yeshiva University, within which is the Florence and
Sol Shenk Synagogue, named for the founder of Consolidated Stores. Gates of Israel is now across the street.

German Evangelical Mission Church. Built in about
1840 at 141 East Houston Street [●E91], the German
Evangelical Mission Church was transformed in 1909
into Kinoland, expanded into the Sunshine Theater in
1917, and revamped as the Chopin, where Polish talkies
were shown. After many years as a warehouse, it was
reopened in 2001 as Landmark's Sunshine Cinema.

Glad Tidings Tabernacle. Pilgrims' Baptist Church was
the name of the sanctuary at 325 West 33rd Street
[●G14]. And pilgrims its members were, building so
large a church in 1867/1868 on what was then the outskirts of town. George Chapman was the architect.
Later called the Thirty-third Street Baptist Church and
Collegiate Baptist Church of the Covenant, it has been
the Glad Tidings Tabernacle since 1914.

Glendale Baptist Church. A windowless stone facade
at 131 West 128th Street [●Q18], adorned by a cross,
conceals the former Manhattan Stables. The Glendale
Baptist Church was founded in 1947 by the Rev. Robert
L. Glenn, and this sanctuary was dedicated in 1954.

God, Church of. Elder Lightfoot Solomon Michaux—once mentioned in the same breath as Father Divine, Sweet Daddy Grace, and Billy Sunday—was a radio evangelist in the 1920s with temples in six cities. The Radio Church of God, at 220 West 145th Street [●T6], was given a new facade in 1979 and is known today simply as the Church of God.

Good Neighbor Church.
See Buen Vecino, Primera Iglesia Evangélica Presbiteriana el

Good Samaritan Cathedral [Q50]

Good Samaritan Cathedral. What may be New York's only storefront cathedral, serving the Ethiopian Orthodox Coptic Church of North and South America, is heralded by proud gold lions at 2018 Adam Clayton Powell Jr. Boulevard [●Q50].

Good Shepherd, Cathedral of the. The tiny Catholic Apostolic denomination had an outsize architectural legacy, including the main church, at 417 West 57th Street [●K32★], and the Harlem church, at 202 West 114th Street [Q61], with its bichromatic arch. The uptown sanctuary was later the Cathedral of the Good Shepherd.

Cathedral of the Good Shepherd [Q61]

Good Shepherd, Chapel of the. Crowning the lovely, timeless quadrangle at the General Theological Seminary on Ninth Avenue [●G42✰] is the Chapel of the Good Shepherd, built from 1886 to 1888, by Charles Coolidge Haight. His father, the Rev. Benjamin I. Haight, was the first rector of St. Peter's Church, a block away.

Chapel of the Good Shepherd [G42]

Good Shepherd, Church of the. Five years before undertaking the Washington National Cathedral, Henry Vaughan designed a chapel for the Church of the Incarnation, at 238 East 31st Street [●H18] in 1902. The Church of the Good Shepherd succeeded Incarnation. Living up to its name in the late 1980s, it offered shelter to homeless men. Residents of the Greentree at Murray Hill condominium next door (paradoxically, the former parish house of Good Shepherd) sued to close the shelter. But the church was upheld by a judge who cited the Bible—"Am I my brother's keeper?"—in his decision.

Church of the Good Shepherd [H18]

Good Shepherd–Faith Presbyterian Church
[K21]

Good Shepherd–Faith Presbyterian Church. Almost lost in the folds of Lincoln Center, at 152 West 66th Street **[●K21]**, is one of the handsomest Romanesque Revival churches in New York, with a broad arched entryway of superimposed brick courses. It was built in 1887 to designs by J. C. Cady & Company for the Church of the Good Shepherd. The Faith half of the hyphenated congregation is descended from the Faith Chapel of the West Presbyterian Church, at 423 West 46th Street **[●I26]**, now St. Clement's Episcopal Church. Quite appropriately, given its location and acoustics, Good Shepherd–Faith Presbyterian Church has been a concert venue since the 1960s. It has also served the Korean Central Church and the Catholic Apostolic Parroquía del Espíritu Santo y de Nuestra Señora de la Caridad.

Good Shepherd Roman Catholic
Church [X2]

Good Shepherd Roman Catholic
Church **[X3]**

Good Shepherd Roman Catholic Church. That is a Celtic cross on this Romanesque sanctuary at the top of Manhattan, at 4967 Broadway **[●X3]**, a testament to the days when Inwood was "the unofficial capital of the Irish diaspora," as Jim Dwyer called it in the *New York Times*. In 1912, a year after the parish was founded, plans were filed by Thomas H. Poole & Company for the first sanctuary, closer to Cooper Street [X2], surrounded by rolling, wooded hills. Plans for the current Good Shepherd Roman Catholic Church were filed in 1935 by Paul Monaghan. In recent years, immigrants from the Dominican Republic have largely supplanted the Irish. But the old neighbors kept their ties to the place, and when a large number of Irish-Americans were killed in the attack of September 11, 2001, Good Shepherd felt the impact terribly. A dented steel cruciform salvaged from the site of the World Trade Center—"Ground Hero," the sign says—stands in the churchyard between two Japanese maples.

Gospel Hall **[R64]**

Gospel Hall. Adjoining brownstones with a unified facade at 27 West 115th Street **[●R64]** have served for decades as Gospel Hall.

Gospel Missionary Baptist Church. There are many painful ways to lose a great building. Temple B'nai

Israel (Sons of Israel) of Washington Heights, at 610 West 149th Street [●S7], an early masterpiece by Emery Roth, was dismantled piece by piece by vandals. Constructed from 1921 to 1923, the sanctuary was designed for 1,300 worshipers under a dome set on arches with 50-foot spans. It also had a gymnasium, swimming pool, classrooms, and kitchen. The congregation was still here through the mid-1970s, but the building was abandoned by 1991 when scavengers made off with copper panels from the dome and one of the 5-foot lion's heads that had adorned the structure. Preservationists could not interest the police in pursuing the thieves. But that was not the end of the story. Today, this is the Gospel Missionary Baptist Church, founded by the Rev. Henry L. Smalls. The dome is still stripped and the central window cinderblocked. But around the arch these words remain: MY HOUSE SHALL BE CALLED A HOUSE OF PRAYER FOR ALL PEOPLES.

Gospel Missionary Baptist Church **[S7]**

Gospel Tabernacle. *See* Crucifixion, Chapel of the

Gospel Temple Church of America. This Beaux-Arts structure at 2056 Fifth Avenue [●R20], designed by Oscar Lowinson and built in 1902, has been the Columbus Club; the Finnish Workers Educational Association; and, since 1955, the Gospel Temple Church of America, founded in 1949 by Bishop Benjamin H. Broadie out of the Church of God in Christ.

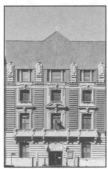

Gospel Temple Church of America **[R20]**

Grace and St. Paul's Church. Squeezed between a row house and an apartment building, this little Romanesque Revival church at 123 West 71st Street [●K6☆] by Stephen D. Hatch was built in 1880/1881 as St. Andrew's Methodist Episcopal Church. St. Andrew's kept moving uptown, to West 76th Street (now the West Side Institutional Synagogue) and then West End Avenue, where it joined with St. Paul's to form the Church of St. Paul and St. Andrew. It sold this building in 1890 to the four-year-old Lutheran Gnaden Kirche, or Grace Church. In 1933, Grace merged with St. Paul Lutheran Church of Harlem, from 147 West 123rd Street [●Q33★], now the Greater Metropolitan Baptist Church.

Grace and St. Paul's Church **[K6]**

Grace Church [A35]

Grace Church **[E33]**

Grace Chapel [E13]

Grace Church. A bend in Broadway gives Grace Church a special setting in the cityscape, allowing its white-marble spire to be seen from as far away as City Hall Park. Legend ascribes the bend to Henry Brevoort, who resisted efforts to straighten the road through his apple orchard. Happily for posterity, the architect James Renwick Jr. (a Brevoort on his mother's side) bestowed on this unique site a slender, crystalline tower that seems to float over Broadway. Working with Walter B. Melvin Architects, the church set out in 2003 to inspect and repair a slight lean in the spire, as part of a long-term restoration project.

The first Grace Church was built on Broadway [A35], in the shadow of Trinity Church, from 1806 to 1808. The present sanctuary, farther up on Broadway [●E33★], was built from 1843 to 1846 and became a bastion for high society, of which Grace's sexton, Isaac Hull Brown, was supreme arbiter. "To be married or buried within its walls has been ever considered the height of felicity," it was said in 1869. Rectors have included the Rev. Thomas House Taylor, under whom the church moved uptown; the Rev. William Reed Huntington, under whom the church undertook much of its late-nineteenth-century development; and the Rev. Henry Codman Potter, who as bishop of New York later commenced work on the Cathedral Church of St. John the Divine.

Grace grew by accretion. Renwick's rectory, a Gothic Revival mansion on Broadway, was added in 1847. The chantry was built in 1879, and Grace House in 1881. Stained-glass windows by Clayton & Bell and Henry Holiday arrived in the late nineteenth century, as did a terra-cotta Roman urn on the lawn, dating perhaps from the time of Nero. On Fourth Avenue are the charming Gothic buildings of the Grace Church School, including the former Day Nursery of 1878 and the Neighborhood House of 1908.

Grace also built four chapels:

The first was constructed in 1850 on Madison Avenue and East 28th Street [H26]. The congregation reorganized in 1852 as the independent Church of the Incarnation and built its own church. The chapel was then reincarnated as the Church of the Atonement.

The second Grace Chapel, also known as the Chapel or Church of the Redemption, was designed by Renwick and built on East 14th Street [E13] in 1861. It burned down in 1872.

The third chapel, on the same site [E14], was consecrated in 1876. It was a vivid, powerful work of Ruskinian Gothic by Potter & Robertson that had an enormous central tracery window under bichromatic voussoirs and a tower with a banded, peaked roof.

The fourth chapel was an ambitious social-service complex—complete with a hospital—designed by Barney & Chapman and built from 1894 to 1896 at 406 East 14th Street [●F1★]. It closed in 1943 and is now the Roman Catholic Church of the Immaculate Conception.

Grace Congregational Church of Harlem. This Romanesque sanctuary at 310 West 139th Street [●S26] was built in 1892/1893 to designs by Joseph Ireland and has served as the Lenox Presbyterian Church, which moved to what is now St. James Presbyterian Church; the Swedish Immanuel Congregational Church; and, since 1923, the Grace Congregational Church of Harlem, organized in 1923 in combination with Harlem Congregational of West 138th Street.

Grace Congregational Church of Harlem [S26]

Grace Faith Church. Like the Chinese Evangel Mission Church, the Grace Faith Church, at 65 Chrystie Street [●B32], declares its religious purpose with a huge cross on the facade.

Grace Gospel Chapel [T34]

Grace Gospel Chapel. Seventy years after it was founded in 1914, Grace Gospel Chapel built its own sanctuary, a gable-fronted building at 102 West 133rd Street [●T34] on the site of its earlier home [T33], which had once been the Salem United Methodist Church.

Grace Reformed Church [I4]

Grace Reformed Church. A delightful country church in midtown, the sanctuary at 845 Seventh Avenue [I4] was built in 1869 as the Seventh Avenue Chapel of the Collegiate Church and was occupied by its successor, Grace Reformed Church, from 1884 to 1921.

Grace to Fujianese, Church of. A former bathhouse at 133 Allen Street [●C1] is now the Chinese Church of Grace to Fujianese. Note the scallop shells.

Church of Grace to Fujianese [C1]

Grace United Methodist Church
[O17]

Grace United Methodist Church. "I believe in miracles," the Rev. Robert W. Emerick told his flock on December 18, 1983. He had to. A week earlier, the old church at 131 West 104th Street [O17] had burned down. Founded in 1869, Grace United Methodist Church commissioned its building from J. C. Cady & Company in 1888. It shared the sanctuary over time with the Greek Orthodox Community of St. Gerasimos and with Iglesia Metodista Grace. The lost church was replaced with a complex at 125 West 104th Street [●O18] designed by Prentice & Chan, Ohlhausen, with a small gabled sanctuary alongside an apartment building with 68 units, 12 for clergy and 56 for low-income families. It was dedicated in 1992.

Gramercy Arts Theater. *See* Trinity Baptist Church

Grace United Methodist Church
[O18]

Greater Bethel A.M.E. Church. The home of the Harlem Library at 32 West 123rd Street [●R37☆] was built in 1891/1892, to designs by Edgar K. Bourne, a decade before the Harlem system merged into the New York Public Library system. It was built next to the Harlem Club, where it is pictured on page 26, and is now home to the Greater Bethel African Methodist Episcopal Church, whose congregation split from the Bethel A.M.E. Church in the 1940s.

Greater Calvary Baptist Church. Designed in 1951 by Joseph Judge and Samuel Snodgrass, 55 West 124th Street [●R34] was a tough response to tough street life. Its presence is softened by the small lawn, a reminder that this was once the site of the Mount Morris Tennis Courts.

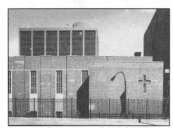

Greater Calvary Baptist Church **[R34]**

Greater Central Baptist Church. The brick box at 2152 Fifth Avenue [●R3], by Richard B. Thomas, was built from 1953 to 1955 for the Greater Central Baptist Church, organized in 1933.

Greater Emmanuel Baptist Church. Fire claimed as its victim in 1984 a splendidly eclectic sanctuary by Starkweather & Gibbs, built from 1881 to 1883 at 323 East 118th Street [R50] for Trinity Methodist

Greater Central Baptist Church **[R3]**

Episcopal Church, which merged into the Jefferson Park Methodist Episcopal Church in 1918. After the fire, Greater Emmanuel Baptist Church, founded in 1935 by the Rev. T. T. Gooden Sr., rebuilt on the site [●R51] in 1988 with an imposing modern version of a Romanesque Revival sanctuary, by Clarence Pete Jr.

Greater File Chapel Baptist Church. The towers of this sanctuary at 505 West 155th Street [●U15] overlook Trinity Cemetery. As the cornerstone attests, this was originally the Welsh Calvinistic Methodist Church, designed by Stoughton & Stoughton and built in 1914. It was rededicated in 1974 as Greater File Chapel Baptist Church, founded in 1953.

Greater Highway Deliverance Temple. The Greater Highway Deliverance Temple occupies an institutional building at 132 East 111th Street [●P8] designed in 1905 by Bernstein & Bernstein as a school and synagogue, Congregation Uptown Talmud Torah. It later served the Harlem Hebrew Institute and as an annex to St. Cecilia's School.

Greater Hood Memorial A.M.E. Zion Church. Cloaked in the Deco architecture of the former Lido Swimming Pool complex at 160 West 146th Street [●T3]—there was even a sandy "beach" on the lot immediately to the east—is the black church with the longest continuous presence in Harlem, though under different names over the years. It began in 1843 as Little Zion, at 236 East 117th Street [R62], a branch of Mother A.M.E. Zion, then on Church Street. In 1911, Little Zion built a sanctuary at 60 West 138th Street [●T19], designed by the pioneering black architects Vertner Woodson Tandy and George Washington Foster Jr., who also designed Mother Zion. At the time, the congregation changed its name to Rush Memorial, in honor of Bishop Christopher Rush. This building is now the Union Congregational Church. In 1937, the congregation moved to 229 Lenox Avenue [●Q48], now the Walters Memorial A.M.E. Zion Church, and took the name Greater Hood Memorial, honoring Bishop J. W. Hood. It held a parade in 1951 as it moved to its current home.

Greater Emmanuel Baptist Church [R50]

Greater Emmanuel Baptist Church **[R51]**

Greater File Chapel Baptist Church **[U15]**

Greater Hood Memorial A.M.E. Zion Church **[T3]**

Greater Metropolitan Baptist Church
[Q33]

Greater Metropolitan Baptist Church. Like the Church of the Blessed Sacrament, this dazzlingly out-of-scale Gothic sanctuary at 147 West 123rd Street **[●Q33★]** dominates the midblock. The cornerstone—CHRISTUS UNSER ECKSTEIN (Christ Our Cornerstone)—hints at its story. The German-American St. Paul Lutheran Church of Harlem was founded in 1864. Its marble sanctuary, designed by Schneider & Herter, was built in 1897/1898. After St. Paul merged with Grace Church in 1933, forming Grace and St. Paul's Church, it sold this building to the Twelfth Church of Christ, Scientist, New York's first African-American branch of Christian Science, now at 2315 Adam Clayton Powell Jr. Boulevard. The Greater Metropolitan Baptist Church, an offshoot of the Metropolitan Baptist Church, bought the building in 1985.

Greater Refuge Temple **[Q31]**

Greater Refuge Temple. Brasilia. The United Nations. Or Lincoln Center, as a companion piece to the Met. Divided into 24 elongated mosaic lozenges—emerald, bronze, gold, jade, periwinkle, and cornflower—this Bossa-Nova facade at 2081 Adam Clayton Powell Jr. Boulevard **[●Q31]**, by Costas Machlouzarides, dates to 1966. But underneath is the much older Loew's Seventh Avenue Theater, originally the Harlem Casino, built in 1889. The congregation is associated with the Church of Our Lord Jesus Christ of the Apostolic Faith, founded by Bishop R. C. Lawson in Columbus, Ohio, in 1919. Lawson established the Refuge Church the same year. It moved from East 131st Street to West 133rd Street and then, in 1945, to the Loew's Theater. Bishop William L. Bonner undertook the 1966 renovation, after which the name was changed to Greater Refuge Temple.

Greater Tabernacle Baptist Church **[S15]**

Greater Tabernacle Baptist Church. The gracious house at 340 Convent Avenue **[●S15]**, home to Greater Tabernacle Baptist Church, was built in 1890 and was once used by the Little Sisters of the Assumption.

Greater Zion Hill Baptist Church. The legend of this Italianate building at 2365 Frederick Douglass Boulevard **[●Q22]**, now the sanctuary of Greater Zion Hill

Baptist Church, can still be read in the entablature: THE PROVIDENT LOAN SOCIETY OF NEW YORK. It was built in 1916 to designs by Renwick, Aspinwall & Tucker and has several identical cousins around town, including a branch on Lexington Avenue at East 124th Street and on Avenue A at Houston Street. Both the Greater Metropolitan Baptist Church and Mount Neboh Baptist Church have worshiped here over the years.

Greater Zion Hill Baptist Church **[Q22]**

Guardian Angel, Church of the. Clear the tracks! That was what the Roman Catholic Church of the Guardian Angel, at 513 West 23rd Street [G26], had to do. But the happy result was a superb bit of twentieth-century Romanesque architecture in the succeeding sanctuary at 193 Tenth Avenue [●G41].

The parish was formed in 1888. Its 1910 building on West 23rd Street by George H. Streeton turned out to be in the path of the elevated viaduct, now called the High Line, that the New York Central planned in the 1920s for its freight trains. The replacement on Tenth Avenue was completed in 1930 to designs by John V. Van Pelt. Inside, above a domed baldachin, are chancel windows that front on the elevated tracks along which boxcars rumbled with meats and produce. Only a block from the waterfront, Guardian Angel ministered to seamen. Its pastor was Port Chaplain of the Archdiocese.

Church of the Guardian Angel **[G41]**

Gustavus Adolphus, Evangelical Lutheran Church of. From 1870 to 1900, the Swedish population of New York increased almost tenfold, from 3,000 to 29,000. This prominent sanctuary by J. C. Cady & Company, at 149 East 22nd Street [●H43], was built during that fertile period, in 1887/1888. It was an early social-service complex, with a gymnasium on the ground floor over which the sanctuary was constructed. Named for the seventeenth-century king of Sweden, the Svenska Lutherska Gustaf Adolf Kyrkan was organized in 1865 and counted among its trustees John Ericsson, designer of the Union ironclad *Monitor*. Today, the Rev. James S. Amos says, the church serves every nation.

Evangelical Lutheran Church of Gustavus Adolphus **[H43]**

H.

Congregation Habonim **[K23]**

Church of Christ in Harlem **[R17]**

Healing from Heaven
Temple **[S29]**

Church of the Heavenly Rest [J34]

Habonim, Congregation. In 1939, a year after Kristall-nacht, as the world was plunging into war, Rabbi Hugo Hahn and a group of refugees from Germany founded the Conservative Congregation Habonim (Builders). Its name was meant to suggest the "promise and challenge of the future as well as the rich foundation of the past." In 1956/1957, the Builders built their synagogue at 44 West 66th Street **[●K23]**, by Stanley Prowler and Frank Faillance. It is a cube rotated 45 degrees and set within another cube. On the facade are the words UNLESS THE LORD BUILDS THE HOUSE, THOSE WHO BUILD IT LABOR IN VAIN. Reminders of the Nazis' destruction were interwoven into the fabric, including a column capital from the Fasanenstrasse Synagogue of Berlin and a scorched Torah from the Great Synagogue of Essen.

Harlem, Church of Christ in. There is no mistaking the creed of this congregation at 340 Malcolm X Boulevard **[●R17]**, etched in stone: FOUNDER: THE CHRIST, THE SON OF THE LIVING GOD / PLACE: JERUSALEM / TIME: A.D. 33 / HEAD: CHRIST / BISHOP: CHRIST JESUS / MINISTER: R. C. WELLS, EVANGELIST. The Church of Christ in Harlem was designed in 1980 by Millard Bresin and dedicated in 1984.

Healing from Heaven Temple. Ringed by lightpost finials that look like human figures with their arms upraised, the bright and exuberant sanctuary of the Healing from Heaven Temple, at 2535 Frederick Douglass Boulevard **[●S29]**, occupies a former Safeway supermarket, built in 1953.

Heavenly Rest, Church of the. It was heavenly rest that Civil War veterans were anticipating when they formed this Episcopal parish in 1865. Their first church, an early Victorian Gothic work by Edward T. Potter, was built from 1868 to 1871 on Fifth Avenue [J34]. The auditorium was set back from the avenue, reached by an entrance barely wider than a brownstone. It appeared outside that the church was tiny, inspiring the comment: "I see the Heavenly—where's the Rest?" Under the Rev. Henry Darlington, the congregation merged with the Church of the Beloved Disciple and acquired a site at Fifth Avenue and East 90th Street [●N3☆] from Andrew Carnegie's widow, Louise, who lived across the street, in a mansion that is now the Cooper-Hewitt National Design Museum. To protect her garden view, she stipulated a 75-foot height limit, but the resulting church was in no way diminished by the design control. This limestone mesa was begun in 1926 by Bertram Grosvenor Goodhue Associates and finished in 1929 by Hardie Phillip of the successor firm Mayers, Murray & Phillip, with sculptures by Lee Lawrie and Malvina Hoffman. During a 1993 restoration, Heavenly Rest suffered a devastating fire. The stained-glass windows were spared because firefighters deliberately used more complicated means to ventilate the 1,000-degree blaze. Rebounding from disaster, the church expanded the restoration project, designed by Gerald Allen and Jeffrey Harbinson.

Church of the Heavenly Rest **[N3]**

Hebrew Tabernacle of Washington Heights. Across West 185th Street from Bennett Park, a great screen of flora-like fans marks the bold, chalky facade of this Art Deco house of worship at 551 Fort Washington Avenue [●V9]. Built as the Fourth Church of Christ, Scientist, in 1931/1932, it was designed by Cherry & Matz. In 1973, it was acquired by Hebrew Tabernacle, a Reform congregation, whose previous home had been the almost equally spectacular synagogue at 609 West 161st Street [●U5]. That sanctuary is well preserved as a Kingdom Hall of Jehovah's Witnesses. Hebrew Tabernacle, founded in 1906, had earlier worshiped at 220 West 130th Street [Q13], which became the Williams Institutional C.M.E. Church. Membership in the synagogue increased significantly with the arrival of German Jews escaping the Holocaust.

Hebrew Tabernacle of Washington Heights **[V9]**

Hedding Methodist Episcopal Church. An imposing Neoclassical church at 337 East 17th Street [H65], this was dedicated in 1854. Hedding Methodist Episcopal Church was founded in 1849—the Rev. Elijah Hedding was a prominent Methodist bishop in the early nineteenth century—and disbanded in 1918.

Hedding Methodist Episcopal Church [H65]

Iglesia Cristiana la Hermosa **[P7]**

Iglesia ACyM Hispana (under construction) **[P13]**

Church of the Holy Agony **[P28]**

Hermosa, Iglesia Cristiana la. Music is the legacy of 3 Central Park North **[●P7]**, once the Park Palace, a catering hall that turned into a concert venue where Joe Cuba, Mario Bauza, Machito and the Afro-Cubans, Eddie Palmieri, Tito Puente, and Ishmael Rivera performed through the 1950s. In 1960, it was converted into a sanctuary for the Hermosa Christian Church (Disciples of Christ), founded in 1938 by the Rev. Pablo Cotto. Although given a new facade on West 110th Street, it retains its original neo-Georgian facade from 1917 on 111th Street.

Hispana, Iglesia ACyM. This large Christian and Missionary Alliance church being built at 155 East 107th Street **[●P13]** was engineered by David Silverman.

Holy Agony, Church of the. Founded in 1930 at 260 East 98th Street, Iglesia de la Santa Agonía was the first church in East Harlem to serve Hispanic parishioners, mostly Puerto Ricans in its early years. It moved in 1952 to 1834 Third Avenue **[●P28]**, a group of buildings by Robert J. Reiley.

Holy Apostles, Church of the | Congregation Beth Simchat Torah. The Church of the Holy Apostles is a Chelsea icon, its soaring steeple undiminished by towers around it. But the high profile of this Episcopal sanctuary on Ninth Avenue **[●G25★]** has as much to do with its embrace of those who are unwelcome elsewhere, a tradition that may be traced to the days when it was reputedly a stop on the Underground Railroad. The parish evolved from a Sunday school founded in 1836 and built its sanctuary, by Minard Lafever, from 1846 to 1848. William Jay Bolton, who had worked with Lafever on the first major stained-glass commission in this country, in Brooklyn, created boldly geometric windows here.

In 1973, the church aided Jacob Gubbay in founding Congregation Beth Simchat Torah (House of Gladness in the Torah), a synagogue where lesbian and gay Jews could "daven to the G—d of Abraham and Sarah in their own secure and loving space." Although the congregation moved in 1975 to a permanent home in the Westbeth complex at 57 Bethune Street, it still uses

Holy Apostles for its main service on Fridays. Sharon Kleinbaum is the very prominent rabbi.

The first woman priest in the Episcopal diocese, the Rev. Ellen Barrett, was ordained at Holy Apostles in 1977. The soup kitchen, begun in 1982, serves anyone who comes to the door. That can mean about 1,000 meals a day. In 1990, fire badly damaged the church. But under the Rev. William A. Greenlaw, Holy Apostles began a second restoration, directed by Ed Kamper, and reopened in 1994. The nave was turned into a flexible space that is now used for the soup kitchen.

Church of the Holy Apostles **[G25]**

Holy Communion, Church of the.
See Calvary and St. George's Church

Holy Cross African Orthodox Pro-Cathedral.
This denomination dates to 1919 when the Rev. George Alexander McGuire, later chaplain general of Marcus Garvey's Universal Negro Improvement Association, organized the Independent Episcopal Church for black communicants. Its sanctuary at 122 West 129th Street **[●Q21]** once served the Rendall Memorial Presbyterian Church.

Holy Cross African Orthodox Pro-Cathedral **[Q21]**

Holy Cross Armenian Apostolic Church.
"Archbishop Assassinated in Procession to Altar; Assassins Swarm About Armenian Prelate and Stab Him." That startling headline in the *New York Times* recorded the awful scene at Holy Cross Armenian Apostolic Church, at 580 West 187th Street **[●V8]**, on December 24, 1933, when Archbishop Leon Elisee Tourian, the supreme head of the Armenian Church in the United States, was attacked by members of the Armenian Revolutionary Federation. The parish was only four years old at the time of the incident. Because blood was shed, the sanctuary—originally the Lutheran Church of Our Saviour—had to be reconsecrated. Plans for Tourian's crypt were filed in 1934 by Manoug Exerjian, who was also responsible for renovating and refacing the church in 1952/1953. In the schism that followed the assassination, the parishes of the original diocese were separated from those of a new prelacy, a division reflected in the existence of two Armenian cathedrals: St. Illuminator's and St. Vartan.

Holy Cross Armenian Apostolic Church **[V8]**

Holy Cross Catholic Church of the Byzantine Rite. A little sanctuary at 323 East 82nd Street [●N31] houses Holy Cross Catholic Church of the Byzantine Rite, founded in 1938. This denomination recognizes the authority of the pope but does not follow the Latin Rite. The building has also been Congregation Atereth Israel and the Greek Orthodox Church of St. John.

Holy Cross Catholic Church of the Byzantine Rite **[N31]**

Holy Cross Church. A great dome nearly 150 feet high marks the summit of the monumental Romanesque Holy Cross Church, at 333 West 42nd Street [●I41], across from the Port Authority Bus Terminal, one of the few nineteenth-century anchors around a percolating, ever-changing Times Square. The parish was founded in 1852 and built on this site [I40] two years later. The church was struck by lightning in 1867. The replacement by Henry Engelbert was finished in 1870 and expanded in 1885 by Lawrence J. O'Connor. This was the pulpit of the Rev. Francis P. Duffy, chaplain to the largely Irish-American Sixty-ninth Regiment in World War I and namesake of Duffy Square, at Broadway and 46th Street. (A statue by Charles Keck stands there, in front of a granite Celtic cross.) Its current celebrated pastor is the Rev. Peter Colapietro—Father Pete—who is known for fighting tenaciously by day for his hardscrabble parish and spending his evenings in the more glamorous precinct of Elaine's.

Holy Cross Church **[I41]**

Holy Cross Mission Church. The sanctuary at 43 Avenue C [F34] housed Holy Cross, a mission church to German Episcopalians, from 1913 to 1934. It has been replaced by a six-story apartment building, but the former clergy house next door, on East 4th Street, is still recognizably ecclesiastical, with its Gothic windows and crenellated roof.

Holy Cross Polish National Catholic Church. The Gothic doorway and windows reveal the religious heritage of the brownstone at 57 St. Mark's Place [●E40], formerly Holy Cross Polish National Catholic Church.

Holy Family, Church of the. Known as the United Nations parish, the handsomely Modernist Church of the Holy Family stands at 315 East 47th Street [● J29].

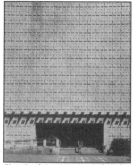

Church of the Holy Family **[J29]**

The planar facade is a latticework made of panels with Greek crosses at the center. Designed by George J. Sole, it was built from 1962 to 1965. The parish was founded in 1924 to serve Italian immigrants. The old church, on the same site [J28], was a converted brewery stable. In 1965, Pope Paul VI visited the church. Fourteen years later, almost to the day, Pope John Paul II extended his blessing to the church after delivering a human-rights message at the UN. In the 1990s, Holy Family sold its air rights to Donald J. Trump, who used them to build the oversize Trump World Tower down the block.

Holy Family Mission. A delightful surprise in East Harlem is a tiny apartment house with a great Gothic window at 236 East 111th Street [●P9]. It was built in 1905 as St. Ambrose's, an Episcopal mission to the Italian population, which lasted until 1936, when it was taken over by Holy Family, an Episcopal mission to Spanish residents.

Holy Family Mission **[P9]**

Holy Fathers Russian Orthodox Church. A Fabergé Easter egg of an architectural treat, this onion-domed sanctuary at 524 West 153rd Street [●U22] is set back from the building line and so comes as a delightful surprise. The Holy Fathers Russian Orthodox Church is one of seven churches clustered around Trinity Cemetery. Plans were filed in 1960 by Vladimir B. Morosov. The congregation was organized in 1927 on West 124th Street and is part of the Russian Orthodox Church Outside Russia, which differs from the Moscow Patriarchate at St. Nicholas Russian Orthodox Cathedral. The cathedral of this denomination is Mother of God of the Sign, on East 93rd Street.

Holy Fathers Russian
Orthodox Church **[U22]**

Holy Innocents, Church of the. The strong resemblance between this Roman Catholic church at 128 West 37th Street [●G12] and the Church of St. Bernard in Greenwich Village is more than coincidental. Both were by Patrick C. Keely. This parish was organized in 1866 and built its sanctuary in 1869/1870. A few blocks north of Herald Square, the Church of the Holy Innocents offered a "shoppers' Mass."

Church of the Holy
Innocents **[G12]**

Church of the Holy Name of Jesus **[O27]**

Holy Name of Jesus, Church of the. When the Upper West Side was still known as the village of Bloomingdale, the Roman Catholic Church of the Holy Name of Jesus was organized in 1868 and built a wood-frame sanctuary on the Bloomingdale Road [O26]. The current church, at 740 Amsterdam Avenue [●O27], was built in stages from 1891 to 1900, with the steeple added in 1918. The architect was Thomas H. Poole.

Holy Rosary, Church of the. The Roman Catholic parish of the Holy Rosary, founded in 1884, opened its church at 444 East 119th Street [●R52] in 1899. Thomas F. Houghton was the architect.

Church of the Holy Rosary **[R52]**

Holy Tabernacle Church. Across from Jefferson Park is the five-story Holy Tabernacle Church, a Pentecostal sanctuary at 407 East 114th Street [●R74]. A kind of proto–Skyscraper Church, its worship space is clearly delineated at the base of a larger structure. Built in 1905/1906, it was designed by Cady & See for the Jefferson Park Methodist Episcopal Church, which had begun as the Italian Church in 1894 during open-air meetings. Jefferson Park merged with Trinity, from East 118th Street, in 1918, and then into the Upper Madison Avenue United Methodist Church in 1977.

Holy Tabernacle Church **[R74]**

Holy Trinity, Archdiocesan Cathedral of the. This Byzantine Moderne sanctuary at 337 East 74th Street [●L3] is the seat of the Greek Orthodox Archdiocese of America, the largest of the Orthodox Christian churches in the Western Hemisphere. In 1892, Holy Trinity rented what is now the Church of St. Benedict the Moor, at 342 West 53rd Street [●I11], and then moved to the former St. James' Church on East 72nd Street [L10]. The building burned down in 1927, and Holy Trinity worshiped at St. Eleftherios Greek Orthodox Church. Plans for the present building were filed in 1931 by Holmes & Converse. It was completed in 1932 and designated the archdiocesan cathedral in 1962, during the long reign of Archbishop Iakovos, the first Orthodox leader to meet with a pope in 350 years. A relic of St. Nicholas himself is kept at Holy Trinity, quite fitting since he was the patron saint of New Amsterdam. In 1990, the cathedral received Dimetrios

I, the first Ecumenical Patriarch of Constantinople to travel to the United States. The dean of the cathedral for many years has been the Rev. Robert G. Stephanopoulos, whose son George is a well-known political commentator. The current archbishop, Demetrios, had to contend with the shocking destruction of St. Nicholas Greek Orthodox Church as a result of the attack on the World Trade Center.

Archdiocesan Cathedral of the Holy Trinity **[L3]**

Holy Trinity, Church of the. The tower at the Episcopal Church of the Holy Trinity, at 316 East 88th Street **[●N10★]**, is almost a prototype for the Woolworth Building, expressing the pure vertical joy in medieval architecture. Adding to its appeal is the setting: a quarter acre of sweetly landscaped grounds, on which are also set St. Christopher House and a parsonage.

Church of the Holy Trinity [J48]

Holy Trinity was always associated with distinctive architecture, beginning with a Victorian "cottage ornée" by Jacob Wrey Mould at Madison Avenue and East 42nd Street [J48]. It was replaced on the same site [J49] in 1873 by Leopold Eidlitz's towering sanctuary—the height of High Victorian Gothic in New York. Holy Trinity's delirious patterning and striking use of color—yellow, brown, red, blue—earned it the nickname Church of the Homely Oilcloth. The rector, the Rev. Stephen H. Tyng Jr., whose father had commissioned Eidlitz to design St. George's Church on Stuyvesant Square, desired a church that would be a "theater with ecclesiastical details."

Church of the Holy Trinity [J49]

The parish weakened as midtown grew more commercial. In 1895, Holy Trinity accepted an invitation to join with St. James' Church on Madison Avenue, which had been offered property on East 88th Street— once the Rhinelander Farm—by Serena Rhinelander. The idea was to establish a landscaped mission in what was then a working-class district, offering a bucolic retreat for worshipers who did not otherwise get to spend time among grass and trees. The mission, run by St. James' but called Holy Trinity, was built from 1895 to 1899 to designs by Barney & Chapman, architects of the mission campus of Grace Church on East 14th Street, now the Church of the Immaculate Conception. Holy Trinity became a freestanding parish in 1951. Under the direction of William Stivale, the bells in that joyous tower were restored in 1995.

Church of the Holy Trinity **[N10]**

Church of the Holy Trinity **[M25]**

Holy Trinity, Church of the. A vast dome of honey-colored, herringbone Guastavino tiles, designed by Joseph H. McGuire, suggests the vaults of the Oyster Bar at Grand Central Terminal. But it also evokes the interior of Hagia Sophia in Istanbul, as intended by the Rev. Michael J. Considine, during whose pastorate the Roman Catholic Church of the Holy Trinity was built, from 1910 to 1912, at 213 West 82nd Street **[●M25]**, for a parish that dates to 1898. Inscribed on the Byzantine facade is the minor doxology: GLORIA PATRI ET FILIO ET SPIRITUI S'O. Deteriorating copper cupolas were removed in 1995, but the interior of the 66-foot-diameter dome was reilluminated to grand effect.

Holy Trinity Chapel **[E55]**

Holy Trinity Chapel. Facing Washington Square Park **[●E55]** is the truncated A-frame chapel of New York University's Catholic Center, designed by Eggers & Higgins and built from 1961 to 1964 with a donation from the family of Generoso Pope, publisher of *Il Progresso Italo-Americano*. Holy Trinity Chapel speaks of an era when architects were seeking to pare down details but retain, however abstractly, traditional ecclesiastical form. As such, it had a close cousin in Edgar Tafel's Protestant Chapel at Kennedy Airport. The stained-glass window wall, mural, and furnishings were designed by Earl C. Neiman.

Holy Trinity Church (Inwood) **[W4]**

Holy Trinity Church (Inwood). Born in Harlem, this Episcopal parish moved to Inwood in "white flight," leaving behind one of New York's architectural treasures: the Romanesque sanctuary that is today St. Martin's Episcopal Church.

Founded in 1868, Holy Trinity built a church in 1869/1870 on upper Fifth Avenue **[R27]**, designed by John W. Welch, that was later Temple Israel. Its next sanctuary, at 230 Lenox Avenue **[●R38★]**, was designed by William A. Potter and completed in 1888. In 1928, the Rev. John Howard Johnson began conducting services in the parish house for black communicants. This group eventually took over the building, establishing St. Martin's. Meanwhile, Holy Trinity, having merged in 1927 with the Church of the Holy Redeemer in Inwood, planned a large complex at

Cumming Street and Seaman Avenue [●W4], with a tall Gothic Moderne sanctuary facing the avenue and a towering flèche at the crossing. But the Depression literally cut these plans short. Only the lower portion of the sanctuary had been built by 1935. Designed by Springsteen & Goldhammer, with an adjoining community house, it is set off on a delightful lawn high above the sidewalk. Membership in the church had dwindled to eight in 1986 but has since rebounded.

Holy Trinity Lutheran Church. There are few beacons as welcoming on the Central Park West skyline as the delicate copper flèche, charmingly illuminated at night, atop this Gothic sanctuary at 3 West 65th Street [●K24☆]. Founded in 1868 by seceders from St. James Lutheran Church, Holy Trinity was once among the few exclusively English-speaking Lutheran congregations in New York, where German predominated. In the closing decades of the nineteenth century, its home

Holy Trinity Lutheran Church [H45]

was at 47 West 21st Street [H45], a sanctuary built as St. Paul's Reformed Dutch Church, founded in 1836. Holy Trinity's present building, by Schickel & Ditmars, was built from 1902 to 1904. In a bit of historical symmetry, the St. James congregation, from which this group had split in 1868, merged back into Holy Trinity in 1938. The pastor from the mid-1950s to the mid-1970s, the Rev. Robert D. Hershey, was known nationally for his broadcasts and locally for Sunday musical vespers focused on Bach. Holy Trinity continues to be cherished for its music, particularly the Bach programs.

Holy Trinity Lutheran Church **[K24]**

Holy Trinity Slovak Lutheran Church. Surprisingly appealing, Holy Trinity Slovak Lutheran Church, at 332 East 20th Street [●H57], is a pared-down, 1964 version of a traditional gabled brick church with tower. But this derivative design by Hyland Dinion succeeds, thanks to the needle-like steeple and ladder-shaped tracery window. The earlier building on this site [H56] served the Colgate Memorial Baptist Church, St. George Ukrainian Catholic Church, and Holy Trinity Slovak Lutheran Church, which moved here in 1911 from 288 East 10th Street [●F10].

Holy Trinity Slovak Lutheran
Church **[H57]**

Holy Trinity Ukrainian Orthodox Church
[B12]

Cathedral of the Holy Virgin Protection
[E80]

Holyrood Church [V17]

Holy Trinity Ukrainian Orthodox Church. Anglicans and Italians once mixed in this richly embellished Romanesque sanctuary at 359 Broome Street [●B12], originally the CHVRCH OF SAN SALVATORE (as it still says over the entrance), run by the New York Protestant Episcopal City Mission Society. Designed by Hoppin & Koen and built in 1901/1902, it is now Holy Trinity Ukrainian Orthodox Church.

Holy Virgin Protection, Cathedral of the. Across from Marble Cemetery at 59 East 2nd Street [●E80]—as peaceful a setting as the Lower East Side has to offer—stands one of Manhattan's three Russian Orthodox cathedrals, heir to a complex history.

The New York City Mission Society built the Olivet Chapel in 1867 on this site [E79], once a small cemetery. Focusing on those not served by the city's mainline churches, the chapel offered services in German, Hungarian, Italian, and Russian. The present Gothic sanctuary, originally the Olivet Memorial Church, was built in 1891 and designed by J. C. Cady & Company. It offered classes, a library, a gymnasium, baths, societies, and clubs.

The building was sold in 1942 to the body now known as the Orthodox Church in America, which traces its origins commonly with those of St. Nicholas Russian Orthodox Cathedral, diverging in 1925 when the Soviet-controlled Living Church won control of the cathedral from Metropolitan (Archbishop) Platon. The followers of Platon moved in 1927 to St. Augustine's Chapel, at 107 East Houston Street [E89], which they subdivided, calling their half St. Mary's Russian Orthodox Cathedral. On acquiring Olivet Memorial, they rededicated it in 1943 as the Cathedral of the Holy Virgin Protection. Christ the Savior Orthodox Church is a parish of this body.

Holyrood Church. If you can ignore the roaring and the fumes of the George Washington Bridge Bus Station across West 179th Street, you will be astonished by this romantic work of Gothic Revival. It is as charming as a work by Alexander Jackson Davis, yet powerful enough to stand up to the concrete forms of the station, by Pier Luigi Nervi. The parish—Holyrood means "Holy Crucifix" or "Holy Cross"—was founded in 1893. Its first sanctuary was a country-style church built two years later on upper Broadway [V17] to designs by R. D. Chandler, at a time when this was still a rural district. As the neighborhood grew a bit more cosmopolitan, Holyrood was converted into the Garfield Theater in 1911. The architects of the present church, at 715 West 179th Street [●V19], were Bannister & Schell, a partnership of William F. Bannister and Richard M. Schell, who also designed the North Presbyterian Church. Holyrood Church was completed in 1914. The building is shared with the Iglesia Santa Cruz (Holy Cross).

Holyrood Church **[V19]**

Hope Baptist Church. Henry F. Kilburn, purveyor of Romanesque design, was the architect of the short-lived Boulevard or Hope Baptist Church, built from 1890 to 1894 at 2720 Broadway [O16]. In 1921, Oscar Konkle planned to replace the sanctuary, by then known as the Metropolitan Tabernacle, with a 17-story church and hotel by Carrère & Hastings and Shreve, Lamb & Blake. The church portion was eliminated before it was built. The hotel is now the Regent Family Residence for the Homeless.

House of God Church Keith Dominion. The House of God Church Keith Dominion, at 127 West 128th Street [●Q19], was designed in 1968 by George Early.

House of Prayer of God in Christ, Baptist. Designed by George Keister and built in 1889, the building at 80 West 126th Street [●R25] served as the Ellerslie Rooms and later the Plantation Club of New York. The Baptist House of Prayer of God in Christ was founded in 1909.

Baptist House of Prayer of God in Christ **[R25]**

Hungarian Baptist Church. The robustly Romanesque building at 225 East 80th Street [●N34], now home to the Hungarian Baptist Church, was once Industrial School No. 7, by Fowler & Hough, built in 1893.

Hungarian Reformed Church. Although the massing and detailing of the facade are fairly anemic, the golden bricks of the Hungarian Reformed Church, a sanctuary built in 1959 at 229 East 82nd Street [●N30], can truly glow of a late-summer afternoon.

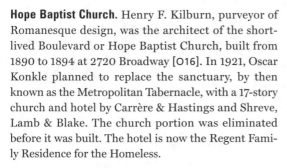

Hungarian Reformed Church **[N30]**

Church of the Immaculate Conception
[F3]

Church of the Immaculate Conception
[F1]

Immaculate Conception, Church of the. That churches and synagogues were once the heart of the social-service infrastructure is evidenced by late-nineteenth- and early-twentieth-century buildings. No sanctuary was complete without classrooms, clubrooms, library, kitchen, and gymnasium. But few of these welfare complexes rivaled this colony of French Gothic buildings at 406 East 14th Street [●F1★], constructed from 1894 to 1896 as a mission chapel of Grace Church. The architect, J. Stewart Barney of Barney & Chapman, was almost simultaneously working on another such complex, for the Church of the Holy Trinity on East 88th Street. (The openwork towers are strikingly similar.) HO, EVERYONE THAT THIRSTETH...proclaims the fountain here. Isaiah 55:1 continues: "Come to the waters; and he who has no money, come, buy and eat!" Grace Hospital had wards for 10 children and 16 elderly men and women, with a bridge leading to the chapel so the disabled could be wheeled to services. It also had a dispensary. Artistry was lavished on the chapel, where stained-glass windows by Clayton & Bell and Henry Holiday were installed. The mission was closed in 1943, and the buildings were sold to the Roman Catholic Church of the Immaculate Conception, founded in 1855. Its previous church, at 505 East 14th Street [F3], finished in 1858, was razed to make way for Stuyvesant Town.

Immanuel Baptist Church. The windowless box at 411 East 75th Street [●N48] is a vestige of the Immanuel Baptist Church, a German congregation founded in 1894. Plans were filed in 1905 by R. E. Dusinberre.

Immanuel Lutheran Church. The foursquare Gothic church at 122 East 88th Street [●N9] stands as enduring testament to a German congregation established in 1863 as "Die Ev.-Luth. Immanuelsgemeinde Ungeaenderter Augsb. Konfession zu Yorkville." Two years later, the pastor and several members withdrew to form the Second Immanuel Lutheran Church, which in 1893 built its own sanctuary at 211 East 83rd Street [●N26], now the Church of St. Elizabeth of Hungary. Second Immanuel rejoined Immanuel in 1912. The present sanctuary, by Arthur Crooks, was built in 1886. Inside the 200-foot tower are three bells given to the congregation by Empress Augusta of Germany, inscribed GLAUBE, HOFFNUNG, and LIEBE (Faith, Hope, and Love). Stained-glass nave windows by Benoit Gilsoul were installed in 1973 after the original windows were destroyed by blasting for the nearby Gimbels East department store.

Imperial (Elks) Lodge No. 127.
See Faith Mission Christian Fellowship

Incarnation, Church of the.
"For by Grace came the Incarnation" is a neat summary of the origins of this historic parish and artistic treasure house. Incarnation began in 1850 as a mission chapel of Grace Church on Madison Avenue and East 28th Street [H26]. The congregation was reorganized two years later as the Church of the Incarnation. In 1864/1865, the parish built its own church at 209 Madison Avenue [●H4★]. Designed by Emlen T. Littel, it is a spare and sober Gothic work of brownstone and contrasting sandstone, lavishly enriched with stained-glass windows by Edward Burne-Jones, John La Farge, the William Morris Company, and the Tiffany Glass and Decorating Company. After a fire in 1882, it was rebuilt and enlarged by D. & J. Jardine. The Rev. Arthur Brooks, rector of Incarnation for 20 years, was the first chairman of Barnard College. Eleanor Roosevelt was confirmed here, and a ramp was later built so Franklin D. Roosevelt could attend his mother's funeral. A 1991 renovation was supervised by Jan Hird Pokorny. Incarnation's chapel at 238 East 31st Street [●H18] is now the Church of the Good Shepherd.

Immanuel Lutheran Church **[N9]**

Church of the Incarnation **[H4]**

Incarnation, Church of the.
La Iglesia de la Encarnación, at 1290 Juan Pablo Duarte Boulevard, or St. Nicholas Avenue [●V34], may fairly be called the St. Patrick's of Washington Heights. The Roman Catholic parish dates to 1908. Plans for this church were filed in 1927 by W. H. Jones, and the cornerstone was laid the next year. Within are side aisles, tall clerestory windows, a ribbed-vault ceiling, and a soaring apse. In the early 1950s, Incarnation was home to the Rev. Ivan Illich, a theologian and author who championed new forms of ministry to Puerto Rican and other Latin Catholics.

Church of the Incarnation **[V34]**

Church of the Intercession [U8]

Church of the Intercession **[U18]**

Intercession, Church of the. No sanctuary in Manhattan has a more expansive yard than the Church of the Intercession, set in the 24-acre Trinity Cemetery **[●U18★]**, the only one on the island still in active use. Resting in peace here are John James Audubon, who lived nearby, and Clement Clarke Moore. The cemetery was begun in 1843, when Trinity Episcopal parish bought a large tract in the suburb of Carmansville. Four years later, Intercession parish was organized. In 1872, it built a stern Gothic church on Broadway [U8], designed by Rembrandt Lockwood. With the coming of the subway, the population exploded. Intercession did not have the money to build a new sanctuary, so it turned to Old Trinity, which made Intercession one of its chapels and took over the construction on its cemetery grounds of the present building, by Bertram Grosvenor Goodhue. The glorious, cathedral-like Gothic church, built from 1911 to 1914, has a strong verticality and assertive massing that recall Goodhue's South Reformed Dutch Church, now the Park Avenue Christian Church. The architect is entombed here, in a monument by his frequent collaborator, the sculptor Lee Lawrie. Intercession regained its independence in 1976. In 1989, its parishioner David N. Dinkins became the first black mayor of New York. His inauguration was celebrated at a service here with Archbishop Desmond M. Tutu of South Africa, the Rev. Jesse Jackson, and a thousand others.

Inwood Hebrew Congregation | Dyckman, Iglesia Adventista del Séptimo Día. The sanctuary at 111 Vermilyea Avenue **[●W1]** is unusual in architecture and operation. The neo-Georgian synagogue, designed in 1921 by George and Edward Blum, currently is shared by the Conservative congregation that built it and a Spanish Adventist church.

Islamic Cultural Center of New York. While it is true that few great houses of worship were constructed in New York City in the late twentieth century, it is not accurate to say that there were none. This, the first purpose-built mosque in Manhattan, was the greatest of all.

It took 48 years to complete St. Patrick's Cathedral and it has taken 112 years and counting to build St. John the Divine, so the 28-year saga of the Islamic Cul-

Inwood Hebrew Congregation **[W1]**

tural Center of New York seems modest by comparison. Founded in 1963, the center established itself in a town house at 1 Riverside Drive [●K1]. The site for the new mosque, at 1711 Third Avenue [●P33], was bought in 1966 by the Kuwaiti, Saudi, and Libyan governments. The project began in earnest under Kuwait's ambassador to the United Nations, Mohammad A. Abulhassan. The Iranian architect Aly S. Dadras drew up a traditional scheme, but it was rejected. Skidmore, Owings & Merrill was given the commission, with Michael A. McCarthy and Mustafa K. Abadan as designers. The 130-foot minaret was designed by Richard Hayden of Swanke Hayden Connell. Although not required for liturgical reasons, the dome and minaret were seen as "the emblem of Islam," said Dr. Abdel-Rahman Osman, the former imam. "They mark a house of God."

Islamic Cultural Center of New York **[K1]**

Sheik Jaber al-Ahmed al-Sabah, the emir of Kuwait, laid the cornerstone in 1988. In 1991, on the Night of Power (Leilat al Qadr), marking the first appearance of the angel Gabriel to Mohammed, worshipers used the main prayer hall for the first time.

The mosque is skewed 29 degrees off the Manhattan street grid, establishing the *qibla*, its orientation toward

Islamic Cultural Center of New York **[P33]**

the Ka'ba in the court of the Grand Mosque in Mecca, the most sacred place of Islam. That direction is indicated by the points of the crescent moons atop the dome and minaret, and by a niche called the *mihrab*, visible as a protrusion on the East 97th Street facade. Within the main hall, the *mihrab* is framed by inscriptions from the Qur'an, including LIGHT UPON LIGHT; GOD GUIDES TO HIS LIGHT WHOM HE WILL. The simplicity of the design stripped the mosque of national attributes, a vital consideration for a project that, though funded largely by Kuwaitis, depended on support from many Islamic countries. The carpet, for example, was a gift from Pakistan. (In prayer, Muslims do not sit in pews but kneel or prostrate themselves.) Simplicity also encourages meditation. The volume is organized around an imaginary 90-foot cube divided in a 5 by 5 by 5 grid. The panels that express this grid are defined by narrow channels that allow light to fill the sanctuary. The milky green color was chosen as representing an oasis, or paradise, in the desert.

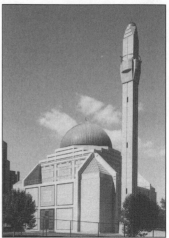

Islamic Cultural Center of New York **[P33]**

A diaphanous cylinder of 90 bulbs hanging by brass rods from the drum of the dome resembles the low-slung oil lamps of Hagia Sophia. Other Islamic elements include a women's gallery and a *minbar*, the staircase topped by a pulpit. Figurative representation is forbidden. What appears to be rectilinear geometric patterning is in fact stylized calligraphy. At the top of the dome, the name Allah is written four times, surrounded by 8 of Allah's 99 attributes, such as the Merciful, the Compassionate, and the Holy. Around the drum of the dome are verses from the Qur'an. One need not be steeped in Islam to appreciate the sanctity of this luminous space, though Jerrilyn D. Dodds noted in *New York Masjid: The Mosques of New York City* that it is not considered possible by Muslims that physical surroundings hasten or encourage spiritual engagement.

Already, the mosque has taken a prominent place in civic life. A 1993 account in the *New York Times* described the scene: "Through its doors came Pakistanis in flowing pastel gowns, black Americans wearing kentecloth hats, an Albanian couple trying to quiet their crying daughter, West Africans in high head wraps, Bahrainis in business suits, Egyptian cab drivers, Yemeni restaurateurs, a young Bosnian who stood up in mid-service and gave an emotional appeal for his countrymen." The mosque was the setting in 1999 of a service for Amadou Diallo, a West African street vendor whose killing by the police brought a firestorm of criticism on the administration of Mayor Rudolph W. Giuliani.

Shortly after the September 11, 2001, attack on the World Trade Center, the imam, Sheik Muhammad Gemeaha, returned abruptly to Cairo. He was succeeded by Imam Omar Saleem Abu-Namous, a native of Palestine who now occupies one of the city's most important pulpits at a critical juncture in history.

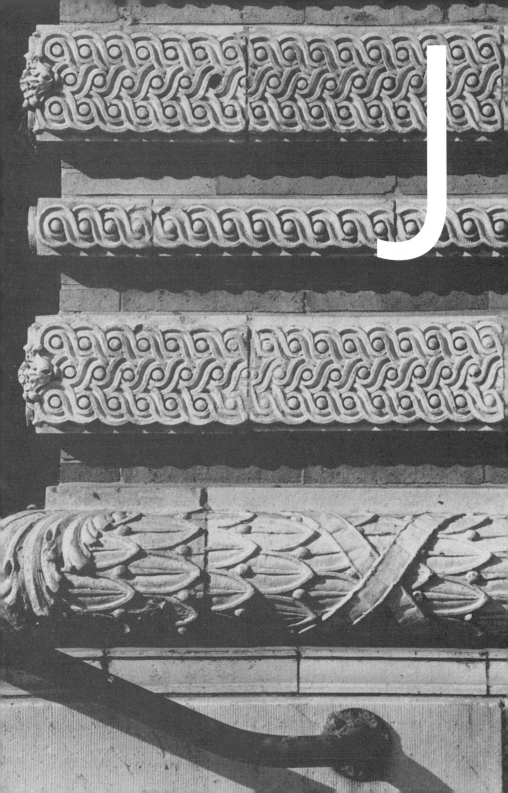

James Chapel **[Q39]**

James Chapel. Two finial-crested towers rise over the Union Theological Seminary. The Brown Memorial Tower, on Broadway, has no liturgical function, but the 85-foot James Tower, on Claremont Avenue [●Q39★], denotes this grand chapel. Union, a nondenominational graduate school, was founded in 1836 in Greenwich Village. It moved to Lenox Hill and then to Morningside Heights, where this complex was constructed from 1908 to 1910, designed by Allen & Collens of Boston, which overshadowed its own work here with the later Riverside Church. James Chapel honors Daniel Willis James, a director of the seminary for 40 years. He gave the land on which the seminary stands and the money needed to build it. The buildings themselves were to be instructive, Daniel J. Fleming wrote in *Education Through Stone and Glass*, with the seminary directors hoping that "ecclesiastical architecture in many a parish would be bettered through the influence of those who had spent their time of preparation in the atmosphere of a carefully studied example of the best period of English Gothic."

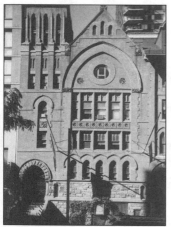

Jan Hus Presbyterian Church **[L4]**

Jan Hus Presbyterian Church. In the early fifteenth century, the Bohemian priest Jan Hus (John Huss) presaged the Reformation by attacking indulgences and denying papal infallibility, among other things. The church that bears his name, Jan Hus Ceskobratrsky Presbyterni Sbor, or Bohemian Brethren Church, was founded in 1877 and built its Victorian Gothic house of worship in Little Bohemia, at 347 East 74th Street [●L4], in 1888. It was designed by R. H. Robertson, and the sanctuary is said to be a replica of Hus's Bethlehem Chapel in Prague.

Jane Street Methodist Episcopal Church. The congregation of the Jane Street Methodist Episcopal Church was founded in 1844 and dissolved in 1920, roughly the same life span of its sanctuary at 13 Jane Street [D6].

Japanese-American United Church of Christ **[G32]**

Japanese-American United Church of Christ. A three-story, midcentury institutional building at 255 Seventh Avenue [●G32], distinguished from workaday neighbors by a large cross, is home to the Japanese-American United Church of Christ. This congregation used to worship in a row house at 323 West 108th Street [●O7], shared with the Japanese Methodist Church.

Jefferson Park Methodist Episcopal Church.
See Holy Tabernacle Church

Jehovah's Witnesses Kingdom Halls.
The Watchtower Bible and Tract Society was incorporated in 1884 under Charles Taze Russell and moved to Brooklyn in 1909. Its adherents, Jehovah's Witnesses, are known for energetic person-to-person missionary work. They meet in Kingdom Halls, most of which are of little architectural consequence, though it is worth noting that the Witnesses were the busiest builders of sanctuaries in Manhattan in the latter twentieth century.

Jehovah's Witnesses Kingdom Hall **[Q15]**

Mario A. Tucciarone designed the 1963 hall at 310 West 129th Street [●Q15], which was rebuilt in 1997 to accommodate duplex meeting rooms used by six separate congregational units; the 1966 hall at 58 West 129th Street [●R7], since sold to the Church of Jesus Christ of Latter-day Saints; and the 1967 hall at 88 Bradhurst Avenue [●S13]. Melvin Leshowitz designed the 1970 hall at 156 East 100th Street [●P30]. The hall at 1763 Madison Avenue [●R67] is marked by a crenellated parapet, while the Salón del Reino at 63 Avenue C [●F29] occupies almost half a block. The hall at 409 Central Park West [●O20] was formerly Congregation Beth Moshe (House of Moses).

Jehovah's Witnesses Kingdom Hall **[U5]**

The remarkable Kingdom Hall at 609 West 161st Street [●U5] was formerly the Hebrew Tabernacle of Washington Heights, by George and Edward Blum and Ludwig Hanauer, completed in 1925. (The cornerstone says 5682 – 1922.) Known for ornamental terra-cotta, the Blums laid it on thick in this deep latticework arch. The Hebrew Tabernacle congregation moved uptown to the former Fourth Church of Christ, Scientist.

Jehovah-Jireh Baptist Church of Christ.
A Renaissance Revival row house at 536 West 148th Street [●S9] was a synagogue for a half century, Congregation Agudas Achim (Association of Brothers), before being acquired by the Jehovah-Jireh Baptist Church of Christ.

Jehovah-Jireh Baptist Church of Christ **[S9]**

Jewish Center **[M17]**

Jewish Center. Looking quite unlike most synagogues, but utterly at one with neighboring apartment houses, the building at 131 West 86th Street [●M17☆] is the home of the Jewish Center, an Orthodox congregation. Designed by Louis Allen Abramson, it was built from 1917 to 1920. The sanctuary is on the second floor, marked by tall arched windows set between two-story fluted pilasters. The center was founded by Rabbi Mordecai M. Kaplan to deter disaffection from synagogue life by offering a Jewish context for youth groups, social gatherings, and athletic events. Later at odds with Orthodox tenets, Kaplan founded the Society for the Advancement of Judaism, spearhead of the Reconstructionist movement. Its home is only a block away, at 15 West 86th Street.

John's Pizzeria. *See* Crucifixion, Chapel of the

John Street Church. Ever since John and Charles Wesley's religious movement took root in American soil in the eighteenth century, 44 John Street has been the home—indeed, the cradle—of Methodist worship. It was born with these words: "Philip, you must preach to us, or we shall all go to hell!" This was Barbara Heck's exhortation to her cousin, a lay preacher named Philip Embury, who responded by organizing a meeting in 1766. The first Methodist church built in America was the Wesley Chapel of 1768, at 44 John Street [A19], a plain barn covered in blue stucco. This was also, indirectly, the birthplace of the African Methodist Episcopal Zion Church, founded in 1796 by a group including Peter Williams, who was sexton here. Embury's lectern and the altar rail are preserved in the Wesley Chapel Museum, part of the current John Street Church. Timber from the chapel later was used to build the Bowery Village Methodist Church and, even later, to serve as beams under the pulpit of the present-day Park Avenue United Methodist Church.

The second John Street Church was built on the same site [A20] in 1817/1818. Its apparent extravagance helped inspire a secession led by the Rev. William Stilwell. Construction of the present church on the site [●A21★] was occasioned by the widening of John Street in 1836. Although the landmark designation is

Wesley Chapel [A19]

John Street Church [A20]

silent about the architect, the building recently has been attributed to William Hurry. The John Street Church sold its air rights, which were used in the development of 33 Maiden Lane in 1984, so it seems safe to hope that it will long continue to offer an island of antebellum tranquillity in the canyons of the financial district.

Judson Memorial Church. If the Washington Arch is the gateway to Greenwich Village, the 10-tiered, golden-brick tower of Judson Memorial Church is the triumphal column—proclaiming an institution that could have evolved only in the Village, with its marvelous jumble of religious, social, political, and cultural missions. Associated over time with Stanford White and John La Farge, with Jim Dine, Claes Oldenburg, and Red Grooms, the church was, at its origin, linked to the Judson family. The Rev. Edward Judson was called in 1881 to the Berean Baptist Church on Downing Street. He expanded it so significantly that new quarters were needed. The present church, at 55 Washington Square South [●E54★], by McKim, Mead & White, was built from 1890 to 1893 and dedicated to Judson's father, Adoniram, a missionary to Burma. Edward's dream was to serve gentry and immigrants. "If the rich and poor are ever to meet together," he said, "it must be in the poor man's territory." The church was open all week, offering health care, employment guidance, sewing classes, even firewood and fresh milk. In the 1950s and 1960s, it opened itself to artists, dancers, poets, and performers. Under the Rev. Peter Laarman in the 1990s, Judson Memorial, affiliated with the Baptist Church and the United Church of Christ, continued to see itself on the side of self-empowerment. It also took care of its physical plant. The stained-glass windows by La Farge were restored by the Cummings Studio to breathtaking result.

John Street Church **[A21]**

Judson Memorial Church **[E54]**

Chevra Kadisha Anshei Podolsk **[C6]**

Kadisha Anshei Podolsk, Chevra. A blend of spiritualism and commerce, this former synagogue at 121 Ludlow Street **[●C6]**—once home to Congregation Kadisha Anshei Podolsk (Burial Society of the People of Podolsk, Ukraine)—had a ground-floor storefront.

Kalvarier Shul. See Sung Tak Buddhist Association

Kehila Kedosha Janina, Congregation. After the destruction of the Second Temple in Jerusalem, a ship bearing Jewish prisoners to Rome was forced ashore by a storm. The Jews made their way to Ioannina in Greece, where they developed a rite called the Romaniote *minhag*. Ioannian immigrants began arriving in New York in the early twentieth century and formed Congregation Kehila Kedosha Janina (Holy Community of Janina) in 1906. Their sanctuary, at 280 Broome Street **[●C8]**, was built from 1925 to 1927 to designs by Sidney Daub. It is now the only Romaniote synagogue in the United States. That makes even more important the efforts to preserve its heritage, through a museum built in the women's gallery.

Congregation Kehila Kedosha Janina **[C8]**

Kehilath Jacob, Congregation. A great sound has been known to come out of this diminutive synagogue at 305 West 79th Street **[●M26]**, popularly referred to as the Carlebach Shul, which was once the garage and laundry for the apartments next door. Rabbi Naftali Carlebach, the chief rabbi of Baden, Austria, until the rise of Hitler, assumed the leadership in 1950. He was succeeded by his son, Rabbi Shlomo Carlebach, called the "foremost songwriter in contemporary Judaism" by the *New York Times*, whose song "Am Israel Chai" served as an anthem for those trapped behind the Iron Curtain. Congregation Kehilath Jacob (Community of Jacob) is known for praying with intensity, fervor, and song.

Congregation Kehilath Jacob **[M26]**

Kehilath Jeshurun, Congregation. Separated by Central Park are two Moorish–Romanesque synagogues, built eight years apart, that bear a remarkable resemblance to each other. The East Side twin is Congregation Kehilath Jeshurun (Community of Israel), at 117

East 85th Street [●N19], an Orthodox synagogue founded in 1871; the West Side twin is Congregation Shaaray Tefila. Kehilath Jeshurun was designed by George F. Pelham in 1902. Like Shaaray Tefila, it had a monumental staircase, but it was removed in 1948. This congregation is well known for sponsoring the Ramaz School, founded in 1937 by Rabbi Joseph H. Lookstein and named for his grandfather, Rabbi Moses Zebulon Margolies (R-M-Z), who was the rabbi here for more than three decades.

Kehilath Jeshurun's earlier synagogue was built in 1890 at 127 East 82nd Street [N28]. It was used for many years by the First Waldensian Church, but wound up in the hands of Congregation Or Zarua, drawing the circle closed.

Congregation Kehilath Jeshurun **[N19]**

Kehillath Yaakov, Congregation.
See Nodah bi Yehuda, Congregation

Kelly Temple Church of God in Christ. Twin staircases create a fairly monumental entrance to the Kelly Temple Church of God in Christ, at 10 East 130th Street [●R5], an otherwise plain brick sanctuary designed in 1949 by Joseph Korwasky. It is one of many Harlem churches whose music has drawn thousands of tourists.

Kelly Temple Church of God in Christ **[R5]**

K'hal Adath Jeshurun, Congregation. The Modernist structure at 85 Bennett Avenue [●V10] has the heft of an institutional powerhouse. So it is. The Orthodox Congregation K'hal Adath Jeshurun (Community of the Congregation of Israel), organized in 1938 and once known as Breuer's—for Rabbi Joseph Breuer— offered its own cradle-to-grave institutions, modeled on the separatist Israelitische Religions-gesellschaft of Frankfurt: elementary school, boys' and girls' high schools, youth groups, women's teaching seminary, yeshiva, *mikvah*, rabbinical court, sisterhood and golden-age club, group health insurance, a committee to visit the sick, supervision over local kosher butchers and bakers, and burial societies. (Note the volunteer ambulances parked out front in the photograph.) Plans were filed in 1950 by Max B. Schreiber.

Congregation K'hal Adath Jeshurun **[V10]**

K'hal Adath Jeshurun with Anshe Lubz, Congregation.
See Eldridge Street Synagogue

King Solomon Grand Lodge.
See Muhammad's Mosque Number Seven

Kingdom Halls. See Jehovah's Witnesses Kingdom Halls

Kingdom of Father Divine. The plaza around the Adam Clayton Powell Jr. State Office Building obliterated any traces of the Kingdom where Father Divine fed Harlem.

George Baker adopted the name Father Divine in 1930 and moved to Harlem three years later. He operated several Kingdoms or Heavens, the most important at 152 West 126th Street [Q28], formerly Hollenders Baths. Father Divine was the preeminent black cult leader of his time, Jervis Anderson wrote in *This Was Harlem*. He preached righteousness, truth, and justice and offered lodging for $2 a week and meals for 15 cents: veal, chicken, or turkey; vegetables, bread, and butter; tea or coffee. At mealtimes, at least, he had "beaten the major churches," Anderson wrote, for "not even the wealthiest of them were able to feed the poor as regularly and as bountifully as he did." He moved to Philadelphia in 1942 and died in 1965. Nothing survives of his Kingdoms on West 126th Street and at 20 West 115th Street (later Sweet Daddy Grace's United House of Prayer for All People) or of his Peace Mission, at 204 West 63rd Street (earlier the Union Baptist Church). But Father Divine's Mansion, at 34 West 123rd Street, still stands and is home to the Bethelite Community Baptist Church.

King's Chapel. Switching denominations, its budget a source of constant contention, influenced by egos and politics, Manhattan's first big house of worship would become an archetype.

AO DO. MDCXLII. W. KEIFTH, DR. GR. HEEFT DE GEMEENTEN DEESE TEMPEL DOEN BOUWEN (A.D. 1642, W. Kieft, Director-General, caused the congregation to build this temple), declared a commemorative stone. The stone building stood in Fort Amsterdam [A48]. John Ogden of Stamford was the contractor.

King's Chapel [A48]

Willem Kieft had raised money among the friends and family of the minister Everardus Bogardus after several rounds of drinks at a wedding. By the time they sobered up, it was too late; they were on the hook.

When the English took over New Amsterdam in 1664, they took over the chapel, too, renaming it for the sovereign and using it for almost 30 years until Governor Benjamin Fletcher told the provincial assembly: "There is likewise the Kings Chappell in the effort which being ready to fall down to the danger of many lives, I thought it convenient to pull it down."

A new chapel was built in the fort [A49] from 1695 to 1697, ornamented with Fletcher's coat of arms. His successor, the earl of Bellomont, was asked to remove the emblem from the chapel, as it symbolized what colonists called Fletcher's "Nautious & Insupportable Pride & Vanity." The building fell into hard times, used as a storehouse, workhouse, and beer garden. But in 1713, Governor Robert Hunter reported that it had been repaired at great expense and was "now one of the most decent & most constantly frequented Houses of Prayer in all America." It also competed with Trinity Church, where "pews are not to be purchased but at a very high rate." At Kings Chapel, by contrast, "all degrees are seated without price or reward."

King's Chapel [A49]

King's Chapel was destroyed by fire in 1741. Almost a half century later, in 1790, the fort itself was leveled. The earth yielded the coffin of the earl of Bellomont, whose silver escutcheon was melted into teaspoons, and the stone placed by Director-General Kieft in the first chapel in 1642, which was taken to the South Reformed Dutch Church on Garden Street and lost when that building burned down in 1835.

King's Chapel of the Apostolic Faith.
See St. Bartholomew's Church

King's House. Among the largest sanctuaries built in recent decades is this two-story structure at 2341 Third Avenue [●R16], designed by Millard Bresin and dedicated in 1975, as inscribed on the facade, as THE TRUE CHURCH OF GOD FOUNDED BY JESUS CHRIST, A.D. 27.

King's House [R16]

Knox Memorial Chapel [I43]

Congregation Kochob Jacob Anshe
Kamenitz de Lite [E63]

Congregation Kolbuszower Teitelbaum
Chevra Banai [F26]

Knesset Israel, Congregation.
See Garment Center Synagogue

Knox Memorial Chapel. Alcoholics Anonymous is
known for making good use of church basements, but
in 1944, it took over an entire church: a Gothic sanctuary at 405 West 41st Street [I43] built in 1898 as the
Knox Memorial Chapel of the Collegiate Church.
Named for the Rev. John Knox, the chapel was organized in 1858 and worshiped first on Ninth Avenue
and then on West 41st Street. AA turned the church
into the headquarters and clubhouse for metropolitan
New York at a time when it had about 1,000 members.
In 1946, 8 of the 11 weekly AA meetings in Manhattan
were held here. The *New York Times* said of the opening ceremony that members "demonstrated that it is
not necessary to be tipsy to have a good time."

Kochob Jacob Anshe Kamenitz de Lite, Congregation.
This Romanesque synagogue at 65 East 3rd Street
[E63], altered in 1908 by Otto Reissmann, served Con-
gregations Beth Haknesseth und Chevra Chochmath
Adam M'Plinsk (Synagogue and Association of
Chochmath Adam of Plinsk, Poland) and Kochob
Jacob Anshe Kamenitz de Lite (Star of Jacob, People
of Kamenitz, Lithuania).

Kol Israel Anshe Poland, Congregation. Congregation
Kol Israel Anshe Poland (Community of Israel, People
of Poland), which once occupied the domed synagogue
at 27 Forsyth Street [●C23] that is now St. Barbara
Greek Orthodox Church, filed plans in 1914 by Sommerfeld & Steckler for a synagogue at 26 West 114th
Street [R70].

Kolbuszower Teitelbaum Chevra Banai, Congregation.
This exquisite synagogue at 622 East 5th Street [F26]
was used by Congregation Kolbuszower Teitelbaum
Chevra Banai (Association of the Sons of Kolbuszowa,
Poland). It was designed by Richard Marzari and Lee
& Samenfeld and was built in 1910, with a sunburst
pediment like those at Congregations Adas Yisroel
Anshe Mezeritch and B'nai Rappaport Anshe Dom-
browa.

Labor Temple [E16]

Labor Temple [E17]

Labor Temple. Four blocks from Union Square is a lesser known working-class landmark: the Labor Temple, New York's most radical church. "It is a well recognized fact that labor has been holding aloof from the Church for some years," said an officer of the Presbyterian Home Mission Board in 1910, when the temple was founded, "perhaps feeling that for it the Church was messageless, and possibly because the men mistrusted the forces back of certain members of the ministry." The founder of the Labor Temple, the Rev. Charles L. Stelze, said its brotherhood would be "entirely unsectarian," welcoming Jews, Catholics, Protestants— even Socialists. "We are going to give the Socialists a fair chance," he said, "and they are going to give us a chance to get at them." The first temple was in the Fourteenth Street Presbyterian Church, at 225 Second Avenue [E16], built in 1851 for a congregation that decamped in 1910 to West 13th Street. A new Labor Temple, by Emery Roth, at 242 East 14th Street [●E17], replaced the church in 1924. The developers built a chapel, an auditorium, and a gymnasium for the temple in exchange for controlling commercial space in the six-story structure. The Presbyterian Church of the Crossroads later met here, as did Congregation Tifereth Israel. The Labor Temple disbanded in 1957.

Lafayette Theater. *See* Williams Institutional C.M.E. Church

LaGree Baptist Church. Harlem's theatrical past is preserved in its churches. The West End Theater, a Spanish Baroque auditorium at 362 West 125th Street [●Q29], was designed by Neville & Bagge in 1902. It was acquired in 1975 by LaGree Baptist Church, founded in 1927 by the Rev. L. S. Taylor, which moved from a parlorfront sanctuary at 139 West 126th Street.

LaGree Baptist Church [Q29]

Lambs Church of the Nazarene. The Lambs in question were not the Lambs of God but the proprietors of a club for actors. The neo-Georgian building at 130 West 44th Street [●I39★] was built as a clubhouse in 1904/1905 to designs by Stanford White (a Lambs Club member) and is best known for its theater, which is still operating. But it is also a house of worship run by the Church of the Nazarene, which acquired the clubhouse in 1975 and kept the Lambs name for its Times Square mission to the homeless and poor and to troubled teen-agers. Reflecting the striking changes in Times Square, the church more recently entered into a partnership with the Hampshire Hotel Group, which planned to build a hotel here while preserving the sanctuary and theater.

Langon Chapel. *See* Notre-Dame-du-Bourg, Chapel of

Lambs Church of the Nazarene **[I39]**

Latter-day Saints, Church of Jesus Christ of. Although their church was established in upstate New York in 1830, Mormons did not have a permanent home in New York City for a century. Their first was the former Manhattan Congregational Church, at the base of the Manhattan Towers hotel at 2162 Broadway [●M36], now the Promenade Theatre, which they used from the 1930s until 1944. They were then at 142 West 81st Street [●M31☆], now the Mount Pleasant Baptist Church, for 30 years. After that, they built a chapel and visitors' center at Two Lincoln Square, an apartment tower on Columbus Avenue [●K22]. The travertine box by Schuman, Lichtenstein & Claman was dedicated by Spencer W. Kimball, president of the church, in 1975.

Church of Jesus Christ of Latter-day Saints **[K22]**

A chapel at 1815 Riverside Drive [●W8], by Frank Fernandez, opened in 2000, becoming Manhattan's first church of the new millennium. The design was old-fashioned. The concept was quite modern: active missionary work in Latino and black neighborhoods. The chapel adjoins a basketball court to offer "slam-dunk salvation," Juan Gonzalez wrote approvingly in the *Daily News*.

Church of Jesus Christ of Latter-day Saints **[W8]**

The church is planning a temple, in which the most sacred ordinances occur, at Two Lincoln Square. Designed by Fernandez, it will be the only temple between Boston and Washington. Fernandez is also designing a new chapel at 360 Malcolm X Boulevard, for a congregation that has used Sylvia's restaurant as a meeting place; another at 217 East 87th Street, replacing the Youth Residence Center; and another created through the renovation of the former St. Vita's Convent, at 141 West 14th Street [●E9].

Swedish Methodist Church
[J14]

Lexington United Methodist Church. The Swedish community of Manhattan, now largely dispersed, left numerous traces. This is one: the former Swedish Methodist Church, organized in 1882, which once occupied a sanctuary at 590 Lexington Avenue [J14] built in 1846 for Lexington Avenue Methodist Episcopal. The present Lexington United Methodist Church, descended from the Swedish congregation, was built at 150 East 62nd Street [●L37] in 1937/1938 to designs by Ford, Butler & Oliver. It opened with a sermon by the bishop of Stockholm. Not far away is Trinity Baptist Church, which was also once a Swedish church.

Liberty Hall. *See* Metropolitan Baptist Church

Limelight. *See* Calvary and St. George's Church

Lexington United Methodist
Church **[L37]**

Lincoln Memorial A.M.E. Church. Scaled like adjoining tenements, 87 Eldridge Street [●C19] declared itself a house of worship with arched window bays, fanlights, and a Star of David. Originally Congregation Anshe Tifereth Jerushelaim, it was acquired in the 1960s by Lincoln Memorial African Methodist Episcopal Church. Today, it is in residential use.

Lincoln Memorial A.M.E. Church
[C19]

Lincoln Square Synagogue. This Orthodox congregation was founded in 1964 by Rabbi Shlomo Riskin, who attracted a cohort missed by so many houses of worship: young, professional, and intellectual. Lincoln Square Synagogue, at 200 Amsterdam Avenue [●K10], a curving travertine structure, was inscribed with a verse from Isaiah 44:22: RETURN TO ME FOR I HAVE REDEEMED YOU. It was designed by Hausman & Rosenberg and built in 1970. Lincoln Square is at the southern end of the West Side *eruv*, which reaches as far north as the Old Broadway Synagogue. In this symbolic extension of home, observant Jews may carry objects or push strollers on the Sabbath, which would otherwise be proscribed. It is defined by the walls of buildings and, where necessary, fishing line at treetop level in the neighborhood.

Lincoln Theater. *See* Metropolitan A.M.E. Church

Lincoln Square Synagogue **[K10]**

Little Church Around the Corner. "I believe there is a little church around the corner where they do that sort of thing," said the Rev. William T. Sabine of the Church of the Atonement in 1870, telling Joseph Jefferson that he would find it distasteful to conduct a funeral for the actor George Holland in his own church. "If that be so, sir," said Jefferson, "God bless the little church around the corner." Around the corner from Atonement was the Episcopal Church of the Transfiguration, at 1 East 29th Street [●H20★], where the Rev. George H. Houghton welcomed the actors. They have come ever since. In the 1920s, the Very Rev. J. H. Randolph Ray helped found the Episcopal Actors' Guild, whose members have included Tallulah Bankhead, Joan Fontaine, Walter Hampden, Rex Harrison, Charlton Heston, and Basil Rathbone. In the 1970s, the church housed the Joseph Jefferson Theatre Company, with such up-and-coming actors as Armand Assante, Tom Hulce, and Rhea Perlman.

Little Church Around the Corner [H20]

Actors were not the only marginalized New Yorkers welcomed at Transfiguration. During the Draft Riots of 1863, African-Americans were in mortal peril from white mobs. The church offered sanctuary to so many people that they filled its schoolroom, library, vestry, and sanctuary. When a mob arrived intent on attacking the fugitives, Houghton greeted them at the gate furiously: "You white devils, you! Do you know nothing of the spirit of Christ?" They dispersed.

Built in 1850 and expanded over the years in a random sort of way that earned it the nickname Holy Cucumber Vine, the beloved complex is entered through a lych-gate, a pavilion where a corpse (*lic* in Old English) is to be set down before being taken inside. This gate, by Frederick Clarke Withers, serves more as a quiet way station for the living.

Transfiguration built a chapel at 120 West 69th Street [●K15☆] that is today Christ and St. Stephen's Church. A subsequent uptown chapel, at 221 West 69th Street [K9], was later Corpus Christi Church.

Transfiguration is noted for long rectorships: only five in a century and a half. As for the very upright Church of the Atonement? That parish dissolved in 1880, and its building is long gone.

Little Mount Zion Pentecostal
Church **[U9]**

Church of the Living Hope
[P19]

Church of the Lord Jesus Christ of the
Apostolic Faith **[R60]**

Little Mount Zion Pentecostal Church. Rock-faced siding on a wood-frame house from 1891 marks Little Mount Zion Pentecostal Church, at 535 West 159th Street **[●U9]**. The cross carries the name of the previous occupant, the Washington Heights A.M.E. Church.

Little Red School House.
See Bethlehem Memorial Presbyterian Church

Living Hope, Church of the. East Harlem needed all the hope it could get, and at this church, at 161 East 104th Street **[●P19]**, it got a wall full of HOPE, inscribed in relief next to the entrance. The structure, originally the Harlem Carriage and Wagon Works, is in an ensemble of buildings, including the former Twenty-eighth Precinct, that was redeveloped by Hope Community, a neighborhood housing-rehabilitation organization founded in 1968. The Church of the Living Hope and the nearby Church of the Resurrection were part of the East Harlem Protestant Parish.

Lowe's 175th Street Theater. *See* United Palace

Lord Jesus Christ of the Apostolic Faith, Church of the. Arguably the most elegant, best preserved facade of the Harlem theater-churches is that of the neo-Georgian Mount Morris Theater of 1911, by Hoppin & Koen, at 1421 Fifth Avenue **[●R60]**. Four blocks south of Mount Morris Park, the former theater is now home to the Church of the Lord Jesus Christ of the Apostolic Faith.

Iglesia Pentecostal Macedonia
[P18]

Macedonia Baptist Church **[S12]**

Madina Masjid **[F5]**

Madison Avenue Baptist Church
[H15]

Macedonia, Iglesia Pentecostal. Reflecting the transformation of East Harlem, this Romanesque sanctuary at 340 East 106th Street **[●P18]** was built as the Presbyterian Church of the Ascension, an Italian mission, in 1912/1913. The architects were Ludlow & Peabody. Seventy years later, it was acquired by the Macedonia Church of the Assemblies of God, founded in 1939 by the Rev. José Belén Hernández of Puerto Rico, at East 104th Street and Lexington Avenue. In the 1960s and 1970s, Macedonia met at 15 East 111th Street [P2], the former Laura Franklin Free Hospital for Children, by Bernstein & Bernstein, built in 1905, where treatment was offered to poor children. Today, Macedonia operates a food pantry helping over 200 people a month.

Macedonia Baptist Church. This sanctuary at 452 West 147th Street **[●S12]** by F. W. Eversley Jr. was built in 1957/1958 for Macedonia Baptist Church, reorganized in 1913.

Madina Masjid. Facing only three requirements—that prayer be oriented to Mecca, that the sexes be separated, and that there be no images of animate beings—a mosque can take humble form. But embellishments do appear. Madina Masjid, at 401 East 11th Street **[●F5]**, founded in 1976, has a small blue-and-white minaret with calligraphic ornament proclaiming ALLAHU AKBAR (God Is Great).

Madison Avenue Baptist Church. A Skyscraper Church ensconced within the Roger Williams Hotel on Madison Avenue **[●H16]**, this is one of the older Baptist congregations, organized in 1839 as the Rose Hill Church. Its first meetinghouse, at 154 Lexington Avenue **[●H21]**, is now the First Moravian Church. Its second home was a Romanesque sanctuary built in 1858 at 133 Madison Avenue [H15]. In 1930, the Madison Avenue Baptist Church leased its property to a hotel corporation with the stipulation that the developers include a sanctuary in the new 15-story structure, which was designed by Jardine, Hill & Murdock. The Rev. John Sanders Bone said the arrangement enabled the church "to maintain itself in an area where it could not otherwise have stayed because of terrific costs, and to provide a 'witness' to the business community in the heart of the city."

Madison Avenue Presbyterian Church. With a tower almost out of Neuschwanstein Castle, and a church house by James Gamble Rogers that overshadows the tower, the Madison Avenue Presbyterian Church, at 921 Madison Avenue [●L7☆], cuts a high profile. So have its members, starting with James Lenox—as in Lenox Hill—who gave the site on which the present church stands.

Madison Avenue Baptist Church **[H16]**

The Manhattan Island Church was organized in 1834 and called the Church in the Swamp (not to be confused with the Swamp Church on Frankfort Street). It united with the Memorial Presbyterian Church, formerly the Eleventh Presbyterian Church. In 1872, Memorial built a Gothic sanctuary at 506 Madison Avenue [J12], designed by D. & J. Jardine, and changed its name again, to Madison Avenue Presbyterian.

Meanwhile, the Fifteenth Street Church, organized in 1844, moved to the Lenox site on Madison Avenue [L6] and renamed itself Phillips Presbyterian in honor of the Rev. William Wirt Phillips, a towering figure in Presbyterianism. Its Victorian Gothic sanctuary by R. H. Robertson was built in 1873. In 1899, Phillips and Madison Avenue decided to merge. The new body would take the name Madison Avenue but occupy the home of Phillips, preserving part of the older structure on the side street for meetings, offices, and choir rehearsals. This annex still stands, visibly distinct, as the Phillips Chapel.

Phillips Presbyterian Church **[L6]**

The present sanctuary was designed by James E. Ware & Son and built in 1899. In 1966, Adams & Woodbridge altered the facade in what one pastor later called the St. Philco style. Leading figures associated with Madison Avenue Presbyterian, many of them Yale graduates, included the Rev. Henry Sloane Coffin, Edward S. Harkness, and Henry R. Luce. During a 1998 renovation, the architect Page Ayres Cowley discovered oak triforium screens hidden by plywood panels. They were beautifully restored.

Madison Avenue Presbyterian Church **[L7]**

Madison Square Presbyterian Church
[H37]

Madison Square Presbyterian Church
[H38]

Mahayana Buddhist Temple **[B31]**

Madison Square Presbyterian Church. New York's shortest-lived landmark and Stanford White's own favorite building were one and the same: the Madison Square Presbyterian Church, completed in 1906 and demolished in 1919, a year after the congregation merged into the First Presbyterian Church. Its first home, at 7 Madison Avenue [H37], designed by Richard M. Upjohn, was built in 1853/1854. As part of its mission work, Madison Square built the Memorial Chapel, at 211 East 30th Street [H17], later renamed to honor the Rev. William Adams and the Rev. Charles Henry Parkhurst. The church's most noteworthy mission—battling Tammany Hall and its links to saloons, gambling dens, and brothels—began in 1892 with Parkhurst's attack from the pulpit on the "lying, perjured, rum-soaked, libidinous lot."

In the early 1900s, needing to expand its home office, the Metropolitan Life Insurance Company gave the church a lot on the north side of East 24th Street and $325,000 to move. Because Upjohn's building was not razed until 1906, there was a brief time when two Madison Square churches flanked 24th Street. White's domed church at 11 Madison Avenue [H38] was dedicated four months after he was mortally wounded at Madison Square Garden, which was then only two blocks away.

Mahayana Buddhist Temple. The joyful yellow Mahayana Buddhist Temple, with its pagoda-like entrance at 133 Canal Street [●B31], serves a branch of the Eastern States Buddhist Temple of America. The building, a former theater, was renovated in 1997 by Yung Foo Don. The bottom character in the big vertical array on the facade is *szu* (Buddhist temple).

Malcolm Shabazz, Masjid. A startlingly plump dome on the angular Harlem skyline marks the *masjid*, or mosque, where El-Hajj Malik El-Shabazz—Malcolm X—once ministered. Founded in 1946 at the Harlem YMCA as Temple Seven of the Nation of Islam, the mosque moved to the Lenox Casino, at 102 West 116th Street [●Q58], built in 1905 to designs by Lorenz F. J. Weiher. Temple Seven was just a storefront in 1954 when Malcolm was named minister by Elijah Muhammad. "One bus couldn't have been filled with the Muslims in New York City," he recalled to Alex Haley in *The Autobiography of Malcolm X*. "Black Christians we 'fished' to our Temple were conditioned, I found, by the very shock I could give them about what had been happening to them while they worshipped a blond, blue-eyed God." Splitting from Elijah Muhammad in 1964, Malcolm opened the Muslim Mosque at the Hotel Theresa and was succeeded at Temple Seven by Louis X, later Minister Louis Farrakhan. Temple Seven was destroyed by a dynamite blast after Malcolm's assassination in 1965 but was rebuilt five years later to designs by Sabbath Brown, gaining the dome and bright yellow window bays. It was renamed to honor Malcolm, as was Lenox Avenue. The West 116th Street *masjid* is now used by orthodox Sunni Muslims. (Another Mosque Number Seven, at 106 West 127th Street [●Q24], serves Farrakhan's Nation of Islam.) Since 1993, the *masjid* has been led by Imam Izak-el Mu'eed Pasha, who has increased its civic role with residential, commercial, and educational projects.

Masjid Malcolm Shabazz **[Q58]**

Manhattan, Iglesia Adventista del Séptimo Día de. The Romanesque treasure at 237 East 123rd Street [●R41] was originally Our Saviour Norwegian Lutheran Church, designed in 1911 by Foster, Gade & Graham. It is now used by Seventh-Day Adventists.

Iglesia Adventista del Séptimo Día de Manhattan **[R41]**

Manhattan Chinese Baptist Church. The storefront with a chevron entablature at 236 West 72nd Street [●K4] was Metro Baptist Church from 1974 to 1984 and is now the Manhattan Chinese Baptist Church.

Manhattan Church of Christ. Kin to Corbusier, this church at 48 East 80th Street [●N36] by Eggers & Higgins lifts the eye across a wall of stained glass by Jean Jacques Duval to an upswept entablature: Brutalism in the service of sacred architecture. The congregation dates to 1920 but traces its origins to an early-nineteenth-century religious restoration movement, from which the Park Avenue Christian Church also stems. In 1941, the Manhattan Church of Christ moved to its present site [N35], and the current sanctuary was dedicated in 1968. Members come from more than 40 countries, said the Rev. Thomas L. Robinson.

Manhattan Church of Christ **[N36]**

Manhattan Congregational Church
(Promenade Theatre) **[M36]**

Manhattan Congregational Church. Great Gothic arches give away the Promenade Theatre, at 2162 Broadway [●M36], as a former Skyscraper Church. What stood on the site [M35] was the Manhattan Congregational Church by Stoughton & Stoughton, built in 1901. Facing development pressure in the 1920s, the Rev. Edward H. Emmett decided "to do what everyone said we were not going to do—stay at the old stand and attend to business," striking a deal with an investment syndicate to replace the church with a 23-story hotel, Manhattan Towers, by Tillion & Tillion, including a new sanctuary. As part of the deal, the developers agreed to lease the shops to only those businesses that would close on Sundays. The church's presence was expressed in a limestone Gothic facade and a cross at the top of the tower that has since been removed. The 800-seat auditorium had a groined ceiling and stained-glass windows. It opened in 1930 but had closed by 1933, with Emmett accused of having misappropriated funds. The Church of Jesus Christ of Latter-day Saints used the sanctuary until 1944. The church was transformed into a theater in 1969, opening with and taking its name from the play *Promenade*, with music by the Rev. Al Carmines. But there are still traces of the old days: a cornerstone visible on Broadway with the chi–rho monogram and the date 1901, and, around the corner, chiseled in a Gothic-arched doorway at 213 West 76th Street: SERVICE ENTRY FOR MANHATTAN CHURCH & TOWERS and CHURCH JANITOR & CHOIR ENTRY.

Manhattan Holy Tabernacle **[S8]**

Manhattan Holy Tabernacle. Originally St. Ann's Church for the Deaf, this Gothic building at 511 West 148th Street [●S8] was designed by Clarence True and built in 1898. St. Ann's ceased operating as a separate church in 1949, and its sanctuary is now the Manhattan Holy Tabernacle.

Manhattan Pentecostal Church **[Q6]**

Manhattan Pentecostal Church. The Manhattan Pentecostal Church, at 541 West 125th Street [●Q6], was formerly an electric- and auto-supply shop.

Manhattan Seventh-Day Adventist Church. Shorn of its towers but still recognizable as a work of Queen Anne revival, 232 West 11th Street [●D10☆], now home to the Manhattan Seventh-Day Adventist Church, was designed by Lawrence B. Valk and built in 1881 for the North Baptist Church.

Manhattanville College of the Sacred Heart Chapel. "Chapel," with its intimation of smallness, is a misnomer for this Gothic sanctuary, which was as large as many full-scale churches. The Roman Catholic Order of the Sacred Heart, devoted to the education of women, bought the Lorillard estate in 1846. The chapel was at the east end of the main building [S30], designed by William Schickel, which was built in 1890. Students at Manhattanville College included Tallulah Bankhead and Rose Fitzgerald, who married Joseph Kennedy. The campus was acquired by and incorporated into City College in 1950.

Manhattan Seventh-Day Adventist Church **[D10]**

Manhattanville Presbyterian Church. Never mind the separation; church became state at 152 Morningside Avenue [Q25]. Designed by Martin E. Thompson, the Manhattanville Presbyterian Church was built around 1852 and remained a church through the late 1870s, after which it was the Eleventh District Municipal Courthouse. It then resumed religious service, as a primary school and convent, for the adjoining Church of St. Joseph of the Holy Family.

Manhattanville College of the Sacred Heart Chapel **[S30]**

Manor Community Church. Bell-shaped and S-curved gables on this structure at 350 West 26th Street [●G29] point architecturally to Dutch provenance. And, indeed, this was originally the Manor Chapel of the South Reformed Dutch Church, built in 1873 and expanded in 1907 by Samuel Edson Gage. The mission was taken over by the Classis of New York in 1914, when South Church disbanded, and became the independent Manor Community Church in 1923.

Manhattanville Presbyterian Church [Q25]

Mar de Galilea, Templo Pentecostal. The Sea of Galilee Pentecostal Church occupies a renovated structure at 166 Eldridge Street [●C2] that was formerly the Panamanian Village restaurant and Golden Star Dance Pavilion.

Manor Community Church **[G29]**

Marble Collegiate Church **[H19]**

Marble Collegiate Church. This Romanesque pile of sugar cubes by Samuel A. Warner was built from 1851 to 1854 as the Fifth Avenue Church, on the corner of West 29th Street **[●H19★]**. The glistening stones imprinted themselves on the civic consciousness, and the church was renamed accordingly in 1906. Marble is one of four bodies in the Collegiate Reformed Protestant Dutch Church of the City of New York, organized in 1628, the oldest Protestant denomination in America with a continuous ministry. (The others are the Fort Washington, Middle, and West End Collegiate Churches.) In the twentieth century, few pulpits and preachers were as intertwined as Marble and the Rev. Norman Vincent Peale, author of *The Power of Positive Thinking*, who is seen standing outside the church in a statue by John Soderberg. Under his successor, the Rev. Arthur Caliandro, Marble installed its first stained-glass window in nearly a century, by J. & R. Lamb Studios, with Asian, black, and white children. In the yard is a bell cast in Amsterdam in 1795 for the North Reformed Dutch Church, which was demolished in 1875. Following an old custom, Marble's weather vane depicts a cock, recalling Peter's denial of Christ.

Mariners' Church **[B58]**

Mariners' Church. Whether they wanted to be churched or not, seafarers were irresistible missionary targets. The New York Port Society was organized in 1819 "for the promotion of the gospel among seamen" and opened the Mariners' Church, at 73 Roosevelt Street [B63], in 1820. In 1854, the Port Society acquired the Fourth Free Presbyterian Church, built in 1836 at Catherine and Madison Streets [B58].

Mariners' Temple Baptist Church **[B53]**

Mariners' Temple Baptist Church. Rough-and-tumble New York is the surprising setting for several Arcadian Greek Revival gems. This one—Manhattan's oldest Baptist church—occupies a site used for worship since the eighteenth century. The Fayette Street, or Oliver Street, Baptist Church [B52] was built in 1795 and burned in 1843. The second Oliver Street Church **[●B53★]**, built in 1844/1845, is attributed to Isaac Lucas or Minard Lafever. In 1863, it was acquired by the Mariners' Temple of Cherry Street. Swedish seamen who worshiped here in the 1880s formed the nucleus of what would become the Trinity Baptist Church. By the early 1980s, Mariners' Temple was down to 60 members. But the Rev. Suzan D. Johnson Cook, the first African-American woman elected senior pastor of any American Baptist congregation, reinvigorated the church with Hour of Power lunchtime services.

Martha Memorial Evangelical Reformed Church. The German congregation at 419 West 52nd Street [I10] was founded in 1880 and merged into the Broadway United Church of Christ in 1965.

Mary Help of Christians, Church of. The Roman Catholic Church of Mary Help of Christians, at 436 East 12th Street [●F6], marks the site of the cemetery of Old St. Patrick's Cathedral, where 41,016 persons were buried between 1833 and 1848 (and exhumed in 1909 for reburial in Calvary Cemetery). The Italian parish was founded in 1908. Plans were filed in 1911 by Domenico Briganti, though the cornerstone was not laid until 1917.

Church of Mary Help of Christians **[F6]**

Master, Presbyterian Church of the. Plump and welcoming as a turn-of-the-century, small-town railroad station, the Presbyterian Church of the Master, at 360 West 122nd Street [●Q45], was designed by William C. Haskell and built in 1893 for the Morningside Presbyterian Church, a white congregation that remained until 1938. That year, the Church of the Master was founded by a black minister, the Rev. James H. Robinson, under whom it grew a hundredfold. In 1972, the church built a community center on Morningside Avenue [●Q46], by Victor Christ-Janer and Roger Glasgow, that it turned into a sanctuary after learning that the main church was unsafe. Although boarded up, the old building still stands.

Presbyterian Church of the Master **[Q45]**

Meek, Church of the. A big gold cross identifies this converted warehouse at 305 West 141st Street [●S22] as the Baptist Church of the Meek, founded by the Rev. Preston W. Duckworth.

Presbyterian Church of the Master **[Q46]**

Memorial Baptist Church **[Q56]**

Memorial Baptist Church. What looks at first to be a daring Vienna Secessionist facade at 141 West 115th Street **[●Q56]** is not quite, since it was intended by Ludlow & Valentine to be the bottom half of a more conventional Romanesque church front. No matter. It is still one of Harlem's finest, built in 1905/1906 as the Northminster Presbyterian Church, which disbanded in 1931. Memorial Baptist Church, founded in 1935 by the Rev. Winfred Willard Monroe, acquired the building in 1940. The Rev. Preston R. Washington, the pastor since 1976, headed Harlem Congregations for Community Improvement, founded the House of Hope for single parents, and spoke early and openly about the impact of AIDS.

Iglesia Pentecostal el Mesías **[C41]**

Mesías, Iglesia Pentecostal el. This may be the largest cross in Manhattan: four stories of stone set into the facade of the Messiah Pentecostal Church, at 189 Madison Street **[●C41]**.

Mesivtha Tifereth Jerusalem. The synagogue and yeshiva at 145 East Broadway **[●C36]** were designed in 1921 by Rudolf P. Boehler for Mesivtha Tifereth Jerusalem, a congregation founded in 1905. The building is also used by Congregation Chai Odom Minski.

Messiah, Chapel of the. A black Episcopal congregation worshiped in the Chapel of the Messiah, at 206 East 95th Street [P36], from 1893 until 1927.

Metro Baptist Church **[I49]**

Metro Baptist Church. Scenes from Polish history are still to be found in the windows at 410 West 40th Street **[●I49]**, by Frederick J. Schwarz, built in 1912/1913 as the Church of St. Clemens Mary, a Polish Roman Catholic parish founded in 1909. Later a Daytop Village drug-rehabilitation facility, the building was acquired in 1984 by Metro Baptist Church, which moved from 236 West 72nd Street **[●K4]** and restored the sanctuary. Metro originated in 1974 as a mission of the Greenwich Baptist Church in Greenwich, Connecticut.

Metropolitan A.M.E. Church. There is great modern exuberance to the sanctuary at 58 West 135th Street **[●T26]**, with lozenge-shaped, tiled fields and semicircular scallops on the facade. The proportions, however, give it away as a former theater: the Lincoln, built in 1915 to designs by Jardine, Hill & Murdock, which welcomed black patrons from its earliest days. It is said that Fats Waller accompanied silent movies on the organ here and that his understudy was Count Basie. When the theater was constructed, it displaced several row houses, including 62 West 135th Street, which was then home to the fledgling Metropolitan African Methodist Episcopal Church. The congregation had been founded in 1901 by the Rev. Daniel W. Wisher in mid-Manhattan. For many years, Metropolitan worshiped at 132 West 134th Street [●T29], now St. John A.M.E. Church. Then, in 1962, under the Rev. Joseph L. Joiner, it returned to West 135th Street by acquiring the Lincoln, which was renovated by John Louis Wilson.

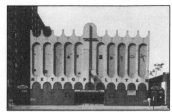

Metropolitan A.M.E. Church **[T26]**

Metropolitan Baptist Church. Although its conical roof is the most striking facet at 151 West 128th Street [●Q16★], a corner tower was planned that would have made this much more like Ephesus Seventh-Day Adventist Church, also by John Rochester Thomas. This sanctuary was originally the New York Presbyterian Church, which moved here from 167 West 11th Street [E24]. The first phase of the building, in 1884/1885, was by Thomas; the second, in 1889/1890, by Richard R. Davis. New York Presbyterian later merged with the Harlem and then the Rutgers Presbyterian Churches.

New York Presbyterian Church **[E24]**

   Metropolitan Baptist Church was formed in 1912 by members of Zion Baptist Church, at 2148 Fifth Avenue, and Mercy Seat Baptist Church, at 45 West 134th Street. In 1916, under the Rev. W. W. Brown, it built the enormous Metropolitan Baptist Tabernacle, by Matthew W. Del Gaudio, at 120 West 138th Street [T17]. After the Baptist congregation bought the New York Presbyterian Church on West 128th Street in 1918, where it remains to this day, the Tabernacle became Liberty Hall. This was the focal point of Marcus Garvey's Back-to-Africa movement, where the first convention was held in 1920 of the Universal Negro Improvement Association. Thousands were drawn to the elaborately ritualistic, almost religious, meetings at the hall.

Metropolitan Baptist Church **[Q16]**

Metropolitan Community Church of New York **[G2]**

Metropolitan Community Church of New York. GERMAN GOSPEL TABERNACLE is what it says under the gable at 446 West 36th Street **[●G2]**, built in 1887. But that is not what you will find inside. The Metropolitan Community Church is a spiritual home to lesbian, gay, bisexual, and transgender people. "We believe, with Isaiah, that the House of God should be a place of prayer and welcome for all of God's children," said the pastor, the Rev. Pat Bumgardner. Founded in 1968 in Los Angeles by the Rev. Troy Perry, the church took root in New York four years later when the Rev. Howard Wells preached in rented space at the Church of the Holy Apostles. Metropolitan helped organize the Lesbian and Gay Community Services Center, at 208 West 13th Street, and was there from 1983 until 1994, when it acquired the West 36th Street property.

Metropolitan Community United Methodist Church **[R23]**

Metropolitan Community United Methodist Church. Among Harlem's oldest churches, this sanctuary stands sentinel at 1975 Madison Avenue **[●R23]**. Methodist services began in 1830, as preachers rode the circuit in upper Manhattan, holding services in the home of John James. The first proper meetinghouse of the Harlem Mission was built in 1833/1834 on East 125th Street [R30]. The present sanctuary, by Rembrandt Lockwood, was built from 1869 to 1871 as St. James Methodist Episcopal Church. The Metropolitan Community United Methodist Church was founded in 1942.

Metropolitan Synagogue.
See Community Church of New York

Metropolitan Temple **[D4]**

Metropolitan-Duane United Methodist Church. The First Wesleyan Chapel, founded in 1833, later became the Central Church and in 1856 built a sanctuary at 50 Seventh Avenue [D4], where Ulysses S. Grant attended services. In 1896, after the arrival of the Rev. Samuel Parkes Cadman, namesake of Cadman Plaza in Brooklyn, the church was rechristened Metropolitan Temple. It was remodeled in the early twentieth century under the Rev. John Wesley Hill. The church burned down in 1928 and was replaced four years later by the present sanctuary, at 201 West 13th Street **[●D5☆]**, designed by Louis E. Jallade in a Collegiate Gothic style reminiscent of his Broadway Presbyterian Church.

The Duane Methodist Episcopal Church, founded in 1797, moved to 294 Hudson Street [B5] in 1864 and was absorbed into Metropolitan in 1939.

Metropolitan-Duane United Methodist Church **[D5]**

Middle Collegiate Church. In the eighteenth century, between the North and South Reformed Dutch Churches, the Middle Dutch Church stood on Nassau Street [A39]. Today, it is the southernmost of the four bodies in the Collegiate Reformed Protestant Dutch Church. (The others are the Fort Washington, Marble, and West End Collegiate Churches.) Its sanctuary, built in 1731, was the most substantial New York had seen. The bell was cast in Amsterdam as EEN LEGAAT AAN DE NEDERDUYTSCHE KERKE NIEUW YORK, a legacy to the Low Dutch Church in New York. It rang out on the signing of the Declaration of Independence. When the British occupied New York during the Revolution, the building was a prison, hospital, and riding school. Restored as a church after the war, it was converted in 1844 to the main post office in New York, which it remained for more than three decades. Inside the sanctuary were 3,226 letter boxes.

Middle Reformed Dutch Church [A39]

The church on Lafayette Place [E59], by Isaiah Rogers, was built from 1836 to 1839. Its Greek Revival portico was made of granite monoliths dragged by 20 yokes of oxen. The spire, Montgomery Schuyler surmised, was to "Christianize the pagan architecture." But it was ridiculed and torn down. The bell was taken to the Collegiate Church of St. Nicholas when the Lafayette Place building was razed.

Middle Collegiate Church [E59]

The present Middle Collegiate Church, at 112 Second Avenue [●E51], by Samuel B. Reed, was built in 1891/1892. The bell returned after the demolition of St. Nicholas and still tolls the inauguration and death of presidents, as it has since the time of Washington. The church was reinvigorated in recent years by the Rev. Gordon R. Dragt with a gospel choir, a jazz ensemble, and free meals for people with AIDS. "Churches have to get less stuffy," he said. "They just have to." Even churches that are 270 years old.

Middle Collegiate Church
[E51]

Milbank Memorial Chapel. Just visible from West 120th Street, thanks to its stained-glass windows, is the Milbank Memorial Chapel of 1897 at Teachers College [●Q40], a Tudor Gothic fantasy designed by William A. Potter and ornamented by the Tiffany Glass and Decorating Company.

Millinery Center Synagogue. Like the nearby Fur Center and Garment Center Synagogues, this Modernist sanctuary at 1025 Sixth Avenue [●I53] was built to serve an apparel trade. When the congregation was founded in 1935, two-thirds of the nation's hat manufacturing occurred in New York. The Millinery Center Synagogue was designed by H. I. Feldman and constructed in 1948.

Millinery Center Synagogue **[I53]**

Minnie Petrie Synagogue. Hebrew Union College of Cincinnati, the oldest Jewish institution of higher education in the Western Hemisphere, merged in 1950 with Rabbi Stephen S. Wise's Jewish Institute of Religion. Its New York center occupied 40 West 68th Street, originally built as the Free Synagogue. In 1979, the institution moved to the new Brookdale Center, designed by Abramovitz, Harris & Kingsland, which includes the Minnie Petrie Synagogue, at 1 West 4th Street [●E58]. Milton Petrie, head of the Petrie Stores chain, contributed to the project, and the synagogue is named for his mother.

Minnie Petrie Synagogue **[E58]**

Misión Evangélica Pentecostal. The sale of air rights to the Aurora apartment tower allowed this congregation to renovate its home at 882 Tenth Avenue [●K31].

Misión Evangélica Pentecostal **[K31]**

Mogen Abram, Congregation. The synagogue at 50 Attorney Street [C12], designed in 1905 by William C. Sommerfeld, served the Russian Congregation Podolsk Unterstuzung Verein, then Congregation Adath Jeshurun Anshe Kamenitz, and, finally, Congregation Mogen Abram (Shield of Abraham).

Monte Hermon, Iglesia Cristiana. A 1950s-style turquoise facade cannot mask the age of 289 East 3rd Street [●F36], which had become a synagogue by the 1920s and now houses Mount Hermon Christian Church.

Congregation Mogen Abram
[C12]

Monte Sion, Iglesia Cristiana. The sanctuary at 297 East 3rd Street [●F37] was built in 1903 by Ebeling & Meyer for Chevra Bachurim Anshie Ungarn (Association of Young Men from the Community of Hungary), and remodeled in 1953 by Kitzler & Nurick. It is now the Pentecostal Mount Zion Christian Church, founded in 1950 by members of the Casa de Oración in Brooklyn to serve Puerto Rican and Dominican neighbors, with the Rev. Gilberto Laguer and his wife, Maria Ugenia, as pastors. The church moved seven times before settling in this sanctuary in 1974, which it renovated in 1980. Under the Rev. Getulio Cruz Jr. and his wife, Lillian Ortiz-Cruz, Mount Zion has become more active in the broader community through Lower Manhattan Together and, as the neighborhood changes, is now offering services in English as well as Spanish.

Iglesia Cristiana Monte Sion **[F37]**

Moran's Townhouse. *See* St. George Chapel

Mormon chapels.
See Latter-day Saints, Church of Jesus Christ of

Morningstar Tabernacle. *See* East Side Tabernacle

Most Holy Crucifix, Church of the. The small Roman Catholic Church of the Most Holy Crucifix, at 378 Broome Street [●B11], was built in 1926 to designs by Robert J. Reiley for an Italian parish founded a year earlier.

Church of the Most Holy Crucifix **[B11]**

Most Holy Redeemer, Church of the. With a Baroque tower soaring 250 astonishing feet into the sky—80 feet shorter but 30 years earlier than St. Patrick's spires—the Church of the Most Holy Redeemer, at 173 East 3rd Street [●F32], looked more like a cathedral than a parish church in Kleindeutschland. It was founded in 1844 and run by the Redemptorist Fathers. The sanctuary was built in 1851/1852 and designed by a Mr. Walsh. In a 1913 renovation, Paul Schulz kept the stupendous form but pared away details and shortened the tower. The church, now known as Santísimo Redentor to many parishioners, is a pilgrimage shrine in honor of Our Lady of Perpetual Help.

Church of the Most Holy Redeemer (original facade) [F32]

Church of the Most Holy Redeemer (present facade) **[F32]**

Church of the Most Precious Blood **[B30]**

Mother A.M.E. Zion Church [T22]

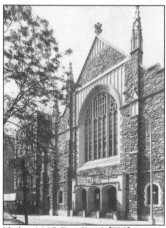

Mother A.M.E. Zion Church **[T23]**

Most Precious Blood, Church of the. As the national shrine of St. Januarius, the patron saint of Naples, this Roman Catholic church at 113 Baxter Street [●B30] is the spiritual home of the lively, raucous San Gennaro Festival every September. Visible from Canal Street, the Church of the Most Precious Blood is a striking vestige of the vanishing Italian community. It was founded in 1891, when building plans were filed by William Schickel & Company.

Mother A.M.E. Zion Church. Behind the vast tracery window at 146 West 137th Street [●T23★] lies the rich story of the oldest black church in New York, associated with Frederick Douglass, Sojourner Truth, Harriet Tubman, and Paul Robeson, whose brother, the Rev. Benjamin C. Robeson, was pastor. Mother African Methodist Episcopal Zion Church is the founding congregation (thus Mother) of a denomination led by the sons and daughters of Africa, under Wesleyan principles (thus Methodist), and supervised by bishops (thus Episcopal). Angered by discriminatory practices at the John Street Church—for example, black members had to wait to take communion until all the white members had done so—James Varick, Peter Williams, and others formed the African Methodist Episcopal Zion Church in 1796. Varick became the first bishop.

In 1800, Mother Zion built its first permanent sanctuary, on Church Street [B38], a site marked by a sidewalk tablet at the corner of Leonard Street. It built a church in 1853 for a small congregation in Seneca Village, which gave way to Central Park. Another uptown outpost, Little Zion of 1843, still exists as Greater Hood Memorial A.M.E. Zion Church [●T3].

In 1864, Mother Zion moved to the former Greenwich Reformed Dutch Church on Bleecker Street [D13], only two blocks from Abyssinian Baptist Church. Its next stop was 127 West 89th Street [M11], where it built a Romanesque church by Edward Alfred Sargent in 1903/1904. This was later the Battery Swedish Methodist Episcopal Church and the Endicott Theater.

During the pastorate of the Rev. James W. Brown, Mother Zion came home to Harlem in 1914, but not to its present building. It moved into a modest Gothic sanctuary at 151 West 136th Street [T22] that had served a succession of Episcopal parishes: Holy Innocents, Holy Nativity, and Redeemer. Behind this building, on West 137th Street, the present sanctuary was built from 1923 to 1925, after which Varick's remains were transferred here for entombment. The architect was George Washington Foster Jr. Under the Rev. George W. McMurray, the James Varick Community Center was constructed in 1972 on the lot once occupied by the Episcopal church.

Mother of God of the Sign, Synodal Cathedral of the. Only five blocks from the onion domes of St. Nicholas Russian Orthodox Cathedral is another Russian Orthodox cathedral. How can this be? Because the Synodal Cathedral of the Mother of God of the Sign, also called Our Lady of the Sign, is the cathedral of a different church: the Russian Orthodox Church Outside Russia, which ministered to Russians displaced by the Revolution and rejected the Moscow Patriarchate, under which St. Nicholas is governed. The synod of bishops moved to New York in 1952. Six years later, it bought the former home of George F. Baker Jr., chairman of the First National Bank (later Citibank), at 75 East 93rd Street [●N1★], begun in 1915 to designs by Delano & Aldrich. There are only a few hints that this is an ecclesiastical building. Over the gate is an Orthodox cross with double crossbars and a diagonal suppedaneum. The Holy Fathers Russian Orthodox Church, at 524 West 153rd Street, also belongs to the Russian Orthodox Church Outside Russia.

Synodal Cathedral of the Mother of God of the Sign **[N1]**

Mount Calvary Baptist Church. A bold Modernist statement of sacred architecture—something of Corbusier's Chandigarh complex comes to mind—Mount Calvary Baptist Church, at 231 West 142nd Street [●T9], was designed by Ifill & Johnson and built in 1970, with Willet Studios stained-glass windows showing biblical scenes. Mount Calvary was founded in 1917 by the Rev. Sterling D. Grayson and occupied four different homes, including 206 West 142nd Street, before moving to this site in 1950.

Mount Calvary Baptist Church **[T9]**

**Mount Calvary United Methodist Church. Some Luther-an churches might be mistaken for Roman Catholic, like this massive Gothic structure at 116 Edgecombe Avenue [●S25] by Henry Andersen, built in 1897/1898 as the Church of the Atonement. After it merged with the Church of Our Saviour in 1927 to become Our Sav-iour's Atonement Lutheran Church in Inwood, its building was acquired by Mount Calvary United Methodist Church, founded in 1925 by a group that had seceded from Bethel A.M.E. Church.

Mount Calvary United Methodist Church
[S25]

Mount Moriah Baptist Church. Similar in massing to the nearby Chambers Memorial Baptist Church, the Romanesque sanctuary at 2050 Fifth Avenue [●R22] was also by Henry F. Kilburn. It was built in 1887/1888 for Mount Morris Baptist, founded in 1843, which had a small chapel on this lot, previously the site of the First Baptist Church of Harlem [R21], by Samuel A. Warner, built around 1854. After Mount Morris left, the building briefly served the Primera Iglesia Bautista de Habla Española de Nueva York before it was acquired in 1935 by Mount Moriah Baptist Church, a black congregation that traces its origins to 1901 and once worshiped at the former Mercy Seat Baptist Church, at 45 West 134th Street [T27].

Mount Moriah Baptist Church [R22]

Mount Morris–Ascension Presbyterian Church. An exquisite copper dome peeks over the top of a wholly original sanctuary by Thomas H. Poole built in 1905/1906 at 15 Mount Morris Park West [●R39☆]. The Harlem Presbyterian Church, whose emblem is still visible on the east facade, was founded in 1844. In 1874, it built a Victorian Gothic church at 43 East 125th Street [R28], by D. & J. Jardine, that later became the Third Church of Christ, Scientist. Harlem Presby-terian merged in 1915 with New York Presbyterian, from West 128th Street. In 1942, as the white popu-lation diminished, Harlem–New York merged into the Rutgers Presbyterian Church and moved downtown. It was succeeded by Mount Morris, a black congrega-tion, which was joined by the Church of the Ascension, from 340 East 106th Street, now the Macedonia Church of the Assemblies of God.

Mount Morris–Ascension Presbyterian
Church [R39]

Mount Neboh Baptist Church. Many sanctuaries have changed hands, but only two in Manhattan seem to have served all three of the city's largest faiths: Jewish, Roman Catholic, and Protestant. The twin-towered building at 1883 Adam Clayton Powell Jr. Boulevard [●Q59] is one; St. Ann's Armenian Catholic Cathedral is the other. Designed by Edward I. Shire, this sanctuary was built for Congregation Ansche Chesed from 1907 to 1909. The building was converted in 1927 by the Spanish Vincentians into the Roman Catholic Church of Our Lady of the Miraculous Medal (Iglesia de Nuestra Señora de la Milagrosa), the third parish in the archdiocese to minister to the Hispanic population. Murals of Our Lady of High Grace, Our Lady of the Angels, and St. Catherine Labouré attest to this period. The sanctuary was acquired in 1980 by Mount Neboh Baptist Church, which was founded in 1937 by the Rev. R. B. Pearson out of Mount Moriah Baptist Church. Mount Neboh had outgrown its space in the former Provident Loan Society building at 2365 Eighth Avenue [●Q22].

Mount Neboh Baptist Church **[Q59]**

Mount Neboh Synagogue. Mount Neboh Synagogue was one of the few official city landmarks ever demolished. Congregation Peni-El of 525 West 147th Street (now the Bethel Holy Church of Deliverance) and Congregation Mount Zion of 37 West 119th Street (now the Emanuel A.M.E. Church) joined to build the Unity Synagogue, at 130 West 79th Street [M33★], in 1927/1928, designed by Walter S. Schneider. The building was acquired in 1930 by Mount Neboh, which moved from 562 West 150th Street [●S3], now the City Tabernacle of Seventh-Day Adventists. It worshiped here until 1978. The Seventh-Day Adventists then used the building as the Crossroads Church before selling it in 1981. It was designated a landmark in 1982 over the new owners' objections. Neighbors tried to find a use for the existing building, but the Landmarks Preservation Commission concluded that the designation had caused a financial hardship that could be relieved only by allowing demolition. The former synagogue was razed in 1984 and replaced by the Austin apartments.

Mount Neboh Synagogue [M33]

Mount Olive Fire Baptized Holiness Church
[Q47]

Mount Olivet Baptist Church **[I9]**

Mount Olivet Baptist Church **[Q51]**

Mount Olive Fire Baptized Holiness Church. This slice of Gothic gingerbread at 308 West 122nd Street **[●Q47]** by James W. Cole, which now serves the Mount Olive Fire Baptized Holiness Church, was built in 1897 for the Second Reformed Presbyterian Church. The Presbyterians' earlier home had been transported whole from Christopher Street to 166 Waverly Place **[E46]**, with the preacher delivering a sermon inside while en route. This was later Abyssianian Baptist Church.

Mount Olivet Baptist Church. Like Abyssinian Baptist, Bethel A.M.E., St. James Presbyterian, and St. Philip's Churches, Mount Olivet Baptist Church moved to Harlem from mid-Manhattan, once a vital African-American neighborhood. Founded as a mission in 1876 and formally organized two years later by the Rev. Daniel W. Wisher, Mount Olivet began worshiping in the Tenderloin, at 112 West 26th Street. In less than a decade, it had its own sanctuary at 161 West 53rd Street **[I9]**, a building constructed of materials salvaged from the Congregational Church of the Puritans. Wisher's successor, the Rev. Charles T. Walker, opened the Colored Men's YMCA at 252 West 53rd Street, a block from the church, predecessor to the 135th Street Y. During the pastorate of the Rev. Matthew W. Gilbert, Mount Olivet was described in the *Colored American Magazine* in 1907 as "the mecca to which Baptists from all parts of the country make pilgrimages." It also gave birth to "daughter" congregations: the Baptist Temple Church, at 20 West 116th Street; Mount Olivet Baptist Church in Queens; and Sharon Baptist Church in the Bronx. It is led today by the Rev. Charles A. Curtis.

Mount Olivet moved in 1925 to the former Temple Israel, at 201 Lenox Avenue **[●Q51☆]**, now Malcolm X Boulevard, which looks like a Roman temple until you notice Stars of David in the column capitals, fanlights, and spandrel panels. It was built in 1906/1907 to designs by Arnold W. Brunner, who broke the Moorish mold, arguing that "synagogues have no traditional lines of architectural expression." Temple Israel occupied this sanctuary for only 13 years, after which it briefly became the Seventh-Day Adventist Temple.

Mount Pleasant Baptist Church. In a little more than a century, this Romanesque sanctuary at 142 West 81st Street [●M31☆] has performed abundant ecclesiastical duty. Designed by Jonathan Capen, it was built in 1892/1893 for the Third Universalist Society, founded in 1834, which was known as the Church of the Eternal Hope when it was here. It leased the building in 1908/1909 to Rabbi Stephen S. Wise's Free Synagogue and sold it in 1910 to the First Church of the Disciples of Christ, which left in 1945 to become the Park Avenue Christian Church. Then the Church of Jesus Christ of Latter-day Saints moved in for 30 years. The Mount Pleasant Baptist Church, founded in 1934, moved here from Harlem, where it had worshiped at 252 West 138th Street [●T15], now the Victory Tabernacle Seventh-Day Christian Church.

Mount Pleasant Baptist Church **[M31]**

Mount Sinai Anshe Emeth, Congregation. The Orthodox Mount Sinai Jewish Center, at 4381 Broadway [●V3], built in 1959 to designs by Murphy & Horowitz, is a medley of Coffee-Shop Modern motifs, including a menorah made of ever-widening, interlocked boomerang forms. But the gravest dignity attaches to the cornerstone, hewn from Mount Zion Israel, which says: BEHOLD I SET A STONE IN ZION, A PRECIOUS STONE, THE CORNERSTONE OF A SURE FOUNDATION. The congregation was formed by the merger of Mount Sinai, at 600 West 181st Street, and Anshe Emeth, at 144 West 131st Street, now the Friendship Baptist Church. The merged group then occupied a synagogue at 109 Wadsworth Avenue [V28], designed in 1921 by William I. Hohauser, before moving to the Broadway building.

Congregation Mount Sinai Anshe Emeth **[V3]**

Mount Washington Presbyterian Church **[W9]**

Mount Washington Presbyterian Church. Only a few thoroughfares in Manhattan are named for clergymen. Payson Avenue in Inwood honors the Rev. George S. Payson, pastor at Mount Washington Presbyterian Church from 1880 to 1920. Its first church, on Broadway [W9], was a wooden, toy-castle version of Gothic, built in 1844 and enlarged in 1856. The present church, at 84 Vermilyea Avenue [●W2], a striking work of modern Gothic, was designed in 1928 by Renwick, Aspinwall & Guard.

Mount Washington Presbyterian Church **[W2]**

Mount Zion A.M.E. Church **[R66]**

Mount Zion A.M.E. Church. UBS monograms at 1765 Madison Avenue **[●R66]** attest to this having been a branch of the Bank of the United States. The building was designed by Louis Allen Abramson in 1921, the year that Mount Zion African Methodist Episcopal Church was founded by the Rev. Louis M. Carpenter. The church moved here in 1943.

Mount Zion Lutheran Church **[S14]**

Mount Zion Lutheran Church. A country church in the middle of Harlem, this sanctuary at 421 West 145th Street **[●S14☆]** by Joseph Wolf was built in 1888 for the Hamilton Grange Reformed Church. In 1906, Hamilton Grange moved out and the Evangelical Lutheran Church of St. Matthew moved in, from Broome Street, bringing with it memorial tablets to the Rev. Georg A. G. Vorberg and the Rev. Carl F. E. Stohlmann that flank the church entrance to this day, notable for their German inscriptions, beginning ZUM ANDENKEN. St. Matthew moved farther uptown, and Mount Zion Lutheran Church acquired this building in 1944 under the Rev. Clemonce Sabourin.

Move of God Cathedral. The small Move of God Cathedral occupied the former St. Catherine of Genoa School at 501 West 152nd Street **[●U24]**.

Muhammad's Mosque Number Seven
[Q24]

Muhammad's Mosque Number Seven. Following the death of Elijah Muhammad in 1975, leadership of the Nation of Islam passed to his son, Warith Deen Mohammed, who reconstituted the movement and gave it a new identity as the World Community of Al-Islam in the West. Three years later, Minister Louis Farrakhan, who had succeeded Malcolm X at Temple Seven on West 116th Street, broke away and set out to rebuild the Nation of Islam, based in Chicago, returning to an adherence to the principles of Elijah Muhammad. Muhammad's Mosque Number Seven, at 106 West 127th Street **[●Q24]**, by Joseph C. Cocker, was built in 1909 as a catering establishment, Carlton Hall. It was later the Second Harlem Church of the Seventh-Day Adventists, after which it was briefly the Twelfth Church of Christ, Scientist. For more than four decades, it was the Masonic King Solomon Grand Lodge before being acquired by the Nation of Islam.

Nachlath Zvi, Congregation. Most Harlem synagogues wound up as churches, but this was a church that wound up as a synagogue. The Methodist Episcopal Church of the Saviour was founded in 1870 and worshiped at 65 East 109th Street [P10] from 1881 until 1905, when it moved to 1791 Lexington Avenue, now the Primera Iglesia Metodista Unida Hispana. Congregation Nachlath Zvi (Inheritance of Zvi [Israel]) was founded in 1909 and was here for several decades.

Church of the Nativity [E64]

Church of the Nativity [E65]

Nativity, Church of the. The Roman Catholic Church of the Nativity, at 44 Second Avenue [●E65], looks more like a firehouse than a house of worship. The pity is that it replaced a great Greek Revival church [E64], built in 1832 for the Second Avenue Presbyterian Church and attributed to Alexander Jackson Davis, James H. Dakin, and James Gallier of Town & Davis. After 10 years, the building was sold to the new parish of the Nativity of Our Lord, which later added the words AD MAJOREM DEI GLORIAM (To the Greater Glory of God) to the entablature. The 1970 church, by Genovese & Maddalene, has a large cross and a bell cote but still seems starkly institutional.

New Church. It would be easy to mistake this Italianate Renaissance Revival gem at 112 East 35th Street [●H8☆] for a courthouse. But it has always been a church: the New Church, also known as Swedenborgian as it is based on the teachings of Emanuel Swedenborg, an eighteenth-century scientist and theologian whose interpretation of Scriptures stressed freedom and individualism. A New York offshoot known as the New Jerusalem Church was organized in 1816 and worshiped for some years on Pearl Street before being deeded the site on 35th Street. The church was built in 1858/1859 to designs by James Hoe and expanded in 1866 by Gambrill & Post. The congregation is still here, representing astonishing continuity for mid-Manhattan. In 2002, after a renovation by Alexander Gorlin, it reclaimed its lovely antebellum sanctuary, an especially chaste yet luminous space, which had been closed for 12 years because of failing roof timbers. Gorlin said he did not know how the inexpertly designed wood truss had stayed up at all. To which the minister, the Rev. Robert E. McClusky, said, looking up: "*We* do."

New Church [H8]

New Covenant Holiness Church. Originally the Day Star Baptist Church and now the New Covenant Holiness Church, the sanctuary at 512 West 157th Street [●U11], by Alfred E. Kehoe, was begun in 1906.

New Covenant Temple. Many of Harlem's former theaters are churches. Some are disguised by new facades; others—like this one at 1805 Amsterdam Avenue [●S4]—are still quite obvious. The Washington Theater, by Lamb & Koehler, was built in 1914 and has long been the New Covenant Temple.

New Covenant Holiness Church [U11]

New Dramatists Theater. *See All Peoples Church*

New Hope Seventh-Day Adventist Church. Very much a row house in scale, 28 Edgecombe Avenue [●S28] has a chevron parapet and Gothic-style windows to signify its religious role. Now home to New Hope Seventh-Day Adventist Church, it was formerly the Church of St. Luke's Beloved Physician.

New Mount Calvary Baptist Church. A former cornice works at 102 West 144th Street [●T8] by Charles M. Sutton, built in 1904, has been New Mount Calvary Baptist Church almost since the day the congregation was founded in 1936 by the Rev. Henry J. Watkins.

New Hope Seventh-Day Adventist Church [S28]

New Mount Zion Baptist Church. The Evangelical Zion Church, a German group, filed plans in 1900 by Niels Toelberg for a sanctuary at 171 West 140th Street [T12]. It was later Congregation Agudath Achim. In 1918, the newly formed Little Mount Zion Baptist Church, under the Rev. William A. Campbell, took title. Having outgrown the building, the church commissioned Maurice Courland to design a new sanctuary, built in 1929 on the site [●T13]. It changed its name five years later to New Mount Zion Baptist Church. The current pastor, the Rev. C. L. Washington Jr., is only the third in the congregation's long history.

New Mount Zion Baptist Church [T13]

New Way Baptist Church. Before the Baptist Temple Church moved to Congregation Ohab Zedek's former synagogue, it was at 159 West 132nd Street [●T32], a sanctuary that has served several congregations, most recently New Way Baptist Church.

New Way Baptist Church [T32]

New York Buddhist Church **[O12]**

New York Chinese Alliance Church **[C3]**

New York United Sabbath Day Adventist Church **[O4]**

New York Zendo Shobo-Ji **[L20]**

New York Buddhist Church. No work of religious art in New York faced as fearsome a journey to its present setting than the 15-foot bronze statue of Shinran Shonin, founder in the thirteenth century of the Jodo Shinshu sect of Buddhism. For it survived the atomic bombing of Hiroshima.

Clad in a robe and sandals, wearing a broad-brimmed *amigasa*, and holding a staff, the figure was installed on Mitaki Hill in 1937 by the businessman Seiichi Hirose. At 8:15 A.M., August 6, 1945, when the bomb exploded a mile and a half away and everything around it was consumed in flames, the statue—though pocked and blistered—endured. Hirose brought it to the United States 10 years later in the spirit of "no more Hiroshimas" and rededicated it on September 11, 1955. The New York Buddhist Church was founded in 1938 by the Rev. Hozen Seki and his wife, Satomi, and is affiliated with the Jodo Shinsu Hongwanji in Kyoto. The American Buddhist Study Center occupies a 1902 town house at 331 Riverside Drive. The sanctuary, at 332 Riverside Drive **[●O12☆]**, was designed in 1955 by Kelly & Gruzen. The church holds an Obon festival in Riverside Park every July and a peace gathering every August 5, during which a bell is tolled at 7:15 P.M. That is 8:15 A.M., August 6, in Japan.

New York Chinese Alliance Church. This distinctive new church with a chamfered glass-block corner at 162 Eldridge Street **[●C3]**, by Peter Poon, was built in 1998. The New York Chinese Alliance Church was founded in 1971 and had worshiped at 4 Rivington Street.

New York United Sabbath Day Adventist Church. The New York United Sabbath Day Adventist Church was founded in the 1920s by James Kemuel Humphrey and worshiped at 144 West 131st Street **[●Q11]**, now the Friendship Baptist Church, and 38 West 135th Street. Its sanctuary, at 145 Central Park North **[●O4]**, by Seymour Gage, was built in 1954/1955.

New York Zendo Shobo-Ji. A carriage house at 223 East 67th Street **[●L20]** was converted in 1968 by the Zen Studies Society and is the New York Zendo Shobo-Ji (Temple of True Dharma), founded in 1956.

Ninth Church of Christ, Scientist. Engine Company 16, at 223 East 25th Street [●H36], is now the Ninth Church of Christ, Scientist, serving a congregation founded in 1919.

Nodah bi Yehuda, Congregation. One of the last synagogues in lower Washington Heights, at 392 Fort Washington Avenue [V29], this was altered from an existing building in 1965 by William Eli Kohn. It was the home of Congregation Kehillath Yaakov (Community of Jacob), an Orthodox German group founded in 1942, and then Congregation Nodah bi Yehuda (Will Be Known in Judah), an Orthodox group founded in 1940.

Congregation Nodah bi Yehuda [V29]

North Presbyterian Church. Far north when it was founded in 1847 at the edge of town—West 32nd Street—North Presbyterian Church is still north, at 529 West 155th Street [●U14], overlooking Trinity Cemetery. The congregation moved here from Ninth Avenue [G19], where the demolition of 500 buildings began in 1903 to make way for Pennsylvania Station and its yards. The uptown church, by Bannister & Schell, was dedicated in 1904.

North Presbyterian Church **[U14]**

North Reformed Dutch Church. Until the 1760s, even as the use of English grew in New York, services at Reformed churches were still in Dutch. To staunch the drift of younger members to the Anglican Church, part-time English services were begun at the Middle Reformed Dutch Church. These filled up quickly, making it clear that an entirely new building would be needed: the North Reformed Dutch Church, designed by Andrew Breested and constructed from 1767 to 1769 on Horse and Cart Lane [A11], later William Street. Two wrought-iron gates survive outside St. Paul's Chapel at Columbia University and are pictured on page 238.

North Reformed Dutch Church [A11]

In 1857, Jeremiah C. Lanphier, a missionary, reasoned that a midday service with singing and testimonials might draw workers. The Noon Prayer Meeting was so successful that it outlived North Church, which was demolished in 1875, leaving behind a chapel at 113 Fulton Street where the prayer meeting continued.

Northwest Reformed Dutch
Church **[G34]**

Northwest Reformed Dutch Church. If there were such a thing as Ruskinian Romanesque, this church at 145 West 23rd Street [G34] would have fit the bill. Consecrated in 1854, it served the Northwest Reformed Dutch Church, organized in 1807 on Franklin Street, which was then the northwest part of town. The West 23rd Street building subsequently served as a stable and an armory and then was lavishly remodeled as the Temple Theater before being rented by the Rev. Albert Benjamin Simpson as the first home of the Christian and Missionary Alliance. The Northwest congregation was later known as the Madison Avenue Reformed Church.

Église de Notre Dame **[Q43]**

Notre Dame, Église de. Within this exquisite Neoclassical sanctuary at 405 West 114th Street [●Q43★], overlooking Morningside Park, is a rough-hewn apsidal grotto. The church was built by Geraldine Redmond, who donated the site after her son was cured at Lourdes, France. The grotto and chapel, which date to 1909/1910, were designed by Daus & Otto. The building was completed in 1914/1915 by Cross & Cross, though a dome modeled on that of the Panthéon in Paris was never constructed.

Notre-Dame-du-Bourg, Chapel of. Surprisingly for a city that began in the seventeenth century, New York has two twelfth-century churches. Both are at The Cloisters [●W10★], the medieval repository of the Metropolitan Museum of Art. The Langon Chapel includes columns, capitals, denticulated courses, and voussoirs from Notre-Dame-du-Bourg, built around 1155 in Langon, near Bordeaux. Chapel lore once had it that the two crowned heads on one of the capitals depicted Eleanor of Aquitaine and King Henry II of England, who visited the monastery with which the church was associated. But the museum now deems that unlikely.

Nueva Gethsemani, Iglesia Pentecostal. Built as the Segunda Iglesia Bautista, now on East 102nd Street, this sanctuary at 112 East 104th Street [●P20] has more recently served the New Gethsemane Pentecostal Church.

Iglesia Pentecostal Nueva
Gethsemani **[P20]**

Congregation Ohab Zedek **[O32]**

Ohab Zedek, Congregation. It is not sight but sound that many associate with this Orthodox congregation: the brilliant coloratura of Josef (Yossele) Rosenblatt, king of the cantors and Ohab Zedek's *hazzan* in the early twentieth century. Incorporated in 1873 as the First Hungarian Congregation Ohab Zedek (Love of Righteousness), it built a synagogue at 70 Columbia Street **[F54]** in 1881 that was later used by Congregation Ahavath Acheim Anshe Ungarn, and then moved to Anshe Chesed's Gothic synagogue at 172 Norfolk Street **[●F45★]**. In 1906/1907, Ohab Zedek built a monumental structure at 18 West 116th Street **[●R65]**, by Hedman & Schoen, with Gothic touches echoing those of the Norfolk Street sanctuary. Here, Rosenblatt reigned with his two-and-a-half-octave range, so popular that tickets were needed for services at which he sang. Ohab Zedek moved in 1926 to 118 West 95th Street **[●O32]**, designed by Charles B. Meyers. Its Harlem sanctuary is now the Baptist Temple Church.

Congregation Ohav Sholaum **[W13]**

Ohav Sholaum, Congregation. Starkly befitting its somber role as a memorial to European synagogues destroyed by the Nazis, Congregation Ohav Sholaum (Love of Peace) was designed by Max B. Schreiber and dedicated in 1951 at 4624 Broadway **[●W13]**. The Orthodox group was organized in 1940 under Rabbi Ralph Neuhaus, composed largely of displaced Jews from Germany and Austria, including survivors of Kristallnacht.

Old Broadway Synagogue **[Q5]**

Old Broadway Synagogue. Among the handful of uptown synagogues outside Washington Heights is Chevra Talmud Torah Anshei Marovi (Torah Study Society, People of the West Side), founded in 1911. Its sanctuary at 15 Old Broadway **[●Q5]**, by Meisner & Uffner, was built in 1923/1924. The synagogue was kept alive by Rabbi Jacob Kret with members drawn from the educational institutions of Morningside Heights. In 2003, it restored the green and blue stained glass of the central window, which had been bricked up since the 1960s.

Congregation Or Zarua
[N28]

Old St. Patrick's Cathedral. *See* St. Patrick's Cathedral

Or Zarua, Congregation. It was a full turn of the circle in 1994, when Congregation Or Zarua inspected what was to be its new home: the First Waldensian Church, at 127 East 82nd Street [N28]. In the basement was a memorial plaque. It turned out that the structure had been built by Congregation Kehilath Jeshurun in 1890 and passed on to B'nai Peyser, Chevra Kadisha Talmud Torah, and others, ending up as the Modern Synagogue, which sold it in 1951 to the Waldensians, who commissioned Merrill & Bradbury to convert it.

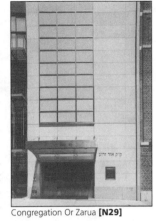

Congregation Or Zarua **[N29]**

Or Zarua was founded in 1989 and met at the 92nd Street Y. It replaced the nineteenth-century building with an icy-white, starkly modern seven-story slab [●N29] in 2001/2002, under a concept by Henry Wollman seen to completion by R G Roesch. The translucent curtain wall glows at night, symbolizing the congregation's name: Light Is Sown.

Orach Chaim, Congregation. Congregation Orach Chaim (Path of Life), composed mostly of German Jews, was founded in 1879 and worshiped at 221 East 51st Street [J15], later the Sutton Place Synagogue. Its present sanctuary, at 1459 Lexington Avenue [●P35], was built in 1906. Stained-glass skylights with Stars of David were uncovered during a 1999 renovation, designed by Alexander Gorlin, under Rabbi Michael D. Shmidman.

Congregation Orach Chaim **[P35]**

Our Lady of Esperanza, Church of. New York's first Spanish-language Roman Catholic parish, Our Lady of Guadalupe, planned at one time to move to Audubon Terrace, a cultural complex developed by Archer M. Huntington and anchored by the Hispanic Society of America. Although the parish ultimately stayed on West 14th Street, its pastor, the Rev. Adrian Buisson, transferred uptown to take charge of a new Spanish parish, the Church of Our Lady of Esperanza, or Nuestra Señora de la Esperanza. As designed by Archer's cousin, Charles P. Huntington, and built from 1909 to 1912, the church, at 624 West 156th Street [●U13☆], had an Ionic portico at the top of a long flight of steps. It was modified in 1924 by Stanford White's son, Lawrence G. White of McKim, Mead & White, who enclosed the steps behind a new facade.

Church of Our Lady of Esperanza **[U13]**

Church of Our Lady of Good Counsel **[N6]**

Church of Our Lady of Guadalupe **[D2]**

Church of Our Lady of Lourdes **[S17]**

Our Lady of Good Counsel, Church of. Thomas H. Poole made stone look like lacework at St. Thomas the Apostle. At 230 East 90th Street **[●N6]** is another Roman Catholic church, Our Lady of Good Counsel, with the same imaginative quality by the same hand, completed in 1892, six years after the parish was founded.

Our Lady of Guadalupe, Church of. Once known as Little Spain, West 14th Street was home to the oldest Spanish-speaking Roman Catholic congregation in New York, Nuestra Señora de la Guadalupe, honoring the patron of the Americas and founded in 1902. The facade, by Gustave Steinback, was added in 1921 to an existing row house at 229 West 14th Street **[●D2]**, bringing a touch of Spanish Baroque to the street with its rounded pediment and iron porch. Over time, reflecting changes in the city's Latin population, Our Lady of Guadalupe has served Spaniards, Spanish-Americans, Puerto Ricans, and Mexicans. Bursting at the seams because of the growing Mexican population, the parish moved in 2003 to the much larger Church of St. Bernard, at 330 West 14th Street **[●D3]**, which was renamed Our Lady of Guadalupe at St. Bernard's.

Our Lady of Loreto, Church of. This institutional building at 303 Elizabeth Street **[E78]**, home to a Sicilian Roman Catholic parish formed in 1891, was marked as a church by the words MADONNA DI LORETO.

Our Lady of Lourdes, Church of. More like a palazzo on the Grand Canal than a parish church, this ebullient structure at 467 West 142nd Street **[●S17★]** is a marvelous recycled hybrid that incorporates the facade of the National Academy of Design and remnants of the A. T. Stewart mansion. Inside, it's like St. Patrick's—literally—with stained-glass windows and other elements that were removed from the eastern end of the cathedral to make way for the Lady Chapel. Cornelius O'Reilly of O'Reilly Brothers was the architect who threaded it all together, from 1902 to 1904. The Church of Our Lady of Lourdes, established in 1901, serves a community as varied as its architecture: African-American, Dominican, Ecuadorean, Eritrean, and Mexican.

Our Lady of Mount Carmel, Church of. Just as Our Lady of Pompei is a towering vestige of the Italian Village, so Our Lady of Mount Carmel, a dazzling Romanesque stalagmite at 449 East 115th Street [●R73], is a vestige of Italian Harlem. It was the village church, Robert Anthony Orsi wrote in *The Madonna of 115th Street:* "The front doors were kept open wide all the time. ... Passersby could see the main altar, glowing with the warm light of hundreds of candles.... The Madonna herself stood high above the altar, watching over Italian Harlem."

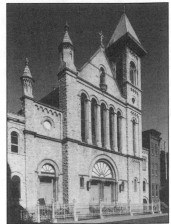

Even before the church opened, devotions had begun in Italian Harlem to the Madonna del Carmine through a mutual-aid society formed by immigrants from Salerno, which organized a *festa* in honor of its patron. From 1884 to 1889, a Roman Catholic church by Lawrence J. O'Connor was being built on East 115th Street. Italian laborers were constructing it, but it was financed by German and Irish neighbors, and after it was finished, Italian parishioners were made to worship in the basement, *la chiesa inferiore*, until 1919. The Madonna statue was moved upstairs in 1923. Four years later, the bell tower was added.

Church of Our Lady of Mount Carmel **[R73]**

The annual *festa* in mid-July was "an old-world spectacle: the ritual procession, headed by a brass band and followed by clergy and the statue of the Virgin borne by the beneficiaries of 'miracles,'" the *WPA Guide* said in 1939, as "donations, fluttering from the tenement windows, are caught and tossed into an outspread cloth or pinned to ornate banners." The *festa* now occurs to the Caribbean beat of Haitian celebrants, who also venerate Our Lady of Mount Carmel. Next door, the abandoned school and convent reopened in 2003 as the eclectic National Museum of Catholic Art and History, designed by Arthur Rosenblatt of RKK Museum and Cultural Facilities Consultants.

Our Lady of Peace, Church of. A Victorian Gothic gem at 237 East 62nd Street [●L35☆] has done triple duty. Built in 1886/1887 to designs by Samuel A. Warner as the Presbyterian Church of the Redeemer, a German congregation, it was Bethlehem Lutheran before being taken over in 1918 by the newly organized Madonna della Pace, a Roman Catholic Italian parish.

Church of Our Lady of Peace **[L35]**

Church of Our Lady of Perpetual Help [L39]

Our Lady of Perpetual Help, Church of. This Romanesque church at 321 East 61st Street [L39] was a proud reminder of Little Bohemia on the outskirts of German and Hungarian Yorkville, and its loss is quite significant. The Bohemian Roman Catholic parish, founded in 1887, began as the Church of SS. Cyrillus and Methodius, at 316 East 4th Street [F35], later Congregation Anshe Baranove. Under the Redemptorist Fathers, the sanctuary on East 61st Street, designed by Henry Bruns, was constructed in 1887 and the parish was rededicated to Our Lady of Perpetual Help. The church was badly harmed by the construction next door of a Queensboro Bridge ramp, which cut the building off from the neighborhood to the west and created an unending stream of traffic outside. The Czech population shrank. The roof leaked so badly that the main sanctuary had to be closed. By the time the archdiocese closed the church, only about 50 parishioners remained. After the Easter Mass in 1998, it was razed. Its site is now just a rubble-filled lot.

Church of Our Lady of Pompei **[E69]**

Our Lady of Pompei, Church of. Italian Greenwich Village is largely a memory, but its cynosure—a copper-domed steeple as slender as a ceremonial *giglio* tower—serves as an exuberant marker of the community. In 1892, the Rev. Pietro Bandini of the Missionaries of St. Charles, or Scalabrinians, opened a chapel to Our Lady of Pompei on Waverly Place. It moved to Sullivan Street and became a parish.

In 1898, the parish moved again, to a Greek Revival church on Bleecker Street [E70] that had been built in 1836 for the Third Universalist Society. Mother Frances Xavier Cabrini, the first American saint, briefly taught at Pompei during this time. The Rev. Antonio Demo, a Scalabrinian, became its pastor in 1900. For the next 35 years, he was a noted figure in the Village, especially in the wake of the Triangle Shirtwaist fire of 1911, which killed at least 18 of his parishioners.

Demo was responsible for building the present Church of Our Lady of Pompei, from 1926 to 1928, after the city extended Sixth Avenue through the old property. For the new site, at 25 Carmine Street [●E69], Matthew W. Del Gaudio designed a combination church, school, convent, and rectory. The statue on the exterior represents St. Charles Borromeo, patron of the Scalabrinians. In 1941, five years after Demo's death, the square outside the church was renamed in his honor. In recent years, the parish has included many Vietnamese and Filipino members, but one Mass every Sunday is still celebrated in Italian.

Our Lady of Sorrows, Church of. This exuberant structure at 103 Pitt Street [●F50]—Victorian, Byzantine, and Romanesque—was designed by Henry Engelbert and built in 1867/1868 for a Roman Catholic parish founded in 1867 by the Order of Friars Minor Capuchin. It is now an English- and Spanish-speaking parish, also known as Nuestra Señora de los Dolores.

Church of Our Lady of Sorrows **[F50]**

Our Lady of the Miraculous Medal, Church of.
See Mount Neboh Baptist Church

Our Lady of the Rosary, Church of. Overlooking Battery Park are the Church of Our Lady of the Rosary and the James Watson house of 1793, at 7 State Street [●A53★], now the Shrine of St. Elizabeth Ann Seton, founder of the Sisters of Charity and the first native-born American to be canonized. As a young woman, Seton belonged to Trinity Church and lived on this site (though not in this house) from 1801 to 1803. In Italy, where she and her husband had gone in hope of reviving his health, she became immersed in Catholicism and, on her return, converted at St. Peter's Church on Barclay Street before moving to Maryland. In 1883, the Watson mansion was turned into the Mission of Our Lady of the Rosary for the care and relief of Irish immigrant girls. It is now the shrine and rectory for the 1964 church, by Shanley & Sturges, which has a figure of Seton over the entrance. After Trinity was shut down on September 11, 2001, the Rev. Peter K. Meehan offered Our Lady of the Rosary as a place of worship for the Episcopal parish, reuniting Seton and Trinity at least temporarily. In the first service on September 16, the Rev. Samuel Johnson Howard, vicar of Trinity, allowed himself the gentle humor of noting, "She was *our* daughter before she was *their* mother." Worshipers laughed, some perhaps for the first time since the attack.

Church of Our Lady of the Rosary **[A53]**

Church of Our Lady of the Scapular–
St. Stephen **[H27]**

Church of Our Lady of the Scapular of
Mount Carmel **[H28]**

Church of Our Lady of Victory **[A42]**

Our Lady of the Scapular–St. Stephen, Church of. With Romanesque arches gushing like a fountain frozen in stone, the Roman Catholic Church of Our Lady of the Scapular–St. Stephen, at 149 East 28th Street **[●H27]**, is a most inventive work by James Renwick Jr. There is also a fully developed facade on East 29th Street, the northward extension of the church, but it is not nearly as compelling, in part because its great rose window is covered in masonry, as are the two subsidiary windows bearing the alpha and omega symbols. The blank window did, however, permit the installation above the main altar of the 46- by 26-foot *Crucifixion* by Constantine Brumidi, who painted *The Apotheosis of George Washington* in the dome of the United States Capitol. Founded in 1848, St. Stephen's was at first on Madison Avenue. It purchased the present site in 1853 and opened the next year. As at the churches of Harlem today, its choir was a prime tourist attraction in the nineteenth century, drawing "so many strangers as to cause annoyance to the devout."

The Scapular side of the parish—a scapular being a vestment symbolizing the cross and yoke of Jesus Christ—was formed in 1889 as Our Lady of the Scapular of Mount Carmel. Its home, dedicated that year, was a Country Gothic sanctuary at 341 East 28th Street [H28]. Just shy of its centenary, this parish was merged with St. Stephen's, and its building was demolished.

Our Lady of the Sign, Cathedral of.
See Mother of God of the Sign, Synodal Cathedral of the

Our Lady of Victory, Church of. Victory was in sight, though not yet assured, in 1944 when Francis Cardinal Spellman, the Military Vicar of the Armed Forces, created this Roman Catholic church. Designed by Eggers & Higgins, the red-brick basilican sanctuary at 60 William Street **[●A42]** was completed in 1946 and "dedicated to Our Lady of Victory in Thanksgiving for Victory won by our valiant dead, our soldiers' blood, our Country's tears, shed to defend men's rights and win back men's hearts to God." It principally serves daytime worshipers rather than residents.

Our Lady of Vilnius, Church of. The yellow-brick Roman Catholic Church of Our Lady of Vilnius, at 570 Broome Street [●B6], by Harry G. Wiseman and built in 1910, has a doughty integrity but still feels overwhelmed by the Holland Tunnel approaches that have criss-crossed the area since its construction. The Lithuanian parish, also known as Our Lady of Vilna, was founded in 1909.

Church of Our Lady of Vilnius
[B6]

Our Lady Queen of Angels, Church of. Trinitarianism finds forceful expression in the Church of Our Lady Queen of Angels, on a cul-de-sac in the Jefferson Houses, at 228 East 113th Street [●P1]. It was designed by William Schickel & Company and built in 1886. The Roman Catholic parish was founded that year by the Order of Friars Minor Capuchin to serve German residents. It now ministers to Puerto Ricans, Dominicans, Mexicans, and African-Americans.

Church of Our Lady Queen of Angels **[P1]**

Our Lady Queen of Martyrs Church. As the twentieth century advanced, many builders of social-service complexes gave up attempts to disguise nonliturgical functions behind church-like facades. Only the sign OUR LADY QUEEN OF MARTYRS CHURCH at 81 Arden Street [●W12] would give this away as anything but a Roman Catholic school, which it was also built to be. The parish, now principally Dominican, was founded in 1927. Plans were filed the next year by Gustave Steinback.

Our Lady Queen of Martyrs
Church **[W12]**

Our Savior, Episcopal Church of. Serving perhaps the only Chinese-speaking Episcopal congregation east of San Francisco, the Episcopal Church of Our Savior, at 48 Henry Street [●C33], is one of the youngest churches in the New York diocese, having gained parochial status in 1987. Its members are first-generation immigrants from China and Hong Kong and second-generation Asian-Americans. Under the Rev. Albany Shiu-Kin To, it reached a development agreement that yielded a 12-story revenue-generating apartment building with a church at its base—a throwback to the Skyscraper Churches of the 1920s. Designed by Seymour Churgin and Bruce Cutler of the Architects Design Group, the 174-seat church was dedicated in 1992.

Episcopal Church of Our Savior
[C33]

Church of Our Saviour **[J56]**

Our Saviour, Church of. Built in 1959, this sanctuary at 59 Park Avenue **[● J56]** is one of the newer Roman Catholic churches in Manhattan and houses one of its youngest parishes, founded in 1955, though it looks far older in its Romanesque garb. Paul W. Reilly was the architect. While statuary niches and tympani in many churches are empty, those in the Church of Our Saviour were filled by craftsmen under Henry J. Pizzutello, in the largest stone-carving program for a church in New York since that of St. Bartholomew's 40 years earlier. Our Saviour's chief claim to fame at the time, however, may have been that it was air-conditioned, something of a novelty in the 1950s.

Our Saviour's Atonement Lutheran Church I Beth Am, The People's Temple. The handsome Collegiate Gothic building nestled in the wooded hills of Inwood at 178 Bennett Avenue **[●V1]** was supposed to have been simply the parish house for a much bigger Our Saviour's Atonement Lutheran Church. The congregation was formed by the merger of two missionary offshoots from St. John's Evangelical Lutheran Church. The Evangelical Lutheran Church of the Atonement was founded by the Rev. Frederick H. Knubel in 1896 and built a sanctuary at 116 Edgecombe Avenue **[●S25]** in 1897/ 1898 that is now Mount Calvary United Methodist Church. The Church of Our Saviour was established farther uptown in 1898, worshiping first at 525 West 179th Street [V24] and then at 580 West 187th Street **[●V8]**, later Holy Cross Armenian Apostolic Church.

Atonement and Our Saviour started to build a major complex on Bennett Avenue, by Mayers, Murray & Phillip: church, parish house, and hospital. The cornerstone was laid in 1928. A year later, the stock market crashed and so did the building plans. The parish house, which functioned as the sanctuary, was transformed in the late 1970s into the Cornerstone Center, with a video studio, dance and performance space, kindergarten, church for the deaf, and Beth Am, The People's Temple, a small Reform Jewish congregation that had worshiped on Thayer Avenue.

Our Saviour's Atonement Lutheran Church (Cornerstone Center) **[V1]**

Padre, Hijo y Espíritu Santo, Iglesia Pentecostal. Formerly a plumbing shop, 2141 Amsterdam Avenue [●U2] is now the Father, Son, and Holy Ghost Pentecostal Church.

Paradise Baptist Church **[U7]**

Paradise Baptist Church. Bold and darkly handsome, with a bravura Modernist sweep, 23 Fort Washington Avenue [●U7] is in its third life. Formerly the Costello Theater, it was turned into a synagogue in 1949 by Fritz Nathan for Congregation Ahavath Torah, which merged in 1965 with Tikvoh Chadoshoh. More recently, this has been the Paradise Baptist Church, founded in 1925 by the Rev. Henry W. Stanley. Although the large circular window remains, the menorah pattern in the tracery is no longer visible.

Park Avenue Christian Church **[N20]**

Park Avenue Christian Church. Often compared with the Sainte-Chapelle because of its 70-foot flèche, the abruptly vertical Gothic church at 1010 Park Avenue [●N20] owes it origins more to the Netherlands than to France—witness the inscription, EEN DRACHT MAKT MACHT (In Unity There Is Strength)—since it was built for the South Reformed Dutch Church from 1909 to 1911, to designs by Cram, Goodhue & Ferguson. South Church formally disbanded in 1914. That year, the sanctuary became the Park Avenue Presbyterian Church as the remaining Reformed congregation merged with the First Union Presbyterian Church. In 1937, Park Avenue Presbyterian merged with the Brick Presbyterian Church and worshiped here until 1940, when the new Brick Church opened. In 1945, the Disciples of Christ moved in. The congregation, which dates to 1810, previously worshiped on West 28th Street [●H29]; at 323 West 56th Street [K40]; and at 142 West 81st Street [●M31☆], now the Mount Pleasant Baptist Church. The congregation is part of a body known officially since 1968 as the Christian Church (Disciples of Christ).

Congregation Beth Israel Bikur Cholim **[L9]**

Park Avenue Synagogue. Approaching this impressive complex, you are neither on Park Avenue nor looking at a synagogue. Instead, you see a five-story building on Madison Avenue, designed by James Rush Jarrett with Schuman Lichtenstein Claman & Efron, that was erected in 1980 to memorialize the 1 million Jewish children who perished in the Holocaust, a theme embodied in reliefs by Nathan Rapoport. The Park Avenue Synagogue itself, on East 87th Street [●N11], was built from 1925 to 1927 to designs by Walter S. Schneider of Deutsch & Schneider. The inscription from Psalm 26 says, I LOVE YOUR TEMPLE ABODE, THE DWELLING-PLACE OF YOUR GLORY. A 1955 annex by Kelly & Gruzen, named for Rabbi Milton Steinberg, with a stained-glass facade by Adolf Gottlieb, was subsumed by the 1980 addition. This Conservative group is descended from Congregation Beth Israel (House of Israel), founded in 1843, which merged in 1855 with Congregation Bikur Cholim (Visitors to the Sick) and worshiped in the former Temple Emanu-El, at 56 Chrystie Street [B33]. In 1886, it built an astonishing Moorish–Romanesque synagogue by Alexander I. Finkle—Middle East meets Mittel Europa—at 143 East 72nd Street [L9]. The current congregation was formed by the merger of Beth Israel Bikur Cholim with Congregation Agudat Yesharim (Association of the Righteous), which had been at 115 East 86th Street [N12], formerly the Gates of Hope Synagogue.

Park Avenue Synagogue **[N11]**

Park Avenue United Methodist Church. Although the church at 106 East 86th Street [●N18] is clearly of the twentieth century, it contains timber from the eighteenth-century birthplace of Methodism in America. The congregation, founded in 1837 as the Yorkville Church, occupied a reassembled version of the Bowery Village Methodist Church—itself reincarnated from the Wesley Chapel on John Street—that had been hauled uptown to East 86th Street [N16]. The congregation's most magnificent church, at 1031 Park Avenue [N17], was designed by J. Cleveland Cady and built from 1882 to 1884, with an unbuttressed 150-foot tower. Park Avenue United Methodist Church moved around the corner in the 1920s, and Cady's church was replaced by a 15-story apartment house. The present sanctuary was built from 1925 to 1927 to designs by Henry C. Pelton, incorporating oak beams from the Wesley Chapel, forerunner of the John Street Church.

Park Avenue Methodist Episcopal Church [N17]

Park Avenue United Methodist Church **[N18]**

Park East Synagogue **[L19]**

Park East Synagogue. There are few flights of architectural fancy on this scale in New York. Designed by Schneider & Herter in Moorish, Byzantine, and Romanesque style, the Park East Synagogue, at 163 East 67th Street [●L19★]—still used by the congregation that built it in 1890—is astonishing, almost hallucinatory. ENTER INTO HIS GATES WITH THANKSGIVING AND INTO HIS COURTS WITH PRAISE, declares a plaque on the facade. Congregation Zichron Ephraim is the memorial to Ephraim Weil from his sons Jonas and Samuel, who gave the land and money for the building. Jonas, a real-estate investor, and Rabbi Bernard Drachman were instrumental in founding the Jewish Theological Seminary. After Drachman resigned from Congregation Beth Israel Bikur Cholim, Weil proposed the creation of a synagogue with a "harmonious combination of Orthodox Judaism and Americanism." The Orthodox congregation has been led in recent decades by Rabbi Arthur Schneier, founder of the Appeal of Conscience Foundation, which promotes religious freedom and human rights. A building restoration by Dan Peter Kopple & Associates was completed in 1997.

Pauline A. Hartford Memorial Chapel **[U1]**

Pauline A. Hartford Memorial Chapel. Sitting serenely in the garden of the Columbia-Presbyterian Medical Center [●U1], almost like a Romanesque rose at the bottom of a cliff-side canyon, is this sanctuary by Eggers & Higgins, dedicated in 1952. The Pauline A. Hartford Memorial Chapel was a gift from the John A. Hartford Foundation. Hartford headed the Great Atlantic & Pacific Tea Company, and the chapel is named for his wife. Roman Catholic, Protestant, Jewish, and Muslim services are conducted in this chapel, which may be the only house of worship on the site of a major-league ball park. These grounds were home to the New York Yankees until 1912.

People's Baptist Church.
See Thy Will Be Done! Christian Ministries

People's Tabernacle. Founded in 1898 as a missionary and benevolent society, the People's Tabernacle complex, at 52 East 102nd Street [P27], included a hotel for young women.

People's Tabernacle **[P27]**

Perry Street Methodist Church. A Gothic stone church was built in 1868 at 132 Perry Street [D15] for the Perry Street Methodist Church, a congregation founded in 1863 that merged into the Jane Street Methodist Episcopal Church in 1910.

Pilgrim Cathedral of Harlem. An imposing temple-front building by Jacob Gescheidt, at 15 West 126th Street [●R19], was constructed in 1922 as the Finnish Progressive Hall and was later the Henry Lincoln Johnson Lodge of the Benevolent and Protective Order of Elks. The Pilgrim Cathedral of Harlem was established in 1992 at 1941 Madison Avenue and moved here under Bishop Charles J. Reed.

Pincus Elijah, Congregation. This briefly lived synagogue at 118 West 95th Street [O31] was designed in 1910 by Moore & Landseidel for Congregation Pincus Elijah and was replaced by Congregation Ohab Zedek.

Postgraduate Center for Mental Health.
See Christ Presbyterian Church

Pilgrim Cathedral of Harlem **[R19]**

Primera Iglesia Bautista de Habla Española de Nueva York. Puerto Ricans who came to New York during and after World War I founded the First Spanish-Speaking Baptist Church in 1921 in Brooklyn. They crossed the river and moved into the Mount Morris Baptist Church, at 2050 Fifth Avenue [●R22], where they remained until 1935, before occupying quarters over the Club Cubanacán on Lexington Avenue. When the Rev. Hipólito Cotto Reyes arrived in 1937, he made one of his highest priorities the location of a permanent home. His attention turned to Grace-Emmanuel Mission Church, a stocky sanctuary at 216 East 116th Street [●R68] that had been built in 1877 for the Grace Episcopal Church of Harlem, founded in 1864. Bishop William T. Manning of the Episcopal diocese strongly supported the idea of placing a church building in the middle of the Barrio at the service of a Spanish-speaking congregation. The inaugural service for the Baptist group was held in 1942, and Cotto Reyes remained the pastor until 1960.

Primera Iglesia Bautista de Habla Española de Nueva York **[R68]**

Primera Iglesia Bautista Hispana de Manhattan **[V30]**

Primera Iglesia Bautista Hispana de Manhattan. The little Baroque brick sanctuary at 96 Wadsworth Avenue **[●V30]** was designed in 1922 by Nathaniel Vickers as a Universalist church and is now the First Spanish Baptist Church of Manhattan.

Primera Iglesia Metodista Unida Hispana. Briefly the "People's Church" during an occupation by the Young Lords, a militant Puerto Rican group, the church at 1791 Lexington Avenue **[●P3]** marks a milestone in political consciousness in the Barrio. It has a distinctive presence, too. Surrounding a modern A-frame are Gothic remnants of the Lexington Avenue Baptist Church of 1880, including the cornerstone: JESUS CHRIST HIMSELF BEING THE CHIEF CORNER STONE. It became the Methodist Church of the Saviour in 1905 and then the First Spanish United Methodist Church. In 1969, the Young Lords seized it and began offering classes, meals, and medical care under the sign: La Iglesia de la Gente. "This is the first time the people of El Barrio have taken over one of the institutions that have so long oppressed them," said Pablo Guzman, the minister of information, who went on to become a well-known journalist, as did Geraldo Rivera and Juan Gonzalez. Another Young Lord, Felipe Luciano, said, "What we are doing is much more Christian, much more brotherly, than anything that any church...is doing." Officials did not agree. After 11 days, they arrested 105 Young Lords and their supporters, who submitted peaceably.

Lexington Avenue Baptist Church (original facade) **[P3]**

Primera Iglesia Metodista Unida Hispana (present facade) **[P3]**

Primitiva, Iglesia Cristiana. The Primitive Christian Church occupies a plain sanctuary at 207 East Broadway **[●C44]** for which plans were filed in 1973 by Robert Bassolino.

Prince of Peace Universal Tabernacle Spiritual Church. The origins of the sanctuary at 557 West 182nd Street **[●V15]**, now home to the Prince of Peace Universal Tabernacle Spiritual Church, is revealed by the Decalogue over the entrance: this was once the Fort Washington Synagogue.

Iglesia Cristiana Primitiva **[C44]**

Promenade Theatre. *See* Manhattan Congregational Church

Prophetic Church of God. An alteration in 1926 by George H. Griebel of a small frame building at 130 West 129th Street [●Q20] yielded what is now the Prophetic Church of God.

Prospect Hill Reformed Church. The Prospect Hill Reformed Church, on Park Avenue [N5], was a plain brick box. The congregation, founded in 1860, worshiped here from 1886 until 1903, before merging with the South Church.

Prince of Peace Universal Tabernacle Spiritual Church
[V15]

Pu Chao Temple. Upswept eaves mark this small Italianate building at 20 Eldridge Street [●C24]—for many years occupied by jewelers—as the Pu Chao Temple of the Buddhist Association of New York, affiliated with the Chinese Pure Land school.

Puerta Estrecha, Iglesia de Dios Pentecostal. The Narrow Gate Pentecostal Church, at 161 Sherman Avenue [●W5], occupies a former Safeway supermarket. Its name recalls Jesus's exhortation: "Enter by the narrow gate, for the gate is wide and the way is easy that leads to destruction."

Prophetic Church of God
[Q20]

Puritans, Congregational Church of the. The Congregational Church of the Puritans was led by the Rev. George B. Cheever, author of *God Against Slavery* and *The Guilt of Slavery and the Crime of Slave-Holding*. James Renwick Jr. designed the church on Union Square West [E12], which was begun in 1846 and razed in 1868 to make way for Tiffany & Company. Materials from the building were numbered and reused to construct the Fifty-third Street Baptist Church, at 161 West 53rd Street [I9], which became the home of Mount Olivet Baptist Church. The Puritans name endured, too, after Cheever gave $87,000—from the sale of the Union Square lease—to the Second Presbyterian Church of Harlem, at 9 West 130th Street [●R4], with the stipulation that it call itself the Presbyterian Church of the Puritans. This is now St. Ambrose Episcopal Church.

Congregational Church of the Puritans [E12]

Quinta Iglesia de Dios Pentecostal. The simple home of the Fifth Latin American Pentecostal Church of God is at 174 East 112th Street [●P5].

Quinta Iglesia de Dios Pentecostal
[P5]

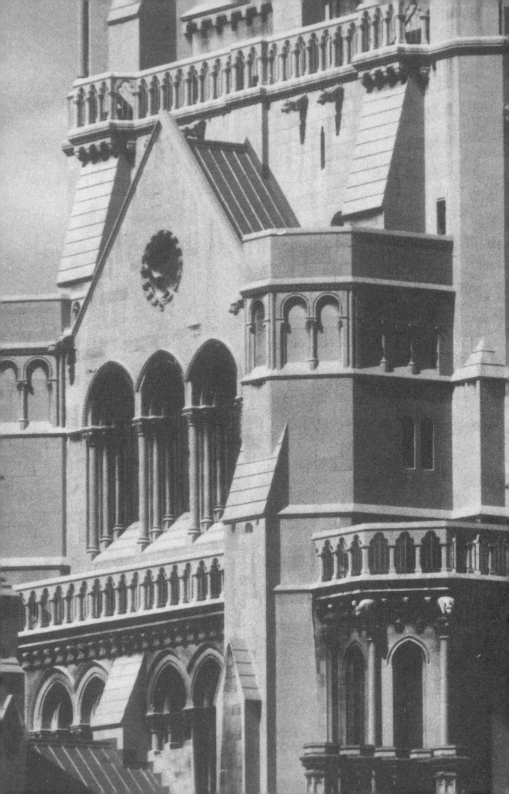

R

Radio Church of God. *See* God, Church of

Ramakrishna-Vivekananda Center [P34]

Ramakrishna-Vivekananda Center. In a row house at 17 East 94th Street [●P34☆], built in 1892 to designs by Cleverdon & Putzel, is a branch of the Ramakrishna Order of India, based on the System of Vedanta, a form of Hinduism explained and demonstrated by Sri Ramakrishna in the nineteenth century and by his disciple Swami Vivekananda. In 1933, Swami Nikhilananda founded the New York center, which acquired this property six years later. The houses at 17 and 19 East 94th Street are being renovated and combined for use by the center.

Congregation Ramath Orah [O5]

Ramath Orah, Congregation. Although contemporary with other neo-Georgian synagogues, the sanctuary at 550 West 110th Street [●O5] was built as a church, designed in 1921 by Hoppin & Koen. It was the West Side Unitarian Church, which merged with the Community Church of New York, before being acquired by Congregation Ramath Orah, cofounded in 1942 by Rabbi Robert S. Serebrenik, who had been the chief rabbi of Luxembourg when the Nazis invaded. The name of the congregation, roughly translated as Light Mountain, is an allusion to the name Luxembourg.

Rauschenbusch Memorial United Church of Christ [I36]

Rauschenbusch Memorial United Church of Christ. CHRISTUS DER ECKSTEIN, says the cornerstone. *The Vagina Monologues*, said the marquee, beginning in 1999, as this former sanctuary at 407 West 43rd Street [●I36], now the Westside Theater, was home to Eve Ensler's play. Designed by Henry F. Kilburn and built in 1889 as the Second German Baptist Church, founded in 1855, it was the pulpit of the Rev. Walter Rauschenbusch, author of *Christianity and the Social Crisis*. Known as a champion of the people, he lost his hearing by ministering to the needy during the Blizzard of 1888, even though he had influenza. The congregation that bears his name began as a study and worship group organized by the Rev. Al Carmines. It moved here after the building was converted into the Westside Theater and shared space until departing for Trinity Presbyterian Church, at 422 West 57th Street [●K37].

Redeemer, Church of the. An early presence on the Upper East Side, this Episcopal parish of 1852 built a country sanctuary at 230 East 85th Street [N21] that was later occupied by the Prospect Hill Reformed and Metropolitan Union American A.M.E. Churches. The Church of the Redeemer moved in 1867 to Park Avenue [N32], where it remained for three decades until merging with Holy Nativity in Harlem.

Church of the Redeemer [N32]

Reformed Dutch Church. "Through the Lord's mercy we have begun to establish here a Christian congregation," the Rev. Jonas Michaëlius wrote back to Holland in 1628. "The people, for the most part, are rather rough and unrestrained, but I find in almost all of them both love and respect towards me.... At the first administration of the Lord's Supper which was observed, not without great joy and comfort to many, we had fully fifty communicants—Walloons and Dutch; of whom, a portion made their first confession of faith before us, and others exhibited their church certificates. Others had forgotten to bring their certificates with them, not thinking that a church would be formed and established here."

Michaëlius was the first clergyman in New Amsterdam and is counted number 1 in a line of Collegiate ministers—the Rev. Norman Vincent Peale is number 40—that runs unbroken to this day.

Under minister number 2, Everardus Bogardus, something like a church was built in 1633 at what would now be 39 Pearl Street [A50]. But it must not have amounted to much, since it was derided as a "mean barn" less than a decade after it was constructed. "The first thing which the English in New England built, after their dwellings, was a fine church, and we ought to do so, too," Captain David De Vries told Director-General Willem Kieft in 1642. Kieft replied that if De Vries was so keen on the idea, he should donate 100 guilders. De Vries retorted that Kieft should do so, as he was the commander. Kieft finally found someone else to help pay, and construction began that year on a second church, inside Fort Amsterdam [A48], that would later be known as King's Chapel. A plaque marking the approximate location of the original church is affixed to the side of the New York Clearing House, at 100 Broad Street.

Reformed Dutch Church (plaque at 100 Broad Street) [A50]

Refuge Church. *See* Greater Refuge Temple

Misión Cristiana Rehoboth **[R55]**

Rehoboth, Misión Cristiana. The sanctuary at 164 East 118th Street **[●R55]** has the unusual distinction among small Harlem churches of having been occupied for more than half a century by the congregation that built it, the Rehoboth Christian Mission. Plans were filed in 1949 by Carl B. Cali.

Rendall Memorial Presbyterian Church **[T20]**

Rendall Memorial Presbyterian Church. This pretty Adamesque sanctuary at 59 West 137th Street **[●T20]**, by Ludlow & Peabody, was built in 1914/1915 as St. James Presbyterian Church, now on West 141st Street. The Rendall Memorial Presbyterian Church is something of an offshoot, having been founded in 1916 as the Washington Mission by the Rev. William R. Lawton, under whose pastorate St. James moved from midtown to Harlem. Lawton renamed the congregation three years later in honor of his teacher, the Rev. Isaac N. Rendall, who was president of Lincoln University in Pennsylvania, one of the oldest historically black colleges. Rendall Memorial moved here in 1927 from 122 West 129th Street **[●Q21]**, now the Holy Cross African Orthodox Pro-Cathedral.

Church of the Resurrection **[P29]**

Resurrection, Church of the. A windowless box of intersecting planes, this sanctuary at 325 East 101st Street **[●P29]** was designed by Victor A. Lundy and built from 1962 to 1965. The Church of the Resurrection is an outgrowth of the East Harlem Protestant Parish, three storefront churches founded in 1948, in what was then among the worst of slums, by a group of young ministers and seminarians that included the Rev. Norman C. Eddy and the Rev. Margaret Ruth Eddy, who served as pastor at Resurrection in the early 1970s. "Fireflies of the spirit" is the name Norman Eddy has given to the human forces that revivified East Harlem in recent decades.

Resurrection, Church of the. No relation to the current Episcopal parish by the same name, the Church of the Resurrection was founded in 1861. Its Romanesque sanctuary at 65 West 35th Street [H2] had been the Murray Hill Baptist Church and later served St. Mark's Methodist Episcopal Church. In 1868, Resurrection built a church on Madison Avenue [J27] by Charles Coolidge Haight. The parish dissolved in 1880.

Resurrection, Church of the. That great Gothic A at 115 East 74th Street [●L2☆] is the oldest extant church on the Upper East Side and still looks very much the country church, as it was when built in 1867/1868 to designs by Renwick & Sands. Organized as the Church of the Holy Sepulchre in 1866 under the Rev. James Oatlands Tuttle Smith, the parish traces itself to the Free Episcopal Church (no pew rentals) begun four years earlier. On the wrong side of the tracks—east of Park Avenue—it was known to socialites as the "Servants' Church." The formal name was changed in 1902 to the Church of the Resurrection, and the parish developed along Anglo-Catholic lines.

Church of the Resurrection **[L2]**

Resurrection, Church of the. Taking institutional form along with its institutional purpose, this Roman Catholic church and school at 276 West 151st Street [●T2] looks more school than church. The Church of the Resurrection was built in 1908 for a parish founded in 1907. In the 1970s, the outspoken Rev. Lawrence E. Lucas became one of the first African-American pastors of a Catholic parish in Harlem. The current pastor, Msgr. Wallace A. Harris, is also pastor of the Church of St. Charles Borromeo and serves as the regional vicar of Harlem.

Church of the Resurrection **[T2]**

Rigging Loft Methodist Meeting Place. In the early seventeenth century, the Reformed Dutch Church met in a "mean barn." In the 1750s and 1760s, the Baptists and then the Methodists convened in a rigging loft on Horse and Cart Lane [A14], now 120 William Street. The Methodists used the loft after Philip Embury could no longer accommodate worshipers in his house and before they opened the Wesley Chapel, precursor to the John Street Church, in 1768. The rigging loft stood until 1854.

Rissho Kosei-Kai New York Center for Engaged Buddhism. A Japanese Buddhist sect, organized in 1938 and said to be the second largest lay religious organization in Japan after Soka Gakkai, occupies a simple sanctuary at 320 East 39th Street [● J53].

Rigging Loft Methodist Meeting Place
[A14]

Fifth Avenue Baptist Church [J33]

Riverside Church (under construction)
[Q36]

Riverside Church [Q36]

Riverside Church. No church in New York commands a more spectacular site, visible for miles from its bluff overlooking the Hudson River. The architecture makes the most of its privileged spot, with a 392-foot sky-scraping tower on Riverside Drive [●Q36★] that houses 22 floors of church rooms and the Laura Spelman Rockefeller Memorial Carillon. In religious and social programs, Riverside Church is also high profile. "Inter-denominational, interracial, and international," it is allied with both the United Church of Christ and the American Baptist Churches. Its senior minister since 1989 has been the Rev. James Alexander Forbes Jr., who succeeded to the pulpit of the Rev. William Sloane Coffin Jr. and the Rev. Harry Emerson Fosdick. The liberal Fosdick resigned from the First Presbyterian Church in 1925 after fundamentalists led by William Jennings Bryan attempted to oust him. John D. Rocke-feller Jr., dissatisfied with what he perceived as the lack of ecumenism at St. John the Divine, put up $8 million to finance an interdenominational church for the charismatic Fosdick.

But Riverside did not spring into existence full blown. At its nucleus is a Baptist congregation founded in 1841. The Norfolk Street Baptist Church worshiped at what is now Congregation Beth Hamedrash Hagodol, at 60 Norfolk Street [●C10★]. As the Fifth Avenue Baptist Church, designed by D. & J. Jardine and built in 1865/1866 at 8 West 46th Street [J33], it counted Rockefellers among its members. Indeed, its men's Bible Class was led by John D. Jr. It was next the Park Avenue Baptist Church, occupying a large sanctuary at 593 Park Avenue [●L30☆], built from 1920 to 1922 to designs by Henry C. Pelton and Allen & Collens of Boston. This is now the Central Presbyterian Church.

John D. Jr. gave to Park Avenue Baptist a 53-bell carillon by Gillett & Johnston of Croydon, England, with a 20,510-pound Bourdon bass bell inscribed IN LOVING MEMORY OF MY MOTHER, LAURA SPELMAN ROCKEFELLER. Recast and expanded into a set of 72 bells, this carillon was taken up to Riverside Church, where it was played passionately for more than a quarter of a century by James R. Lawson.

At Riverside Church, built from 1927 to 1930, Allen & Collens were once again the architects. The original complex had a sanctuary and tower, modeled loosely on those of Chartres Cathedral. Quite loosely, since Chartres is not a 22-story office and classroom building.

The Martin Luther King Jr. Wing, by Collens, Willis & Beckonert, was completed in 1955. In 2000, the Landmarks Preservation Commission designated the sanctuary and tower a landmark, saying that the city's tallest church "still dominates the skyline, symbolizing the progressive beliefs of its congregation." This was a far cry from 1931, when the magazine *American Architect* ridiculed the choice of thirteenth-century motifs for a pulpit occupied by a modern churchman like Fosdick, huffing, "We would not require Gershwin to perform and compose on a harpsichord."

Rock Church **[L34]**

Rock Church. Incorporated in 1929, the Rock Church was an outgrowth of the First Swedish Pentecostal Church. In 1946, it acquired the former Tonsil Hospital at 153 East 62nd Street **[●L34]** for its sanctuary.

Rocky Mount Baptist Church **[W14]**

Rocky Mount Baptist Church. An aptly named sanctuary in the high altitudes of 37 Hillside Avenue **[●W14]**, the Rocky Mount Baptist Church was formerly the Wilhelm Weinberg Center.

Rodeph Sholom, Congregation. Rodeph Sholom (Pursuers of Peace), a Reform congregation, is one of the oldest in New York, founded by German immigrants in 1842. It built a sanctuary at 8 Clinton Street **[●F46]** in 1853 that is still in use by Congregation Chasam Sopher and is the second oldest surviving purpose-built synagogue in the city. It moved to a madly Victorian Romanesque sanctuary at Lexington Avenue and East 63rd Street **[L33]** designed by D. & J. Jardine and built in 1872/1873 for Congregation Anshe Chesed. Its present home, at 7 West 83rd Street **[●M23☆]**, was designed by Charles B. Meyers and built in 1929/1930. Unlike many synagogues of this period, which had a single portal, Rodeph Sholom has three great arched windows under an inscription from the book of Micah: WALK HUMBLY WITH THY GOD. In 2003, it added a rooftop chapel by Pasanella + Klein Stolzman + Berg.

Congregation Rodeph Sholom **[L33]**

Congregation Rodeph Sholom **[M23]**

Rutgers Presbyterian Church [H25]

Rutgers Riverside Presbyterian Church [K2]

Rutgers Presbyterian Church **[K3]**

Rutgers Presbyterian Church. Does the name Rutgers ring a bell? Both Rutgers Presbyterian Church and the State University of New Jersey are namesakes of Col. Henry Rutgers, who fought in the Revolutionary War and farmed on the Lower East Side. The colonel gave a parcel from his farm at Rutgers and Henry Streets [C37] to the First Presbyterian Church for an adjunct congregation called the Rutgers Street Church, built in 1797/1798. Its second home on that site [●C38], built in 1841/1842, still stands as the Roman Catholic Church of St. Teresa. Rutgers moved in 1863 to 90 Madison Avenue [H24], which had been constructed in 1844 for the Madison Avenue Presbyterian Church. On this site [H25], working with Samuel A. Warner, Rutgers built a Victorian Gothic sanctuary from 1873 to 1875 that later served as the Masonic Scottish Rite Hall. In 1888, Rutgers opened a chapel by R. H. Robertson on West 73rd Street [K2] and restyled itself Rutgers Riverside. The chapel was followed by Robertson's powerful Romanesque church, like a masonry locomotive, which extended to Broadway and was dedicated in 1890.

The church then leased its valuable Broadway frontage to a bank and moved to a modest midblock sanctuary by Henry Otis Chapman at 236 West 73rd Street [●K3], built from 1921 to 1926. "It is no more than a question of putting real estate values, which are lying idle, to work for the kingdom of God," said the Rev. Daniel Russell. Rutgers merged in 1942 with the Harlem–New York Presbyterian Church. Russell's investment continues to pay dividends, as the church today is a hub of social-service activity. It also plays chimes daily that are audible in the neighborhood. So it really does ring a bell.

Rzeszower-Korczyner, Congregation. Members of this congregation, at 70 Willett Street [F52], founded in 1888, came from the Polish towns of Rzeszow and Korczyn.

St.

St. Agnes, Chapel of. *See* Trinity Church

Church of St. Agnes [J42]

Church of St. Agnes [J43]

Church of St. Aloysius [T31]

St. Agnes, Church of. One of Manhattan's newest houses of worship is one of its most traditional in design, befitting the conservative pastoral and political role of a Roman Catholic parish where the Latin Mass is celebrated. The Church of St. Agnes was founded in 1873 to serve Irish laborers at Grand Central Depot. Its first church, at 141 East 43rd Street [J42], was designed by Lawrence J. O'Connor and built from 1873 to 1877. Eamon de Valera, later prime minister and president of Ireland, was baptized here in 1882. Archbishop Fulton J. Sheen, known for his radio and television broadcasts, preached here for 50 years. From this church, John Cardinal O'Connor led an important antiabortion march. In 1992, the building was destroyed by fire. The pastor, Msgr. Eugene V. Clark, vowed to rebuild. And he kept his word. The new church opened on the same site [● J43] in 1998. Designed by Acheson, Thornton, Doyle, it is a pared-down version of Il Gesù in Rome, flanked by the reclad remains of the old towers. St. Agnes, a Roman martyr, can be seen in a niche in the facade. And on each door is her emblem in art: the lamb. Or, in Latin, *agnus*.

St. Aloysius, Church of. If this church were in Italy— and it could be—it would be a compelling draw, its facade a scintillating quiltwork of decorative masonry. But at 209 West 132nd Street [●T31], it is a little-known treasure, one of many in which Harlem abounds. Like the astonishing All Saints Church, it came from the Renwick shop, bearing the hand of William W. Renwick. The Roman Catholic Church of St. Aloysius was founded in 1899, and the sanctuary was built in 1902. The exuberance continues inside, where gospel music, not typically part of the Catholic liturgy, has been incorporated into services for what is now an African-American parish.

St. Alphonsus Liguori, Church of. The chic Soho Grand Hotel marks the site of one of the great Lombard Romanesque churches, built less than a century after the death of its namesake. The Roman Catholic parish was founded in 1847 under the Redemptorist Fathers, who ministered to German Catholics. The first Church of St. Alphonsus Liguori was built in 1847 at 10 Thompson Street [B16]. After the lot was extended through to 310 West Broadway [B17], a new church was built from 1870 to 1872, credited to Francis G. Hempler. The enormous building was closed in 1980, having settled into the bed of an underground stream. The statue of St. Alphonsus was salvaged and moved to a spot outside the Church of St. Anthony of Padua.

Church of St. Alphonsus Liguori [B17]

St. Ambrose, Church of. Often, the multipurpose nature of Roman Catholic facilities makes them look more like institutions than sanctuaries. In deft hands, as at 539 West 54th Street [●I1], the result can be a structure with Gothic flair. Plans were filed in 1911 by John V. Van Pelt for a four-story church, school, and rectory. The parish was founded in 1897 and disbanded in 1938. The former Church of St. Ambrose is now Centro María, a women's residence run by the Sisters of Mary Immaculate, but Sunday Masses are still celebrated in the chapel.

Church of St. Ambrose (Centro María) [I1]

St. Ambrose Episcopal Church. This Gothic sanctuary at 9 West 130th Street [●R4] was designed by James W. Pirsson and built from 1873 to 1875 as the Presbyterian Church of the Puritans, originally the Second Presbyterian Church of Harlem, organized in 1872. It renamed itself as a condition of a gift from the Rev. George B. Cheever of the Congregational Church of the Puritans. The building was acquired in 1936 by St. Ambrose, a black Episcopal parish founded in 1925 under the Rev. Elliott E. Durant that had worshiped at 125 West 130th Street, now the Beulah Baptist Church, and at 160 West 129th Street [●Q17], now the Faith Mission Christian Fellowship.

St. Ambrose Episcopal Church [R4]

SS. Anargyroi Greek Orthodox Church. A touch of Greece at 1547 Juan Pablo Duarte Boulevard, or St. Nicholas Avenue [●V4], SS. Anargyroi Greek Orthodox Church welcomes worshipers with a deep porch and small bell tower. It was designed in 1967 by Pedro F. Lopez.

SS. Anargyroi Greek Orthodox Church [V4]

Church of St. Andrew
[B49]

Church of St. Andrew **[B50]**

St. Andrew's Episcopal Church
[R14]

St. Andrew's Episcopal Church
[R11]

St. Andrew, Church of. Surrounded by courthouses and government buildings, the Roman Catholic Church of St. Andrew proclaims a higher authority: BEATI QUI AMBULANT IN LEGE DOMINI (Blessed are they who walk in the law of the Lord). The first church was built in 1818 on Duane Street [B49] for the Society of United Christian Friends. In 1841, as Carroll Hall, it was where Catholics gathered to fight the denial of public financing to parochial schools. Patrick J. Hayes, a future cardinal, was born in a house next door and baptized at St. Andrew in 1867. Five people died in 1875 when the collapse of an adjoining crockery factory brought the church ceiling down as worshipers listened to a sermon on death.

In 1900, the Rev. Luke J. Evers initiated a 2:30 A.M. Mass for night workers, since the church was so close to Printing House Square, where the *Sun, Telegraph, Times,* and *World* were published. The present sanctuary was dedicated in 1939 on the same site [●B50]. The architects were Maginnis & Walsh and Robert J. Reiley. Andrew, the first called of the apostles, was said to have been martyred on an X-shaped cross, which is his emblem. It can be seen in the pediment, within a medallion surrounded by two angels.

St. Andrew's Episcopal Church. Most parishes simply leave old buildings behind. This group, the first Episcopal parish in Harlem, disassembled its Victorian Gothic sanctuary and moved it two and a half blocks west, to 2067 Fifth Avenue [●R11★]. St. Andrew's Episcopal Church was organized in 1829 under the Rev. George L. Hinton. A church was built on East 127th Street [R13] in 1829/1830. It burned and was replaced in 1873 with a Gothic structure by Henry M. Congdon, set in a large yard on the same site [R14], between Park and Lexington Avenues. Sixteen years later, Congdon was commissioned for the remarkable task of dismantling, moving, reorienting, enlarging, and reerecting the building. The tower was heightened in the process and given a clock. A decision in 1942 to abolish pew rentals effectively opened St. Andrew's to black parishioners, chiefly of Caribbean descent, who quickly came to compose the vast majority of members.

St. Ann's Armenian Catholic Cathedral I St. Ann's Roman Catholic Church.

This was once Temple Emanu-El. Of all the facets of this old church at 120 East 12th Street [●E29], that may be the most amazing: that it served for 13 years as the home of the congregation now so venerably ensconced on Fifth Avenue. Perhaps only one other sanctuary in Manhattan, Mount Neboh Baptist Church in Harlem, has served all three of the city's major faiths. And St. Ann's days of diversity are not over. Used by Armenians and Ecuadoreans, it also celebrates a Latin Mass called the Tridentine Rite.

St. Ann's Church [E39]

Constructed in 1847 as the Twelfth Street Baptist Church, it was purchased in 1854 by Congregation Emanu-El, which moved from Chrystie Street. By 1862, conditions were so crowded, as the congregational minutes noted, "that small children and adolescents wander aimlessly about in the Temple." Emanu-El built a new synagogue on Fifth Avenue. Then came the Roman Catholic parish of St. Ann, founded in 1852.

St. Ann's first sanctuary, on East 8th Street [E39], was a building with a complex history of its own. Designed by John McComb Jr., it was constructed in 1811/1812 on Murray Street as the Third Associate Reformed Presbyterian Church, among the most sophisticated of New York's Georgian buildings. In 1842, as downtown real estate grew more valuable, the congregation sold the site and moved its building to 8th Street, at the head of Lafayette Place. In 1852, it was rededicated as St. Ann's Church. After the parish moved out, this building was used as an upholstery factory and then, beginning in 1879, as a theater, known over time as Aberle's, the Grand Central, John Thompson's, the Monte Cristo, the Comedy, and, in 1894, the Germania (pictured at right). It was razed in 1904 during the construction of the subway.

St. Ann's Church (as a theater) [E39]

St. Ann's left nothing of the East 12th Street building except the front walls. Behind that façade Napoleon Le Brun created a French Gothic sanctuary that was dedicated in 1871. In 1983, it was established as St. Ann's Armenian Catholic Cathedral. The Armenian Church is one of several Eastern Catholic churches in communion with Rome, unlike the "separated" Orthodox churches.

St. Ann's Armenian Catholic Cathedral [E29]

St. Ann's Church for the Deaf [H61]

St. Ann's Roman Catholic Church [P11]

Church of St. Anthony of Padua (as a stable) [E84]

St. Ann's Church for the Deaf. Thomas Hopkins Gallaudet established the first free school for the deaf in 1817. His son Edward founded a school that evolved into Gallaudet University in Washington, D.C., and his son Thomas, an Episcopal priest known as the "apostle to the deaf," founded St. Ann's Church for the Deaf in 1852, the first such church in the country. In 1859, the parish acquired the former Christ Church, at 7 West 18th Street [H61]. In 1898, it moved uptown and constructed a Gothic building by Clarence True at 511 West 148th Street [●S8]. Counseling, lectures, and entertainment were offered. "In a chapel flooded with light for those who must depend on sight alone, the pastor delivers his sermons in sign language and the choir 'sings' with its hands," the *WPA Guide* said in 1939. Ten years later, St. Ann's ceased to be a separate church. The building is now the Manhattan Holy Tabernacle.

St. Ann's Roman Catholic Church. A Roman Catholic parish founded in 1911, St. Ann's occupies a church at 312 East 110th Street [●P11] that was designed that year by Nicholas Serracino.

St. Anthony of Padua, Church of. The first Roman Catholic parish organized for an Italian congregation in the United States, St. Anthony of Padua was founded in 1859 out of the Church of St. Vincent de Paul and reestablished in 1866 by the Franciscans, under the Rev. Leo Pacilio. Its first home, at 149 Sullivan Street [E84], was a church built in 1839 for the Sullivan Street Methodist Episcopal Church, now known as the Washington Square United Methodist Church. From 1886 to 1888, the present church was built at 155 Sullivan Street [●E85], designed by Arthur Crooks. The plain brick Houston Street facade was never meant to be seen. It originally was hidden by tenements that were torn down when the street was widened, leaving an unbuildable gore. St. Anthony turned this space into a garden where it erects a Nativity scene every Christmas. Father Fagan Square, two blocks away, honors the Rev. Richard Fagan, who died after rescuing other priests from a fire in the rectory in 1938.

St. Augustine's Episcopal Church. St. Augustine's claim on our conscience is all but hidden from view: two crude galleries flanking the organ loft, tucked under the eaves. The people who worshiped in this wretched space must have experienced a vast, immutable gulf separating them from the gentry below. It is enormously moving to get a visceral sense of how rigidly society was stratified and segregated, even in a house of the Lord. But were they actually used by slaves, as tradition holds and the church sign board proclaims: HOME OF NEW YORK CITY'S ONLY EXISTING SLAVE GALLERY?

Church of St. Anthony of Padua **[E85]**

By the time the sanctuary at 290 Henry Street [●C48★] was consecrated in June 1828 as All Saints' Church, almost a year had passed since emancipation had taken effect in the state. Yet New York still recognized as slaves people from other states who came here in the company of their masters. And All Saints', being close to the piers, might have seen more than its share of nonresidents. So the answer may be unknowable.

St. Augustine's Episcopal Church began in 1869 as a chapel of Trinity parish. Its enormous Victorian Gothic sanctuary and mission house by Potter & Robertson was built in 1876/1877 at 107 East Houston Street [E89], largely on the grounds of an old Quaker cemetery, in the densest and poorest quarter in the city. In 1927, the sanctuary was divided by a soundproof partition to create an Episcopal chapel on one side and, on the other, St. Mary's Russian Orthodox Cathedral, seat of Metropolitan Platon, who had been displaced from St. Nicholas Russian Orthodox Cathedral.

St. Augustine's merged in 1945 with All Saints' and moved to Henry Street. The Rev. C. Kilmer Myers chronicled his experience in this violent and lawless neighborhood in *Light the Dark Streets*. "A parish not in tension is not, in our day, a Christian parish," he wrote in 1957. The Henry Street sanctuary, credited to John Heath, was made a landmark in 1966. St. Augustine's was spun off from Trinity in 1976 as an independent parish. In the 1990s, under the Rev. Errol A. Harvey, it offered one of the first programs of AIDS counseling for convicts and addicts—still in service to the most desperate New Yorkers.

St. Augustine's Chapel [E89]

St. Augustine's Episcopal Church **[C48]**

St. Barbara Greek Orthodox Church
[C23]

St. Barbara Greek Orthodox Church. If the sanctuary at 27 Forsyth Street [●C23] isn't Greek to you, your perception is keen. Designed by Schneider & Herter in 1892, it was Congregation Kol Israel Anshe Poland, before that group moved to Harlem, and then Congregation Mishkan Israel Anshei Suwalk. St. Barbara Greek Orthodox Church has been here since 1932.

St. Barnabas' Chapel. St. Barnabas' Chapel was one of a group of buildings dedicated in 1865 at 306 Mulberry Street [E77] by the New York Protestant Episcopal City Mission Society to house and care for destitute women and children.

St. Bartholomew's Church [E60]

St. Bartholomew's Church [J41]

St. Bartholomew's Church. Years have passed since the battle for St. Bart's ended. The church is recovering. But the fight over one of the most valuable parcels of real estate in New York is likely to resonate for many years as a defining moment in parish history. That is no small thing, since St. Bartholomew's Church goes back to 1835.

Its first sanctuary, on Lafayette Place [E60], was built in 1835/1836. It moved to a site on Madison Avenue [J41] bought from William H. Vanderbilt. James Renwick Jr. designed the Lombardic church, built from 1872 to 1876. An elaborate portal by Stanford White, inspired by the abbey of Saint-Gilles-du-Gard in Provence, was added as a memorial to Cornelius Vanderbilt. In 1892, St. Bartholomew's opened a mission to the Swedish population of Harlem, at 121 East 127th Street [R15]. It operated for 40 years, after which the building served as St. Mary's Eastern Orthodox Cathedral and the Kings Chapel of the Apostolic Faith.

When it came time for the parish to relocate from Madison Avenue, Alice Gwynne Vanderbilt offered to pay for moving her husband's memorial. So that served as the starting point for the design of the new church, built from 1917 to 1919 on Park Avenue [●J21★]. Bertram Grosvenor Goodhue did much more than provide a setting for the portal, however. He brilliantly synthesized ancient and modern forms in a Byzantine–Romanesque style. The golden-hued sanctuary occupies the northern half of the block. On the south are a garden and community house. In the 1980s, under the Rev. Thomas D. Bowers, a divided congregation sought to replace the community house with a 47-story office tower. But the Landmarks Preservation Commission would not allow it. A legal battle began that lasted until 1991, when the Supreme Court refused to hear St. Bartholomew's challenge to the landmark designation.

St. Bartholomew's Church **[J21]**

St. Benedict the Moor, Church of. The first church in the North for black Roman Catholics was founded in 1883 in Greenwich Village and named for a Franciscan venerated as a counselor and healer, who was born in Sicily to enslaved African parents. The Rev. Thomas Farrell, pastor of the Church of St. Joseph, on Sixth Avenue, and one of the earliest priests to espouse racial equality, had left $5,000 in his will to establish a church for blacks, stipulating that the sum go to a Protestant orphanage if the church had not been founded within three years.

The Church of St. Benedict the Moor opened at 210 Bleecker Street [E70], a splendid Greek Revival temple constructed in 1836 for the Third Universalist Society. Following the black migration uptown, St. Benedict moved in 1898 to 342 West 53rd Street [●I11], the former Second German Church of the Evangelical Association, built in 1869 to designs by R. C. McLane & Sons. "This was the steppingstone for blacks from the Village to Harlem," Bishop Emerson J. Moore said at St. Benedict's centenary. "It was the first Catholic church to welcome blacks and was always used to call attention to racial prejudices in America." Far larger than an ordinary parish, St. Benedict's boundaries extended until 1921 into the dioceses of Newark, New Jersey, and Brooklyn. It was vital enough in the early twentieth century to sponsor its own charitable institution: St. Benedict's Home for Destitute Colored Children in Rye, New York. Today, it is a largely Hispanic congregation, San Benito, operated by the nearby Church of the Sacred Heart of Jesus. But it is also a rare and handsome vestige of the days not so long ago when the West Side was a thriving African-American neighborhood.

Church of St. Benedict the Moor [E70]

Church of St. Benedict the Moor **[I11]**

Church of St. Bernard **[D3]**

St. Bernard, Church of. St. Bernard of Clairvaux had little use for vast, immoderate churches. Yet he has an imposing Victorian Gothic sanctuary in his honor at 330 West 14th Street **[●D3]**. The parish was organized in 1868 in a wagon factory on West 13th Street. The present sanctuary was built from 1873 to 1875 to designs by Patrick C. Keely, architect of the similarly detailed Church of the Holy Innocents. The Church of St. Bernard was the first church dedicated by an American cardinal, the newly created John Cardinal McCloskey. In 2003, it became the home for the nearby parish of Our Lady of Guadalupe and was renamed Our Lady of Guadalupe at St. Bernard's.

Church of St. Boniface [J32]

St. Boniface, Church of. Named for the Apostle of Germany, the German Roman Catholic parish of St. Boniface was created in 1858. Its church, at 882 Second Avenue [J32], was built in 1868/1869.

Church of St. Brigid (original facade) **[F16]**

St. Brigid, Church of. Among the oldest Roman Catholic church buildings in New York and one of the first in the Gothic style, the twin-towered Church of St. Brigid, at 119 Avenue B **[●F16]**, was used from 1848 until 2001, when Edward Cardinal Egan closed it for safety reasons, as engineers had noticed small but significant movement in the structure.

St. Brigid was organized in 1848, and its sanctuary, attributed to Patrick C. Keely, was ready within the year, though a chilling augury occurred at the cornerstone ceremony, when one of the newly laid walls sank from the weight, causing some alarm.

Originally an Irish parish, named for one of the triad of wonder-working Irish saints—Columba and Patrick are the others—Santa Brígida has served the Hispanic community in recent decades, as the Lower East Side underwent wrenching change. "If Jesus says to feed the poor, and the political climate is anti-poor, then the gospel has political implications," said the Rev. George Kuhn, who arrived in 1986. Kuhn denounced the police as "agents of the businesses and real-estate communities who only care about protecting property values." He took food across police lines to squatters and turned the school cafeteria into a weekend homeless shelter. Opponents saw him siding

Church of St. Brigid (present facade) **[F16]**

with fringe elements rather than the working poor. What doomed the old church, though, was neither politics nor social change but gravity. When the rear wall was found to be pulling away from the building, the main sanctuary was closed. It still is not clear what its fate will be. But a sign on the door in 2001 expressed the parish sentiment: "¡Que viva Santa Brígida!"

St. Catherine of Genoa, Church of. A crowstep gable marks the Roman Catholic Church of St. Catherine of Genoa, at 500 West 153rd Street [●U23], like Our Lady of Good Counsel by the same architect, Thomas H. Poole. One of seven churches clustered around Trinity Cemetery, the parish was founded in 1887 and built this sanctuary in 1889/1890.

Church of St. Catherine of Genoa **[U23]**

St. Catherine of Siena, Church of. A rare example of Arts and Crafts style in a New York sanctuary, the Roman Catholic Church of St. Catherine of Siena, at 411 East 68th Street [●L18], has springing arches that sweep over the nave. Among them, you feel as though you're in the rib cage of an enormous masonry whale. The parish was founded in 1897 by the Dominican Fathers of the Church of St. Vincent Ferrer, chaplains to the nearby hospitals. Its first sanctuary was a church and school building at 420 East 69th Street [L17]. The present church was built in 1930/1931 to designs by Wilfred E. Anthony.

Church of St. Catherine of Siena **[L18]**

St. Cecilia, Church of. Camels, donkeys, and sheep are not the sort of traffic one expects on East 106th Street, but on January 6 they parade by this big Roman Catholic church on Three Kings' Day. The Church of St. Cecilia is a focal point of life in the Barrio at other times, too, a center of devotion for Puerto Rican, Mexican, Ecuadorean, black, and Filipino parishioners, a diversity reflected in the creation of small shrines within the church honoring national patron saints. The parish was founded in 1873 and occupied the Red House hotel on Second Avenue [P17]. The present sanctuary, at 120 East 106th Street [●P16★], was built from 1883 to 1887 to designs by Napoleon Le Brun & Sons. On the facade is a terra-cotta relief of St. Cecilia, playing an organ as she looks out over East Harlem.

Church of St. Cecilia **[P16]**

Church of St. Charles Borromeo
[T11]

Church of St. Clare **[G3]**

St. Clement's Episcopal Church
[E67]

St. Charles Borromeo, Church of. "We are the Easter people and hallelujah is our song." The preacher was Pope John Paul II, and the setting in 1979 was the Church of St. Charles Borromeo, at 211 West 141st Street **[●T11]**, a building and an institution that loom large in Harlem. The parish was founded in 1888. Its first church was on West 142nd Street [T10]. Plans were filed for the present sanctuary in 1901 by George H. Streeton, architect of the somewhat similar Church of St. Raphael. In 1929, Msgr. Thomas M. O'Keefe was transferred to St. Charles Borromeo from St. Benedict the Moor to work with African-American parishioners. Almost 40 years passed before the first black pastor, the Rev. Harold A. Salmon, was named. In 1968, the church was gutted by fire, though the outer walls survived. In 1972/1973, L. E. Tuckett & Thompson created a Modernist sanctuary within the great Gothic envelope. Msgr. Emerson J. Moore, who grew up in Harlem, became pastor in 1975. In 1982, the pope made Moore—whom John Cardinal O'Connor called the "most popular preacher in town"—the first black bishop in the New York archdiocese.

St. Christopher's Chapel. *See* Trinity Church

St. Chrysostom, Chapel of. *See* Trinity Church

St. Clare, Church of. A Baroque confection from the pastry chef who served up St. Jean Baptiste, the Roman Catholic Church of St. Clare, also known as Santa Chiara, stood at 438 West 36th Street [G3]. It was designed in 1905 by Nicholas Serracino.

St. Clemens Mary, Church of. *See* Metro Baptist Church

St. Clement's Episcopal Church. The Victorian Gothic structure at 423 West 46th Street **[●I26]** could be a London schoolhouse, with its prim but frankly institutional air. Edward D. Lindsey designed the building, constructed from 1870 to 1872 as the Faith Chapel of the West Presbyterian Church. It was sorely tested in the winter following the Panic of 1873, when it distributed bread, groceries, coal, shoes, and clothing. After Faith (now Good Shepherd–Faith Presbyterian

Church) moved out, this building was used by St. Cornelius, which merged into St. Clement's Episcopal Church, whose first sanctuary, on Amity Street [E67], opened in 1831. The parish moved uptown in 1920, taking in members of the Chapel of St. Chrysostom, a mission of Trinity Church. It embarked on a notable experiment in 1963 when the Rev. Sidney Lanier and Wynn Handman founded the Off-Broadway American Place Theatre, opening with Robert Lowell's *The Old Glory*. After American Place moved to a home of its own in 1971, St. Clement's continued to serve as an Off-Broadway theater as well as a religious sanctuary.

St. Columba, Church of. One of the oldest extant Roman Catholic churches in New York, St. Columba was built in 1845 at 343 West 25th Street [●G30]. The parish, founded in 1845, honors one of the triad of Irish saints (Brigid and Patrick being the others). Its current claim to secular fame is having Tony Orlando and Whoopi Goldberg among its school alumni.

St. Clement's Episcopal Church **[I26]**

Church of St. Columba **[G30]**

St. Cyprian's Chapel. Testament to San Juan Hill and—through the Johnson family—indirect forerunner of St. Martin's Episcopal Church in Harlem, this chapel at 171 West 63rd Street [K26] was numbered among the leading black churches in the city. San Juan Hill was an area in the West 50s and 60s that may have taken its name from black veterans of the Spanish-American War who settled there or from the racial tensions that often flared into full-fledged battles. St. Cyprian's Chapel, founded in 1905 and run by the New York Protestant Episcopal City Mission Society, had industrial, cooking, and sewing schools; a gymnasium; a laundry; an employment bureau; a home for immigrant girls; and a soup kitchen. The minister in charge was the Rev. John Wesley Johnson, assisted by his son, the Rev. John Howard Johnson, who founded St. Martin's. The Gothic structure was about where the stage house of the Metropolitan Opera is today.

St. Cyprian's Chapel [K26]

St. Cyril, Church of. The Roman Catholic Slovenian parish at 62 St. Mark's Place [●E45]—SLOVENSKA CERKEV SV. CIRILA, the cornerstone says—was founded in 1916.

Church of St. Cyril **[E45]**

Church of SS. Cyril and Methodius
[I45]

St. Edward the Martyr Church
[P12]

St. Eleftherios Greek Orthodox Church [G27]

St. Eleftherios Greek Orthodox
Church [G28]

SS. Cyril and Methodius, Church of I St. Raphael, Church

of. Watching over the Lincoln Tunnel like a twin-peaked fortress, this Roman Catholic church at 502 West 41st Street [●I45] was built in 1902 to designs by George H. Streeton. To the sides and rear, intricate and monumental Gothic detail is expressed in common red brick. As the Church of St. Raphael, founded in 1886, it served the Irish of Hell's Kitchen. Daniel Patrick Moynihan worshiped and cast his first vote here. In 1974, it began to serve a Croatian Roman Catholic parish founded in 1913 that had worshiped for almost 60 years at 552 West 50th Street [●I17], now SS. Kiril and Methodi Bulgarian Eastern Orthodox Diocesan Cathedral. Under the Rev. Slavko Soldo, the Church of SS. Cyril and Methodius was a hub of Croatian relief efforts in the early 1990s during the war in the former Yugoslavia.

St. Dumitru, Romanian Orthodox Church of. A parlor-front sanctuary, the Romanian Orthodox Church of St. Dumitru has been at 50 West 89th Street [●M13☆] since 1940, a year after its founding. John H. Knubel and John Solomon altered the 1892 row house, designed by Thom & Wilson.

St. Edward the Martyr Church. The Gothic St. Edward the Martyr Church, at 14 East 109th Street [●P12], houses an Episcopal parish organized in 1883. The sanctuary, by George A. Bagge, was built in 1887 and financed by Elbert Gary of U.S. Steel, after whom Gary, Indiana, was named.

St. Eleftherios Greek Orthodox Church. St. Eleftherios Greek Orthodox Church was organized in 1918 and worshiped in the former Twenty-fourth Street Methodist Episcopal Church of 1860, at 359 West 24th Street [G27]. It was in this sanctuary in 1931 that Athenagoras was enthroned as archbishop, 17 years before his elevation to the Patriarchate of Constantinople. (That is why a bust of Patriarch Athenagoras stands outside.) Spared by the development of Penn South Houses, the church burned in 1973. Plans were filed the next year by Steven Papadatos, and the present church, on the same site [●G28], was built in 1976.

St. Elizabeth, Church of. Few sanctuaries in Manhattan enjoy as commanding a situation as the Roman Catholic Church of St. Elizabeth, rising atop a steep bluff at 268 Wadsworth Avenue **[●V6]**. The first church, at 4381 Broadway [V2], by Napoleon Le Brun, was dedicated in 1872, three years after the founding of the parish. James Gordon Bennett of the *New York Herald*—namesake of nearby Bennett Park—was the benefactor, having embraced Catholicism in his later years. The present church was designed in 1927 by Robert J. Reiley. Santa Isabel is so interwoven into Dominican life that Edward Cardinal Egan came here in 2001 to honor those who had died in the crash of a jetliner flying from New York to the Dominican Republic.

Church of St. Elizabeth **[V6]**

St. Elizabeth Ann Seton, Shrine of.
See Our Lady of the Rosary, Church of

St. Elizabeth of Hungary, Chapel of. A small-scale, red-brick Sainte-Chapelle was appended to the New York Cancer Hospital on Central Park West **[●O15★]** by Charles Coolidge Haight, built from 1884 to 1890. Run by the New York Protestant Episcopal City Mission Society, the Chapel of St. Elizabeth of Hungary was dedicated to Elizabeth Hamilton Cullum, who had been instrumental in establishing the hospital, forerunner of the Memorial Sloan-Kettering Cancer Center. The building was later the notorious Towers Nursing Home, which closed in 1974 amid allegations of patient neglect. After long years of abandonment, a luxury residential redevelopment got under way in 2001.

Chapel of St. Elizabeth of Hungary **[O15]**

St. Elizabeth of Hungary, Church of. To trace the story of the Upper East Side Church of St. Elizabeth of Hungary, begin on the Lower East Side, at San Isidoro y San Leandro Orthodox Catholic Church of the Hispanic Rite, at 345 East 4th Street **[●F31]**, where the cornerstone says SLOV. KOSTOL SV. ALZBETY. The Slovak Roman Catholic parish was founded in 1891. In 1917, it moved to its present sanctuary, at 211 East 83rd Street **[●N26]**, built in 1893 as the Second Immanuel Lutheran Church and altered by Francis J. Berlenbach.

Church of St. Elizabeth of Hungary **[N26]**

Church of St. Emeric [F4]

St. Emeric, Church of. Unlike mission churches that brought some beauty to their surroundings, postwar churches in poor neighborhoods were frankly spartan. The Roman Catholic parish of St. Emeric was founded in 1949 and laid the cornerstone in 1950 for a brick box at 740 East 13th Street [●F4], designed by Voorhees, Walker, Foley & Smith, that has at least been blanketed in ivy.

Église Française du St.-Esprit [B37]

St.-Esprit, Église Française du. Defying the typical trajectory toward increasing grandeur, the French Church of the Holy Ghost *now* occupies the most modest in its series of sanctuaries.

After King Louis XIV revoked the Edict of Nantes, which had guaranteed toleration of Protestantism by the Catholic state, Huguenot refugees formed the Église des Réfugiés Français à la Nouvelle York in 1688. Their first church stood on Petticoat Lane [A47], now Marketfield Street. The Temple du St.-Esprit was built in 1704 on King's Street [A41], now Pine Street, and drew Huguenot worshipers from as far as New Rochelle, New York. Perhaps on the theory that the enemy of my enemy is my friend, the Huguenots and Anglicans united in 1803. Almost 20 years earlier, Elias Desbrosses had bequeathed £1,000 to Old Trinity to establish a French Episcopal church. Unable to comply, Trinity set aside the sum. St.-Esprit claimed the Desbrosses legacy by conforming to the Anglican liturgy.

Église Française du St.-Esprit [H46]

Ithiel Town of Town & Davis designed St.-Esprit's third and most exquisite church, built from 1832 to 1834 on Church Street [B37]. In 1862, St.-Esprit laid a cornerstone at 30 West 22nd Street [H46] for a Gothic Revival church. The fifth St.-Esprit, at 45 East 27th Street [H30], was designed by Brun & Hauser and built in 1899/1900. As the French community dwindled, this large building had to be relinquished. The parish spent eight itinerant years until 1934, when it moved to the Sixty-first Street Methodist Episcopal Church, at 229 East 61st Street [L38], built in 1874/1875. Shrinking even further, in 1941 it bought the former Kirmayer School, at 109 East 60th Street [●L42], and built a 70-seat chapel, designed by A. Herbert Mathes, where it still celebrates the Edict of Nantes. "It is

Église Française du St.-Esprit [H30]

wonderful," said the Rev. Nigel Massey, "to be a part of a church which counts among its most important festivals a celebration of tolerance."

Église Française du St.-Esprit **[L38]**

Saints Faith, Hope, and Charity, Chapel of.
See St. Patrick's Cathedral

St. Frances Xavier Cabrini, Shrine of.
Larger than life, a two-story stained-glass Mother Cabrini, patron saint of immigrants and the first American citizen to be made a saint, overlooks the Hudson River from a stunning spot just south of The Cloisters. Why here?

Frances Xavier Cabrini, founder of the Missionary Sisters of the Sacred Heart of Jesus, was sent to New York in 1889 by Pope Leo XIII to help Italian immigrants. She established a number of institutions, including Columbus Hospital, now Cabrini Medical Center. She also bought property in Washington Heights from C. K. G. Billings and made her headquarters in the Sacred Heart Villa at 701 Fort Washington Avenue, where Mother Cabrini High School now stands. (That's why she's here.) In her travels through Europe, in the Americas, and around the United States, Mother Cabrini established 67 schools, hospitals, and orphanages—one for each year of her life. She died in Chicago in 1917. After the high school was built, her remains were returned to Washington Heights and enshrined. She was canonized in 1946. The Shrine of St. Frances Xavier Cabrini, on Fort Washington Avenue [●W15], by De Sina & Pellegrino, was completed in 1960. The plan is a parabolic arch. Mosaics depicting her life wrap around an altar in which a wax effigy is displayed for veneration. (The saint's actual remains are kept in an urn.)

Église Française du St.-Esprit **[L42]**

Shrine of St. Frances Xavier Cabrini **[W15]**

St. Francis de Sales, Church of.
There are few houses of worship as luminous as this Roman Catholic church at 135 East 96th Street [●P32]. The parish was founded in 1894. The Baroque church was designed in 1896 by O'Connor & Metcalf and expanded six years later by George H. Streeton. As early as the 1930s, the Church of St. Francis de Sales was an important center of worship for Spanish Harlem. Today, it is run jointly with the Church of St. Lucy.

Church of St. Francis de Sales **[P32]**

Church of St. Francis of
Assisi **[G21]**

Church of St. Francis Xavier **[E2]**

Church of St. Francis Xavier **[E3]**

St. Francis of Assisi, Church of. Spiritual home to the Rev. Mychal F. Judge, the Church of St. Francis of Assisi was founded in 1844 by the Rev. Zachary Kunz, a Franciscan who broke from the Church of St. John the Baptist. The first St. Francis, at 137 West 31st Street [G20], was dedicated in 1844. "If the Saint loved poverty," the historian John Gilmary Shea wrote, "he must have loved the church in his honor." The present sanctuary was designed by Henry Erhardt and built in 1891 on the same site [●G21]. *The Glorification of the Mother of Jesus* by Rudolph Margreiter, once the largest mosaic in the United States, was installed in 1925. Four years later, the Franciscans began operating a bread line that continues to this day. In 1958, a courtyard was added, designed by the Rev. Cajetan J. B. Baumann. Certainly the most renowned of the friars at St. Francis was Father Judge, the Fire Department chaplain who was officially the first casualty of the attack on September 11, 2001. The image of his ashen body being carried from the World Trade Center was one of the most powerful expressions of the human toll that day.

St. Francis Xavier, Church of. Exuberantly complex, a bit offbeat, and impossible to ignore—both the architecture and the Jesuit-run Roman Catholic parish itself. After a false start on Elizabeth Street, the Jesuits began building the College of St. Francis Xavier on West 15th Street and a church on 16th Street [E2], designed by William Rodrigue. It was dedicated in 1851. In March 1877, someone shouted "Fire!" during a service, and seven people died in the panicked evacuation. After this calamity, the Jesuits resolved to build a new church. The present Church of St. Francis Xavier, at 30 West 16th Street [●E3], designed by Patrick C. Keely, was built from 1878 to 1882. Its great, domed crossing, with murals by William Lamprecht, is a space of considerable grandeur and majesty. But the church also had more earthly concerns. The Xavier Institute of Industrial Relations helped longshoremen and tunnel workers fight union corruption. One of its members, the Rev. John M. Corridan, was the model for Father Barry in the 1954 movie *On the Waterfront*. Later, for eight years, the church offered a Mass for members of Dignity, a group of gay and lesbian Catholics, until the archdiocese ordered an end to it in 1987.

St. Gabriel, Church of. The Angel of the Annunciation could not compete with the Queens Midtown Tunnel, which claimed this Roman Catholic sanctuary at 310 East 37th Street [H12] in 1939. But the Church of St. Gabriel was, in its day, a powerhouse, producing two American cardinals: James Farley and Patrick J. Hayes. The parish was founded in 1859, but the Civil War delayed construction of the church, designed by Henry Engelbert, until 1864. It was dedicated in 1865. St. Gabriel's Park to the south, truncated by the tunnel construction, is now St. Vartan Park, named for the nearby St. Vartan Armenian Cathedral.

Church of St. Gabriel [H12]

SS. George and Demetrios, Hellenic Orthodox Church of. On a hilly corner at 140 East 103rd Street [●P25] stands a Romanesque sanctuary built in 1891 to designs by Franklin Baylies. Now the Hellenic Orthodox Church of SS. George and Demetrios, it was the Blinn Memorial Methodist Episcopal Church, serving a German congregation, until 1930. The Greek Orthodox parish of St. George was begun here in 1931, joined three years later by St. Demetrios, founded in 1927.

Hellenic Orthodox Church of SS. George and Demetrios **[P25]**

St. George Chapel. Steaks? Yes. Seafood? Naturally. But what's a dragon doing above the entrance to Moran's Townhouse, a restaurant at 103 Washington Street [●A30]? Being slain, of course. For this white terra-cotta structure was once St. George Chapel, where services were held for Syrians of the Melchite Rite, in communion with the Roman Catholic Church. Its presence here is a reminder of the days when Washington Street was a Syrian quarter. The Melchite group began worshiping in the chapel of St. Peter's Church on Barclay Street in 1890 and was formally organized in 1920. This sanctuary, the alteration of an existing building, was designed in 1929 by Harvey F. Cassab.

St. George's Chapel. See Trinity Church

St. George's Church. See Calvary and St. George's Church

St. George Chapel (Moran's Townhouse) **[A30]**

St. George Tropeoforos Church. On West 54th Street, where most activity involves the Midtown North Precinct and Midtown Community Court, St. George can be seen in a stained-glass window slaying the dragon. Originally the New Amsterdam Building and now St. George Tropeoforos Church, 307 West 54th Street [●I3] dates from 1886 and was designed by H. J. Grant. The Greek Orthodox parish, founded in 1920, worshiped at 451 West 39th Street [I48] before moving here.

St. George Tropeoforos Church **[I3]**

St. George Ukrainian Catholic Church. As many other ethnic enclaves vanished in the latter twentieth century, the Catholics of Little Ukraine built this domed Byzantine Moderne church, firmly rooted on the spot where they had worshiped for more than six decades. The street outside St. George Ukrainian Catholic Church, Taras Shevchenko Place, honors the nineteenth-century nationalist poet, novelist, and artist. At the end of the 1990s, the church estimated that about 25,000 Ukrainians still lived in this area.

St. George Ukrainian Catholic Church **[E49]**

The Ukrainian Catholic Church is in communion with the Roman Catholic Church. Its first services in New York were at the Church of St. Brigid, on Tompkins Square. This parish was founded in 1905 at 332 East 20th Street [H56]. It moved in 1911 to the former Seventh Street Methodist Church, built in 1836 at 30 East 7th Street [E49], creating a lovely incongruity: five onion domes atop a distyle-in-antis Greek Revival facade. Plans for the present building on the site [●E50] were filed in 1973 by Apollinaire Osadca. The church was dedicated on Pussy Willow Sunday in 1978. Rich mosaic panels on the facade show St. George Cathedral in Lviv and St. Sophia Cathedral in Kiev.

St. Gerasimos, Greek Orthodox Community of. Built almost at the same time as Lever House, the Greek Orthodox Community of St. Gerasimos, at 149 West 105th Street [●O14], looks as though it could be several centuries older. It is a contemporary of the strikingly similar Holy Cross Armenian Apostolic Church, in what might be called Postwar Romanesque Revival. The Greek Orthodox parish was founded in 1926 and

St. George Ukrainian Catholic Church **[E50]**

shared the Grace United Methodist Church, at 131 West 104th Street [O17]. Plans for the present building were filed in 1949 by Kokkins & Lyras, who also designed the Washington Heights Hellenic Church of St. Spyridon.

St. Gregory the Great, Church of. Browne and Berrigan. Paragons of progressivism, activism, or radicalism—as you will—they are linked inextricably to this Upper West Side Roman Catholic church.

St. Gregory the Great parish was founded in 1907 and originally worshiped at 119 West 89th Street [M9]. In 1912/1913, it built a parochial school at 144 West 90th Street [●M10], designed by Elliott Lynch, with an interim ground-floor chapel that was to serve until a much grander main church could be built. But that development never happened, so the schoolhouse still serves as the sanctuary.

Greek Orthodox Community of St. Gerasimos **[O14]**

The Rev. Henry J. Browne—"a large man of Old Testament bearing and new politics taste," as Philip Nobile described him in *The Berrigans*—was pastor during the 1960s. The street in front of St. Gregory was renamed in his honor. "We need to listen to the poor themselves," Browne said. He denounced the city for not building enough housing, called the governor a fink because he had no housing program, and battled a proposed Alexander's department store on Broadway. Capping this tumult, the Rev. Philip F. Berrigan arrived in April 1970 to address a peace rally. He was wanted by the FBI for having destroyed draft files and then failing to surrender to begin a prison term. Federal agents broke through a locked door in the rectory to arrest him. For his part, Browne informed the agents of the hours of Sunday Masses, "should you wish to return."

Church of St. Gregory the Great **[M10]**

St. Gregory the Illuminator Church. This former sanctuary at 314 East 35th Street [●H11], across from St. Vartan Park, was long ago the Girls and Boys Kindergarten before serving as St. Gregory the Illuminator Church, an Armenian congregation, in the 1950s and 1960s. The building is now used by YAI, serving people with disabilities.

St. Gregory the Illuminator Church **[H11]**

Church of St. Lawrence O'Toole **[N24]**

Church of St. Ignatius Loyola **[N25]**

Church of St. Ignatius of Antioch **[J51]**

St. Ignatius Loyola, Church of. In 1994, the eyes of the world focused on the lusciously Baroque, Jesuit-run Church of St. Ignatius Loyola, at 980 Park Avenue **[●N25★]**, for the funeral of Jacqueline Kennedy Onassis, who had been baptized here 64 years earlier. It says much about the prominence of this Roman Catholic parish that it played a central role at the beginning and the end of the life of one of New York's First Citizens. It also says much about the parish and its high regard for liturgical art that in 1993 it installed the largest mechanical-action organ in New York, a four-manual, 5,000-pipe instrument built by N. P. Mander of London. Commemorating an entirely different kind of music, St. Ignatius was the site of the funeral in 2001 of the popular singer Aaliyah.

The parish, founded in 1851, was first dedicated to St. Lawrence O'Toole before being entrusted to the Society of Jesus in 1866. It built a modest brick Romanesque sanctuary on East 84th Street [N24] in 1854. Thirty years later, it began building a Gothic Revival church on Park Avenue. That project was abandoned, but the rough-faced basement story is still evident along the East 84th Street side. The Baroque, basilica-like upper sanctuary, by Schickel & Ditmars, was dedicated in 1898. The facade recalls Il Gesù, the Jesuits' mother church in Rome, and is inscribed with the society's motto: AD MAJOREM DEI GLORIAM (To the Greater Glory of God). Originally, the side towers were to have been topped with four-tiered steeples. In 2002, Edward Cardinal Egan halted a plan by the Rev. Walter F. Modrys to renovate the interior along the lines prescribed by the Second Vatican Council by moving the altar closer to the people and removing the communion rail. In the *New York Times*, Daniel J. Wakin described the tension in part as a "struggle between the need to maintain the church as a living institution that serves today's parishioners and the integrity of a beautiful, historic building."

St. Ignatius of Antioch, Church of. The Church of St. Paul and St. Andrew is a tough architectural act with which to compete. The critic Montgomery Schuyler credited the Episcopal Church of St. Ignatius of Antioch, immediately next door, with not even trying.

Instead, he said, it "preaches a sermon on moderation and restraint that is especially needed and welcome." Architectural simplicity was one thing; liturgical simplicity, another. In the 1860s, Episcopalians were torn between the evangelical Low Church and the ritualistic High Church. The Rev. Ferdinand C. Ewer resigned as rector of the Low Christ Church in 1871 to found St. Ignatius, where the Eucharist was called the Mass, incense was burned, candles were lit, and full colored vestments were worn. Its first permanent home was at 56 West 40th Street [J51], across from Bryant Park, where the parish worshiped from 1874 to 1902. The present sanctuary, at 552 West End Avenue [●M14], was designed by Charles Coolidge Haight and built in 1901/1902, with further interior work by Ralph Adams Cram. Consecrated in 1925, it was so close to being Catholic that it had a built-in holy-water stoup at the door. Although membership declined in the postwar years, St. Ignatius began to grow again with the revitalization of the Upper West Side and embarked on a long-term rehabilitation program.

Church of St. Ignatius of Antioch **[M14]**

St. Illuminator's Armenian Apostolic Cathedral. The assassination in 1933 of Archbishop Leon Elisee Tourian in upper Manhattan created a schism, dividing the Armenian Church into the diocese based at St. Vartan Armenian Cathedral (under the Mother See of Holy Etchmiadzin in Armenia) and the prelacy based at St. Illuminator's Armenian Apostolic Cathedral (under the Holy See of Cilicia in Antelias). St. Illuminator's, founded in 1910 to serve Armenians in the old Gashouse District, occupies a Greek Revival sanctuary at 221 East 27th Street [●H31] that was built in 1843, rebuilt in 1849, and used until 1917 by the Rose Hill Methodist Episcopal Church.

St. Illuminator's Armenian Apostolic Cathedral **[H31]**

San Isidoro y San Leandro Orthodox Catholic Church of the Hispanic Rite. At 345 East 4th Street [●F31] is the birthplace of the Church of St. Elizabeth of Hungary. The Roman Catholic church left in 1917, and the building was later the Holy Trinity Eastern Orthodox Church and the Russian Greek Orthodox Church of St. Nicholas before becoming San Isidoro y San Leandro Orthodox Catholic Church of the Hispanic Rite.

San Isidoro y San Leandro Orthodox Catholic Church of the Hispanic Rite **[F31]**

St. James' Church [L14]

St. James' Church [L10]

St. James' Church (original facade) [L11]

St. James' Church (present facade) [L11]

St. James' Church. An architectural history lesson in three dimensions, St. James' Church, at 865 Madison Avenue [●L11☆], has the bones of a robust 1884 Romanesque design by R. H. Robertson that was reclad with a Gothic overlay by Ralph Adams Cram in 1924 and topped with a tin-can steeple by Richard A. Kimball in 1950. It is lovelier inside than outside, ornamented with a great rose window and carved reredos. A leading Episcopal congregation—one of its rectors, the Rev. Horace W. B. Donegan, went on to become the bishop of New York—St. James' began as a country chapel for a summer colony on the East River, sharing its rector with the equally bucolic St. Michael's Episcopal Church, on the Hudson. A clapboard church was built in 1809/1810 on Hamilton Square [L14]. The second church was built in 1869 on East 72nd Street [L10], with a lively Victorian Gothic facade by James Renwick Jr. The building found a second ecclesiastical life in the early twentieth century as Holy Trinity Greek Orthodox Church. It burned down in 1927.

Work began on the present church in 1884. It opened in 1885, though it never received the very tall tower that Robertson had planned. It was deliberately disoriented, facing west, with the apse on the avenue end so that no new construction would block sunlight from reaching the chancel windows. Ten years after it opened, St. James' merged with the Church of the Holy Trinity from East 42nd Street and built a mission, known as the Church of the Holy Trinity, at 316 East 88th Street [●N10★].

In the 1920s, Cram & Ferguson undertook a radical reorientation and redesign of the building. Under the Rev. Brenda G. Husson, a plan for the restoration of the church and parish house was drawn up in 1999 by the architect Lee Harris Pomeroy. It includes renovating the east hall, building a new atrium, and adding a columbarium. But not changing that steeple. "We all know it doesn't fit architecturally," Husson said. "But it's our steeple. And it's been our steeple for a very long time."

St. James Church. The Greek Revival nobility of the Roman Catholic St. James Church, at 32 James Street [●B57★], has been no guarantee against hard times.

But its intrinsic beauty helps conjure the days in the 1880s when this was the "leading Catholic parish in New York, not excepting the cathedral itself," in the words of Alfred E. Smith, who was an altar boy here. He went on to become governor of New York and the first Roman Catholic candidate for the presidency.

Dedicated in 1836, St. James is one of the oldest Catholic churches in Manhattan and has unusually sophisticated architectural elements. But no one knows who designed it. Contemporary historians have punctured the once-common attribution to Minard Lafever. The structure was at one time topped by a domed cupola, perhaps to de-paganize the Greek temple front, on which was inscribed D.O.M. S. JACOBO DEO OPTIMO MAXIMO (To God, the Best and Greatest). In 1836, the first United States branch of the Ancient Order of Hibernians was organized here. A century and a half later, a citizens' group headed by Hibernians financed the restoration of St. James at a dire moment, after city officials ordered it closed in 1983 because the roof was in danger of collapsing.

St. James Church **[B57]**

St. James Lutheran Church. Lutherans in the nineteenth century were divided over whether services should be in German or English. The Rev. Frederick Christian Schaeffer organized an English-speaking congregation, St. James Lutheran Church, on Orange Street. In 1843, it moved to Mulberry Street and then, in 1857, to 216 East 15th Street [●E7], a building greatly altered by Otto L. Spannhake, in 1905, into the German Masonic Temple. It is now used by the Friends Seminary.

William A. Potter, the architect of the Chapel of St. Agnes and St. Martin's Episcopal Church, designed a small but richly Richardsonian sanctuary at 902 Madison Avenue [L8], built in 1889/1890. It was filled with Tiffany decorative work inside and overshadowed outside by the 50-room home of Louis Comfort Tiffany; indeed, it almost looked like a forecourt to the Tiffany residence. In 1938, St. James merged with Holy Trinity Lutheran Church and moved to 3 West 65th Street, at Central Park West [●K24☆], drawing a historical circle closed, since Holy Trinity had seceded 70 years earlier from St. James.

St. James Lutheran Church [L8]

St. James Presbyterian Church
[I14]

St. James Presbyterian Church [S20]

St. Jean Baptiste Roman Catholic Church [N44]

St. James Presbyterian Church. It is a splendid Gothic tableau: in the foreground, the ornate tower of St. James Presbyterian Church, a bit of Neuschwanstein fantasy; high on the hill beyond, over the treetops of St. Nicholas Park, the spires of City College.

St. James is as important an institution historically as it is a commanding presence architecturally, descended from one of the earliest black congregations in New York. It was founded in 1895 at the Odd Fellows Hall on West 32nd Street by members of the former Shiloh Presbyterian Church. St. James moved to 211 West 32nd Street but was displaced by Pennsylvania Station. In 1903, it took over the West Fifty-first Street Presbyterian Church, at 359 West 51st Street [I14]. Then it moved to Harlem and into a lovely new church by Ludlow & Peabody at 59 West 137th Street [●T20], dedicated in 1915. This is now Rendall Memorial Presbyterian Church.

St. James moved to its present home, 409 West 141st Street [●S20☆], in 1927. Designed by Ludlow & Valentine, it was built in 1904/1905 as the Lenox Presbyterian Church, which had been at 310 West 139th Street [●S26]. The Lenox congregation changed its name to St. Nicholas Avenue Presbyterian and merged in 1927 into North Presbyterian Church. During St. James's first decades on West 141st Street, it was led by the Rev. William Lloyd Imes, whom the Rev. Adam Clayton Powell Jr. described as having "the mind of a scholar, the soul of a saint, the heart of a brother, the tongue of a prophet and the hand of a militant."

Dorothy Maynor, the wife of the pastor, the Rev. Shelby Rooks, was an operatic soprano who was barred from a career in opera because of her race, though she was a famous recitalist. In 1964, she founded the Harlem School of the Arts in the basement of St. James, teaching piano to a dozen children. The school is now housed in a building north of the church, by Ulrich Franzen & Associates, attended by 3,000 children and adults annually.

St. Jean Baptiste Roman Catholic Church. Although this twin-towered structure could nobly crown the Spanish Steps in Rome, it is descended from humble roots. When the French Canadians of Yorkville joined to worship in 1882 as St. Jean Baptiste Roman Catholic Church, they had to use a stable at 202 East 77th Street that now is a Housing Works thrift shop. Their next home, by Napoleon Le Brun, was built from 1882 to 1885 at 159 East 76th Street [N44]. In 1892, St. Jean became a shrine to St. Anne, with the presentation of a relic from Sainte-Anne-de-Beaupré in Quebec. When Thomas Fortune Ryan, a financier and street railway monopolist, had to stand in the church one day because there was no room, he is said to have asked the Rev. Arthur Letellier how much a new building would cost. The priest answered, at least $300,000. "Very well," said Ryan. "Have your plans made, and I will pay for the church." The result was the present sanctuary by Nicholas Serracino, built from 1912 to 1914 at 184 East 76th Street [●N47★], with a 175-foot-high dome. Under the Rev. John A. Kamas, the church undertook a renovation in the 1990s, made possible by the sale of air rights to the adjacent Siena apartment tower. The once somber interior was redecorated by Felix Chavez in vivid colors that play off the newly vibrant windows, restored by Patrick Clark.

St. Jean Baptiste Roman Catholic Church [N47]

St. John A.M.E. Church [R12]

St. Joachim, Church of. The Romanesque tower of the Roman Catholic Church of St. Joachim, at 22 Roosevelt Street [B56], built in 1888 for an Italian parish, was a harbinger for Judson Memorial Church.

St. John A.M.E. Church. Arrow-headed windows mark this sanctuary at 132 West 134th Street [●T29]. Once part of a row, it was altered in 1917 by Joseph C. Cocker for the Metropolitan A.M.E. Church. St. John African Methodist Episcopal Church, founded in 1919, previously worshiped at 72 East 128th Street [R12], originally a Lutheran church and later the Church of God in Christ.

St. John A.M.E. Church [T29]

St. John's Baptist Church. Since 1932, St. John's Baptist Church, founded in 1917 by the Rev. Wilson Major Morris, has made its home in an elaborate old house, at 448 West 152nd Street [●S1☆], built in 1887 by James B. Gillie to designs by M. V. B. Ferdon.

St. John's Baptist Church [S1]

St. John's Chapel. *See* Trinity Church

St. John's Evangelical Lutheran Church
[D14]

St. John's Evangelical Lutheran Church. Hiding in plain sight on a raucous Greenwich Village thoroughfare, at 81 Christopher Street [●D14☆], is the sixth oldest house of worship in Manhattan, built in 1821/1822 as the Eighth Presbyterian Church. You might be fooled at first by some of the Victorian gewgaws added in 1886 by Berg & Clark, but the essential form is a three-bay, gabled barn, like its contemporaries.

The Presbyterians built their church where the first Lutheran seminary classes had been held in the 1790s. They relinquished the property in 1842 to St. Matthew's Episcopal Church, which was here until 1858, when the building was turned over to the German Lutherans, who inscribed the pediment: DEUTSCHE EVANGELISCH-LUTHERISCHE ST. JOHANNES KIRCHE. While the principal German area was east of the Bowery, there was also a community in Greenwich Village that all but disappeared after World War I.

St. John's in the Village **[D8]**

St. John's in the Village **[D9]**

St. John's in the Village. The modest recall of Greek Revival in this modern Episcopal church at 220 West 11th Street [●D9☆] is deliberate, for it replaces just such a gem. The parish is descended from St. Jude's Free Episcopal Church, which worshiped in what is now the Waverly Theater until 1853. Reorganized as St. John the Evangelist, the parish took possession in 1856 of the Hammond Street Presbyterian Church [D8☆], built 10 years earlier. (Hammond was the name of 11th Street.) Congregationalists followed the Presbyterians, and Baptists followed the Congregationalists. As the South Baptist Church, it was expanded along Factory Street, now Waverly Place, with the addition in 1854 of a Greek Revival parish house at no. 224. Gardens behind the church and adjoining properties created a midblock common, St. John's Colony. In 1971, St. John's in the Village burned down. Its Ionic columns were made of wood, and a fire chief called it a "lumberyard." In re-creating it, Edgar Tafel, a protégé of Frank Lloyd Wright, evoked Greek Revival style and massing in a modern vernacular. The new church, built from 1972 to 1974, presents a windowless pedimented facade, with inscribed panels to suggest an octastyle portico. It kindly complements the parish hall, which survived the fire and is connected to the new church.

St. John Nepomucene Church. Bad King Wenceslas had John of Nepomuk, Bohemia, thrown into the river. Five hundred years later, in 1895, this Slovak Roman Catholic parish—Slovensky Kostol Sv. Jana Nepomuckeho—was founded. In its early years, it worshiped at 289 East 4th Street [●F28], now the Iglesia Pentecostal Camino a Damasco, and then at 350 East 57th Street [L49], formerly Congregations Adath Israel and Shaarey Beracha. The present sanctuary of St. John Nepomucene Church, at 411 East 66th Street [●L23], was completed in 1925 to designs by John V. Van Pelt, architect of the Church of the Guardian Angel. At both, Van Pelt mixed building materials randomly, creating an unusual sense of antiquity. In the tympanum, the figure of John holds fingers to lips, a reference to the legend that he perished because he would not divulge to Wenceslas the queen's confession of adultery. (The Bohemian church of St. John of Nepomucene, now called St. John the Martyr, is at 252 East 72nd Street.)

St. John Nepomucene Church **[L23]**

St. John's Pentecostal Church **[R1]**

St. John's Pentecostal Church. The sanctuary at 440 Malcolm X Boulevard [●R1] that is now home to St. John's Pentecostal Church was once the Franklin Theater cinema.

St. John the Baptist, Church of. Among the more powerful churches by a master of ecclesiastical architecture, Napoleon Le Brun, is the Church of St. John the Baptist. The parish was organized in 1840 to serve German Catholics. Its first home, on West 31st Street, burned in 1847. Its second home, at 125 West 30th Street, closed in 1870. The parish was then placed under the Order of Friars Minor Capuchin. The cornerstone for Le Brun's church, at 207 West 30th Street [●G23], was laid in 1871. It was dedicated in 1872, but obscured 60 years later by the adjacent Pennsylvania Terminal Building, a 17-story office tower.

Church of St. John the Baptist
[G23]

Greek Orthodox Church of St. John the Baptist **[H63]**

Leake and Watts Orphan Asylum **[O3]**

Cathedral Church of St. John the Divine (Heins & La Farge) **[O3]**

Cathedral Church of St. John the Divine (Ralph Adams Cram) **[O3]**

St. John the Baptist, Greek Orthodox Church of. The very simple yellow-brick Greek Orthodox Church of St. John the Baptist, at 143 East 17th Street **[●H63]**, once had a Baroque facade, designed in 1885 by Schwarzmann & Buchman. It was altered in 1957 by Kyriacos A. Kalfas.

St. John the Divine, Cathedral Church of. Gothic in every sense, the Cathedral Church of St. John the Divine is as much saga as structure, though there is quite a lot of structure. Wandering among the giant columns of one of the world's largest cathedrals is an experience akin to an awe-struck journey through a grove of sequoias. But after 112 years—and counting—it is far from finished.

As the towers of St. Patrick's Cathedral rose in the 1880s, Episcopalians who had long enjoyed a sense of preeminence in New York resolved to build something grander. The 13-acre campus of the Leake and Watts Orphan Asylum suggested itself as part of a modern acropolis, with Columbia University and St. Luke's Hospital. (The asylum itself, an 1843 Greek Revival temple by Ithiel Town, still stands.) Many of the nation's leading architects competed for the cathedral commission: J. C. Cady & Company; Carrère & Hastings; Bertram Grosvenor Goodhue; Richard Morris Hunt; Potter & Robertson; Renwick, Aspinwall & Russell; Richard M. Upjohn. But it was won in 1891 by George L. Heins and Grant La Farge, who later designed the first subway stations. Their plans called for a Romanesque–Gothic hybrid structure, with an enormous cimborio over the crossing.

From 1894 to 1903, the former Church of the Epiphany, at 130 Stanton Street **[F44]**, was designated the Pro-Cathedral. The construction of St. John the Divine on Amsterdam Avenue **[●O3]** began on St. John's Day, December 27, 1892. (Divine, incidentally, is not an adjective to describe this saint; it is a noun, meaning St. John the Theologian.) The building was about one-third complete in 1911, including the 55-foot granite apsidal columns, when La Farge was replaced by Ralph Adams Cram, the ultimate Gothicist.

The implementation of Cram's revised Gothic

design began in 1916. The building was extended by 81 feet, to 601 feet. The west front, the baptistery, and part of the north transept were built. On November 30, 1941, the opening of the interior was celebrated. But construction ceased after the attack on Pearl Harbor on the following Sunday, December 7, and did not begin again until 1979, under Bishop Paul Moore Jr. and the Very Rev. James Parks Morton. At the Cathedral Stoneworks on the grounds of St. John the Divine, journeymen from England trained local residents as stonecutters. The 150-foot south tower began to rise toward its intended 300-foot height. There was even bold talk of completing the south transept as a biosphere designed by Santiago Calatrava. But as the cathedral entered its second century, money ran out and the stoneworks went bankrupt. The south tower had reached 200 feet.

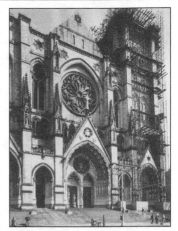

Cathedral Church of St. John the Divine **[O3]**

Furthering the unending drama was a fire on December 18, 2001, that destroyed the gift shop, damaged the north transept, and consumed two seventeenth-century tapestries, though firefighters kept the flames from reaching the roof. For a city just beginning to recover from a devastating terrorist attack, it seemed a crippling blow. But the cathedral managed to open—the smell of smoke still in the air—for the Christmas Eve Eucharist, attended by Senator Hillary Rodham Clinton and her husband, former President Bill Clinton. (There is a chilling augury of September 11 in the Portal of Paradise, carved from 1988 to 1997 by Simon Verity and Jean Claude Marchionni: a statuary pedestal showing the World Trade Center toppling under a cloud of smoke.)

Cathedral Church of St. John the Divine (apsidal facade) **[O3]**

The cathedral trustees are exploring a plan to develop the edges of the grounds, known as the Close, working with Columbia University to build something like a medieval village with the cathedral at the center. They agreed to accept landmark designation of the main building, though neighbors and preservationists, who wanted the entire Close made a landmark, persuaded the City Council to overturn the designation in 2003, since it was not all-encompassing. So the saga continues.

Portal of Paradise **[O3]**

Church of St. John the Evangelist [J20]

Church of St. John the Evangelist [J4]

Church of St. John the Evangelist [J5]

St. John the Evangelist, Church of. Modern bas-relief sculptural panels at the base of an otherwise nondescript office tower at 1011 First Avenue [● J5] scarcely hint that this Roman Catholic parish has a history that can be traced back almost two centuries and was interwoven with the development of St. Patrick's Cathedral.

The story began with the purchase in 1810 by the Rev. Anthony Kohlmann of a large countryside tract bordered by Fourth (Park) and Fifth Avenues, and East 50th and East 51st Streets—not yet divided by Madison Avenue. On the land was a mansion that housed a Jesuit college and chapel, dedicated to St. Ignatius. The college closed after three years, and the property was acquired by St. Peter's Church and St. Patrick's Cathedral, on Mulberry Street, for use as a burial ground. The chapel reopened in 1840 as the Church of St. John the Evangelist, which soon moved into a frame sanctuary on a Fifth Avenue lot [J18] that had been excised from the planned cemetery, at the corner of 50th Street. Its parishioners included workers at the nearby Deaf and Dumb Asylum.

As plans were drawn up for a new St. Patrick's on Fifth Avenue, St. John built a sanctuary in 1859 on the east side of Madison Avenue [J19]. A large successor church [J20] was built in 1871, with the intention that it would be converted into a boys' parochial school after the cathedral was completed. In 1881, however, the cathedral sold the land under St. John to Henry Villard, on condition that "no other than first-class private dwellings should be erected." McKim, Mead & White designed exactly such an ensemble. Closing the circle, the Villard Houses were acquired by the archdiocese in 1946 and turned into offices and residences for clergy.

St. John, meanwhile, built a Gothic church at 351 East 55th Street [J4] from 1881 to 1886. In 1971, the archdiocese announced that it would move from the Villard Houses to a tower on the site of St. John. The 20-story Catholic Center by Ferrenz & Taylor opened in 1974 with a new Cathedral Girls' High School and a new sanctuary for St. John the Evangelist, which once again had given way to the greater needs of the archdiocese.

St. John the Martyr, Church of. Even at a modest scale, the confident hand of R. H. Robertson can be seen in this Romanesque sanctuary at 252 East 72nd Street [●L12], built in 1887 as the Knox Presbyterian Church. In 1904, it was acquired by a Bohemian Roman Catholic parish founded a year earlier as St. John of Nepomucene and now known as St. John the Martyr.

Church of St. John the Martyr **[L12]**

St. Joseph, Church of. Visible over the tenement landscape of the Lower East Side are the twin domed towers of this Roman Catholic sanctuary—San Giuseppe— at 5 Monroe Street [●C27], designed by Matthew W. Del Gaudio. Built in 1924 to serve an Italian population, St. Joseph is now designated an Italian and Chinese parish.

St. Joseph, Church of. The second oldest purpose-built Roman Catholic parish church in Manhattan is the Church of St. Joseph, at 371 Avenue of the Americas [●E47☆], a robust Greek Revival temple whose randomly coursed fieldstone side walls hint at its considerable age. The building was designed by John Doran and erected in 1833/1834 for a parish founded in 1829. Catholics regarded the new St. Joseph proudly, since it was second in size only to St. Patrick's Cathedral, on Mulberry Street. And it served a large territory: from Canal Street to 20th Street, Broadway west to the Hudson River. (To give some idea of its scope, by the late 1870s, the same territory was also served by the Churches of St. Alphonsus Liguori, St. Anthony of Padua, St. Bernard, and St. Francis Xavier.) Fire damaged St. Joseph in 1885, after which the building was renovated by Arthur Crooks. The parish supported St. Joseph's Half Orphan Asylum in a building later used by St. Vincent's Hospital. And it was the cradle in the nineteenth century of the Accademia movement, whose members questioned the inerrancy of Scripture, papal infallibility, priestly celibacy, vestments, the Latin liturgy, and the suitability of nuns to teach future wives and mothers. It first met at St. Joseph under the Rev. Thomas Farrell, who was also responsible by his bequest for the creation of New York's first church for black Catholics: St. Benedict the Moor.

Church of St. Joseph **[C27]**

Church of St. Joseph **[E47]**

St. Joseph's Asylum Chapel **[N7]**

Church of St. Joseph [N14]

Church of St. Joseph **[N15]**

St. Joseph, Church of. On the side of a modern apartment building at 402 East 90th Street **[●N7]** is a remarkable palimpsest: a three-dimensional, Neoclassical facade with pediments, pilasters, keystones, and arched window openings. This was once the chapel of St. Joseph's Asylum, which cared for poor orphans. The chapel, designed by Anthony F. A. Schmitt, served neighboring Catholics, many of them German. The parish of St. Joseph was organized in 1873, taking the name of the asylum. Its first church was built in 1873/1874 on East 87th Street [N14], designed by Lawrence J. O'Connor. It was replaced by the present Church of St. Joseph, at 408 East 87th Street **[●N15]**, by William Schickel & Company, constructed in 1895.

St. Joseph's Chapel. *See* St. Peter's Church

St. Joseph Maronite Church. St. Joseph Maronite Church, for Syrian Catholics, was organized in 1890 under the Rev. Butros Korkemas and opened its own sanctuary at 57 Washington Street [A36] in 1916. "At all hours devotees can be found kneeling and prostrating themselves, very much in the Moslem manner, before the candy-white decorative altars," Konrad Bercovici wrote in 1924, describing scenes that "make one think of the beginnings of Christianity."

St. Joseph of the Holy Family, Church of. The oldest existing church in Harlem—indeed, the oldest existing church north of 44th Street—is a modest Romanesque sanctuary at 405 West 125th Street **[●Q26]**. Constructed before the Civil War, it is a reminder of how deep Harlem's history runs. The parish was founded in 1860 for German Catholics, and the red-brick Church of St. Joseph of the Holy Family was dedicated the same year. The building was enlarged in 1871 and altered again in 1889 by Herter Brothers. The window over the entrance was turned into a statuary niche for St. Joseph, who can be seen standing over 125th Street with the infant Jesus in his arms. For a time, an affiliated school and convent were housed in the former Manhattanville Presbyterian Church, a Greek Revival sanctuary directly behind St. Joseph.

St. Jude, Church of. Brutalist architecture in the service of sanctuaries often seems a paradoxical impulse. But in the Church of St. Jude, at 3815 Tenth Avenue [●W7], it frankly acknowledges a tough setting, across from a Gaseteria and under rumbling El tracks. This Spanish Roman Catholic parish, also known as San Judas, was founded in 1949. Two years later, Voorhees, Walker, Foley & Smith filed plans for a church and school on West 204th Street [●W6]. A jazzy mosaic, worthy almost of Stuart Davis, adorns the rectory. The firm Clark & Warren filed plans in 1975 for the Tenth Avenue sanctuary, in which a massive concrete entablature wraps around a red-brick wall, with huge diagonal incisions at the corner to mark the entrances. It is hard to like but possible to respect as an effort to express sacred architecture in a modern idiom.

Church of St. Joseph of the Holy Family **[Q26]**

SS. Kiril and Methodi Bulgarian Eastern Orthodox Diocesan Cathedral. Sometimes, it seems, the smaller the sanctuary, the longer the roster of congregations that have used it. This building at 552 West 50th Street [●I17] was the home of a Lutheran church; then the Church of St. Clemens Mary, before that Roman Catholic parish moved to 410 West 40th Street; and then, for almost 60 years, the Church of SS. Cyril and Methodius, before that Croatian Catholic parish moved in with the Church of St. Raphael, at 502 West 41st Street. SS. Kiril and Methodi Bulgarian Eastern Orthodox Diocesan Cathedral, where services are conducted in Church Slavonic and Bulgarian, had been at 312 West 101st Street for 40 years before moving here in 1979, under Metropolitan Joseph.

Church of St. Jude **[W7]**

St. Leo, Church of. This Roman Catholic parish was organized in 1880. That year, Lawrence J. O'Connor filed plans for the church at 11 East 28th Street [H23], with a prominent Gothic tracery window and slender side tower. Under the Rev. Thomas J. Ducey in the late nineteenth century, the Church of St. Leo was for a time favored by some of the city's wealthiest and most prominent Catholic families. The building later served as the chapel of the convent of Mary Reparatrix. Its site is now the plaza of the Madison Belvedere apartment tower.

SS. Kiril and Methodi Bulgarian Eastern Orthodox Diocesan Cathedral **[I17]**

Church of St. Lucy **[P23]**

St. Lucy, Church of. The church at 338 East 104th Street [●P23] was built for an Italian Roman Catholic parish founded in 1900 out of Our Lady of Mount Carmel. The first architects were Lynch & Combs, but only a basement was finished by 1914 when a new church was designed by Thomas J. Duff. Now mostly Hispanic—the Marian Shrine has a statue of Nuestra Señora de la Providencia, patron of Puerto Rico—the Church of St. Lucy is administered by St. Francis de Sales.

St. Luke A.M.E. Church **[U25]**

St. Luke A.M.E. Church. There may be no better place to sense the bucolic past of Washington Heights than in front of this piece of Victorian Gothic gingerbread at 1872 Amsterdam Avenue [●U25], the oldest church north of 125th Street, set against the verdant backdrop of Trinity Cemetery. It was dedicated in 1869 as the Washington Heights Methodist Episcopal Church. St. Luke African Methodist Episcopal Church was founded in 1926 and, before moving here in 1946, worshiped at 139 West 126th Street, a parlorfront sanctuary that later served the LaGree Baptist Church.

St. Luke Baptist Church
[Q32]

St. Luke Baptist Church. The building at 103 Morningside Avenue [●Q32] has served the Universal Holy Temple of Tranquillity, the Knights of Columbus, and the Southern Baptist Church. St. Luke Baptist Church was founded in 1937.

St. Luke's Church. This mountainous sanctuary on a steep embankment, at 435 West 141st Street [●S19☆], is like a cathedral in an Italian hill town. St. Luke's Church descends from the Church of St. Luke in the Fields. After a fire at the Greenwich Village sanctuary in 1886, the congregation moved uptown. Looking for temporary quarters, the Rev. Isaac H. Tuttle found a weathered but distinguished old house on Convent Avenue that turned out to be the Grange, Alexander Hamilton's country home in the first years of the nineteenth century. The house was moved a block and a half south to the present site and served as chapel and rectory. It is now the Hamilton Grange National Memorial, sitting in the big embrace of the front porch of the church, designed by R. H. Robertson and built

St. Luke's Church **[S19]**

in 1891/1892. St. Luke's merged with St. Martin's Episcopal Church in 1942 under the Rev. John Howard Johnson. The rectorate passed in turn to his sons, the Rev. David Johnson and the Rev. Johan Johnson.

St. Luke's Hospital Chapel. A stained-glass window on the West 114th Street facade reveals the presence of the St. Luke's Hospital Chapel, a central feature of Ernest Flagg's design for this Episcopal-affiliated hospital on Amsterdam Avenue [●Q44], built in 1896.

St. Luke's Hospital Chapel [Q44]

St. Luke in the Fields, Church of. The country village of Greenwich served in the early nineteenth century as a haven from yellow fever. Honoring Luke, the physician Evangelist, Episcopal villagers founded the church in 1820. Clement Clarke Moore drew up a plan, but the building contract was given to John Heath. Both have been credited with the Church of St. Luke in the Fields, built in 1821/1822 at 487 Hudson Street [●D17☆], as has James N. Wells. After a fire in 1886, the congregation moved to Convent Avenue. The Hudson Street sanctuary became the Chapel of St. Luke, a mission of Trinity Church, in 1891, but gained independence as a parish in 1976, so there are now two Episcopal St. Lukes. Fire struck again in 1981, gutting the building ruinously. But under the Rev. Ledlie I. Laughlin Jr., St. Luke rebuilt, to designs by Hardy Holzman Pfeiffer Associates, and was reconsecrated in 1985. With its embrace of gay Villagers, the parish was hard hit by AIDS. Fittingly, its chaste sanctuary was the setting of a memorial service in the movie *Longtime Companion*. Its lush, labyrinthine 2-acre garden is open to the public, a great gift of verdant tranquillity.

Church of St. Luke in the Fields [D17]

St. Luke's Lutheran Church [I42]

St. Luke's Lutheran Church. Can Gothic and Deco marry and find happiness? They can, as this sanctuary at 308 West 46th Street [●I29] on Restaurant Row attests. Founded in 1850, St. Luke's Lutheran Church moved in 1875 to 233 West 42nd Street [I42], the former Forty-second Street Presbyterian Church. The present sanctuary, by Tilton & Githens, was completed in 1923. The nave facade is virtually all window, designed by F. X. Zettler.

St. Luke's Lutheran Church [I29]

St. Luke Methodist Church. A Congregational church at 108 West 41st Street [I47] was rebuilt as St. Luke Methodist Church in 1872. Used as a sanctuary until 1899, it became the Shuberts' Comedy Theater.

St. Malachy's Church **[I19]**

St. Malachy's Church. Its chimes played "There's No Business Like Show Business" and its pastor, the Rev. George Washington Moore Jr., was awarded a special Tony in 1991. Ever since the 1920s, when it was the setting for the funeral of Rudolph Valentino and the wedding of Douglas Fairbanks Jr. to Joan Crawford, St. Malachy's Church, at 239 West 49th Street [●I19], has been closely identified with Broadway. The Roman Catholic parish was founded in 1902 and soon had a basement sanctuary. Plans for the main church were filed in 1910 by Thomas J. Duff. The Actors' Chapel was constructed in 1920. Its pews have been occupied by Fred Allen, Don Ameche, George M. Cohan, Perry Como, Irene Dunne, Jimmy Durante, Sir Alec Guinness, Florence Henderson, Hildegarde, Bob Hope, Ricardo Montalban, Pat O'Brien, Carol O'Connor, Cyril Ritchard, Rosalind Russell, Danny Thomas, and Spencer Tracy. Under Moore, St. Malachy's expanded its mission to the elderly, poor, homeless and homebound.

St. Mark's Church in-the-Bowery
(Stuyvesant vault) **[E35]**

St. Mark's Church in-the-Bowery. "I don't know if the East Village is 'way out' because of St. Mark's or if St. Mark's is 'way out' because of the East Village," Bishop Paul Moore Jr. said in 1986. "But certainly the church and the neighborhood share a free spirit." Built before the gridiron street plan was implemented, St. Mark's Church in-the-Bowery does not even conform to Manhattan's orthogonal layout. Instead, it sits on crooked Stuyvesant Street, remnant of the road that led to the farm, or *bouwerie*, to which Director-General Peter Stuyvesant retired after New Amsterdam surrendered to the British. Here he built a chapel [E35] in 1660 and was buried in 1672 (in a vault whose location is marked on the east wall of the present church), after which the chapel fell into disuse and decay.

In 1793, Stuyvesant's grandson offered the site [●E36★] for an Episcopal church. St. Mark's was begun in 1795 and finished in 1799, making it the second oldest church building in Manhattan. Atop the Georgian structure, a Greek Revival steeple by Ithiel Town was erected in 1828. The Italianate cast-iron portico was added in 1854.

St. Mark's built a memorial chapel and parish house in 1883 at 288 East 10th Street [●F10], by James Renwick Jr. and W. H. Russell. Now St. Nicholas of Myra Orthodox Church, it overlooks Tompkins Square Park, named after Daniel Tompkins, James Monroe's vice president, who is buried at St. Mark's, as are Colonel Nicholas Fish and Mayor Philip Hone. The churchyard on Stuyvesant Street was to have been the site of St. Mark's Towers, three Frank Lloyd Wright apartment buildings commissioned by the Rev. William Norman Guthrie, who also commissioned from Wright the 1,500-foot "Steel Cathedral including Minor Cathedrals for a Million People" for an unspecified site in New York. While Guthrie's building projects were never realized, he had a profound effect on St. Mark's, exploring in ritual the notion of the unity of religion. The church attracted, as parishioners or visitors, W. H. Auden, Ted Berrigan, Isadora Duncan, Kahlil Gibran, Allen Ginsberg, Martha Graham, Vachel Lindsay, Robert Lowell, Edna St. Vincent Millay, and Sam Shepard. It welcomed Theater Genesis and the Danspace Project.

Fire ravaged St. Mark's in 1978, but it was restored under the Rev. David A. Garcia, to designs by the Edelman Partnership, and reopened in 1983. The rectory at 232 East 11th Street, by Ernest Flagg, was rebuilt in 1999 as the Neighborhood Preservation Center.

St. Mark's Church in-the-Bowery **[E36]**

St. Mark the Evangelist, Church of. The first Catholic parish for blacks in northern Manhattan was founded in 1907 as an outgrowth of All Saints Church. Its sanctuary, the Church of St. Mark the Evangelist, at 65 West 138th Street [●T14], was designed by George F. Pelham and built in 1907/1908. It began serving African-American parishioners in 1912, under the care of the Holy Ghost Fathers. What looks like a little Romanesque church next door is the pre-kindergarten Montessori program of St. Mark's School.

Church of St. Mark the Evangelist **[T14]**

St. Mark's Methodist Episcopal Church [H2]

St. Mark's United Methodist Church [S27]

Church of San Martín (The Cloisters)
[W11]

St. Martin's Episcopal Church [R38]

St. Mark's United Methodist Church. St. Mark's United Methodist Church looms into view at the confluence of Edgecombe and St. Nicholas Avenues, bringing to mind the cliff-side Gothic of West Point, and its finials are echoed in the City College campus up the hill. Like so many older black churches, St. Mark's traces in its own journey the dislocation of the African-American community from the Tenderloin in midtown, to San Juan Hill on the West Side, to Harlem.

Founded in 1871 out of Mother A.M.E. Zion Church by the Rev. William Butler, St. Mark's worshiped at 65 West 35th Street [H2], the former Church of the Resurrection, and then moved to the former All Souls' Church, at 139 West 48th Street [I22]. Its next sanctuary, at 231 West 53rd Street [I8], was the former St. John's Methodist, designed by D. & J. Jardine and built in 1870. St. Mark's was there until 1926. (Much later, this was the site of Studio 54.) The present church, at 49 Edgecombe Avenue [●S27], by Sibley & Fetherston, was built from 1921 to 1926. St. Mark's was the mother church of Salem United Methodist Church in Harlem and congregations in the Bronx and Queens.

San Martín, Church of. St. Martin gazes serenely from the apse, as he has for eight and a half centuries, ever since San Martín was built on a hillside in the village of Fuentidueña, about 100 miles north of Madrid. In 1957, after two decades of negotiations, the Spanish government agreed to lend indefinitely the surviving portion of the ruined church to The Cloisters [●W11★], which houses much of the medieval art in the collection of the Metropolitan Museum of Art. The apse was dismantled into 3,300 stones, shipped to America, and reerected in 1961 as the Fuentidueña Chapel.

St. Martin's Episcopal Church. This Episcopal complex at 230 Malcolm X Boulevard [●R38★] is Manhattan's best extant work of Richardsonian Romanesque design. Two others by the same architect, William A. Potter—the Chapel of St. Agnes and St. James Lutheran Church—were lost.

The Harlem grouping was built in 1887/1888 for Holy Trinity Church, which merged in 1927 with the

Church of the Holy Redeemer in Inwood. The buildings were taken over by St. Martin's Episcopal Church, a black congregation organized in 1928 by the Rev. John Howard Johnson, who was also a leader in the fight to integrate the stores of 125th Street under the banner "Don't buy where you can't work."

St. Martin's became a full parish in 1940 and merged with St. Luke's Church two years later. Among its members were the artist Romare Bearden and Robert L. Douglas, owner of the all-black Renaissance basketball team. In 1949, the church bought a 42-bell carillon from the Van Bergen foundry in the Netherlands, prompting a visit from Queen Juliana herself in 1952. Contrasted to the carillon across town at Riverside Church, given by the Rockefellers, these are proudly called the "poor people's bells" by the Rev. David Johnson, John Johnson's son. By the end of the 1990s, however, for want of a carillonneur and the money to keep the tower in good repair, the bells went silent.

Church of St. Mary (original facade) [C13]

St. Mary, Church of. What is the "oldest" Catholic church in Manhattan? St. Peter's Church has worshiped on the same site since 1786, but in two buildings. The Church of the Transfiguration dates to 1801, but the building was originally an Episcopal church. Old St. Patrick's was finished in 1815, but as a cathedral. The Church of St. Mary, therefore, qualifies: its cornerstone was laid in 1832, and it was dedicated in June 1833. The parish was founded in 1826 and worshiped on Sheriff Street [C17] in the former Seventh Presbyterian Church. The Greek Revival facade of the present sanctuary, at 440 Grand Street [●C13], was turned Romanesque by Patrick C. Keely in 1864, with more work by Lawrence J. O'Connor in 1871. But the fieldstone side walls are still visible.

Church of St. Mary (present facade) **[C13]**

St. Mary's American Orthodox Greek Catholic Church. The Slavic cross gives away this sanctuary at 121 East 7th Street [●F15] as an Orthodox church. Altered in 1902 by John P. Voelker, it served the First Hungarian Reformed Church. It was later the Resurrection Greek Catholic Church and the Eastern Orthodox Church of SS. Peter and Paul before becoming home to St. Mary's American Orthodox Greek Catholic Church.

St. Mary's American Orthodox Greek Catholic Church **[F15]**

St. Mary's Catholic Church of the Byzantine Rite [E15]

St. Mary's Catholic Church of the Byzantine Rite. The most startling of the four houses of worship around Stuyvesant Square is a Modernist jewel box at 246 East 15th Street [●E8], built in 1964 with a tower of glistening metal strands that reach up flame-like, whipped and wrapped around the bell. Founded in 1912, St. Mary's is Catholic but not Roman. It follows the Byzantine Rite of the Church of Constantinople (Byzantium). It occupied a Gothic sanctuary at 225 East 13th Street [E15] that was the Welsh Presbyterian Church in the late nineteenth century. In 1959, St. Mary's filed plans for a new building on East 15th Street. The architect was the Rev. Cajetan J. B. Baumann, a former cabinetmaker and sculptor who was both OFM (Order of Friars Minor, or Franciscan) and FAIA (Fellow of the American Institute of Architects).

St. Mary's Catholic Church of the Byzantine Rite [E8]

St. Mary Magdalene, Church of. The Church of St. Mary Magdalene, at 529 East 17th Street [H66], served a German Catholic parish that was founded in 1873.

St. Mary the Virgin, Church of. Something very innovative undergirds the Gothic masonry of the Episcopal Church of St. Mary the Virgin. This structural pioneer was one of the first churches with a skeletal-steel framework. Steel was useful because the building had to carry a heavy symbolic load. St. Mary the Virgin is a leader in Anglo-Catholicism, the ritual-rich evocation of pre-Reformation liturgy and architecture. (Its use of incense inspired the fondly irreverent nickname Smoky Mary's.) The first church, by William Hallett, was dedicated in 1870 at 228 West 45th Street [I32]. This was later the Lutheran Church of the Redeemer and the Fifth Church of Christ, Scientist. The present complex, at 139 West 46th Street [●I28★], was built in 1894/1895 to designs by Pierre Le Brun of Napoleon Le Brun & Sons. The use of steel allowed many functions to be squeezed into the midblock site, which runs to West 47th Street, with room left over for a lofty and impressive sanctuary. In 1996/1997, under the Rev. Canon Edgar F. Wells, the church underwent a restoration designed by J. Lawrence Jones & Associates. The 80-foot ceiling was painted deep blue with golden stars. To step under that sky is to leave mid-Manhattan's tumult far behind.

Church of St. Mary the Virgin [I32]

Church of St. Mary the Virgin [I28]

St. Mary's–Manhattanville, Church of. Across from the Twenty-sixth Precinct is a sweet evocation of country-side life, an Episcopal parish dating to the days of Manhattanville. Its first sanctuary was built from 1824 to 1826, to plans by Robert Oughton, at what is now 521 West 126th Street [Q2], with a parsonage added in 1851. The present Church of St. Mary's–Manhattanville [●Q3★] was built in 1908/1909. The architect was Theodore E. Blake of Carrère & Hastings. St. Mary's was one of the first parishes to abolish pew rentals in the nineteenth century, and it cut a progressive profile in the 1980s and 1990s under the Rev. Robert W. Castle, a forceful social activist. On his watch, the former Speyer School across the street was turned into a 40-bed shelter for homeless people with AIDS.

Church of St. Mary's–Manhattanville [Q2]

Church of St. Mary's–Manhattanville **[Q3]**

St. Matthew, Evangelical Lutheran Church of. You might not think of searching as far uptown as 202 Sherman Avenue [●W3] for "America's Oldest Lutheran Church," chartered in 1664—after all, shouldn't it be somewhere in lower Manhattan?—but here it is nonetheless: "rich in heritage," as its president said in 1998, but today "a poor inner-city congregation serving the poor."

Unable to make headway under the Dutch, Lutherans secured a charter in 1664 when the English took over New York. In 1676, they built Trinity Church on Broadway [A34], two decades ahead of the nearby Episcopal church of the same name. Trinity Lutheran burned in 1776. In 1784, Trinity merged with Christ Church, which was known as the Swamp Church, on Frankfort Street [B62]. The combined congregation moved in 1826 to a sanctuary on Walker Street [B34] that had been built for St. Matthew's Church and, after doing so, adopted that name. As the Evangelical Lutheran Church of St. Matthew, the congregation moved to 354 Broome Street [B13] in 1868 and then jumped far uptown in 1906 to 421 West 145th Street [●S14], bringing along memorials to several pastors. The commemorative stones can still be seen outside Mount Zion Lutheran Church. The present St. Matthew, in Inwood, a Modernist A-frame with a rough-hewn wood cross, was designed in 1956 by Brown & Guenther.

Christ Church [B62]

Evangelical Lutheran Church of St. Matthew **[W3]**

Church of Zion and St. Timothy [K39]

Church of St. Matthew and
St. Timothy [M22]

St. Matthew's Baptist Church [T1]

St. Matthew and St. Timothy, Church of. Two centuries of history lie behind the inscrutably Brutalist facade of the Church of St. Matthew and St. Timothy, at 26 West 84th Street [●M22☆], beginning with Zion Church, founded in 1797 as a Lutheran congregation. It built a church at 25 Mott Street [B44] in 1801 and then converted en masse to Episcopalianism. Its sanctuary burned in 1815 and was rebuilt as the structure we see today [●B45★], now the Church of the Transfiguration. Zion moved in 1854 to 245 Madison Avenue [J55], designed by Frank Wills, where it was joined by the Church of the Atonement.

St. Timothy's Church was founded in 1853. It worshiped at 310 West 54th Street [I6], later Amity Baptist Church, and in a chapel on West 56th Street [K38] that opened in 1867.

Zion and St. Timothy merged in 1890 and, on the West 57th Street side of St. Timothy's chapel site [K39], built a fantastic Victorian Gothic sanctuary in 1891/1892, by William Halsey Wood.

Wood also designed St. Matthew's Church of 1894, at 26 West 84th Street [M21], for a parish founded in 1887. St. Matthew's merged in 1922 with Zion and St. Timothy to create the present body. The building burned in 1965 and was replaced two years later by a stark concrete sanctuary designed by Victor Christ-Janer & Associates.

St. Matthew's Baptist Church. St. Matthew's Baptist Church occupies a sprawling modern sanctuary at 43 Macombs Place [●T1], designed in 1963 by Donald F. White and dedicated in 1967 under the Rev. John J. Sass. The congregation was founded in 1925 by the Rev. Jerome D. Harris.

St. Matthew's Church. Cleared to create the Lincoln Towers superblock, the Roman Catholic St. Matthew's Church, at 215 West 67th Street [K17], was designed in 1903 by John J. Deery. The parish was founded in 1902.

St. Michael, Church of. The most unusual transportation associated with Pennsylvania Station had nothing to do with trains, but with the Romanesque Revival sanctuary of this Roman Catholic parish.

The Church of St. Michael was founded in 1857. From 1861 to 1868, it built a Gothic church on West 31st Street [G17] that burned down in 1892. Two years later, Archbishop Michael Corrigan dedicated a new sanctuary on the West 32nd Street side of the same lot [G18]. Unfortunately, in less than a decade this property was needed for the rail yard leading into the new Pennsylvania Station. Plans were filed by Napoleon Le Brun & Sons in 1905 for a series of church buildings at 414 West 34th Street [●G13] to be constructed by the Pennsylvania, New York & Long Island Rail Road Company. At a reported cost of $1 million (real money in those days), the railroad numbered every stone at St. Michael, took apart the church, and reassembled it on the new site. It was dedicated in 1907.

Church of St. Michael [G13]

St. Michael's Episcopal Church. This parish served the Upper West Side long before it was the Upper West Side, when it was the country village of Bloomingdale. The first St. Michael's Episcopal Church was built on the Bloomingdale Road [O21] in 1806/1807, followed by a Gothic structure made of oak on the same site [O22], built in 1853/1854. Until 1842, St. Michael's shared its rector with another country parish, St. James' Church, across the island. The present Romanesque sanctuary, at 225 West 99th Street [●O23], was completed in 1891 to designs by Robert W. Gibson. It occupies the site of the older churches and part of the Bloomingdale roadbed.

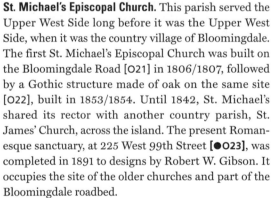

St. Michael's Episcopal Church [O22]

St. Michael's operated St. Jude's Chapel, designed by Ludlow & Peabody and built in 1921 at 19 West 99th Street [O25] as a mission to African-Americans.

The greatest of St. Michael's treasures is *St. Michael's Victory in Heaven*, a suite of 22-foot apsidal windows by Louis Comfort Tiffany and the Tiffany Glass and Decorating Company. Viewed together, the five windows form a unified composition, like celestial Cinerama. They were restored in the 1980s, but a protective glazing system turned out to cause problems of its own and so, under the Rev. Canon George W. Brandt Jr., the windows were re-restored.

St. Michael's Episcopal Church [O23]

St. Michael's Russian Catholic Church **[E87]**

Church of St. Monica **[N38]**

Collegiate Church of St. Nicholas [J25]

St. Michael's Russian Catholic Church. This delightful work of Gingerbread Gothic at 266 Mulberry Street [●E87★], built as a chancery in 1859, is a bridge between the two St. Patrick's Cathedrals, since it stands on the old grounds but was designed by the architects of the new cathedral: James Renwick Jr. and William Rodrigue. It has been St. Michael's Russian Catholic Church since 1936.

St. Monica, Church of. A Flamboyant window dominates the Roman Catholic Church of St. Monica, at 413 East 79th Street [●N38], finished in 1907 to designs by Schickel & Ditmars. The parish was founded in 1879.

St. Nicholas, Church of. A spiritual home of an American saint, John Nepomucene Neumann, the Gothic Revival Church of St. Nicholas, at 127 East 2nd Street [F42], was built in 1848. Founded in 1833 by the Rev. John Stephen Raffeiner, it was the first Roman Catholic church to minister specifically to Germans.

St. Nicholas, Collegiate Church of. More than half a century has elapsed since the demolition of the Collegiate Church of St. Nicholas, a landmark at 600 Fifth Avenue [J25], but one still mourns its loss. The congregation was intimately linked with New York history, and its sanctuary was a thrillingly original, almost Expressionistic work of Gothic architecture, with acutely battered and flying buttresses, a wildly disproportionate steeple, and a complex gabled roof scape that seem to have presaged the work of Antonio Gaudí. "It is simply Gothic gone roaring mad," said the critic Montgomery Schuyler. He meant no compliment, but he was quite right. Designed by W. Wheeler Smith, the church was built from 1869 to 1872. It was known first as the Fifth Avenue, or Forty-eighth Street, Church and then as St. Nicholas. Pew no. 39, a spiky organic work of High Victorian Gothic, was dedicated in 1920 to Theodore Roosevelt, "who in his youth listened here to the Gospel and became a member of this church." When the church was demolished in 1949, the pew was sent to the Theodore Roosevelt Birthplace National Historic Site on East 20th Street, where it remains.

St. Nicholas Albanian Orthodox Church. An unusual flourish in the seven-story apartment building at 359 West 48th Street [●120]—two tall buttresses with rosettes—is a remnant of its years as a house of worship, built in 1873 and designed by D. & J. Jardine. Faith Chapel moved here in 1896 from 423 West 46th Street [●126] and remained until 1942, when it moved uptown to join the Church of the Good Shepherd and the West 48th Street sanctuary was acquired by St. Nicholas Albanian Orthodox Church. In 1968, the building was turned into an Off-Broadway theater, originally called the Playhouse, then the Jack Lawrence. It was sold to residential developers in 1987.

St. Nicholas Albanian
Orthodox Church [120]

St. Nicholas Greek Orthodox Church. Two suitcases hold all that remains of St. Nicholas Greek Orthodox Church, at 155 Cedar Street [A26]: a paper icon of St. Dionysios of Zakynthos, a *kalyma* ornamental cloth used to cover the Bible on a reading stand, a *kandelion* oil-burning lamp, a bell clapper. While the world focused on the unspeakable horror across the street on September 11, 2001, Greek Orthodox Americans felt the additionally acute pain of losing a cherished little sanctuary, crushed by the collapse of 2 World Trade Center. "This just rendered everything into dust," said Archbishop Demetrios, who visited Ground Zero frequently after the attack.

Founded in 1916 in what was then a Middle Eastern quarter, St. Nicholas was said to be the third oldest Greek Orthodox church in the New York area. It moved into the former Cedar House tavern in 1919 and filed plans for a new church by Kyriacos A. Kalfas, but apparently contented itself with renovating the existing building. Its bell cote was a gentle spiritual counterpoint to the gigantism of the nearby trade center. St. Nicholas was best known for its Epiphany celebration in January, in which divers recovered a cross from the Hudson.

Within a month of the September 11 attack, Demetrios pledged that the church would "rise in glory once more in the same sacred spot as a symbol of a determined faith." Just what it will look like is unclear, but it was given a place in the plan developed for the World Trade Center site by Studio Daniel Libeskind.

St. Nicholas Greek Orthodox
Church (original facade) [A26]

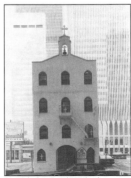

St. Nicholas Greek Orthodox
Church (later facade) [A26]

St. Nicholas of Myra Orthodox Church
[F10]

St. Nicholas of Myra Orthodox Church. On Tompkins Square Park is a splendid complex at 288 East 10th Street [●F10] by James Renwick Jr. and W. H. Russell, built in 1883 as a memorial chapel and parish house for St. Mark's Church in-the-Bowery. A bas-relief lion on the facade testifies to its origins under the patronage of St. Mark. After serving as the Holy Trinity Slovak Lutheran Church, this building was occupied in 1925 by the newly formed St. Nicholas of Myra Church of the American Carpatho-Russian Orthodox Diocese. It rented the building until 1937 and then bought it. The church today draws worshipers from New Jersey, Long Island, and Connecticut. Services are conducted in English and Church Slavonic. And Christmas comes in January.

St. Nicholas Russian Orthodox Cathedral
[P31]

St. Nicholas Russian Orthodox Cathedral. Commenced, as the cornerstone says, in the reign of the MOST PIOUS AUTOCRAT AND GREAT EMPEROR NICHOLAS ALEXANDROVICH OF ALL RUSSIAS, the cathedral at 15 East 97th Street [●P31★] was built in 1901/1902 and dedicated to St. Nicholas the Wonder-worker. The Muscovite Baroque design by John Bergesen—especially the five great onion domes—inspires wonder to this day.

The dramatic story of St. Nicholas Russian Orthodox Cathedral lives up to the setting. The Rev. Alexander Hotovitzky of Ukraine came to the fledgling St. Nicholas parish in 1895. To raise money for a new church, he traveled to Russia in 1900. Czar Nicholas II gave the first 5,000 rubles toward construction. The cornerstone was laid in the presence of the crew from the battleship *Retvizan*, then under construction in a Philadelphia shipyard for the Russian navy. The cross from the ship's chapel was brought to St. Nicholas after the *Retvizan* was sunk in 1904, during the Russo-Japanese War. St. Nicholas was elevated to a cathedral in 1905 when the seat of the vast American diocese of the Russian Orthodox Church was transferred from California to New York.

The chaos in Russia after the 1917 Revolution echoed profoundly on East 97th Street. In 1923, the Rev. John Savva Kedrovsky was appointed in Moscow by the Soviet-controlled Living Church as the American metropolitan, or archbishop, displacing Metropolitan Platon. But church leaders here refused to recognize Kedrovsky, on the grounds that he was essentially a Bolshevik agent. The battle for "the crook and mitre of St. Nicholas Cathedral," as the *New York Times* put it, involved "raids, riots, court injunctions and the wielding of axes against the church doors." A state court awarded the cathedral to Kedrovsky in 1925, but he still needed police assistance to claim it. Meanwhile, the followers of Platon declared themselves autonomous from the church in Russia, reaffirmed Platon as their leader, and, in 1927, established St. Mary's Russian Orthodox Cathedral in St. Augustine's Chapel on East Houston Street.

The struggle over St. Nicholas continued for another quarter century. It eventually turned on the question of whether New York State had the constitutional authority to require, as it did in 1945, that Russian Orthodox churches generally—and thus St. Nicholas specifically—be administered by the American separatist movement rather than the Moscow Patriarchate, which had by then been recognized by the Soviet government and was therefore suspect in the eyes of many. In 1952, the Supreme Court overturned the New York law, guaranteeing control of St. Nicholas by the Moscow Patriarchate. "Under our Constitution," Justice Felix Frankfurter wrote, "it is not open to the governments of this Union to reinforce the loyalty of their citizens by deciding who is the true exponent of their religion."

St. Nicholas Russian Orthodox Cathedral **[P31]**

St. Patrick's Cathedral. Because of its place in the heart of Manhattan, because of its size and beauty, and because of the power and influence its bishops have long enjoyed, St. Patrick's Cathedral [● J17★] is the image of the Roman Catholic Church in America. It comes as close as any single religious institution to being synonymous with New York. "It happens to transcend all faiths," said Edward I. Koch, who was mayor during the cathedral's centenary.

For Archbishop John J. Hughes, who conceived it and laid the cornerstone in 1858, the cathedral was to stand for the "increasing numbers, intelligence and wealth" of the Catholic community and serve as a "public architectural monument of the present and

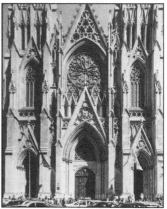

St. Patrick's Cathedral **[J17]**

Old St. Patrick's Cathedral (east facade)
[E88]

Old St. Patrick's Cathedral (west facade)
[E88]

St. Patrick's Cathedral (Lady Chapel) [J17]

prospective greatness of this metropolis." In its patron and in the identity of those on its throne, it is also an Irish monument, as an 1878 couplet made plain: "New York's Cathedral, peerless in our land, / Tribute of faith to Erin's saint shall stand."

But it is neither New York's only St. Patrick's Cathedral nor its first. That was Old St. Patrick's Cathedral, at 260 Mulberry Street [●E88★], designed by Joseph François Mangin and built from 1809 to 1815 on the site of the cemetery used by St. Peter's Church downtown. St. Patrick's was the largest religious structure in New York at the time, but not quite the right size for windows donated by King Louis Philippe of France, which were installed instead at the Fordham University Church in the Bronx. Tensions between nativist agitators and Irish Catholics reached a peak in 1836 when a mob gathered to sack the cathedral. Defenders cut musket ports in the wall and stationed armed sentinels outside, discouraging the attack. But a fire achieved in 1866 what the Know-Nothings could not: the destruction of St. Patrick's, which was rebuilt by Henry Engelbert and rededicated in 1868.

By then, construction was well under way on a larger and grander cathedral uptown on Fifth Avenue, designed by James Renwick Jr. and William Rodrigue, Hughes's brother-in-law. The soaring, twin-towered Gothic structure was strongly influenced by Cologne Cathedral, which was then being completed after a hiatus of several centuries. The new St. Patrick's was consecrated in 1879, after which the old one on Mulberry Street became a parish church for generations of Italians, Dominicans, and Chinese.

The 330-foot towers of the Fifth Avenue cathedral were finished in 1888. Between 1901 and 1906, the Lady Chapel, by Charles T. Matthews, was added on the east end. St. Patrick's also maintained the Chapel of Saints Faith, Hope, and Charity, first at 487 Park Avenue [L46] and then at 128 East 58th Street [●L48], the former Fine Arts Theater.

The graveyard on Mulberry Street yielded the remains in 1990 of Pierre Toussaint, whose canonization is being considered as America's first black saint. He is now entombed in the Fifth Avenue cathedral, along with the cardinal archbishops, some represented by scarlet galeros hanging from the ceiling. The crypt was opened in 2000 to receive John Cardinal O'Connor, who—though he publicly deplored the idea of the archbishopric as "Powerhouse"—was a most influential political leader, using the cathedral so effectively as a bully pulpit for his conservative social beliefs that the identities of man and institution merged, which brought protesters to—and sometimes inside—the great bronze doors. He was succeeded by Edward Cardinal Egan, who presided when the attack of September 11, 2001, turned St. Patrick's into a focal point of the city's mourning and its quest for some kind of spiritual response to the horror.

St. Patrick's Cathedral **[J17]**

St. Paul and St. Andrew, Church of. The tower of this United Methodist church is a lighthouse, a spiritual beacon at 540 West End Avenue **[●M15★]**. The Church of St. Paul and St. Andrew results from the merger in 1937 of St. Andrew's Methodist Episcopal Church and St. Paul's, which began as the Mulberry Street Methodist Episcopal Church **[E76]**, founded and built in 1834 at 305 Mulberry Street. Renamed St. Paul's, the congregation moved to a church designed by Ebenezer L. Roberts on Fourth Avenue **[H42]**, where it remained until 1893. It then built the present West End Avenue sanctuary, by R. H. Robertson, in 1897.

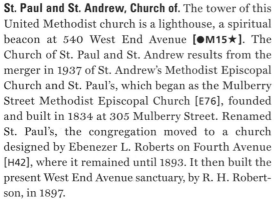

St. Paul's Methodist Episcopal Church **[H42]**

St. Andrew's was organized in 1875. Its first permanent home was at 123 West 71st Street **[●K6☆]**, built in 1880/1881 and designed by Stephen D. Hatch. This sanctuary is now Grace and St. Paul's Church. In 1889, St. Andrew's commissioned a sanctuary at 120 West 76th Street **[●M37☆]** from Cady, Berg & See that is now the West Side Institutional Synagogue.

In 1989, when St. Paul and St. Andrew was denied permission to raze its landmark sanctuary on West End Avenue, the Rev. Edward C. Horne said "preservationists have a clear interest in preserving the building at all costs—including the congregation." But the church has endured and is now shared with Congregation B'nai Jeshurun. Indeed, when a four-year-old at B'nai Jeshurun's Hebrew school was asked where Jews went for Yom Kippur, the youngster said, "To church!"

Church of St. Paul and St. Andrew **[M15]**

St. Paul Baptist Church **[T30]**

St. Paul's Chapel **[Q41]**

North Reformed Dutch
Church gate outside St.
Paul's Chapel **[Q41]**

St. Paul's Church [R53]

St. Paul Baptist Church. From the architects of 1 Fifth Avenue and the Master Apartments comes this blend of Deco and Romanesque at 249 West 132nd Street [●T30], designed in 1928 by Helmle, Corbett & Harrison. St. Paul Baptist Church dates to 1893, when west midtown was an important black neighborhood. The congregation moved from West 43rd Street to West 29th Street to the former Congregation Beth Israel, at 352 West 35th Street [G5], before coming to Harlem.

St. Paul's Chapel. *See* Trinity Church

St. Paul's Chapel. There is reason enough to marvel at the herringbone Guastavino-tiled crossing in St. Paul's Chapel. But structurally it represents another marvel: perhaps the first church in the United States with a self-supporting dome.

St. Paul's was built on the Columbia University campus [●Q41★] from 1904 to 1907. Olivia Egleston Phelps Stokes and Caroline Phelps Stokes donated the money for the chapel on condition that the commission be awarded to their nephew, Isaac Newton Phelps Stokes, author of *The Iconography of Manhattan Island* and partner in Howells & Stokes. Nepotism rarely had better effect. The Byzantine interior—almost every possible curving surface, even the undersides of staircases, is made of Guastavino tiles—is a complete surprise after the Renaissance Revival exterior, which complements McKim, Mead & White's master plan for the campus. There are also windows by D. Maitland Armstrong, John La Farge, Henry Wynd Young, and J. Gordon Guthrie.

PRO ECCLESIA DEI (For the Assembly of God) reads the entablature. President Nicholas Murray Butler said that the chapel declared to the "whole University in terms of the God of Christianity the ultimate force in the whole universe." These days, it is far more ecumenical, home to some 600 religious services for many different communities of faith every year. Outside the chapel stand two lacy wrought-iron gates, relics of the North Reformed Dutch Church, which stood until 1875 on William Street [A11]. Columbia held its 1809 commencement at this church, so its students have been walking through these gates for almost two centuries.

St. Paul's Church. The great twin limestone towers at 115 East 117th Street **[●R54]** are among the more distinctive ecclesiastical presences in Harlem, which is only fitting, since the Roman Catholic St. Paul's Church, founded in 1834, is one of the oldest institutions in Harlem. The parish's first sanctuary stood on roughly the same site [R53]. The cornerstone was laid in 1835. In its early days as a northern outpost, St. Paul's ministry extended into Westchester County. The building was enlarged and rededicated in 1871. The present sanctuary was built in 1907/1908 to designs by Neville & Bagge. The annual Good Friday procession through the neighborhood ends here.

St. Paul's Church **[R54]**

St. Paul's Church, German Evangelical Lutheran. The second oldest Lutheran congregation in Manhattan was founded in 1841 by the Rev. Frederick William Geissenhainer Jr. and occupied a Romanesque church on Sixth Avenue [E10], built in 1860/1861. Its present sanctuary, at 315 West 22nd Street **[●G36☆]**, was designed by Francis A. Minuth and built in 1897/1898. Its ethnic heritage is spelled out on the facade: DEUTSCHE EV.-LUTHERISCHE ST. PAUL'S KIRCHE and ICH BIN DER WEG DIE WAHRHEIT UND DAS LEBEN (I Am the Way, the Truth, and the Life).

German Evangelical Lutheran St. Paul's Church [E10]

German Evangelical Lutheran St. Paul's Church **[G36]**

St. Paul's Community Church. A ghostly palimpsest on the east wall—ODEON 145TH ST. THEATRE—tells the story of St. Paul's Community Church, at 256 West 145th Street **[●T4]**, constructed as a theater in 1910 to designs by Thomas W. Lamb. The theater made an appearance in *Manchild in the Promised Land*, as Claude Brown would come here to watch Westerns. (The Odeon Theater Annex of 1919 is now the Union Baptist Church.) In 1952, it was acquired by St. Paul's, which emerged in 1947 out of turmoil within the African Methodist Episcopal Church. After the attempted removal of the Rev. Hale B. Thompson as pastor of Bethel A.M.E. Church, a group of Bethel congregants—many from South Carolina—formed St. Paul's with Thompson as their pastor. "They wanted a church that would place their spiritual needs before those of the denomination and its leadership," Cynthia Hickman wrote in *Harlem Churches*.

St. Paul's Community Church **[T4]**

Church of St. Paul the Apostle (as planned) [K30]

Church of St. Paul the Apostle (before 2 Columbus Avenue) **[K30]**

St. Peter's Church **[G43]**

St. Paul the Apostle, Church of. This vast treasure house of ecclesiastical art on Columbus Avenue [●K30] was once the second largest church in the nation. (Only St. Patrick's Cathedral was larger.) Yet the Church of St. Paul the Apostle may fairly be credited to a single man: the Rev. Isaac Thomas Hecker, who worked in his family's flour and baking business before joining the Roman Catholic priesthood. In 1858, he founded the Missionary Society of St. Paul the Apostle, or the Paulist Fathers.

Their first church was built in 1859 on part of the present lot [K29]. In its stead, Jeremiah O'Rourke conceived a Victorian Gothic fantasy with 300-foot towers. The cornerstone was laid in 1876. Six years later, an engineer, the Rev. George Deshon, took over the project, using stones salvaged from the Croton Aqueduct. The exterior was so forbidding that the Paulists called it Fort Deshon. It was dedicated in 1885. Within the basilican interior are Stanford White's gleaming baldachin and Bertram Grosvenor Goodhue's robust floor mosaics. Hecker's tomb is marked by the *Angel of the Resurrection* by Lumen Martin Winter, also the sculptor of the 60-foot-long blue-and-white bas-relief over the main entrance depicting the conversion of St. Paul. Hecker founded the *Catholic World*, the first national Catholic magazine, and the Catholic Publication Society, which evolved into the Paulist Press. Radio station WLWL, the "apostolate of the air," broadcast from towers on church property.

By selling its air rights, St. Paul was able to build a new parish center on West 59th Street, incorporating a three-story cross on its facade. But the monolithic 40-story apartment tower that resulted from the deal, 2 Columbus Avenue, butts up against the south tower and considerably diminishes the church's presence.

St. Peter's Church. A venerable Chelsea landmark whose glowing tower clock evokes the cobblestoned past, St. Peter's Church, at 344 West 20th Street [●G43☆], is also a lesson in architectural history. What is now the rectory, at 346 West 20th Street, was built in 1831/1832 as St. Peter's Chapel. It was to have been part of a Greek Revival complex centered on a Theseion-like church, by Clement Clarke Moore, who donated land from his family estate to the Episcopal parish. However, ecclesiastical favor shifted abruptly to Gothic Revival. So did St. Peter's sanctuary, as designed by James W. Smith and built from 1836 to 1838. The iron railing once enclosed the yard of Trinity Church, where Moore's father, the Rev. Benjamin Moore, had been rector.

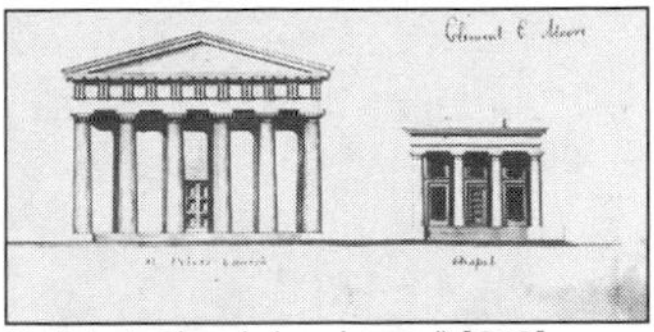

St. Peter's Church (as planned) **[G43]**

St. Peter's Church. A real-estate transaction paved the way for New York's most architecturally successful postwar sanctuary. St. Peter's Church **[● J11]** is not flawless, but it is an ambitious and largely successful attempt to create a serene, voluminous, contemplative spiritual space without resorting to traditional liturgical iconography. The Lutheran congregation was founded in 1861. A decade later, it bought the former Lexington Avenue Presbyterian Church on East 46th Street [J35], before being uprooted by Grand Central Terminal.

St. Peter's Church [J35]

A settlement from the New York Central Railroad enabled the congregation to build a church in 1903 on Lexington Avenue [J10], by J. G. Michel. Not far from the West 52nd Street clubs, St. Peter's was home to the Jazz Pastor, the Rev. John Garcia Gensel, who held jazz vespers for the musicians. Asked whether this might attract a bad element, he said: "That's the kind we want in church. The good ones can stay home. A church is a congregation of sinners, not an assembly of saints."

St. Peter's Church [J10]

In 1970, the First National City Bank agreed to pay St. Peter's $9 million for its property and build a new church alongside the 59-story tower that it planned on the site. Designed by Hugh Stubbins & Associates, architects of the tower, the church was finished in 1977. Stubbins described it as "two hands held up in prayer with light coming between them." The interior was by Vignelli Associates. Louise Nevelson created sculpture for the Erol Beker Chapel of the Good Shepherd. Sensitive to criticism that commerce had overpowered spirituality, the Rev. Ralph Edward Peterson said: "Some people might view us an eternal life-savings unit of Citicorp. But we are totally separate." (The tower is now known as Citigroup Center.)

St. Peter's Church **[J11]**

St. Peter's Church [A2]

St. Peter's Church. This somber temple, the cradle of Catholicism in New York, nobly bears the mantle of three centuries of history. Established in 1785, after a Revolution won with the aid of Catholic France and Catholic Spain, St. Peter's was the first Roman Catholic parish in New York State. The campaign for a church was led by the French consul, Hector St. John de Crèvecoeur, and the Spanish minister, Don Diego de Gardoqui, who laid the cornerstone on Barclay Street [A2]. St. Peter's Church opened in 1786. The first free public Catholic school in New York was established here in 1800. Elizabeth Ann Seton converted to Catholicism at St. Peter's, and Pierre Toussaint belonged to the parish. The present Greek Revival church [●A3★], built on the same site from 1836 to 1840, was once attributed to Isaiah Rogers, but is now more commonly assigned to John R. Haggerty and Thomas Thomas. St. Peter's was the first church in the diocese to offer midday services for office workers, beginning in 1906. Within the parish were two mission churches for Syrians. In 1983, St. Joseph's Chapel opened at Battery Park City [●A25], overlooking the Rev. Msgr. John J. Kowsky Plaza, named for a priest who served at St. Peter's. The body of the Rev. Mychal F. Judge, officially the first casualty at the World Trade Center, was brought to St. Peter's by firefighters on September 11, 2001, and laid before the altar.

St. Peter's Church [A3]

St. Philip's Church [B43]

St. Philip's Church. "As the emergence of the year's first crocus announces that spring is on its way, so did the arrival of so important a church as St. Philip's signify that Harlem was sure to be the next major settlement of blacks in Manhattan," Jervis Anderson wrote in *This Was Harlem*. Every bit a landmark, St. Philip's is the oldest black Episcopal parish in New York and one of the most influential institutions in Harlem.

In the eighteenth century, Elias Neau instructed African- and Native American men and women and presented them at Trinity Church for baptism. His African Episcopal Catechetical Institution evolved into the Free African Church of St. Philip, named for an evangelist whose baptism of an Ethiopian official led to the introduction of Christianity in that land. The

St. Philip's Church [E76]

parish was led by the Rev. Peter Williams Jr., whose father was a founder of Mother A.M.E. Zion Church. Its first church was on Centre Street [B42], as was its second [B43], which anti-abolitionists sacked in 1834. Rather than denouncing the desecration, however, the Episcopal bishop of New York called on Williams to resign from the Anti-Slavery Society. St. Philip's moved in 1857 to 305 Mulberry Street [E76], formerly the Mulberry Street Methodist Episcopal Church, a predecessor of the Church of St. Paul and St. Andrew. During the Draft Riots of 1863, the building was used as a barracks for federal troops. The Rev. Hutchens Chew

St. Philip's Church [G33]

Bishop moved the parish in 1886 to the West Twenty-fifth Street United Presbyterian Church, at 161 West 25th Street [G33], which was altered two years later by Herman Kreitler. The cornerstone for the church at 204 West 134th Street [●T28★] was laid in 1910, and the building was dedicated the next year. It was designed by two pioneering African-American architects: Vertner Woodson Tandy, the first registered black architect in the state, and George Washington Foster Jr., who also designed Mother A.M.E. Zion. The reredos came from West 25th Street. Members of or worshipers at St. Philip's Church have included W. E. B. Du Bois, Langston Hughes, and Justice Thurgood Marshall. The archbishop of Canterbury visited in 1981 and presented the Order of the Cross of St. Augustine to the Rev. M. Moran Weston, under whom St. Philip's developed five nonprofit housing projects.

St. Philip's Church [T28]

St. Raphael, Church of.
See SS. Cyril and Methodius, Church of

St. Rose, Church of. The Gothic Church of St. Rose, at 34 Cannon Street [C18], was built in 1871 for an Italian Roman Catholic parish.

St. Rose of Lima, Church of. The bold Romanesque Revival Church of St. Rose of Lima, at 510 West 165th Street [●U4], was designed in 1902 by Joseph H. McGuire for a Roman Catholic parish that had been founded a year earlier.

Church of St. Rose of Lima [U4]

St. Sava Serbian Orthodox Cathedral
[H35]

St. Sava Serbian Orthodox Cathedral. "The tide of uptown emigration has left the church and its present chapels almost bare of parishioners," George Templeton Strong wrote in 1848, speaking of Old Trinity on Wall Street and the plans to build an uptown annex. Trinity Chapel, at 15 West 25th Street [●H35★], was built from 1851 to 1856 to designs by Richard Upjohn, complemented by Jacob Wrey Mould's Trinity Chapel School, built next door in 1860. Edith Newbold Jones was married in the lofty sanctuary in 1885, taking the name of her husband, Edward Wharton. She chronicled the class whose patronage made the West 25th Street chapel the only one of Trinity's outposts that could have sustained itself without aid from the mother church.

But the gentry had long departed by 1942, when the building was sold to the fledgling Serbian Eastern Orthodox Church of St. Sava, dedicated to the patron saint of the Serbs. The church was consecrated in 1944, under the Rev. Dushan Shoukletovich. Peter II, the last king of Yugoslavia, attended services here. Gradually, the building has been remade from a Protestant chapel to an Orthodox cathedral. In 1962, an oak iconostasis was added, carved at a monastery in southern Serbia. Byzantine-style windows were commissioned to replace those destroyed when a bomb went off at the nearby Communist Party headquarters on West 26th Street in 1973. The gilded bust is of Bishop Nikolai Velimirovich, who helped organize the Serbian Orthodox Church in America and was in later years the "luminary-in-residence" at the cathedral, unable to return to his homeland under Marshal Tito. St. Sava Serbian Orthodox Cathedral held prayer services in the 1990s "for victims of the NATO aggression."

Church of St. Sebastian
[H39]

St. Sebastian, Church of. The Church of St. Sebastian, at 312 East 24th Street [H39], was the home until 1971 of an Italian Roman Catholic parish founded in 1915. Plans were filed in 1916 by Nicholas Serracino.

St. Spyridon, Washington Heights Hellenic Church of. An exuberant Byzantine–Romanesque sanctuary at 124 Wadsworth Avenue [●V22], designed by Kokkins & Lyras, houses a Greek Orthodox parish founded in

Washington Heights Hellenic Church of St. Spyridon **[V22]**

1931. Archbishop Michael laid the cornerstone in 1951, and the Washington Heights Hellenic Church of St. Spyridon was finished in 1954. It replaced a sanctuary on the same site [V21] by Gross & Kleinberger, built in 1914, that had served as Fort Washington Baptist Church, Wadsworth Avenue Baptist Church, and the Equality Temple.

Church of St. Stanislaus Bishop and Martyr [E92]

St. Stanislaus Bishop and Martyr, Church of. In the churchyard at 101 East 7th Street [●F14] stands a monumental bust of Pope John Paul II, who visited the Church of St. Stanislaus Bishop and Martyr as Karol Cardinal Wojtyla of Cracow. This Polish Roman Catholic parish was the first in Manhattan, founded in 1873. It occupied a Greek Revival temple at 43 Stanton Street [E92], built in 1845 as the Stanton Street Reformed Dutch Church, that had served Congregation B'nai Israel. The present sanctuary, by Arthur Arctander, was built in 1900 /1901 under the Rev. John H. Strzelecki. To minister to the Poles of Harlem, the Rev. Felix F. Burant opened the ancillary St. Hedwig's Church, at 62 East 106th Street [P15], in 1934. He also broadcast into Poland on the Voice of America and Radio Free Europe. Today, despite the changes all around, Polish is still spoken at St. Stanislaus.

Church of St. Stanislaus Bishop and Martyr **[F14]**

St. Stephen, Church of.
See Our Lady of the Scapular–St. Stephen, Church of

St. Stephen's Community A.M.E. Church. A simple sanctuary at 2139 Eighth Avenue [●Q54] is home to St. Stephen's Community African Methodist Episcopal Church, a congregation founded in 1966.

St. Stephen's Community A.M.E. Church **[Q54]**

St. Stephen of Hungary, Church of. Named for the first king of Hungary—Szent István—this parish started downtown in 1902. Its early home was at 420 East 14th Street [F2], a sanctuary that had been the Episcopal Chapel of the Bread of Life under St. George's Church and then the Romeyn Chapel under the Fifth Avenue Presbyterian Church. Plans for the present Church of St. Stephen of Hungary, at 408 East 82nd Street [●N33], were filed in 1926 by Joseph H. McGuire.

Church of St. Stephen of Hungary **[N33]**

St. Stephen's United Methodist Church
[X1]

St. Stephen's United Methodist Church. Designed by Alexander McMillan Welch, St. Stephen's United Methodist Church was built in 1897 on Terrace View Avenue in Manhattan. Not having moved an inch, it stands today in the Bronx, at 144 West 228th Street **[●X1]**. Yet it still looks very much like the hillside home of a country parish: a handsome oak-frame structure covered in weathered shingles, with a fine little tower and open belfry. As part of Marble Hill, fused to the mainland when the Spuyten Duyvil Creek was filled in 1913, it is technically under Manhattan's jurisdiction, which is how one Bronx church finds itself uniquely in this book.

Church of St. Teresa **[C38]**

St. Teresa, Church of. This was once *the* Rutgers Presbyterian Church, on the old Rutgers Farm, at the corner of Henry and Rutgers Streets **[●C38]**—as in Col. Henry Rutgers. It was built in 1841/1842 and has what is said to be the city's oldest public clock. After the Presbyterians left, the church was rededicated in 1863 as the Church of St. Teresa, serving a Roman Catholic parish founded three years earlier. A nineteenth-century church historian, John Gilmary Shea, said of the building that "those who reared it as a continuation of the protest against the Church of Rome . . . were, in fact, building better than they knew—erecting an edifice where the Mass was one day to be offered." That is still the case today; now in English, Spanish, and Chinese.

St. Thomas Church **[E74]**

St. Thomas Church. Although it has lost most of its Gilded Age mansions, Fifth Avenue still has some of the grandest houses of worship in America, including St. Thomas Church **[● J9★]**, a masterpiece by Cram, Goodhue & Ferguson. The Episcopal parish, founded in 1823, was no less conspicuous at Broadway and Houston Street **[E74]**. Its first church of 1826, designed by Joseph R. Brady and the Rev. John McVickar, was a forerunner of Gothic Revival. Its octagonal towers rose over the countryside like a castle. The first church at the present site [J8] was built from 1865 to 1870, designed by Richard Upjohn, working with his son Richard M. Upjohn. It was finished by Arthur Crooks. The 260-foot tower dominated the skyline. An Easter procession to the nearby St. Luke's Hospital evolved into the Easter Parade. St. Thomas's inner-city mission was a chapel at 230 East 60th Street [●L45] that gained its independence as All Saints' Church.

After the Upjohns' church burned in 1905, it was replaced with the present sanctuary, built from 1911 to 1916, combining Bertram Grosvenor Goodhue's forcefully modern manipulation of medieval forms and Ralph Adams Cram's spiritual embrace of pure Gothicism: "There will be no steel columns masked by applied stone, no girders doing the work supposed to be accomplished by vaults and arches, no thin curtain walls, no subterfuges of any sort." As striking as the exterior is Goodhue's great reredos, 80 feet high, with 60 figures by Lee Lawrie. Music is at the heart of parish life, and the new St. Thomas Choir School, at 202 West 58th Street, was completed in 1987.

St. Thomas Church [J8]

St. Thomas Church **[J9]**

St. Thomas More, Church of. The second oldest sanctuary on the Upper East Side, at 65 East 89th Street [●N4], is a Country Gothic church. It was built in 1870 as the Church of the Beloved Disciple to serve residents of the Home for Indigent Christian Females, financed by the philanthropist Caroline Talman and designed by Hubert & Pirsson. The parish merged in 1929 with the Church of the Heavenly Rest, within which is a Beloved Disciple chapel. The older sanctuary became the East Eighty-ninth Street Reformed Church, a new home for the Second Collegiate Church of Harlem. A memorial window from that time honors the Rev. Joachim Elmendorf, whose name survives in Harlem at the Elmendorf Reformed Church. In 1950, the building was transformed to plans by William Boegel for a Roman Catholic parish named after the chancellor of England who was beheaded for having refused to recognize King Henry VIII as head of the English church. (A pointed choice of patron for a sanctuary originally built by Anglicans.) Tranquil and venerable, the Church of St. Thomas More was a little-known local treasure until 1999, when it fell under the national spotlight as the setting of a memorial Mass for John F. Kennedy Jr., whose mother had been a parishioner.

Church of St. Thomas More **[N4]**

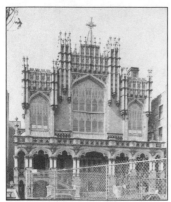

Church of St. Thomas the Apostle **[Q53]**

St. Thomas the Apostle, Church of. Rising over the tough edges of St. Nicholas Avenue like a fantastic lace scrim, the Roman Catholic Church of St. Thomas the Apostle, at 262 West 118th Street **[●Q53]**, is even more awesome inside, with windows by Mayer of Munich that form virtual walls of color, interspersed with elaborate Stations of the Cross, under a spidery fan-vaulted ceiling almost worthy of Kings College Chapel at Cambridge. The parish was founded in 1889. In 1904, Thomas H. Poole & Company filed plans for the upper church, dedicated in 1907. St. Thomas evolved into a mission church as the black population of Harlem grew. Harry Belafonte's family belonged; Kareem Abdul-Jabbar was said to have been baptized in the church; and Hulan E. Jack, the first black borough president of Manhattan, was buried from here. St. Thomas was rescued from extinction in 1979 by the Salesians of Don Bosco, but they withdrew in June 2003. Two months later, the church was padlocked without warning, leaving parishioners adrift.

St. Thomas the Apostle Liberal Catholic Church **[T7]**

St. Thomas the Apostle Liberal Catholic Church. Liberal Catholicism combines the ritualism and mysticism of the Catholic rite with what it calls a wide measure of intellectual liberty and respect for the individual conscience. St. Thomas the Apostle Liberal Catholic Church, at 147 West 144th Street **[●T7]**, by Kitzler & Nurick, was built in 1950. Murals by Amar Ghose depict saints of the islands of the Caribbean. St. Thomas was founded in 1926 by Bishop James P. Roberts Sr., whose son, Bishop James P. Roberts Jr., now leads the church.

St. Vartan Armenian Cathedral **[H10]**

St. Vartan Armenian Cathedral. As distinctive as the onion domes of St. Nicholas Russian Orthodox Cathedral, a great drum and conical dome, rising 140 feet over Second Avenue **[●H10]**, makes St. Vartan Armenian Cathedral unlike any other house of worship in Manhattan, though it is strikingly similar to the great churches of Armenia, the first country to adopt Christianity as a state religion, in 301. A century and a half later, Vartan Mamigonian was slain in battle defending the faith. He is the namesake of this cathedral and can be seen in relief over the entrance, helmet at his feet.

New York is the seat of the eastern diocese of the Armenian Church of America, which was established in 1898 as Armenians poured into this country seeking refuge from the Ottoman Turks. The campaign to erect this remarkable structure was led by Archbishop Sion Manoogian and his successor, Archbishop Torkom Manoogian, who later became the patriarch of Jerusalem. Designed by Steinmann & Cain, the successor firm to McKim, Mead & White, the cathedral was built from 1966 to 1968. It borrows designs and motifs from the churches of Aghtamar and Hripsime, as well as the 1,500-year-old Cathedral of Holy Etchmiadzin, from which Vasken I, Supreme Patriarch and Catholicos of All Armenians, traveled to consecrate St. Vartan. Inside, the dome is adorned at its apex with an Armenian letter representing the expression "He is."

Church of St. Veronica **[D16]**

St. Veronica, Church of. You can see just about anything on Christopher Street, even a Roman Catholic church, at no. 153 [●**D16**]. The parish was founded in 1887, and the cornerstone laid three years later. The architect was John J. Deery. Parishioners worshiped for years in a basement sanctuary while awaiting the construction of the upper church. The Church of St. Veronica was finished in 1903.

Church of St. Vincent de Paul (original facade) **[G35]**

St. Vincent de Paul, Church of. If it was French enough for Edith Piaf—who was married here in 1952 to the composer Jacques Pills—it ought to be French enough for anyone. Indeed, it was the bishop of Nancy, the comte de Forbin-Janson, who urged the French Catholics of New York to build their own church. The first layman to contribute to the project was Pierre Toussaint. The sanctuary was built in 1842, a year after the parish was founded, on Canal Street [B28]. The cornerstone for the present Church of St. Vincent de Paul, at 123 West 23rd Street [●**G35**], was laid in 1857, but the sanctuary was not dedicated until 1868. Henry Engelbert's original monumental Neoclassical facade was toned down a bit by Anthony De Pace, who designed a new limestone front in 1939.

Church of St. Vincent de Paul (present facade) **[G35]**

Church of St. Vincent Ferrer **[L25]**

Church of St. Vincent Ferrer **[L26]**

St. Vincent Ferrer, Church of. For this magnificent Roman Catholic church by Bertram Grosvenor Goodhue, at 881 Lexington Avenue **[●L26★]**, an ancient architectural vernacular is swept into the industrial age with piston-like buttresses, not unlike a great ecclesiastical locomotive. The Church of St. Vincent Ferrer was founded in 1867 and is run by the Dominicans, or Order of Preachers, whose symbols include a black mantle from which they get the name Blackfriars and the dog, a punning reference to *Domini canes* (watchdogs of the Lord). Their first church on this site [L25] was built from 1867 to 1869 to designs by Patrick C. Keely. It was a Gothic barn, joined in 1881 by a convent on the corner of East 65th Street, designed by William Schickel, that still stands.

Impressed by St. Thomas Church on Fifth Avenue, the Very Rev. E. G. Fitzgerald commissioned Goodhue to design the present St. Vincent, built from 1916 to 1918. Goodhue considered it his best church. The sculptor Lee Lawrie, a frequent collaborator, produced the Great Rood over the main entrance, believed to be the first representation of Christ on the cross to be carved on the exterior of a Catholic church in New York. Inside, the cobalt of Charles Connick's stained glass is so rich that it appears almost too deep to admit light. The church has drawn worshipers as diverse as Andy Warhol and Hugh L. Carey, the former governor of New York.

St. Volodymyr, Ukrainian Autocephalic Orthodox Church of. The sanctuary at 160 West 82nd Street **[●M27☆]**, designed by Arnold W. Brunner of Brunner & Tryon, was built in 1893/1894 as the home of Congregation Shaaray Tefila, also known as the West End Synagogue. In 1959, the congregation moved to a new synagogue on the Upper East Side, where it remains. Its West 82nd Street sanctuary was acquired by the Ukrainian Autocephalic Orthodox Church of St. Volodymyr, founded in 1926. Creating denominational symmetry, the Ukrainians' former church, at 334 East 14th Street **[●E18]**, became a synagogue for Congregation Tifereth Israel.

Ukrainian Autocephalic Orthodox Church of St. Volodymyr **[M27]**

Church of the Sacred Heart of Jesus **[I13]**

Church of the Sacred Hearts of Jesus and Mary **[H14]**

Salem United Methodist Church **[Q14]**

Salvation and Deliverance Church **[R57]**

Sacred Heart of Jesus, Church of the. A bit out of the way, at 457 West 51st Street **[●I13]**, is one of the largest sanctuaries in midtown. The parish was formed in 1876 and converted the Plymouth Baptist Church on West 51st Street [I12]. In 1884, it built a huge Victorian Romanesque church by Napoleon Le Brun & Sons. The Church of the Sacred Heart of Jesus was, in 1965, the first in the diocese to be redesigned under the liturgical requirements of the Second Vatican Council. It oversees the Church of St. Benedict the Moor and the chapel in the former Church of St. Ambrose.

Sacred Hearts of Jesus and Mary, Church of the. The Church of the Sacred Hearts of Jesus and Mary is an elegant Neoclassical temple in white brick at 307 East 33rd Street **[●H14]**, designed in 1915 by Nicholas Serracino. It was built to serve an Italian Roman Catholic parish that had been founded a year earlier.

Salem United Methodist Church. One of Harlem's most imposing churches is the broad, towering, and ruddy Romanesque sanctuary at 211 West 129th Street **[●Q14]**. It was described in 1893 as the largest Protestant church auditorium in the city, serving the largest Methodist congregation, Calvary Church, founded in 1883. The sanctuary was designed by John Rochester Thomas, whose Metropolitan Baptist Church is just one block south. Calvary was built in 1887 and enlarged in 1890.

Salem United Methodist Church was founded in 1902 by the Rev. Frederick A. Cullen, adoptive father of the poet Countee Cullen, as a mission of St. Mark's United Methodist Church. In 1908, it became a separate church and moved to 102 West 133rd Street [T33], later Grace Gospel Chapel. It acquired Calvary in 1923. Marian Anderson belonged to this church, and James Weldon Johnson's funeral was held here. Under the Rev. Charles Young Trigg, it was renovated from 1949 to 1953 by Joseph Judge and Samuel Snodgrass, an ecclesiastical design specialist.

Salvation and Deliverance Church. Once the home of Columbia Typewriters, the building at 37 West 116th Street **[●R57]** was designed by Bruno W. Berger and

built in 1903. It has since been the Institutional Synagogue, founded in 1917 by Rabbi Herbert S. Goldstein,
and the Walker Memorial Baptist Church. Now it is
Salvation and Deliverance Church, established in 1975
by the Apostle William Brown.

Salvation Army
Headquarters [E21]

Salvation Army. Yes, these are the folks with bells and
kettles at Christmastime, but the Salvation Army is
more than a social-service agency. It is a religious
denomination, founded by William Booth in 1865 and
brought to New York in 1880 by George Scott Railton.
In 1895, the Army opened a headquarters, at 120 West
14th Street [E21], designed by Gilbert A. Schellenger
to resemble a medieval citadel. Under Evangeline
Booth, William's daughter, work began in 1929 on a
new headquarters on the same site [●E22], designed
by Ralph Walker of Voorhees, Gmelin & Walker, a master of the Ziggurat Moderne style. Within the complex
is a 1,600-seat auditorium called the Centennial
Memorial Temple (1929 was the hundredth anniversary of Booth's birth). The exterior presents a grand
entry arch framed by curtain-like folds. The building
was dedicated in 1930, the jubilee of Railton's arrival
in New York. National headquarters moved to New
Jersey in 1982, but the building on West 14th Street
continues to serve as the Greater New York divisional
headquarters. Other Army outposts include:

Salvation Army Centennial
Memorial Temple [E22]

The Times Square Ministries, at 315 West 47th
Street [●I25], which opened in 2002 as a replacement
for the Glory Shop, at 161 West 49th Street, whose
glass doors allowed meetings within to be witnessed
from outside. The new five-story building, designed by
the Hillier Group, includes a space that doubles as a
chapel and theater.

Salvation Army Times
Square Ministries [I25]

The Central Citadel, at 221 East 52nd Street [●J13],
an institutional building designed in 1940 by
Voorhees, Walker, Foley & Smith.

The Manhattan Citadel, at 175 East 125th Street
[●R31], a plain brick box built at the corner of Third
Avenue in 1978.

The Harlem Temple, at 540 Malcolm X Boulevard
[●T18], by the Eggers Group, built from 1985 to 1987,
whose deep recessed entrances echo the portal at
headquarters.

Salvation Army Harlem Temple
[T18]

Iglesia Pentecostal Sarepta **[F20]**

Sarepta, Iglesia Pentecostal. A former stable at 701 East 6th Street **[●F20]** is home to a Pentecostal church named for Zarephath, where Elijah extended a poor woman's handful of meal and raised her son from death.

Schottenstein Center. *See* Gates of Israel, Congregation

Scientology, Church of. The New York center of Scientology, founded by L. Ron Hubbard, author of *Dianetics*, is at 227 West 46th Street **[●I27]** in the theater district—not inappropriate, since celebrity adherents like Tom Cruise, John Travolta, and Kirstie Alley have helped keep Scientology in the public eye. It was designed by Harde & Short and built in 1912 for the White Rats Club, but the current facade dates to a 1917 alteration by Thomas W. Lamb. The Church of Scientology bought the building in 1980.

Floating Church of Our Saviour
[C51]

Floating Church of Our Saviour
(rebuilt) [C51]

Seaport Chapel. A tranquil Modernist chapel is heir to a tradition going back to 1834 and the founding by Episcopal laymen of the Young Men's Auxiliary Missionary and Education Society, now known as the Seamen's Church Institute, a counseling, educational, and welfare service for merchant mariners. Its first sanctuary rocked in the waves off Pike Street [C51]. Launched in 1844, it was the Floating Church of Our Saviour, a Gothic Revival sanctuary by Richard Upjohn on two catamaran-type hulls. "Sailors needed something a little peculiar," an 1851 guidebook noted, "and hence the idea of…a floating temple, moored in some dock, so that 'Jack in his roundabout' should feel perfectly at home." It burned in 1866, was rebuilt in 1870, and was used until 1910.

The institute's second sanctuary, the Floating Church for Seamen, also known as the Chapel of the Holy Comforter, was anchored in the Hudson River off Dey Street from 1846 until 1856, and then was floated to Laight Street and finally to Hubert Street [B26]. Holy Comforter was also the name of the society's first upland church, whose tall tower on Houston Street [D18] greeted seamen along the West Side piers. It was built in 1888 to designs by Charles Coolidge Haight, with a bequest from William H. Vanderbilt, part of a complex with recreation and residence halls.

In 1906, the Seamen's Church Institute undertook its largest project, a 13-story headquarters by Warren & Wetmore at 25 South Street [A51], with a chapel, hotel, reading room, lecture hall, bank, employment bureau, and merchant-marine school. Rising from a corner turret was a lighthouse with a range of 12 miles, installed as a memorial to the *Titanic*. With the addition of an annex in 1929, the institute could lodge 1,614 men. The lighthouse was salvaged—and now stands in the South Street Seaport—when the institute moved in 1968 to 15 State Street [A52], overlooking Battery Park. At the rounded prow of the 23-story building by Eggers & Higgins was an extruded cross, running the height of the building.

Chapel of the Holy Comforter [D18]

The institute's current headquarters, which opened in 1991 at 241 Water Street [●A10☆], in the South Street Seaport, was by James Stewart Polshek & Partners. By tradition, the Seaport Chapel has a votive ship model hung from the ceiling. Atop the building, a cruciform yardarm testifies to a 170-year-old association with the church.

Seamen's Church Institute **[A10]**

Second Canaan Baptist Church. A radiant stained-glass cross now adorns the former Lenox Theater, at 10 Malcolm X Boulevard [●P6], by George F. Pelham, built in 1911. The Rev. John P. Ladson founded the Second Canaan Baptist Church in his kitchen in 1947.

Second Church of Christ, Scientist. It is not written that the second shall be first, but that was the case on Central Park West, where the Second Church of Christ, Scientist, was completed in 1901 at 10 West 68th Street [●K20☆], two years ahead of the First Church. In 1891, Laura Lathrop, one of the disciples whom Mary Baker Eddy had sent to New York, parted ways with Augusta Emma Stetson of the First Church and formed the Second, commissioning as her architect Frederick R. Comstock, who had been an associate on the Mother Church in Boston. This Beaux-Arts cube with a broad copper dome was begun in 1899 and dedicated in 1911, once the mortgage was paid off. In 2003, the Second was joined by the First, when that congregation—far too small for its sanctuary on West 96th Street—moved here for worship.

Second Canaan Baptist Church **[P6]**

Second Church of Christ, Scientist **[K20]**

Second Friendship Baptist Church [Q35]

Scotch Presbyterian Church [B19]

Scotch Presbyterian Church [O29]

Second Presbyterian Church
[O30]

Second Friendship Baptist Church. A whitewashed former garage at 215 West 122nd Street [●Q35] houses the Second Friendship Baptist Church, founded by the Rev. E. G. Clarke.

Second Methodist Protestant Church. The Second Methodist Protestant Church was built at 101 Sullivan Street [B2] in 1828. Turned into a stable in about 1867, it ended up as a garage—a reverse version of the Second Friendship Baptist Church.

Second Presbyterian Church. In a disagreement over what Psalms to use, the Second Presbyterian Church separated from the First in 1756 and called a pastor, the Rev. John Mitchell Mason, from Scotland. Widely known as the Scotch Presbyterian Church, it built a sanctuary on Cedar Street [A37] in 1768. In 1836/1837, it constructed a Greek Revival church on Grand Street [B19] that was sold in 1852 to the Fourth Presbyterian Church. The Scotch Church made its home from 1853 to 1894 at 53 West 14th Street [E11].

It then moved far uptown, to 6 West 96th Street [O29], overlooking Central Park. This church was built in 1893/1894, to designs by William H. Hume & Son, with a grand corner tower and open-air belfry. It was replaced by a Skyscraper Church by Rosario Candela, built in 1928/1929. This 16-story apartment tower, at 360 Central Park West [●O30☆], incorporates a sanctuary for the Second Presbyterian Church at its base, expressed as a sheer limestone wall with a great Gothic portal. The developers, Vincent J. Slattery and Morris H. Rothschild, had just completed a similar project with the Church of the Strangers and were about to embark on one with the Calvary Baptist Church.

Second Providence Baptist Church. The building at 11 West 116th Street [●R59], now home to the Second Providence Baptist Church, opened in 1913 as the Jewel Theater, designed by Victor Hugo Koehler.

Second Reformed Presbyterian Church. The twin-towered Romanesque sanctuary at 227 West 39th Street [I51] was one of the earliest of New York's grand synagogues. It was built in the 1860s for Congregation Adas Jeshurun, which merged with Anshe Chesed, builders of the first grand synagogue on Norfolk Street, to form Congregation Beth El, later absorbed by Emanu-El. The building was acquired by the Presbyterians in 1874. Founded in 1830, the Second Reformed Presbyterian Church once worshiped at 166 Waverly Place [E46], later Abyssinian Baptist Church, and then at 167 West 11th Street [E24].

Second Providence Baptist Church **[R59]**

Second St. John Baptist Church. This unusual free-standing building at 141 West 118th Street **[●Q52]** was once the St. Thomas Academy. It was acquired in 1965 by the Second St. John Baptist Church, an outgrowth of St. John's Baptist Church. It began at Broadway and West 131st Street in 1950, under the Rev. Norman O. Williams, who led the church until his death in 1982. The West 118th Street sanctuary was expanded between 1988 and 1990. Orange, yellow, green, and blue windows enliven the plain masonry facade.

Second Shiloh Baptist Church. This wood-frame house at 26 West 127th Street **[●R18]** has been the Second Shiloh Baptist Church for more than three decades.

Second Reformed Presbyterian Church **[I51]**

Second Street Methodist Church. The Second Street Methodist Church, built in 1832 at 276 East 2nd Street [F40], was razed in 1915 for the Israel Orphan Asylum.

Second Universalist Church. A distyle-in-antis Greek Revival sanctuary was built around 1827 at 97 Orchard Street [C9] for the Reformed Dutch Church. It was acquired by the Universalists in 1832 and torn down three decades later. The building that is now the Lower East Side Tenement House Museum stands on part of the old church site.

Second St. John Baptist Church **[Q52]**

Segunda Iglesia Bautista. A sparkling blue mosaic cross sets apart this gray-brick institutional building at 163 East 102nd Street **[●P26]**, designed by Kempa & Schwartz. The cornerstone was laid in 1963. The Second Baptist Church had been at 112 East 104th Street **[●P20]**, now the Iglesia Pentecostal Nueva Gethsemani.

Segunda Iglesia Bautista **[P26]**

Senier and Wilno, Congregation. Built as Congregation Makower of Poland in 1893, this Romanesque synagogue at 203 Henry Street [C45] later became the Wilno Shul (for Vilnius, Lithuania), which was joined by Congregation Anshe Sineer after its synagogue on Madison Street burned in 1972. Only three years later, Congregation Senier and Wilno was destroyed by arson.

Seventh Avenue United Presbyterian Church. A late Greek Revival sanctuary was built in 1853 at 29 Seventh Avenue [E23] by the Greene Street Reformed Dutch Church. It was acquired in 1865 by the Seventh Avenue United Presbyterian Church, also known as the Second Associate Church, which worshiped here until 1907.

Seventh Avenue United Presbyterian Church [E23]

Seventh Church of Christ, Scientist. It can happen on occasion that an architecturally distinguished church is replaced by something equally notable. The oversize oculus of the Seventh Church of Christ, Scientist, at 520 West 112th Street [●O2], designed by William Fryer and completed in 1990, clearly sets it apart from the adjoining 22-story apartment tower. They both replace a 1919 church on the same site [O1], designed by Griffin & Wynkoop, an intriguing interpretation of Greek Revival whose nearly windowless facade made it look a bit like a secret-society headquarters.

Seventh Church of Christ, Scientist [O1]

Seventh Presbyterian Church. A barn-like sanctuary at 142 Broome Street [C14] served the Seventh Presbyterian Church from 1827 to 1935, after which it was the Ukrainian-Russian-American All Saints Church. Downtown Talmud Torah Synagogue replaced it.

Shaaray Tefila, Congregation. Having engaged three important architects for its earlier sanctuaries—Eidlitz, Fernbach, and Brunner—it is paradoxical that the Reform Congregation Shaaray Tefila (Gates of Prayer) should end up in a former Trans-Lux Theater. Founded in 1845 as a breakaway from Congregation B'nai Jeshurun, Shaaray Tefila built a synagogue in 1847 at 112 Wooster Street [B3], by Leopold Eidlitz and Otto Blesch. What set it apart was its forceful Romanesque design and the impulse behind it. "The style cho-

Seventh Church of Christ, Scientist [●O2]

sen is Byzantic which flourished centuries back, and was especially used by the Portuguese and other Jews when persecuted in the Middle Ages," wrote the *hazzan*, Samuel M. Isaacs, in 1846. "The spectator will at once receive the impression that the building is intended as a place of worship, not of the poetical deities of the Greeks, nor the pompous trinity of the Christians, but of the mighty God of the Jews."

After worshiping briefly in an armory, the congregation moved in 1865 to 127 West 44th Street [133], a Moorish–Romanesque sanctuary by Henry Fernbach. In 1893/1894, it built a Byzantine–Moorish sanctuary, by Arnold W. Brunner, at 160 West 82nd Street [●M27☆], known as the West End Synagogue. This building, still standing, is now the Ukrainian Autocephalic Orthodox Church of St. Volodymyr.

Congregation Shaaray Tefila [133]

Shaaray Tefila's present sanctuary, at 250 East 79th Street [●N39], was built as the Colony movie theater, which later came under Trans-Lux management. It was converted into a synagogue in 1959 by John J. McNamara and Horace Ginsbern & Associates. The windowless exterior on the Second Avenue side is ornamented with an enormous menorah. Like so many synagogues, it was ringed with concrete barriers after the attack on New York in 2001.

Congregation Shaaray Tefila **[N39]**

Shaare Hatikvah Ahavath Torah v'Tikvoh Chadoshoh, Congregation.

This congregation's complex name reflects the amalgamation of Shaare Hatikvah (Gates of Hope), founded in 1935, with Ahavath Torah (Love of Torah) and Tikvoh Chadoshoh (New Hope), both established in 1938. Shaare Hatikvah, the first German-Jewish institution in Washington Heights, grew as Jews fled the Nazis. Its synagogue at 711 West 179th Street [●V20], by Maurice Courland, was built in 1957 in memory of perished Jewish congregations in Europe. Ahavath Torah was in the former Costello Theater, at 23 Fort Washington Avenue [●U7], where it was joined in 1965 by Tikvoh Chadoshoh. In 1975, they merged with Shaare Hatikvah on West 179th Street. Also worshiping here is the Orthodox Congregation Nodah bi Yehuda (Will Be Known in Judah), which had been at 392 Fort Washington Avenue, in the former Kehillath Yaakov synagogue.

Congregation Shaare Hatikvah Ahavath Torah v'Tikvoh Chadoshoh **[V20]**

Shaare Zedek, Congregation. *See* Civic Center Synagogue

Congregation Shaare Zedek **[M3]**

Shaare Zedek, Congregation. Polish Jews formed the city's third oldest synagogue, Congregation Shaare Zedek (Gates of Righteousness), in 1839. They worshiped on Pearl Street before acquiring 38 Henry Street [C28] in 1850. This sanctuary had been built in 1828 by the orthodox branch of the Religious Society of Friends and converted into a synagogue in 1840 by Anshe Chesed. At 40 Henry Street [C29], Shaare Zedek built a new synagogue in 1891. An offshoot group of the same name was established in Harlem in 1900 at 25 West 118th Street [●R49], now the Bethel Way of the Cross Church of Christ.

After the Henry Street shul was sold in 1911 to Congregation Mishkan Israel Anshei Suwalk, the original Congregation Shaare Zedek also moved to Harlem, renting the New York Presbyterian Church on West 128th Street for High Holy Days until the two Shaare Zedeks reunited in 1914 on West 118th Street. The present Neoclassical sanctuary, designed by Sommerfeld & Steckler, was built at 212 West 93rd Street [●M3] in 1922/1923.

Shaarey Shamoyim, Congregation.
See First Roumanian-American Congregation

Sharon Baptist Church. The synagogue at 65 East 113th Street [R72] was Mount Zion at the turn of the twentieth century. In 1909, it became the Harlem branch of Congregation K'hal Adath Jeshurun—the Eldridge Street Synagogue—though relations were tense with the downtown brethren. The uptown sanctuary was sold in 1930 to the Sharon Baptist Church.

Shearith Israel, Congregation. Like counterpoints to the oaks across the street in Central Park, four great columns dominate the facade of this Orthodox sanctuary, the Spanish and Portuguese Synagogue, at 8 West 70th Street [●K11★]. Shearith Israel (Remnant of Israel) is the oldest Jewish congregation in North America, tracing itself to 23 Jews, mostly Spanish and Portuguese, who arrived in New York from Recife, Brazil, in 1654.

Congregation Shearith Israel Cemetery **[B55]**

The oldest physical remnant of Shearith Israel is the tombstone of Benjamin Bueno de Mesquita, who died in 5444, or 1683. He is buried in a little cemetery overlooking Kimlau (Chatham) Square [●B55★]. So are Rabbi Gershom Mendes Seixas, the first American-born Jewish clergyman, and Lewis Moses Gomez, the president of the congregation when the first synagogue was built in 1730 on Mill Street [A45], now South William Street. Eighteen members of the congregation who fought in the Revolutionary War are also buried in the first cemetery. The second cemetery of 1805, on West 11th Street [●E30☆], sat among the apple trees and cow pastures of Greenwich Village.

Congregation Shearith Israel [A45]

A larger synagogue was built on Mill Street [A46] in 1817/1818, and a third cemetery was established in 1829 on West 21st Street [●G45☆], later surrounded by the Hugh O'Neill dry-goods store. A Greek Revival synagogue was built at 56 Crosby Street [B9] in 1833/1834 that was later Henry Wood's Minstrel Hall. The next synagogue was a grand Neoclassical structure at 5 West 19th Street [H53] by Robert Mook, built in 1859/1860. Although it was razed in 1898, the *hazzan*'s residence, at 7 West 19th Street, still stands.

Shearith Israel almost moved to Harlem, but picked the Upper West Side for its present sanctuary, built in 1896/1897 to designs by Brunner & Tryon, echoing Greco-Roman synagogue ruins found in Galilee to gain what Arnold W. Brunner called "the sanction of antiquity." The doors were first opened by the great-great-grandson of Lewis Moses Gomez. They are not where you think they might be, behind the monumental arcade. That is the location of the Ark, since the sanctuary is oriented to Jerusalem. On the lot immediately west of the landmark synagogue, the congregation planned a 14-story community house and apartment building in 2002. It was also burnishing its sanctuary with the help of the architect Stephen Tilly. "When you come into the synagogue, you realize you're in the presence of God," Rabbi Marc D. Angel said. "You feel the span of the centuries." You can also see it in a smaller sanctuary within the building, known as the Little Synagogue, where relics of the eighteenth and early nineteenth centuries are kept, including Torah scrolls desecrated by British soldiers during the Revolutionary War.

Congregation Shearith Israel [H53]

Congregation Shearith Israel [K11]

Shiloh Baptist Church **[Q9]**

Shiloh Baptist Church. The mosaic mural that has dominated the facade of this sanctuary at 2226 Adam Clayton Powell Jr. Boulevard **[●Q9]** since 1979 depicts the "reaching up of hands and hungry souls for the saving grace of God through Jesus Christ." Shiloh Baptist Church, organized in 1899, was led for more than eight decades by the Rev. Edward W. Wainwright and his son, the Rev. Leslie E. Wainwright. The congregation moved to this site in 1918 and doubled the size of the church in 1953/1954 in an alteration designed by Charles W. B. Mitchell.

Shiloh Church of Christ **[R9]**

Shiloh Church of Christ. Proving that modest architecture can be exuberant, the Shiloh Church of Christ, at 7 West 128th Street **[●R9]**, has a giant cross in a Gothic portal. The facade is a 1953 alteration by Richard B. Thomas.

Shiloh Presbyterian Church. The spiritual forerunner of St. James Presbyterian Church was founded downtown on Rose Street in 1822 as the First Colored Presbyterian Church, or African Church, under the Rev. Samuel E. Cornish, who was black. Two years later, the congregation built a substantial sanctuary at 119 Elm Street [B29], now Lafayette Street. But the debt was too much, and the building had to be relinquished. (It was acquired by Congregation B'nai Jeshurun.) In 1831, the African-American Presbyterians moved into the old Swamp Church on Frankfort Street [B62], where they stayed for 20 years. As the black population moved uptown, so did Shiloh Presbyterian Church, spending its final years until 1888 at 167 West 26th Street. Members of this group were responsible seven years later for founding St. James Presbyterian.

First Colored Presbyterian Church [B29]

Congregation Austria-Hungary Ansche Sfard **[C47]**

Shtiebl Row. On arriving in the golden city, immigrants from Eastern Europe promptly redrew their village boundaries around their own tiny congregations. Too independent to be subsumed into larger synagogues and too poor to build their own, they used any space they could afford, including storefronts and tenements. The small rooms in which they worshiped were called *shtieblach*. Hundreds of them lined East Broadway and surrounding streets, and Shtiebl Row was known as the citadel of Orthodoxy. The densest remaining concentration on East Broadway, between Clinton and Montgomery Streets [●C47], includes Congregations Beth Hachasidim de Polen, at no. 233; Shearyth Adas Israel, at no. 237; Austria-Hungary Ansche Sfard, at no. 239; Zemach Zedek Nusach Hoari, at no. 241; and Thilom Anshei Wishkowe, at no. 257, founded in 1865, which had been at 169 Clinton Street [C22], designed in 1904 by Benjamin Steckler.

Sinagoga, Iglesia Pentecostal la. The Sinagoga Pentecostal Church, at 115 East 125th Street [●R29], looks like a storefront sanctuary at first glance. But it occupies the former Harlem Grand Theater of 1916 by George Mort Pollard.

Iglesia Pentecostal la Sinagoga **[R29]**

Sion, Iglesia Luterana. A charming vestige of German Harlem, 217 East 119th Street [●R48] was built in 1873 as the Deutsche Evangelische Lutherische St. Johannes Kirche, founded in 1864 and closed 90 years later. Today, it does triple duty as Zion Lutheran Church, Iglesia Pentecostal Amor y Vida (Love and Life), and Iglesia Pentecostal La Senda Antigua (Ancient Path).

Iglesia Luterana Sion **[R48]**

Sixteenth Street Baptist Church. A Romanesque sanctuary built in about 1857 at 253 West 16th Street [D1] was home to the Sixteenth Street Baptist Church, founded in 1833 and dissolved in 1927.

Sixth Street Community Center.
See Ahawath Yeshurun Shara Torah, Congregation

Sixteenth Street Baptist Church **[D1]**

Society for the Advancement of Judaism. Having established the Jewish Center but finding himself at odds with Orthodox tenets, Rabbi Mordecai M. Kaplan founded the Society for the Advancement of Judaism—Reconstructionism—in 1922. While keeping many traditional practices, the movement also embraced the equality of women. (Kaplan's daughter was the first bat mitzvah.) In 1925, it bought the Alcuin School, at 15 West 86th Street [●M18☆], which was altered by Deutsch & Schneider and given a new facade in 1937 by Albert Goldhammer.

Society for the Advancement of Judaism **[M18]**

South Reformed Dutch Church [A44]

South Reformed Dutch Church. An inscription on the Park Avenue Christian Church, EEN DRACHT MAKT MACHT (In Unity There Is Strength), is a reminder of one of New York's oldest congregations: South Reformed Dutch Church, whose first sanctuary, completed in 1693, stood on Garden Street [A43], now Exchange Place. A new church was built on the site [A44] in 1807. For 120 years, this was the southernmost Collegiate church, as the name suggests. Although the South Church separated from the Collegiate charge in 1812, it kept the name as it moved northward. It built a new church in 1837 on Murray Street [B61], later used by the Fourth Universalist Society. Its next home was a Gothic Revival church of 1849 on Fifth Avenue [H52]. In 1890, the congregation bought Zion Episcopal Church, completed in 1854 on Madison Avenue [J55]. It made its last stand at 1010 Park Avenue [●N20], built from 1909 to 1911 to designs by Cram, Goodhue & Ferguson, before going out of existence in 1914.

South Reformed Dutch Church [J55]

Southern Baptist Church. An enormous tracery window dominates this bold Eclectic Gothic sanctuary at 12 West 108th Street [●O9], designed by Frank E. Wallis and built from 1903 to 1905 for the First United Presbyterian Church, which had worshiped at 250 West 34th Street [G15]. Following the Presbyterians, the building was used as the parish hall of the nearby Roman Catholic Church of the Ascension. The Southern Baptist Church, organized in 1922 under the Rev. Macon Osborne, arrived here in 1953 from 103 Morningside Avenue [●Q32], now St. Luke Baptist Church.

First United Presbyterian Church [G15]

Spanish and Portuguese Synagogue. *See* Shearith Israel, Congregation

Spring Street Presbyterian Church. "Much of the neighborhood was lost in a kind of sodden apathy to which drunken quarrels brought release," recalled the Rev. Norman Thomas, who was assigned to the Spring Street Presbyterian Church in 1905. In the midst of this poverty stood a Greek Revival sanctuary built at 250 Spring Street [B7] in 1835/1836. It endured until the 1960s, a noble ruin of a genteel past.

Southern Baptist Church [O9]

Stanton Street Synagogue.
See B'nai Jacob Anshei Brzezan, Congregation

Stephen Wise Free Synagogue. Although houses of worship sometimes are informally known by the name of their rector, rabbi, or pastor, it rarely happens that a congregation formally identifies itself with an individual. But Rabbi Stephen Samuel Wise was in every sense synonymous with the Free Synagogue, a Reform congregation he founded in 1907, having turned down an invitation in 1905 to the pulpit of Temple Emanu-El when he was told that he would be subject to control by the board of trustees. "How can a man be vital and independent and helpful, if he be tethered and muzzled?" asked Wise. "A free pulpit will sometimes stumble into error; a pulpit that is not free can never powerfully plead for truth and righteousness." The Free Synagogue was to be free in another sense—"pewless and dueless," in the words of its first president, Henry Morgenthau Sr.

Spring Street Presbyterian Church **[B7]**

Wise began conducting services near Emanu-El, in the Hudson Theater at 139 West 44th Street, now preserved and incorporated into the Millennium Broadway Hotel. The synagogue next occupied 142 West 81st Street **[●M31☆]**, now the Mount Pleasant Baptist Church, before moving to Carnegie Hall. The Free Synagogue House was built at 40 West 68th Street **[●K18☆]** in 1922/1923, to designs by Eisendrath & Horowitz. Its 600-seat auditorium could not contain the crowds that came to hear Wise, however, so services continued at Carnegie Hall. This building was later used by the Hebrew Union College–Jewish Institute of Religion and is now York Preparatory School. Next door, at 30 West 68th Street **[●K19☆]**, a new synagogue by Bloch & Hesse, with more than twice the capacity of the older auditorium, was begun in 1940 with a cornerstone from the Temple in Jerusalem. Delayed by World War II, the building was not completed until January 1950, nine months after Wise had died. The first woman ordained as a rabbi, Sally J. Priesand, served here in the 1970s as an assistant to and associate of Rabbi Edward E. Klein.

Free Synagogue House **[K18]**

Rabbi Balfour Brickner was perhaps the best known of Wise's successors, an outspoken voice in the 1980s for abortion rights, civil rights, and the environment.

Stephen Wise Free Synagogue **[K19]**

Church of the Strangers
[E42]

Church of the Strangers [K33]

Church of the Strangers (Le
Bar Bat) **[K34]**

Sung Tak Buddhist Association **[C35]**

Strangers, Church of the. Of all the names to call a church in New York, none may be as poignantly perfect, since this is a city of the transient. One such was the Rev. Charles Force Deems, from North Carolina, who founded the nondenominational Church of the Strangers in 1868, especially to minister to sojourners. Commodore Cornelius Vanderbilt bought the Mercer Street Presbyterian Church—built in 1834 at 299 Mercer Street [E42] and later the birthplace of the YMCA of the City of New York—and presented it to Deems in 1870. It was the setting in 1877 of Vanderbilt's funeral, over which Deems presided.

In 1898, the Church of the Strangers moved to a Victorian Gothic sanctuary at 309 West 57th Street [K33] that had been the Sixth Universalist Church, also known as the Church of Our Saviour, and the Central Congregational Church. This site **[●K34]** was redeveloped in 1927/1928 with a Skyscraper Church: a 16-story apartment tower by Rosario Candela with a new home at its base for the church, known as the Deems Memorial, expressed as a large Gothic portal. The developers, Vincent J. Slattery and Morris H. Rothschild, went on to build similar projects with the Second Presbyterian and Calvary Baptist Churches. The West 57th Street sanctuary was used by Christian Scientists and Baptists until 1969, when it became the Media Sound Recording Studio, whose acoustics drew performers like Aretha Franklin, John Lennon, Frank Sinatra, and Stevie Wonder. Then it was transformed into Le Bar Bat, which the Zagat Survey called a "great place to dance and be merry late at night with young BATs (bridge and tunnelers)." In other words, strangers.

Subud Chelsea Center. *See* Fur Center Synagogue

Sung Tak Buddhist Association. This structure is a kind of architectural metaphor for the Lower East Side: built to serve a vital Jewish community, transmogrified into an abandoned eyesore, and then revived—though modified—in Chinese hands. Immigrants from Kalwarie on the Polish–Lithuanian border joined in 1899 with Congregation Beth Hamedrash Livne Yisroel Yelide Polen to form Congregation B'nai Israel Kalwarie (Sons of Israel). They built the Kalvarier

Shul, at 13 Pike Street [●C35★], in 1903/1904 to designs by Alfred E. Badt. This was, indirectly, the birthplace of the Young Israel movement in 1911, as Rabbi Judah L. Magnes lectured here to Orthodox youths. The synagogue closed in 1977 and slowly went to ruin. At the same time, though, the Chinese population was growing, in part because of the abolition of the national-origins quota system. Chinatown pushed beyond its traditional borders. In the mid-1990s, the Kalvarier Shul was converted into the Sung Tak Buddhist Association, a temple affiliated with the Chinese Pure Land school. On the porch is a statue of Kwan-Yin, the incarnation of compassion.

Sutton Place Synagogue [J15]

Sunshine Cinema. *See German Evangelical Mission Church*

Sutton Place Synagogue. The sanctuary at 221 East 51st Street [J15] was home to Congregation Orach Chaim until 1906, after which it was acquired by Congregation Beth Hamedrash Hachodosh Talmud Torah (New House of Study for the Study of the Torah), founded in 1901 and now known as the Sutton Place Synagogue. A new sanctuary on the site [● J16] was designed for the Conservative congregation in 1974 by Herbert Fleischer Associates.

Sutton Place Synagogue **[J16]**

Swedenborgian Church. *See New Church*

Swedish Bethesda Evangelical Church. Among the polyglot tesserae of the gorgeous mosaic in Manhattan, one rarely thinks of Scandinavians, but they once were here in great numbers. Swedish Bethesda Evangelical Church was founded in 1879 and worshiped at 240 East 45th Street [J38], later the German Evangelical Zion Church, and 138 East 50th Street [J24], formerly Congregation Shaarey Beracha.

Swedish Seamen's Church. A center of Swedish life, the Svenska Kyrkan, at 5 East 48th Street [● J26], was altered into its present neo-Gothic form by Wilfred E. Anthony in 1921 for the New York Bible Society. The Swedish Seamen's Church, founded in 1873 on Water Street, bought this building in 1978. A *högmässa*, or morning service, is celebrated every Sunday.

Swedish Seamen's Church **[J26]**

T

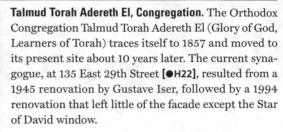

Talmud Torah Adereth El, Congregation. The Orthodox Congregation Talmud Torah Adereth El (Glory of God, Learners of Torah) traces itself to 1857 and moved to its present site about 10 years later. The current synagogue, at 135 East 29th Street [●H22], resulted from a 1945 renovation by Gustave Iser, followed by a 1994 renovation that left little of the facade except the Star of David window.

Congregation Talmud Torah Adereth El (before 1994 renovation) [H22]

Talmud Torah Anshei Marovi, Chevra. *See* Old Broadway Synagogue

Temple Beth El. *See* Beth El, Congregation

Temple Emanu-El. *See* Emanu-El, Congregation

Temple Israel [R27]

Temple Israel **[L1]**

Temple Israel. Most Jewish congregations of the Harlem diaspora moved into that neighborhood. Temple Israel was Harlem born and bred, going back to the incorporation in 1873 of Congregation Yod b'Yod (Hand-in-Hand), which reorganized as Temple Israel in 1888 and acquired Holy Trinity Church, on Fifth Avenue [R27], designed by John W. Welch and built in 1869/1870. Among the trustees of Temple Israel was Cyrus L. Sulzberger, great-grandfather of the current publisher of the *New York Times*. In 1907, Temple Israel built its own sanctuary at 201 Lenox Avenue [●Q51✩], designed by Arnold W. Brunner, which may rank as the single best Neoclassical synagogue in Manhattan. Today, it is Mount Olivet Baptist Church. Temple Israel was joined in 1909 by Shaarey Beracha, a congregation of Alsatian Jews.

The temple moved downtown in 1920 to a Neoclassical synagogue by William Tachau at 210 West 91st Street [●M8] that is now Young Israel of the West Side. After staying in this sanctuary for more than 45 years, the Reform congregation moved across Central Park to a Brutalist synagogue by Peter Claman of Schuman & Lichtenstein at 112 East 75th Street [●L1✩], built from 1964 to 1967. In 2002, Temple Israel planned a significant alteration designed by Gruzen Samton that would open up the rather inscrutable facade.

Temple of the Covenant. *See* Congregación Mita, Iglesia

Templo Bíblico. The little Biblical Temple, at 503 West 126th Street [●Q4], was built in 1882 as the firehouse of Engine Company 37, to designs by Napoleon Le Brun.

Templo Bíblico Capilla Evangélica. A frame structure with a brick facade, the Biblical Temple Evangelical Chapel, at 461 West 166th Street [●U3], was the Norwegian Free Lutheran Brethren Church and St. Paul's Evangelical Lutheran Church.

Templo Bíblico [Q4]

Tenth Church of Christ, Scientist. Probably no Christian denomination in modern times has tried as many varieties of architectural expression as the Church of Christ, Scientist. At 171 Macdougal Street [●E41☆] is the modern impulse: a brick wall at the end of Macdougal Alley, penetrated by corbeled openings, including a monumental shaft that serves the Gothic purpose of lifting the eye upward. The Tenth Church of Christ, Scientist, is not a new structure but a remodeling, in 1966/1967, by Victor Christ-Janer & Associates, of a nineteenth-century factory and store.

Templo Bíblico Capilla Evangélica [U3]

Tenth Street Church of Christ. The building at 257 East 10th Street [●F9], formerly a Polish church and a Russian restaurant, became the Church of Christ New York City Mission in 1958, under the Rev. David Vaughan Elliott, with a largely Puerto Rican congregation.

Tercera Avenida, Iglesia de Dios. In the retail bustle of Third Avenue, the arched facade of the Church of God, at no. 2137 [●R61], serves as a reminder of a spiritual presence.

Tenth Church of Christ, Scientist [E41]

Tercera Iglesia Cristiana (Discípulos de Cristo). The Third Christian Church (Disciples of Christ) was founded in 1952 by lay members of the Second Church in the Bronx, four of whom survived for the semicentenary. In 1997, Ira Oaklander of OCV Architects wrapped a curving screen around a mansard-roofed house at 46 Hamilton Place [●S24]. The new facade does not wholly obscure the old house, so it is an appealingly frank expression of the building's conversion.

Tercera Iglesia Cristiana (Discípulos de Cristo) [S24]

Third Church of Christ, Scientist
[R28]

Third Church of Christ, Scientist [L31]

Broome Street Reformed Dutch
Church [B8]

Thirty-fourth Street Reformed Dutch
Church [G7]

Theater Four. *See* First Church of the Evangelical Association

Third Church of Christ, Scientist. On the quintessential Upper East Side site, 583 Park Avenue [●L31☆], the quintessential Upper East Side architects, Delano & Aldrich, produced the quintessential Georgian meetinghouse, proper as teatime.

It offers quite a contrast to the eclectic exuberance of the First and Second Churches and to the earlier Third Church, an enormous Victorian Gothic sanctuary at 43 East 125th Street [R28], designed by D. & J. Jardine and built in 1874 for the Harlem Presbyterian Church, which used it for 30 years until moving to what is now the Mount Morris–Ascension Presbyterian Church.

The Third Church of Christ, Scientist, was organized in 1895 and occupied the Harlem sanctuary in the 1910s. Its present sanctuary was built from 1922 to 1924. Right down to the elliptical oculus in the pediment, it is a perfect bookend to the Colony Club one block south—by Delano & Aldrich.

Thirty-fourth Street Reformed Dutch Church. Where the New Yorker Hotel stands, at 307 West 34th Street [G7], was a Gothic church built in 1860 for a Reformed group founded as the Broome Street Reformed Dutch Church. Its earlier sanctuary, on the corner of Greene Street [B8], was dedicated in 1824. The Thirty-fourth Street Reformed Dutch Church dissolved in 1920.

Thirty-seventh Street Methodist Episcopal Church. The Thirty-seventh Street Methodist Episcopal Church, at 225 East 37th Street [J57], was dedicated in 1859. The congregation disbanded in 1911, and its sanctuary was replaced by a telephone company building.

Thomas Memorial Wesleyan Methodist Church. The Rev. Ingraham Thomas of Beulah Wesleyan Methodist Church is remembered in the name of this congregation, formed in 1946 by members of Beulah. They worshiped at 252 West 138th Street [●T15] until 1962, when they took over their present sanctuary at 270 West 126th Street [●Q27].

Thy Will Be Done! Christian Ministries. The People's Baptist Church, founded in 1930, moved to 165 East 103rd Street [●P22] in 1966. The sanctuary is now home to Thy Will Be Done! Christian Missionaries, an interdenominational fellowship.

Tifereth Israel, Congregation. Pure Gingerbread Romanesque fantasy, this vivacious sanctuary at 334 East 14th Street [●E18] was designed in 1866 by Julius Boekell as the First German Baptist Church, at the edge of Kleindeutschland. In 1926, it became the Ukrainian Autocephalic Orthodox Church of St. Volodymyr, which added the onion domes. The Conservative Town and Village Synagogue, Congregation Tifereth Israel (Glory of Israel), was founded in 1949 and worshiped at the Labor Temple, at 242 East 14th Street [●E17]. It acquired its current home in 1962, after St. Volodymyr moved to the Congregation Shaaray Tefila synagogue on the Upper West Side.

Thomas Memorial Wesleyan Methodist Church [Q27]

Tiffereth Israel, Congregation. The Allen Street Methodist Episcopal Church, built in 1836 at 126 Allen Street [C4], was occupied by Congregation Tiffereth Israel after the Methodists moved out.

Thy Will Be Done! Christian Ministries [P22]

Tikvath Israel of Harlem, Congregation.
See Christ Apostolic Church of U.S.A.

Tillman Chapel. What kind of spiritual message can be conveyed to a community drawn from around the world? The facade of the Tillman Chapel at the Church Center for the United Nations, at 777 First Avenue [● J45]—part sculpture by Benoit Gilsoul, part stained-glass window by Henry Lee Willet—aspires to represent "Man's Search for Peace," with humanoid forms around an encompassing, elliptical eye. "Man cannot escape the all-seeing eye of the Almighty which penetrates the darkness of his despair," declares a plaque signed by Willet. The Church Center was built in 1962 to designs by William Lescaze. The ground-floor chapel was donated in 1963 by the Women's Division of the Board of Missions of the Methodist Church, honoring one of its members, Sadie Wilson Tillman.

Congregation Tifereth Israel [E18]

Tillman Chapel [J45]

Times Square Church **[I15]**

Iglesia Metodista Unida Todas las Naciones **[E44]**

Trans World Buddhist Association Buddha Virtue Temple **[B51]**

Times Square Church. Times Square was at its nadir in 1986, when the Rev. David Wilkerson, an evangelist and the author of *The Cross and the Switchblade*, founded the nondenominational, fundamentalist Times Square Church. Its services were held first in Town Hall and then in the Nederlander Theater, before the church settled in the Mark Hellinger Theater, at 237 West 51st Street **[●I15★]**, which it bought in 1991. The theater opened in 1930 as the Warner Hollywood, one of the last great movie palaces, designed by Thomas W. Lamb and the Rambusch Studios. Behind the stark Deco–Secessionist facade lies an interior that is pure, unbridled, Baroque fantasy. In its days as a playhouse, it housed the long-running *My Fair Lady* and in 1971—perhaps an augury of sorts— *Jesus Christ Superstar*.

By the beginning of the twenty-first century, the 1,600-seat church had 8,000 members. Overflow crowds watched services on closed-circuit television in adjoining halls. The former projection booth was a center where sermons were translated for worldwide distribution. Wilkerson credited the turnaround of the neighborhood less to secular authorities than to the power of prayer. In any case, the day had come when "Times Square" and "Church" did not seem mismatched on the same bill.

Todas las Naciones, Iglesia Metodista Unida. One of several row-house churches on St. Mark's Place, the sanctuary at no. 48 **[●E44]** tells of its origins in an ornate terra-cotta entablature: FIRST GERMAN METHODIST EPISCOPAL CHURCH, founded in 1842. The church was at 254 East 2nd Street **[F39]**, later the East Side Tabernacle, until it moved here in 1900. First German closed in 1975. The United Methodist Church of All Nations now shares this sanctuary with Manhattan Central United Methodist.

Town and Village Synagogue.
See Tifereth Israel, Congregation

Trans World Buddhist Association Buddha Virtue Temple. The four-story red-brick Trans World Buddhist Association Buddha Virtue Temple is at 7 East Broadway **[●B51]**.

Transfiguration, Church of the.
See Little Church Around the Corner

Transfiguration, Church of the. Built by Anglicans who had converted from Lutheranism and then sold to Roman Catholics for a parish founded by a Cuban priest to serve an Irish and Italian population, this sanctuary at 25 Mott Street [●B45★] is a center of the Chinese community, with a school where most of the children are Buddhist. Transfiguration, indeed!

Church of the Transfiguration **[B45]**

The sanctuary was originally home to Zion Episcopal Church, which endures as the Church of St. Matthew and St. Timothy. Zion rebuilt the structure after an 1815 fire and sold it in 1853 to the Church of the Transfiguration, known as the Church of the Immigrants. This Roman Catholic parish was founded in 1827 by the Rev. Félix Varela y Morales, whom Pope John Paul II described as the "foundation-stone of the Cuban national identity." An advocate of Cuban independence from Spain—which is why he was in exile here—Varela was a social reformer, philosopher, vicar general of the archdiocese, and publisher of an early Spanish-language newspaper, *El Habañero* (The Havanan).

Transfiguration added a steeple by Henry Engelbert in 1868. In the 1950s, Masses began being celebrated in Cantonese, as well as in Italian and English. And in 1976, the Rev. Mark Cheung became the first Chinese pastor of a New York Roman Catholic church. The school, founded by Varela in 1832, was opened to all faiths in 1969.

Transfiguration Lutheran Church **[R26]**

Transfiguration Lutheran Church. The three-story Gothic sanctuary at 74 West 126th Street [●R26] was altered in 1912 by Nathan G. Kelsey for the Lenox Avenue Union Church–Disciples of Christ, which had been at 39 West 119th Street. Transfiguration Lutheran Church, founded by the Rev. Paul Edward West, moved to this building in 1928.

Trinity A.M.E. Church. This building at 259 West 126th Street [●Q23] was a carpenter's shop before the arrival in 1943 of Trinity African Methodist Episcopal Church, founded in 1933 in San Juan Hill by the Rev. Robert Kinlock.

Trinity A.M.E. Church **[Q23]**

Trinity Baptist Church **[L43]**

Trinity Baptist Church. Could this be a church? Your eye is caught by a stepped facade in graduated colors of brick, from loamy brown to bright marigold. You are transported momentarily to Stockholm. The Scandinavian sensibility continues within: blond woods, bottle-blue glass, bold geometry, and expressionistic ornament. If you arrived doubting that Art Deco exuberance could be put to liturgical purpose, you'll leave wishing that there were more buildings like this gem at 250 East 61st Street **[●L43☆]**.

The First Swedish Baptist Church, founded in 1867, conducted services at the Mariners' Temple Baptist Church. By the 1890s, the congregation was at 138 East 27th Street **[●H33]**, later the Davenport Theater and now the Gramercy Arts Theater and Teatro Repertorio Español. It then moved to the former Trinity Baptist Church, at 141 East 55th Street [J3], which later became the American Music Hall.

Plans for the present sanctuary were filed in 1930 by Martin Gravely Hedmark, a Swede, who created a sampler of native motifs, with bell steeples modeled on historic originals and a stepped profile recalling buildings along the Baltic. Major services were conducted in Swedish until 1942, when English was adopted, along with a new name that echoed the past: Trinity.

Trinity Church Graveyard **[A33]**

Trinity Church. King William III was sovereign of New York when Anglican citizens first worshiped in a barnlike church on the Broad Way. More than 300 years later, Trinity Church remains on the same spot. Its continuity alone gives it venerable status, as does its symbolic role as a spiritual counterpoint to Mammon, embodied by the nearby financial houses of Wall Street.

No mere relic, however, Trinity played a vital role on September 11, 2001, and in the months that followed. Indeed, it offered what may have been the very first institutional response to the attack, just after the second jetliner hit the World Trade Center: an impromptu service for those who streamed into the church for shelter and solace. In the midst of a hymn—"O God, our help in ages past"—there came the thunderous collapse of the south tower, casting the church into Stygian pitch and ash. Both Trinity and its chapel,

St. Paul's, survived the attack and ministered to the
needy. Having survived wars, rebellion, riots, and
plagues, it was a role for which this parish was well
suited.

A royal charter granted in 1697 called for Trinity to
pay an annual rent of one peppercorn to the Crown.
The first church [A31] was built in 1698, but the oldest
object in the churchyard is the gravestone of five-year-
old Richard Churcher, who died in 1681 when this was
the town burial ground. Trinity's destiny as an extraordinarily powerful institution was cast by Queen Anne
in 1705 when she enlarged its holdings to 215 acres,
with a parcel stretching along the Hudson River from
Fulton to Christopher Street. The Queen's Farm
encompassed much of what it is today Tribeca and the
West Village. The second Trinity Church [A32], attributed to James Robinson or Josiah Brady, was consecrated in 1790. It lasted until a heavy snowfall in 1839
compelled its demolition.

Trinity Church [A32]

Richard Upjohn designed the present Trinity
Church [●A33★], which was consecrated in 1846.
Astonishing in many ways, it was, first of all, the tallest
building in New York and remained so for four
decades, with a 280-foot, 5-inch spire. The Astor
Memorial, by Frederick Clarke Withers, was added in
1877; the Chapel of All Saints, by Thomas Nash, in
1913; the Bishop William T. Manning Memorial Wing,
by Adams & Woodbridge, in 1966. The Queen's Farm
properties, though vastly depleted, are still a vital part
of Trinity's portfolio, with about two dozen commercial buildings. As for its own real-estate obligations
under the charter of 1697, Trinity presented Queen
Elizabeth II with a jar of 279 peppercorns in 1976, to
cover the rent for all the intervening years.

Trinity Church **[A33]**

Trinity maintained a network of chapels around
town for the ease of its own communicants and for the
performance of inner-city missionary work. Perhaps
the closest rival to the mother church in wealth and
power was Trinity Chapel, at 15 West 25th Street
[●H35★], now St. Sava Serbian Orthodox Cathedral.
The other chapels were:

Trinity Cemetery **[U18]**

Chapel of the Intercession. The hand of Trinity gives
itself away, for what other parish would have had the
resources to build a cathedral-like chapel on upper

Chapel of St. Agnes [M6]

Chapel of St. Chrysostom [I52]

St. John's Chapel [B25]

Broadway [●U18★], now the Church of the Intercession? It sits within Trinity Cemetery, which the parish opened in 1843.

Chapel of St. Agnes. Designed by William A. Potter and built from 1890 to 1892 on West 92nd Street [M6], the Chapel of St. Agnes was simply the best Richardsonian Romanesque church in Manhattan. The Rev. William T. Manning, later bishop of New York, was vicar here at the turn of the twentieth century, when membership exceeded 2,000. But St. Agnes was deemed expendable when the adjoining Trinity School needed an athletic field. It was closed in 1943 and torn down the next year. Happily, something remains. The parish house at 121 West 91st Street is used by Trinity School and protected as a landmark.

St. Augustine's Chapel. The second Trinity mission chapel, St. Augustine's, was organized in 1869. Its Victorian Gothic sanctuary was at 107 East Houston Street [E89]. The chapel moved to 290 Henry Street [●C48★] in 1945 and gained its independence, as St. Augustine's Episcopal Church, in 1976.

St. Christopher's Chapel. St. Christopher's Chapel occupied the Trinity Mission House, at 209 Fulton Street [A4], built in 1887 and closed in 1956. Another chapel opened at 48 Henry Street in 1953 and closed in 1971. This is now the site of the Episcopal Church of Our Savior.

Chapel of St. Chrysostom. St. Chrysostom was the first Trinity mission chapel, designed not to accommodate the well-to-do but to serve the poor. Designed by Richard Upjohn, it was built in 1868/1869 on Seventh Avenue [I52] and stood until 1924.

St. George's Chapel. In 1748, Trinity decided that it was "absolutely Necessary to build a Chappell of Ease," which was constructed in 1752 on Beekman Street [A8] to designs by Robert Crommelin. After St. George's moved as an independent parish to Stuyvesant Square, this rebuilt sanctuary [A9] was Holy Evangelists and then the Free Church of St. George's Chapel before being replaced by the St. George Building.

St. John's Chapel. Rivaling St. Paul's in its beauty, St. John's Chapel was built at 46 Varick Street [B25] from 1803 to 1807, to designs by John McComb Jr. and Isaac McComb. It faced a lovely park of the same name. The idyll was shattered in 1868 with the construction in the park of the New York Central & Hudson River Rail Road Freight Depot. The chapel closed in 1909, but the old church building endured for another nine years, until the city widened Varick Street. St. John's Burying Ground, where Edgar Allan Poe once spent time walking among the 800 gravestones, is now James J. Walker Park. On the north side of the park is a poignant remnant of the cemetery: a marble coffin, topped by two firemen's helmets, containing the remains of 20-year-old Eugene Underhill and 22-year-old Frederick A. Ward, who lost their lives in 1834 "by the falling of a building."

St. Paul's Chapel **[A5]**

Chapel of St. Luke. The parish of St. Luke sold its sanctuary at 487 Hudson Street [●D17☆] to Trinity in 1891 and received assistance in meeting the cost of its new building on Convent Avenue. For more than 80 years, Trinity operated and added to the Chapel of St. Luke. Like Intercession, it was spun off again, as the Church of St. Luke in the Fields, in 1976.

St. Paul's Chapel. In ephemeral New York—miraculously—stands the chapel where thanksgiving prayers were offered by the first president of the United States immediately after his inauguration on April 30, 1789. The chaste architecture of Manhattan's oldest church [●A5★] practically invites you to listen for the sound of the Founders' ghosts, the excited clamor and heartfelt petitions as both Houses of Congress gathered here following the inauguration. Quite literally Colonial in

St. Paul's Chapel **[A5]**

style, St. Paul's Chapel was built from 1764 to 1766. The building seems to have been patterned on St. Martin-in-the-Fields in London. Thomas McBean is frequently credited with the design, though recent scholarship assigns a role to Andrew Gautier.

Surrounded by wheat fields, St. Paul's served Trinity communicants out in the countryside. The honor of conducting the 1789 thanksgiving service fell to St. Paul's—not Trinity—because the mother church had burned in the great fire of 1776 and was not yet rebuilt. President Washington worshiped at St. Paul's until the capital moved to Philadelphia. (Only later, in 1794, was the noble wooden steeple added, by James Crommelin Lawrence.) The presidential pew is still set aside and was occupied by George H. W. Bush on a visit in 1989

St. Paul's Chapel
(September 11, 2001,
memorial fence) **[A5]**

to commemorate the bicentenary of George Washington's inauguration. But it is not only presidents who are welcomed. The balcony has served for 20 years as a shelter for homeless men.

St. Paul's noblest and most tireless role came after September 11, 2001, when it sheltered and comforted the police officers, firefighters, rescue workers, and laborers engaged in the heroic effort of combing through and carting off the ruins of the World Trade Center, directly across Church Street. Washington's pew became the podiatrist station. St. Paul's offered its great iron fence as the setting of a magnificently impromptu people's memorial. For months, it was covered with missing-person posters, family snapshots, baseball caps, T-shirts, teddy bears, origami cranes, candles, and poems—inspiring a reverential hush from almost everyone who approached.

Trinity Community Church. What may be Manhattan's last neon "Jesus Saves" sign hangs outside the Trinity Community Church, at 138 Henry Street [●C39].

Trinity Evangelical Lutheran Church
[O24]

Trinity Evangelical Lutheran Church. Spared the urban-renewal wrecking ball, Trinity Evangelical Lutheran Church, at 168 West 100th Street [●O24], still dominates its setting. This German congregation was founded in 1888, and the present sanctuary, designed by George W. Conable, was built in 1908.

Trinity Lower East Side Lutheran Parish
[F11]

Trinity Lower East Side Lutheran Parish. The imaginatively unconventional church at 602 East 9th Street [●F12] houses the fourth-oldest Lutheran congregation in Manhattan. Trinity Lower East Side Lutheran Parish was founded in 1843. Its earlier Greek Revival home [F11] was built in 1847 as the Ninth Street Church–Dry Dock Mission. The present sanctuary, with a 100-seat chapel, was designed by Robert Litchfield and built in 1993. Concrete-block quoins around red-brick walls create a spirited facade on a limited budget.

Trinity Lower East Side
Lutheran Parish **[F12]**

Trinity Lutheran Church. A Gothic tower at 542 West 153rd Street [●U21], overlooking Trinity Cemetery, marks this former sanctuary, which now serves the

New York Foundling Hospital. The Washington Heights German Evangelical Lutheran congregation, founded in 1895, built a church on this site [U20] in 1897/1898, by Dodge & Morrison. A new church was designed by Francis Averkamp in 1921, the same year the congregation changed its name to Christ Evangelical Lutheran. It was known for a time as Trinity Lutheran, after a merger with the church at 168 West 100th Street.

Trinity Lutheran Church [U21]

Trinity Presbyterian Church | Rauschenbusch Memorial United Church of Christ. The Mizpah Chapel of the Central Presbyterian Church moved in 1886 to 422 West 57th Street [●K37] and remained an outpost of Central Presbyterian until 1947, when Trinity Presbyterian Church was organized. It has since been joined by the Rauschenbusch Memorial United Church of Christ.

Trinity Presbyterian Church [K37]

True Buddha Diamond Temple. At the base of the former Down Town Community House, built in 1925 at 105 Washington Street [●A29], is the True Buddha Diamond Temple, the primary New York temple for the True Buddha school, founded by Grand Master Sheng-yen Lu.

True Buddha Diamond Temple [A29]

True Light Lutheran Church. If such a thing can be imagined as Sino-Deco-Gothic, 195 Worth Street [●B47] is it. The True Light Lutheran Church was founded in 1936 on Canal Street. Its sanctuary was built in 1948/1949 to designs by Bernard W. Guenther and Ralph S. Meyers. The roof was supposed to have been in the form of a pagoda.

True Reformed Dutch Church. Buttresses and grotesques mark a row house at 21 Bank Street [●D7✫] that was converted in 1893 into a sanctuary for the short-lived True Reformed Dutch Church.

Twirl. *See* Chelsea Presbyterian Church

True Light Lutheran Church [B47]

U-V

Ulanower, Congregation. The synagogue at 630 East 5th Street [F27] served Congregation B'nai Sholom and then Congregation Ulanower, founded in 1906.

Unification Church. The denomination founded in 1954 by the Rev. Sun Myung Moon, the Holy Spirit Association for the Unification of World Christianity, acquired the former Columbia University Club, at 4 West 43rd Street [● J47], in 1974.

Union Baptist Church **[T5]**

Union Baptist Church. Like other black churches, Union Baptist, founded in 1898 by the Rev. George H. Sims Sr., testifies in its origins to the days when Lincoln Square was an African-American community. After a brief spell at 223 West 67th Street [K16], Union built a church in 1901 at 204 West 63rd Street [K25] by W. A. Gorman, adding a larger sanctuary next door in 1905. It remained there until 1927, when it moved to 240 West 145th Street [●T5], the Odeon Theater Annex of 1919 by Thomas W. Lamb. (The Odeon itself is now St. Paul's Community Church.) The sanctuary was modernized in 1989 under the Rev. Ollie B. Wells Sr.

Union Congregational Church **[T19]**

Union Congregational Church. The pioneering black architects Vertner Woodson Tandy and George Washington Foster Jr. designed this sanctuary at 60 West 138th Street [●T19] in 1911 for the Rush Memorial A.M.E. Zion Church, named for Bishop Christopher Rush. This congregation is the black church with the longest continuous presence in Harlem and now worships at 160 West 146th Street as Greater Hood Memorial. In 1935, the 138th Street building was acquired by Union Congregational Church, which was founded in 1920 by the Rev. James E. Sargeant as the Ebenezer Moravian Church.

Union Methodist Episcopal Church **[I21]**

Union Methodist Episcopal Church. "Union Church Social Center Always Open," declared the sign in front of this Neoclassical church by Weary & Kramer, built in 1894 at 229 West 48th Street [I21] for a congregation founded that year as a merger of the Forty-third Street and St. John's Churches. Its motto was "99 Steps from Broadway," and its nickname, the Actors' Church. The Union Methodist Episcopal Church had a theater in its attic and, in its basement restaurant, fed unemployed actors during the Depression.

Union Reformed Church. The Waverly Theater, at 325 Avenue of the Americas [●E66], has a surprise in plain sight: a high peaked roof that gives it away as something more than a 1937 cinema. Its bones may be as old as 1831, when a church on this site was built for the Third Universalist Society. After four years as the Third Associate Presbyterian Church, it was acquired by St. Jude's Free Episcopal Church, forerunner of St. John's in the Village. It was then home to the Union Reformed Church until 1893. That year, J. & R. Lamb filed alteration plans of their own design, and the building—fittingly—became the studio of the Lamb Ecclesiastical Art Works, which it remained until 1935. It was altered again, by Harrison Wiseman, into the Waverly. But as that peaked roof reveals, there is still a bit of church to it yet.

Union Reformed Church (J. & R. Lamb) [E66]

Union Reformed Church (Waverly Theater) [E66]

United House of Prayer for All People. "Praise him with trumpet sound," says Psalm 150. And this congregation does. The United House of Prayer for All People has been a charismatic presence since the arrival in 1920 of its founder, Bishop C. M. Grace—Sweet Daddy Grace—at 20 West 115th Street [R69], where thousands came for an exultant form of worship called "shouting," accompanied by brass bands. The building was razed in 1947, but the block is still used every August for a mass baptism by fire hose. The present sanctuary, the Mother House, at 2320 Frederick Douglass Boulevard [●Q30], is in a block-long complex that includes a popular soul-food cafeteria and commercial space on West 125th Street. A conflict in 1995 between a Jewish-owned clothing store and its subtenant, a popular black-owned record store, ended dreadfully when a gunman set fire to the clothing store, killing himself and seven others. A renovation and expansion of the building by Edward E. Cherry, which the church had planned before the incident, was completed in 1997, when the new sanctuary was dedicated.

United House of Prayer for All People [Q30]

United Moravian Church **[R24]**

United Moravian Church. The congregations united in this large sanctuary at 200 East 127th Street **[●R24]** are the Third and Fourth Moravian Churches. The Third, a group drawn mostly from the West Indies, worshiped in the 1930s at 410 West 45th Street **[●I31]**. The merged groups were at 2100 Lexington Avenue before building this sanctuary, designed by Johnson Hanchard in 1977.

United Nations, Church Center for the. *See* Tillman Chapel

United Palace. Could there be a better setting for a charismatic evangelist who liked to say, "You don't have to wait for your pie in the sky by and by; have it now with ice cream and a cherry on top"? The Rev. Frederick J. Eikerenkoetter II—Reverend Ike—had the sense in 1969 to acquire the Loew's 175th Street Theater **[●V31]**, a 1930 movie palace by Thomas W. Lamb, who seems to have borrowed from the Alhambra in Spain, the Kailasa rock-cut shrine in India, and the Wat Phra Keo temple in Thailand, adding Buddhas, bodhisattvas, elephants, and honeycomb stonework in an Islamic pattern known as *muqarnas*. Reverend Ike's United Church takes far better care of the former theater, now known as the United Palace, than any exhibitor would have. Places like this were meant to make you feel like a million dollars, and that was just right for the church "under the spout, where the blessings pour out." With a cherry on top.

United Palace **[V31]**

Universal Church **[E62]**

Universal Church. Formerly the New York Jewish Evangelization Society, the pediment-topped building at 56 Second Avenue **[●E62]** houses the Universal Church and the East Side Church of Christ.

Universal Hagar's Spiritual Church **[S2]**

Universal Hagar's Spiritual Church. Father George William Hurley has a place in the pantheon of Harlem evangelists. His movement, named for a brown-skinned damsel whom he had seen in a vision, was founded in 1923. To the notion that one finds reward in heaven—a concept, it might be argued, by which white oppressors seek to palliate black suffering—Universal Hagar's Spiritual Church answers, in its commandments: "Thou shall believe in heaven and hell here on earth." It has long occupied the former Duroyd Gasket and Die Manufacturing Company building at 419 West 150th Street [●S2].

University Place Presbyterian Church. Richard Upjohn seemed unsure that Gothic was the right style for Reformed churches, which had originated after the Gothic period. So he devised an even more inventive hybrid style for the University Place Presbyterian Church, built in 1844/1845 at 49 University Place [E32]. Organized by members of the Duane Street Church in 1845 and joined by the Mercer Street Church in 1870, this congregation was folded into the First Presbyterian Church in 1918.

University Place Presbyterian Church [E32]

Upper Madison Avenue United Methodist Church. Part of the community center for the Taft Houses, 1723 Madison Avenue [●R71] was designed in 1967 by Edgar Tafel. It was occupied in 1977 by the new Upper Madison Avenue United Methodist Church, under the Rev. John Warner, which was a merger of the Taft Church and the Jefferson Park Methodist Episcopal Church. The center continues to accommodate community programs like Head Start.

Upper Madison Avenue United Methodist Church [R71]

Urban Outfitters. *See* Baptist Tabernacle

Vermilye Chapel. A Reformed Dutch sanctuary built in 1890 in the rear yard of 414 West 54th Street [I5], the Vermilye Chapel closed in 1935.

Victory Tabernacle Seventh-Day Christian Church. This delightful little Venetian Romanesque confection at 252 West 138th Street [●T15] was born to be a sanctuary, even though it was constructed as an office of the Equitable Life Assurance Society in 1895, to designs by Jardine, Kent & Jardine. Remodeled by Vertner Woodson Tandy in 1923, it housed the Coachmen's Union League Society, whose members were photographed here by James VanDerZee. For a time, it was home to the Mount Pleasant Baptist Church. The Victory Tabernacle Seventh-Day Christian Church arrived in 1942 and shared the building for a time with the Thomas Memorial Wesleyan Methodist Church.

Victory Tabernacle Seventh-Day Christian Church [T15]

Village Presbyterian Church **[E20]**

Village Presbyterian Church. With a stately, sheltering portico that seems to embrace the whole block, the Thirteenth Street Presbyterian Church opened in 1847 at 143 West 13th Street [●E20☆]. The design, attributed to Samuel Thomson, is based on the Theseion in Athens. This is one of the most sweetly tranquil cityscapes in Manhattan; a white, wooden Greek temple snuggled in among nineteenth-century homes.

But not all has been tranquil within. The Rev. Samuel C. Burchard was indirectly credited—or blamed—for the election of Grover Cleveland in 1884 after the backlash among Catholics to his description of Democrats as the party of "rum, Romanism and rebellion."

In 1954, the Rev. Jesse W. Stitt, pastor of the Village Presbyterian Church, as the sanctuary was then called, welcomed the Brotherhood Synagogue, founded by Rabbi Irving J. Block. "God does not favor one religious institution over another or the cloak of one minister over another," Stitt said. For 20 years, the Christian and Jewish congregations shared a house of worship. But this celebrated ecumenical arrangement dissolved in a battle of words during the Yom Kippur War of 1973. After Block posted a sign outside the church wishing "victory and peace for Israel," the gesture was denounced by the Rev. William Glenesk, Stitt's controversial successor. The synagogue moved to Gramercy Park, and the church closed in 1975.

Seven years later, the building was converted into a co-op. To preserve the dignity of this noble temple front, the architect Stephen B. Jacobs moved the new residential entrance to the side. Equally beguiling is the signboard for "The Village Presbyterian Church" out front, posted with what look like hymn numbers—141, 143, 145—but are in fact the street address.

Village Temple **[E28]**

Village Temple. The Village Temple, at 33 East 12th Street [●E28], has been home since 1957 to Congregation B'nai Israel (Sons of Israel), a Reform group founded in 1948.

Wadsworth Avenue Baptist Church **[V13]**

Wadsworth Avenue Baptist Church. A rocket burst of Georgian energy, complete with a slender steeple, the Wadsworth Avenue Baptist Church occupies a dramatic bluff-side setting at 210 Wadsworth Avenue **[●V13]**. Plans were filed in 1924 by Ludlow & Peabody. The congregation moved here from 124 Wadsworth Avenue [V21], which later became the Washington Heights Hellenic Church of St. Spyridon.

Wall Street Synagogue. The Wall Street Synagogue is an Orthodox congregation founded in 1929. On the roof of its sanctuary, at 47 Beekman Street **[●A7]**, it built a 12- by 20-foot replica of the humble cabin that housed Congregation Shearith Israel, on South William Street, preserving in three dimensions the memory of New York's earliest synagogue.

Wall Street Synagogue
[A7]

Walters Memorial A.M.E. Zion Church. Once the Central Republican Club, 229 Malcolm X Boulevard **[●Q48]** served as the home from 1937 to 1951 of the Greater Hood Memorial A.M.E. Zion Church, the oldest black church in Harlem, and now is Walters Memorial African Methodist Episcopal Zion Church.

Warren Hall. *See* Baptist Tabernacle

Warshawer Shul. *See* Erste Warshawer, Congregation

Iglesia Pentecostal de Washington Heights
[V25]

Washington Heights, Iglesia Pentecostal de. The oldest Spanish Pentecostal church in Washington Heights was founded in 1935 out of the Bethel Church. In 1966, it acquired a two-story commercial building at 281 Audubon Avenue **[●V25]** for its sanctuary. The Rev. Carlos R. Reyes has been the pastor here for 45 years.

Washington Heights Congregation. A Modernist castle with a crenellated facade at 815 West 179th Street **[●V18]** is home to the Orthodox Washington Heights Congregation, founded in 1914. It had worshiped in a synagogue at 510 West 161st Street [U6] by Mitchell Bernstein. The present sanctuary was designed in 1965 by David Kraus for Temple Beth Sholom, founded in 1931.

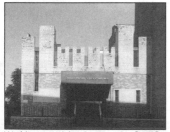

Washington Heights Congregation **[V18]**

Washington Heights Presbyterian Church. Among the very first houses of worship in upper Manhattan, the

Washington Heights Presbyterian Church was built in 1860 at 1920 Amsterdam Avenue [U16]. The congregation merged with the nearby North Presbyterian Church in 1905.

Washington Heights United Presbyterian Church.

See Camino, Iglesia el

Washington Square United Methodist Church. Among the 50 oldest houses of worship in Manhattan can be counted one of its most progressive congregations, the "Peace Church," housed in an ornate Romanesque Revival sanctuary built before the Civil War at 135 West 4th Street [●E53☆]. The congregation emerged from the Sullivan Street Methodist Episcopal Church, at 149 Sullivan Street [E84], a reorganized Episcopal group founded in 1842. Its sanctuary became the Church of St. Anthony of Padua. The present church was built in 1859/1860 to designs by Charles Hadden, and the congregation changed its name to reflect its new location. In 1893, the Asbury Methodist Episcopal Church, on the other side of Washington Square, merged with the Washington Square United Methodist Church.

This was a center for antiwar activism during the Vietnam War and has stayed true to that course. "The United States military does not dominate the skies over Iraq," the Rev. Bryan Travis Hooper preached in March 2003. "The skies over Iraq, like the skies everywhere, are the domain of God alone." The church is also a sanctuary for gay New Yorkers. The Harvey Milk School for lesbian and gay youth began at Washington Square in 1985, and the Rev. Paul M. Abels, pastor from 1973 to 1984, was the first openly gay minister with a congregation in a major Christian denomination.

Washington Heights Presbyterian Church [U16]

Washington Square United Methodist Church [E53]

Waverly Theater. See Union Reformed Church

Way of the Cross Tabernacle of Christ. There are not many parlorfront churches in this book, but an exception is made for 126 West 136th Street [●T24] because it has served as a sanctuary for more than 80 years. It was formerly the Fourth Moravian Church and then the Mount Pleasant Baptist Church. The Way of the Cross Tabernacle of Christ acquired it in 1977.

West End Collegiate Church
[M34]

West End Presbyterian
Church **[O13]**

West Forty-fourth Street United
Presbyterian Church (Actors Studio) **[I34]**

West Side Institutional Synagogue **[M37]**

West End Collegiate Church. In 1891/1892, the Collegiate Reformed Protestant Dutch Church built a sanctuary that actually looks Dutch, at 368 West End Avenue [●M34★], standing out from Manhattan gray with its yellow-orange brickwork. The architect Robert W. Gibson drew on Dutch cityscapes—in particular, the seventeenth-century Vleeshal in Haarlem—for the crowstep gables and picturesque dormers of the West End Collegiate Church, affiliated with Fort Washington, Marble, and Middle. The complex included a home for the Collegiate School, which was established in 1628 as part of the Reformed Dutch Church.

West End Presbyterian Church. The Amsterdam Avenue skyline is blessed with great church towers, including this tall and exquisitely detailed Romanesque Revival spire at 165 West 105th Street [●O13], designed by Henry F. Kilburn and built in 1891. The West End Presbyterian Church is a beacon in yellow brick and terra-cotta. Founded in 1888, it was once the largest Presbyterian congregation in the city.

West End Synagogue. "Jews like to think of themselves as children of the Book," said the architect Henry Stolzman of Pasanella + Klein Stolzman + Berg. So he found especially felicitous the assignment in 1997 to transform the 30-year-old Riverside Branch of the New York Public Library, at 190 Amsterdam Avenue [●K12], into the West End Synagogue, for a Reconstructionist congregation founded in 1985.

West Forty-fourth Street United Presbyterian Church. This sanctuary at 432 West 44th Street [●I34★] was one of the last Greek Revival churches, built in 1858 or 1859 for the Seventh Associate Presbyterian Church, founded in 1855, when this area was farmland. In its latter years of religious service, it was the West Forty-fourth Street United Presbyterian Church, which disbanded in 1944. The most famous preacher in this pulpit was Lee Strasberg, the artistic director of the Actors Studio, which acquired the building in 1955. And in the pews sat Marilyn Monroe and Marlon Brando.

West Side Institutional Synagogue. The Romanesque sanctuary at 120 West 76th Street [●M37☆], designed by Cady, Berg & See, was built from 1888 to 1890 for St. Andrew's Methodist Episcopal Church. After that congregation merged with and moved into St. Paul's in 1937, this building became the West Side Institutional Synagogue. Founded in 1917 by Rabbi Herbert S. Goldstein to "integrate the sanctuary, study and social halls and gymnasium within an Orthodox Jewish atmosphere attractive to an American constituency," the Institutional Synagogue had been at 37 West 116th Street [●R57], now the Salvation and Deliverance Church. The grilles and entrance screen on the West 76th Street synagogue were added in 1965.

West Side Methodist Episcopal Church [I30]

West Side Methodist Episcopal Church. The sanctuary at 461 West 44th Street [I30] was built in 1863 as the Janes Methodist Episcopal Church, later known as the Forty-fourth Street Church, which merged in 1917 with the Thirty-fifth Street Church to form the West Side Methodist Episcopal Church.

West Presbyterian Church [E81]

West-Park Presbyterian Church. One of the finest Romanesque sanctuaries in Manhattan, West-Park Presbyterian Church is a landmark in every sense but the official one. And its fate is uncertain. What is at stake—besides a neighborhood icon—is an institution, created by merger in 1911, that can be traced to 1829. The first sanctuary of the West Presbyterian Church [E81], or Carmine Street Church, was built in 1831 to designs by Town & Davis. The congregation next built an exuberant Victorian Gothic church in 1862 at 31 West 42nd Street [J46].

Park Church was founded in 1854 as the Eighty-fourth Street Presbyterian Church, with a wood-frame sanctuary on West End Avenue [M20] by Leopold Eidlitz. Under the Rev. Anson Phelps Atterbury, it built a chapel by Eidlitz in 1884 on West 86th Street. Complementing the chapel, Henry F. Kilburn designed a rugged and ruddy main church in 1890 at 539 Amsterdam Avenue [●M16]. It is marked on the skyline by a corner tower with bell-shaped roof so vigorous that it stands in confident counterpoint to even the enormous Belnord apartment block across the avenue. But architectural power alone is not enough to sustain a congregation.

West Presbyterian Church [J46]

West-Park Presbyterian Church [M16]

Westside Theater.
See Rauschenbusch Memorial United Church of Christ

Williams Institutional C.M.E. Church
(original facade) [Q10]

Williams Institutional C.M.E. Church
(present facade) **[Q10]**

Buddhist Society of Wonderful
Enlightenment **[C31]**

Williams Institutional C.M.E. Church. "The most stylish black showplace in Harlem," as Jervis Anderson called the Lafayette Theater, forms the structural core of the Williams Institutional Christian Methodist Episcopal Church, at 2225 Adam Clayton Powell Jr. Boulevard **[●Q10]**. But its great facade is gone. Designed by Victor Hugo Koehler, the Lafayette opened in 1912. Two years later, Lester Walton, the theater critic of the *Age*, was appointed manager. And two years after that, Charles Gilpin (who went on to an acclaimed turn with the Provincetown Players in *The Emperor Jones*) formed the Lafayette Players, black Harlem's first legitimate-theater group. In the 1930s, the Lafayette was the home of the WPA's Negro Theater Project, where Orson Welles directed the all-black *Macbeth*.

The Williams congregation was founded in 1919 and worshiped for many years at 220 West 130th Street [Q13], the former Hebrew Tabernacle. It bought the theater in 1951 and kept the facade largely intact until 1990, when Percy Griffin designed a new front. The idea was "to make it look more like a church than a theater," said the Rev. James Arthur Jones. That it does, a gabled pavilion with a stained-glass rose window, flanked by three steel crosses on one side and three bells on the other.

Wonderful Enlightenment, Buddhist Society of. Upswept eaves denote the Buddhist Society of Wonderful Enlightenment, a small storefront temple of the Ch'an school at 99 Madison Street **[●C31]**.

Y-Z

DEUTSCHE EV. KIRCHE V.
YORKVILLE.

Yorkville Synagogue **[N42]**

Yorkville Synagogue. The Yorkville Synagogue, at 352 East 78th Street **[●N42]**, home to the Orthodox Congregation B'nai Jehudah (Sons of Judah), is ornamented only by a Decalogue. Plans were filed in 1925 by Benjamin H. Whinston.

Young Israel of Fifth Avenue. The inscription LABOR OMNIA VINCIT over the sanctuary window at 3 West 16th Street **[●E4]**, now Young Israel of Fifth Avenue, reflects the fact that this little 1920 building, designed by Charles H. Higgins, once housed the International Ladies Garment Workers Union, Misses and Children's Dressmakers Union, Waterproof Garment Workers Union, White Goods Workers Union, and radio station WEVD—as in Eugene V. Debs, the Socialist leader.

Young Israel of Fifth Avenue **[E4]**

Young Israel of the West Side. By far the most aesthetically distinguished of the Young Israel synagogues is Young Israel of the West Side, at 210 West 91st Street **[●M8]**, built in 1920 to designs by William Tachau. It was originally Temple Israel, whose name is still inscribed on the facade even though it moved out in 1967.

Young Israel of the West Side **[M8]**

Young Israel Synagogue. The oldest congregation in the worldwide Orthodox movement called Young Israel stands in the midst of Shtiebl Row. Young Israel formed in 1912 among second-generation Americanized students who were seeking to bring about a revival of Judaism through innovative religious, educational, and social programs. During a lecture at the Kalvarier Shul, on Pike Street, Rabbi Judah L. Magnes suggested that this movement have a name. Someone in the crowd answered, "We in America are the young of Israel!" In 1929, Young Israel opened its present sanctuary at 235 East Broadway **[●C46]**, formerly the Hebrew Immigrant Aid Society.

Young Israel Synagogue **[C46]**

Yung Kee Wholesale Center.
See Disciples of Christ, Church of the

Zichron Ephraim, Congregation. See Park East Synagogue

Zichron Moshe, Congregation. A spartan sanctuary at 342 East 20th Street [●H58], designed by Joseph J. Furman in 1955, is home to Congregation Zichron Moshe, founded in 1917.

Congregation Zichron Moshe [H58]

Zion Baptist Church. An African-American congregation founded in 1832, Zion Baptist Church moved in 1839 to 488 Pearl Street [B48], which had served Zion Lutheran Church, the First Universalist Society, the Church of the New Jerusalem, and St. James Lutheran Church. At the turn of the twentieth century, before relocating uptown to 2148 Fifth Avenue, Zion briefly occupied 166 Waverly Place [E46], formerly Abyssinian Baptist Church. It can therefore be said that one sanctuary in this book actually went from Abyssinian to Zion.

Zion–St. Mark's Lutheran Church. At 339 East 84th Street [●N22] stands Yorkville's last German-speaking church, even in its facade: DEUTSCHE EV. KIRCHE V. YORKVILLE. St. Mark's Lutheran Church, the older half of this merged body, worshiped at 325 East 6th Street [●E52] from 1847 to 1940. It is destined to be remembered for having suffered a most appalling loss of 784 members—including 511 children and 191 mothers—aboard the excursion steamer *General Slocum*, which burned in the East River in 1904. Until September 11, 2001, the *Slocum* disaster was the most devastating single incident in New York City history.

Zion Church, incorporated in 1893, bought the East 84th Street sanctuary, which had been built in 1888 to designs by J. F. Mahoney for the German Evangelical Church of Yorkville. In recent years, though the German population had almost disappeared, a *deutscher Gottesdienst* (German service) continued to be celebrated at Zion–St. Mark's Lutheran Church every Sunday.

Zion–St. Mark's Lutheran Church [N22]

BIBLIOGRAPHY

RELIGIOUS INSTITUTIONS AND COMMUNITIES
Books and Bound Volumes

*An Account of the Proceedings Incidental to the Opening for
    Public Worship of the Bloomingdale Reformed Church,
    Broadway and 68th Street, in New York City.* New York:
    The Consistory, 1886.
All Saints Church: A Profile. New York: All Saints Church, 1992.
Anstice, Henry. *History of St. George's Church in the City of
    New York, 1752–1811–1911.* New York: Harper, 1911.
Beasley, Norman. *The Cross and the Crown: The History of
    Christian Science.* Boston: Little, Brown, 1952.
Bennett, William Harper. *Catholic Footsteps in Old New York.*
    New York: Schwartz, Kirwin & Fauss, 1909.
———. *Handbook to Catholic Historical New York City.* New
    York: Schwartz, Kirwin & Fauss, 1927.
Bergman, Edward F. *The Spiritual Traveler: New York City:
    The Guide to Sacred Spaces and Peaceful Places.* Mahwah,
    N.J.: HiddenSpring, 2001.
Birstein, Ann. *The Rabbi on Forty-seventh Street.* New York:
    Dial, 1982.
Block, Irving J. *A Rabbi and His Dream: Building the Broth-
    erhood Synagogue, a Memoir.* Hoboken, N.J.: KTAV, 1999.
Bridgeman, Charles Thorley. *A History of the Parish of Trini-
    ty Church in the City of New York.* Vol. 6. New York: Trini-
    ty Church, 1962.
Brolin, Brent C. *The Battle of St. Bart's.* New York: Morrow,
    1988.

Brower, William Leverich. *Tercentenary of the City of New York: A Tribute to the Settlement of Manhattan Island, Now New York, by the Dutch, Early in the Seventeenth Century.* New York: Consistory of the Collegiate Reformed Dutch Church, 1926.

Brown, Mary Elizabeth. *From Italian Villages to Greenwich Village: Our Lady of Pompei, 1892–1992.* New York: Center for Migration Studies, 1992.

Bruckbauer, Frederick. *The Kirk on Rutgers Farm.* New York: Revell, 1919.

Bunker, John. *From Holystones to Gantry Cranes: A Brief History of the Seamen's Church Institute of New York and New Jersey.* New York: Seamen's Church Institute, 1984.

Burton, Katherine. *The Dream Lives Forever: The Story of Saint Patrick's Cathedral.* New York: Longmans, Green, 1960.

Carmer, Carl. *The Years of Grace, 1808–1958.* New York: Grace Church, 1958.

Carthy, Mary Peter. *A Cathedral of Suitable Magnificence: St. Patrick's Cathedral, New York.* Wilmington, Del.: Glazier, 1984.

——. *Old St. Patrick's: New York's First Cathedral.* New York: United States Catholic Historical Society, 1947.

Chambers, Talbot W. *The Noon Prayer Meeting of the North Dutch Church, Fulton Street, New York.* New York: Board of Publication of the Reformed Protestant Dutch Church, 1858.

Chorley, E. Clowes. *The Centennial History of Saint Bartholomew's Church, 1835–1935.* New York: St. Bartholomew's Church, 1935.

——, ed. *Quarter of a Millennium: Trinity Church in the City of New York, 1697–1947.* Philadelphia: Church Historical Society, 1947.

Church Directory, 1986–87. New York: Council of Churches of the City of New York, 1986.

Church Directory, 1993–94. New York: Council of Churches of the City of New York, 1993.

The Church of the Puritans, Presbyterian: 130th Street, near 5th Avenue, New-York. New York: De Vinne, 1889.

Churchyards of Trinity Parish in the City of New York. New York: Trinity Parish, 1947.

Clarkson, David. *History of the Church of Zion and St. Timothy of New York, 1797–1894.* New York: Putnam, 1894.

Cohalan, Florence D. *A Popular History of the Archdiocese of New York.* 2d ed. Yonkers, N.Y.: United States Catholic Historical Society, 1999.

Competitive Designs for the Cathedral of St. John the Divine in New York City. Reprint. New York: Da Capo, 1982.

Cook, Leland. *St. Patrick's Cathedral: A Centennial History.* New York: Quick Fox, 1979.

Cook, Terri. *Sacred Havens: A Guide to Manhattan's Spiritual Places.* New York: Crossroad, 2001.

Cox, John, Jr. *Quakerism in the City of New York, 1657–1930*. New York: Privately printed, 1930.

Davis, Nancy, and Joy Levitt. *The Guide to Everything Jewish in New York*. New York: Adama, 1986.

De Sola Pool, David. *Portraits Etched in Stone: Early Jewish Settlers, 1682–1831*. New York: Columbia University Press, 1952.

De Sola Pool, David, and Tamar de Sola Pool. *An Old Faith in the New World: Portrait of Shearith Israel, 1654–1954*. New York: Columbia University Press, 1955.

De Witt, Thomas. *A Discourse Delivered in the North Reformed Dutch Church (Collegiate) in the City of New-York*. New York: Board of Publication of the Reformed Protestant Dutch Church, 1857.

Dedication of the Meeting-House of the Society for Ethical Culture of New York. New York: Society for Ethical Culture, 1910.

DeMille, George E. *Saint Thomas Church in the City and County of New York, 1823–1954*. Austin, Tex.: Church Historical Society, 1958.

Disosway, Gabriel P. *The Earliest Churches of New York and Its Vicinity*. New York: Gregory, 1865.

Dix, John A., and Leicester C. Lewis, ed. *A History of the Parish of Trinity Church in the City of New York*. Vol. 5. New York: Columbia University Press, 1950.

Dix, Morgan, ed. *A History of the Parish of Trinity Church in the City of New York*. Vols. 1–4. New York: Putnam, 1898–1906.

Dodds, Jerrilynn D., with photographs by Edward Grazda. *New York Masjid: The Mosques of New York City*. New York: PowerHouse, 2002.

Dunlap, David W., and Joseph J. Vecchione. *Glory in Gotham: Manhattan's Houses of Worship*. New York: City & Company, 2001.

Dupré, Judith. *Churches*. New York: HarperCollins, 2001.

Edelblute, Lucius A. *The History of the Church of the Holy Apostles (Protestant Episcopal), 1844–1944*. New York: Church of the Holy Apostles, 1949.

Emhardt, William Chauncey, Thomas Burgess, and Robert Frederick Lau. *The Eastern Church in the Western World*. Milwaukee: Morehouse, 1928.

Evanzz, Karl. *The Messenger: The Rise and Fall of Elijah Muhammad*. New York: Pantheon, 1999.

Farley, John M. *History of St. Patrick's Cathedral*. New York: Society for the Propagation of the Faith, 1908.

Farr, James McCullough. *A Short History of the Brick Presbyterian Church in the City of New York, 1768–1943*. New York: Brick Presbyterian Church, 1943.

Fleming, Daniel J. *Education Through Stone and Glass*. New York: Union Theological Seminary, n.d.

Force, Benjamin Q. *The History of the Charter Church of New York Methodism, Eighteenth Street, 1835–1885*. New York: Phillips & Hunt, 1885.

Fort Washington Collegiate Church, 1909–1959. New York: Fort Washington Collegiate Church, 1959.

Fowler, Dorothy Ganfield. *A City Church: The First Presbyterian Church in the City of New York, 1716–1976.* New York: First Presbyterian Church, 1981.

Francois, Edgard, with illustrations by Romare Bearden. *St. Martin's: A New York Landmark.* New York: St. Martin's Church, 1967.

Fuld, Stella F., ed. *Central Synagogue, 140 Years.* New York: Central Synagogue, 1979.

Goldstein, Israel. *A Century of Judaism in New York: B'nai Jeshurun, 1825–1925.* New York: Congregation B'nai Jeshurun, 1930.

Gore, Robert L., Jr. *We've Come This Far: The Abyssinian Baptist Church, a Photographic Journal.* New York: Stewart, Tabori & Chang, 2001.

Greenleaf, Jonathan. *A History of the Churches, of All Denominations, in the City of New York, from the First Settlement to the Year 1846.* New York: French, 1846.

Grinstein, Hyman B. *The Rise of the Jewish Community of New York, 1654–1860.* Philadelphia: Jewish Publication Society of America, 1947.

Grove, Harold E. *St. Thomas Church.* New York: St. Thomas Church, 1965.

Gurock, Jeffrey S. *American Jewish Orthodoxy in Historical Perspective.* Hoboken, N.J.: KTAV, 1996.

——. *When Harlem Was Jewish, 1870–1930.* New York: Columbia University Press, 1979.

Haberstroh, Richard. *The German Churches of Metropolitan New York: A Research Guide.* New York: New York Genealogical & Biographical Society, 2000.

Haldeman, I. M. *A History of the First Baptist Church in the City of New York.* Rev. ed. New York: First Baptist Church in the City of New York, 1953.

Hall, Edward Hagaman. *A Guide to the Cathedral Church of Saint John the Divine in the City of New York.* 17th ed. New York: Dean and Chapter of the Cathedral Church, 1965.

Hickman, Cynthia. *Harlem Churches at the End of the Twentieth Century: An Illustrated Guide.* New York: Dunbar, 2001.

Historical Records Survey. *Guide to Vital Statistics in the City of New York: Churches.* New York: Works Progress Administration, 1942.

——. *Inventory of the Church Archives in New York City: Eastern Orthodox Churches and the Armenian Church in America.* New York: Works Progress Administration, 1940.

——. *Inventory of the Church Archives in New York City: Lutheran.* New York: Works Progress Administration, 1940.

——. *Inventory of the Church Archives of New York City: The Methodist Church.* New York: Works Progress Administration, 1940.

——. *Inventory of the Church Archives of New York City: Presbyterian Church in the United States of America.* New York: Works Progress Administration, 1940.

———. *Inventory of the Church Archives of New York City: Protestant Epis-copal Church in the United States of America, Diocese of New York.* New York: Works Progress Administration, 1940.

———. *Inventory of the Church Archives of New York City: Reformed Church in America.* New York: Works Progress Administration, 1939.

———. *Inventory of the Church Archives in New York City: Roman Catholic Church, Archdiocese of New York.* New York: New York City Works Progress Administration, 1941.

Holmes, John Haynes. "Charles Henry Parkhurst." In Dumas Malone, ed., *Dictionary of American Biography,* vol. 14, pp. 244–246. New York: Scribner, 1934.

Holy Trinity Church, New York, New York. Hackensack, N.J.: Custombook, 1973.

In This Place: A Centennial History of All Angels' Church in the Diocese of New York. New York: All Angels' Church, 1959.

Israelowitz, Oscar. *Synagogues of New York City: History of a Jewish Com-munity.* Brooklyn, N.Y.: Israelowitz, 2000.

———. *Synagogues of New York City: A Pictorial Survey in 123 Photographs.* New York: Dover, 1982.

Johnston, J. Wesley. *Old John Street: A Historical Sketch, 1766–1905.* New York: John Street Church, 1905.

Jolowicz, Kathy, ed. *Zion–St. Mark's Lutheran Church, 1892–1992/ 1847–1992, a History.* New York: Zion–St. Mark's Evangelical Lutheran Church, 1992.

Kennedy, James W. *The Unknown Worshipper.* New York: Morehouse-Bar-low, 1964.

Knapp, Shepherd. *A History of the Brick Presbyterian Church in the City of New York.* New York: Brick Presbyterian Church, 1909.

Krasno, Nicholas. *A Guide to the Church of Saint Mary the Virgin, New York City.* New York: St. Mary the Virgin, 1999.

Kring, Walter Donald. *Liberals Among the Orthodox: Unitarian Beginnings in New York City, 1819–1839.* Boston: Beacon, 1974.

Lefévre, Kamiel, and Grace H. Patton. *The Laura Spelman Rockefeller Memorial Carillon of the Riverside Church.* New York: Riverside Church, 1939.

Liberman, Herman N. "Houses of Worship, Manhattan, 1966–1968." Her-man N. Liberman Photograph Collection, New-York Historical Society.

———. "Houses of Worship, Manhattan, 1968–1969." Herman N. Liberman Photograph Collection, New-York Historical Society.

———. "Houses of Worship, Manhattan, 1969–1971." Herman N. Liberman Photograph Collection, New-York Historical Society.

———. "Houses of Worship, Manhattan, 1971–1973." Herman N. Liberman Photograph Collection, New-York Historical Society.

Lincoln, C. Eric. *The Black Muslims in America.* Boston: Beacon, 1973.

Lindsley, James Elliott. *A History of Saint James' Church in the City of New York, 1810–1960.* New York: St. James' Church, 1960.

——. *This Planted Vine: A Narrative History of the Episcopal Diocese of New York.* New York: Harper & Row, 1984.

Livingstone, Elizabeth A. *The Concise Oxford Dictionary of the Christian Church.* Oxford: Oxford University Press, 1977.

Lomax, Louis E. *When the Word Is Given: A Report on Elijah Muhammad, Malcolm X, and the Black Muslim World.* New York: New American Library, 1964.

Lowe, David. *Three St. Bartholomew's: An Architectural History of a Church.* New York: Victorian Society in America, 1983.

Lowenstein, Steven M. *Frankfurt on the Hudson: The German-Jewish Community of Washington Heights, 1933–1983, Its Structure and Culture.* Detroit: Wayne State University Press, 1989.

Makulec, Louis L. *Church of St. Stanislaus Bishop and Martyr on East Seventh Street in New York City, 1874–1954.* New York: Roman Catholic Church of St. Stanislaus, 1954.

Malloy, Joseph I. *The Church of St. Paul the Apostle, New York.* New York: Paulist Press, n.d.

Manning, William Thomas. *The Progress of the Cathedral of Saint John the Divine, 1934.* New York: Cathedral of St. John the Divine, 1934.

Manzella, Joseph, and Robin Dawson. *The Windows of St. Patrick's Cathedral.* Strasbourg: Signe, 1998.

The Marble Collegiate Church. New York: Marble Collegiate Church, 1954.

Mardiguian, Armine, Shakeh Kadehjian, and Nishan Bakalian. *A History of the Armenian Evangelical Church of New York.* New York: Armenian Evangelical Church, 1996.

Martignoni, Angela. *"My Mission Is the World": The Life of Mother Cabrini.* New York: Vatican City Religious Book, 1949.

McKitrick, Edyth. *Grace Church in New York: A Guide to the Windows and Other Memorials.* New York: Grace Church, 1997.

Mead, Frank S., and Samuel S. Hill. *Handbook of Denominations in the United States.* 9th ed. Nashville, Tenn.: Abingdon, 1990.

Merriam, Dena, with photographs by David Finn. *Trinity: A Church, a Parish, a People.* New York: Cross River, 1996.

Metropolitan Baptist Church 80th Anniversary Souvenir Journal. New York: Metropolitan Baptist Church, 1992.

Miller, Kenneth D., and Ethel Prince Miller. *The People Are the City: 150 Years of Social and Religious Concern in New York City.* New York: Macmillan, 1962.

Miller, Lina D. *The New York Charities Directory.* New York: Charity Organization Society in the City of New York, 1918.

Monsky, Jacob. *Within the Gates: A Religious, Social and Cultural History, 1837–1962.* New York: Congregation Shaare Zedek, 1964.

Morehouse, Clifford P. *Trinity: Mother of Churches, an Informal History of Trinity Parish in the City of New York*. New York: Seabury, 1973.

Moulton, Elizabeth. *St. George's Church, New York*. New York: St. George's Church, 1964.

Murray, Peter, and Linda Murray. *The Oxford Companion to Christian Art and Architecture*. Oxford: Oxford University Press, 1996.

Myers, C. Kilmer. *Light the Dark Streets*. Greenwich, Conn.: Seabury, 1957.

Neher, John. *1855–1995: Celebrating 140 Years*. New York: St. John's Evangelical Lutheran Church, 1995.

Nichols, L. Nelson. *History of the Broadway Tabernacle of New York City*. New Haven, Conn.: Tuttle, Morehouse and Taylor, 1940.

Nickerson's Illustrated Church Musical and School Directory of New-York and Brooklyn. New York: Nickerson & Young, 1895.

The Official Catholic Directory: Anno Domini 2001. New Providence, R.I.: Kenedy, 2001.

Oldboy, Felix [John Flavel Mines]. *Walks in Our Churchyards, Old New York, Trinity Parish*. New York: Peck, 1896.

One Hundred Thirteenth Yearbook of the Collegiate Church of the City of New York. New York: Reformed Protestant Dutch Church, 1992.

Orsi, Robert Anthony. *The Madonna of 115th Street: Faith and Community in Italian Harlem, 1880–1950*. New Haven, Conn.: Yale University Press, 1985.

Parkhurst, Charles H. *A Brief History of the Madison Square Presbyterian Church and Its Activities*. New York: Printed by request, 1906.

Patterson, Samuel White. *Old Chelsea and Saint Peter's Church: The Centennial History of a New York Parish*. New York: Friebele, 1935.

Peck, George T. *A Noble Landmark of New York, the Fifth Avenue Presbyterian Church: 1808–1958*. New York: Fifth Avenue Presbyterian Church, 1960.

Peters, John Punnett, ed. *Annals of St. Michael's: Being the History of St. Michael's Protestant Episcopal Church, New York, for One Hundred Years, 1807–1907*. New York: Putnam, 1907.

A Pictorial Pilgrimage to the Cathedral of St. John the Divine in the City of New York. New York: Laymen's Club of the Cathedral of St. John the Divine, 1950.

Pokrovsky, M., ed. *St. Nicholas Cathedral of New York: History and Legacy*. New York: St. Nicholas Cathedral Study Group, 1968.

Post, W. Ellwood. *Saints, Signs and Symbols*. 2d ed. Harrisburg, Pa.: Morehouse, 1974.

Postal, Bernard, and Lionel Koppman. *Jewish Landmarks in New York: An Informal History and Guide*. New York: Hill and Wang, 1964.

Quirk, Howard E. *The Living Cathedral, St. John the Divine: A History and Guide*. New York: Crossroad, 1993.

Ray, J. H. Randolph. *My Little Church Around the Corner.* New York: Simon and Schuster, 1957.

Read, Newbury Frost. *The Story of St. Mary's: The Society of the Free Church of St. Mary the Virgin, New York City, 1868–1931.* New York: St. Mary the Virgin, 1931.

The Riverside Church in the City of New York: A Handbook of the Institution and Its Building. New York: Riverside Church, 1931.

Roberts, Vera Mowry. *The Story of Rutgers Church.* New York: Rutgers Presbyterian Church, 1998.

Rogers, Raynor R. *The Story of Old John Street Church.* New York: John Street Press, 1984.

Ross, Ishbel. *Through the Lich-Gate: A Biography of the Little Church Around the Corner.* New York: Payson, 1931.

Rutgers Presbyterian Church 175th Anniversary, 1798–1973. New York: Rutgers Presbyterian Church, 1973.

Ryan, Leo Raymond. *Old St. Peter's: The Mother Church of Catholic New York (1785–1935).* New York: United States Catholic Historical Society, 1935.

Saint Martin's Church: Dedication of the Carillon, Dedicatory Recital. New York: St. Martin's Church, 1949.

Saint Patrick's Cathedral. Newton, Mass.: Conroy, n.d.

Saint Patrick's Cathedral: The 100th Year. New York: St. Patrick's Cathedral, 1979.

Saint Patrick's Cathedral, New York. New York: Archbishopric of New York, 1942.

Saint Vartan Cathedral, New York City. New York: Diocese of the Armenian Church of America, n.d.

St. Vincent Ferrer's Church. New York: Dominican Fathers, 1944.

Schopler, Ernest H., ed. "John Kedroff v. Saint Nicholas Cathedral of the Russian Orthodox Church in North America." In *Cases Argued and Decided in the Supreme Court of the United States, October Term, 1952.* Rochester, N.Y.: Lawyers Co-Operative, 1953.

Scott, Joseph. *A Century and More of Reaching Out: An Historical Sketch of the Parish of St. Paul the Apostle.* New York: Missionary Society of St. Paul the Apostle, 1983.

Serbian Orthodox Cathedral of Saint Sava in New York, 50 Years, 1944–1994. New York: Serbian Orthodox Cathedral of St. Sava, 1994.

Shea, John Gilmary. *The Catholic Churches of New York City, with Sketches of Their History and Lives of the Present Pastors.* New York: Goulding, 1878.

Shelley, Thomas J. *The History of the Archdiocese of New York.* Vol. 1. Strasbourg: Signe, 1997.

Shoemaker, Samuel M. *Calvary Church, Yesterday and Today: A Centennial History.* New York: Revell, 1936.

Shokeid, Moshe. *A Gay Synagogue in New York.* New York: Columbia University Press, 1995.

Silber, William B. *A History of St. James' Methodist Episcopal Church at Harlem, New York City, 1830–1880: With Some Facts Relating to the Settlement of Harlem.* New York: Phillips & Hunt, 1882.

Smith, Christine. *St. Bartholomew's Church in the City of New York.* New York: Oxford University Press, 1988.

Smith, Jane I. *Islam in America.* New York: Columbia University Press, 1999.

Souvenir Album Containing Illustrations of the Churches, Academies and Institutes in Commemoration of the Centennial Anniversary of the Archdiocese of New York, 1808–1908. New York: Fleming, 1908.

Stewart, William Rhinelander. *Grace Church and Old New York.* New York: Dutton, 1924.

Tabor, Paul, and Laurie Lambrecht. *St. Ignatius Loyola: A Pictorial History and Walking Guide of New York City's Church of St. Ignatius Loyola.* New York: Church of St. Ignatius Loyola, 1999.

Taddiken, John G. C., ed. *The History of St. John's Evangelical Lutheran Church.* New York: St. John's Evangelical Lutheran Church, 1905.

To Build Again. New York: Cathedral Building and Conservation Fund, n.d.

Trinity Church Bicentennial Celebration, May 5th, 1897. New York: Trinity Parish, 1897.

True Light Lutheran Church, 50th Anniversary, 1936–1986. New York: True Light Lutheran Church, 1986.

VanNorden, Luanne. *A Short History of the Brick Presbyterian Church in the City of New York, 1944–1968.* New York: Brick Presbyterian Church, 1968.

Walker, Wyatt Tee. *A Prophet from Harlem Speaks: Sermons and Essays.* New York: Martin Luther King Fellows Press, 1997.

Ward, Emory. *Faith of Our Fathers Living Still: The Story of Marble Collegiate Church.* New York: Marble Collegiate Church, 1978.

Ward, Susan Hayes. *The History of the Broadway Tabernacle Church.* New York: Broadway Tabernacle Church, 1901.

Wenner, George U. *The Lutherans of New York, 1648–1918.* New York: Petersfield, 1918.

West End Collegiate Church, the First Hundred Years, 1892–1992. New York: West End Collegiate Church, 1992.

White, Frederic C., comp. *Historical Sketch of the South Church (Reformed) of New York City.* New York: Gilliss & Turnure, 1887.

Wilson, Jeff. *The Buddhist Guide to New York.* New York: St. Martin's Griffin, 2000.

Winston, Diane. *Red-Hot and Righteous: The Urban Religion of the Salvation Army.* Cambridge, Mass.: Harvard University Press, 1999.

Wolfe, Gerard R., with photographs by Jo Renée Fine. *The Synagogues of New York's Lower East Side.* New York: New York University Press, 1978.

Year Book of the (Collegiate) Reformed Protestant Dutch Church of the City of New York. Nos. 11–15. New York: The Church, 1890–1894

Periodicals, Reports, and Pamphlets

About Us: Park Avenue United Methodist Church [pamphlet]. New York: Park Avenue United Methodist Church, n.d.

Allon, Janet. "Harlem: A Legend Reviews His Housing Legacies." *New York Times*, March 3, 1996, sec. 13, p. 8.

Anderson, Susan Heller, and Maurice Carroll. "New York Day by Day / A Celebration of Spanish Heritage." *New York Times*, July 30, 1984, p. B4.

——. "New York Day by Day / Centennial Mass." *New York Times*, November 7, 1983, p. B2.

Anderson, Susan Heller, and David W. Dunlap. "New York Day by Day / A Country-Like Parish Surrounded by Change." *New York Times*, April 21, 1986, p. B2.

"Apse Previewed at the Cloisters." *New York Times*, June 2, 1961, p. 35.

"Archbishop Assassinated in Procession to Altar; Laid to Old-World Feud." *New York Times*, December 25, 1933, p. 1.

"Architecture and Symbolism of the Riverside Church." *Church Monthly*, December 1930, pp. 1–58.

Berger, Joseph. "Converted Buildings." *Newsday*, March 30, 1983, pt. 2, p. 4.

——. "A Man Battles to Save Cherished Synagogue." *New York Times*, July 21, 1986, p. B3.

——. "O'Connor's Way: Assertive and Heard." *New York Times*, February 17, 1986, p. A1.

Berger, Meyer. "About New York / Stone Carver Comes Out of Retirement at 71 to Do Pointing on Church Edifice." *New York Times*, November 11, 1957, p. 34.

Bernstein, Richard. "Immigration Magnet: The Lower East Side Changes Its Face." *New York Times*, June 28, 1994, p. B1.

Berwick, Carly. "Neighborhood Report / Lower East Side: A Synagogue's Artistic Route to a Rebirth." *New York Times*, December 19, 1999, sec. 14, p. 6.

Binder, David. "Churches Found in Unlikely Sites." *New York Times*, May 7, 1961, sec. 8, p. 1.

Blair, William G. "St. Luke's Church, Ruined by Fire, Plans to Rebuild." *New York Times*, March 8, 1981, p. 28.

Blau, Eleanor. "Bishop Praises Church Merger." *New York Times*, January 5, 1976, p. 32.

"Blaze Ruins Church in Chelsea, 3d Such Fire There in a Month." *New York Times*, August 6, 1973, p. 20.

Bloch, Eric. "A Barometer of Immigrant Need and Immigrant Success." *Aufbau, the Transatlantic Jewish Paper*. Available at: aufbauonline.com/ 2002/issue16/12.html.

Booklet Showing Some Phases of the Work of the New York City Mission and Tract Society. New York: New York City Mission and Tract Society, n.d.

Bradley, John A. "St. Nicholas Church to Be Razed to Make Way for Office Building." *New York Times*, April 1, 1949, p. 1.

Brady, Thomas F. "Nile Temple on Its Way Here." *New York Times*, July 12, 1968, p. 33.

A Brief History of the New Church (Swedenborgian) in New York City [pamphlet]. New York: New Church, n.d.

Briggs, Kenneth A. "Construction of Cathedral of St. John Will Resume." *New York Times*, December 5, 1978, p. A1.

———. "Cooke Marks 175 Years of Diocese in New York." *New York Times*, April 9, 1983, p. 27.

———. "For Rev. Carmines, Church in Theater." *New York Times*, September 19, 1982, p. 40.

———. "Renewed Church a Symbol of Easter." *New York Times*, April 6, 1985, p. 23.

Brown, Patricia Leigh. "The Soot Is Gone, But What Is Lost?" *New York Times*, August 30, 1990, p. C1.

Brozan, Nadine. "For Houses of God, a Devilish Market." *New York Times*, June 18, 2000, sec. 11, p. 1.

Bruni, Frank. "Child Care, Unisex Prayers and More Attract Parishioners to Failing Church." *New York Times*, November 8, 1996, p. B1.

Butler, Charles. "The Temple Emanu-El, New York." *Architectural Forum*, February 1930, pp. 151–154.

Caulfield, Brian. "Air Rights: Manhattan Parishes Enhance Ministry with Profits from Real Estate Deals." Catholic New York Online. Available at: cny.org/archive/ld/ld012199.htm.

Cenacle of St. Regis, New York, 1894–1952 [pamphlet]. New York: Cenacle of St. Regis, 1952.

"Center Is Dedicated to Victims of Hitler." *New York Times*, January 15, 1951, p. 19.

"Church Converted into Labor Temple." *New York Times*, February 24, 1910, p. 5.

"Churches on the West Side." *Real Estate Record and Builders Guide*, May 12, 1888, pp. 599–600.

Cohn, Lynne M. "A Church by Any Other Name." *Our Town*, October 21, 1993, p. 12.

"Collegiate Reformed Dutch Church, West End Avenue and Seventy-seventh Street, New York." *Architecture and Building*, October 29, 1892, p. 217.

Collins, Glenn. "Hellinger Theater Is Sold to Church." *New York Times*, December 7, 1991, p. 13.

A Comprehensive Guide to the St. Mark's Church in-the-Bowery Historical Site [annotated map]. New York: St. Mark's Church in-the-Bowery, 1999.

Cook, Joan. "Rev. George W. Moore, 64, Pastor Who Invigorated 'Actors' Chapel.'" *New York Times*, May 4, 1991, p. 10.

"Cram Will Build Gothic Cathedral." *New York Times*, June 22, 1911, p. 1.

Crane, Charles. "Why We Made It Gothic." *American Architect*, July 1931, pp. 26–124.

"Croatian-Americans Send Aid to Victims of Yugoslav Battles." *New York Times*, November 24, 1991, p. 42.

Croly, Herbert D. "The Skyscraper in the Service of Religion." *Architectural Record*, February 1924, pp. 203–204.

"Crowd at Opening of Labor Temple." *New York Times*, April 11, 1910, p. 3.

Davis, Ossie. "Eulogy Delivered at the Funeral of Malcolm X, Faith Temple Church of God, February 27, 1965." Available at: cmgww.com/historic/malcolm/eulogy.html.

"Dedication of the Pauline A. Hartford Memorial Chapel." *Stethoscope*, July 1952, pp. 1–3.

Dewan, Shaila K. "Synagogue from 1800's Is Damaged in a Fire." *New York Times*, December 7, 2001, p. D3.

"Dr. Holmes Dies: Crusading Cleric." *New York Times*, April 4, 1964, p. 1.

"Dr. Reisner Dies: Noted Clergyman." *New York Times*, July 18, 1940, p 24.

Dreyfuss, Joel. "Harlem's Ardent Voice." *New York Times Magazine*, January 20, 1991, p. 19.

Dugan, George. "Harlem Gets Church-in-a-Church." *New York Times*, November 6, 1972, p. 45.

——. "Protestant Church Moves During Service." *New York Times*, March 3, 1969, p. 26.

Dunlap, David W. "Architecture / A New Mosque for Manhattan, for the 21st Century." *New York Times*, April 26, 1992, sec. 2, p. 38.

——. "Battle of St. Bart's Goes to Landmarks Panel." *New York Times*, February 1, 1984, p. B1.

——. "Blocks / Messages in Concrete: The Aesthetics of Safety." *New York Times*, August 15, 2002, p. B3.

——. "Bush, the Homeless and the Past to Meet at Service at St. Paul's." *New York Times*, April 24, 1989, p. B3.

——. "The Changing Look of the New Harlem." *New York Times*, February 10, 2002, sec. 11, p. 1.

——. "The Church: From the Rubble, Icons of Disaster and Faith." *New York Times*, December 25, 2001, p. B1.

——. "Church v. State: Landmark Case." *New York Times*, February 2, 1997, sec. 9, p. 1.

——. "Churches Bask in Restored Brilliance of Windows." *New York Times*, December 23, 1988, p. B2.

——. "Church's Landmark Status Is Upheld." *New York Times*, September 13, 1990, p. B4.

——. "City Awards $1 Million to Aid Synagogue." *New York Times*, October 22, 2000, p. 39.

——. "Columbia in Talks to Build at St. John." *New York Times*, October 31, 2002, p. B3.

——. "Commercial Real Estate / Nightclub to Reopen in Gothic Church." *New York Times*, May 27, 1998, p. B8.

——. "A Firm Foundation, Starting at the Roof." *New York Times*, December 26, 1999, sec. 11, p. 1.

——. "For Churches, Births and Rebirths." *New York Times*, December 22, 2002, sec. 11, p. 1.

——. "For Sale: 1 Church, W. 96th St., Park Vu." *New York Times*, July 10, 2003, p. 84.

——. "4 Cornerstones of Harlem Life Are Designated as Landmarks." *New York Times*, July 14, 1993, p. B3.

——. "Gutted Church to Rebuild on Same Midtown Site." *New York Times*, December 21, 1992, p. B3.

——. "Heaven's Palette in Bolder Hues." *New York Times*, December 25, 1998, p. E39.

——. "In Remembrance of Sorrow from Other Times." *New York Times*, January 25, 2002, p. E39.

——. "In Spiritual Places, Mundane Problems." *New York Times*, December 26, 1993, secs. 9–10, p. 1.

——. "In Synagogue Design, Many Paths." *New York Times*, December 8, 2002, sec. 11, p. 1.

——. "Landmarks Panel Permits Owner to Raze Synagogue." *New York Times*, February 9, 1983, p. B3.

——. "Landmarks Panel Vetoes Request to Raze Church." *New York Times*, May 10, 1989, p. B3.

——. "Landmarks Panel Vetoes Tower Plans for St. Bart's and Historical Society." *New York Times*, June 13, 1984, p. B1.

——. "Manhattan Journal / Tale of Past Jewish Life, Told in Tile." *New York Times*, November 4, 2001, p. 38.

——. "Near Ground Zero, Unbowed Spires." *New York Times*, September 30, 2001, sec. 11, p. 1.

——. "New Life Is Envisioned for Historic Synagogue." *New York Times*, February 18, 1987, p. B2.

——. "On Lower East Side, a Synagogue Begins a New Life." *New York Times*, September 24, 1984, p. B1.

——. "Parish Forced Out of Fragile Church." *New York Times*, May 15, 1989, p. B3.

——. "Polished Marble and Sacramental Scuffs." *New York Times*, August 25, 2002, sec. 11, p. 1.

——. "Postings / For Grace Church at Broadway and 10th Street: $2 Million Project to Repair Leaning Spire and Leaky Roof." *New York Times*, April 20, 2003, sec. 11, p. 1.

——. "Postings / A Home of Their Own: Neo-Classic Synagogue for a Historic District." *New York Times*, December 13, 1992, sec. 10, p. 1.

——. "Postings / 1923 Harlem Synagogue: Stolen Community Assets." *New York Times*, May 19, 1991, sec. 10, p. 1.

——. "Postings / $1 Million Window Project at West End Collegiate Church: Conserving Stained Glass." *New York Times*, December 24, 2000, sec. 11, p. 1.

——. "Postings / Renovation at All Saints Episcopal: 1894 Church Will Receive New Facade, Its Third." *New York Times*, July 29, 2001, sec. 11, p. 1.

——. "Postings / Temple Israel on East 75th Street to Be Clad in Jerusalem Stone: A New Facade that Lets in the Light." *New York Times*, February 10, 2002, sec. 11, p. 1.

——. "Postings / $10 Million Restoration of Madison Avenue Presbyterian Church: Under Plywood, an 1899 Legacy." *New York Times*, March 28, 1999, sec. 11, p. 1.

——. "Preserving Churches: A Quandary." *New York Times*, September 22, 1986, p. B3.

——. "Quakers Get $10,000 to Fix a Landmark." *New York Times*, May 18, 1987, p. B3.

——. "Restoration Job: Chapel and Lives." *New York Times*, November 22, 2001, p. B1.

——. "Restoring the Luster to Sacred Sites." *New York Times*, April 15, 2001, sec. 11, p. 1.

——. "Returning Gleam to Marble Church: Crumbling Piece of City History Is Getting Its Stones Restored." *New York Times*, August 12, 1999, p. B1.

——. "St. Bart's to Open Its Doors to an Adversary." *New York Times*, May 4, 1991, p. 25.

——. "St. Nicholas: Hulking Neighbor Buries a Church." *New York Times*, September 17, 2001, p. A8.

——. "Seamen Institute Finds a Haven on Water Street." *New York Times*, October 31, 1988, p. B2.

——. "Sensuous Curves Ascend Above the Hard-Edged City." *New York Times*, March 3, 2000, p. E47.

——. "Tower Proposed for Central Park West." *New York Times*, August 24, 1983, p. B1.

——. "Trinity Church: Amid the Rubble, a Steeple Stands." *New York Times*, September 17, 2001, p. A8.

——. "Vestiges of Harlem's Jewish Past." *New York Times*, June 7, 2002, p. E33.

——. "West-Park Presbyterian Weighs Revamping." *New York Times*, January 24, 2003, p. B4.

——. "Xanadus Rise to a Higher Calling." *New York Times*, April 13, 2001, p. E29.

Dunning, Jennifer. "A Church Celebrates Its First Century of Creative Growth." *New York Times*, April 11, 1990, p. C11.

Dwyer, Jim. "Sonovagun, if It Isn't Dominion." *New York Times Magazine*, November 11, 2001, p. 83.

Emerging Church, Emerging Nation: Historic Wesley Chapel [pamphlet]. New York: John Street Church, n.d.

"Father T. J. Ducey, Long Ill, Is Dead." *New York Times*, August 23, 1909, p. 1.

Feuer, Alan, and Daniel J. Wakin. "Fire Damages St. John the Divine, Gutting Gift Shop and Scorching Art." *New York Times*, December 19, 2001, p. D1.

"Fire at St. John's in 'Village' Linked to Break-in at Church." *New York Times*, March 7, 1971, p. 60.

First Baptist Church of New York City, Then and Now [pamphlet]. New York: First Baptist Church in the City of New York, n.d.

Fiske, Edward B. "$21-Million First Ave. Complex to House Archdiocesan Offices." *New York Times*, August 12, 1971, p. 1.

——. "War Dispute Helps End Brotherhood Effort." *New York Times*, November 10, 1973, p. 35.

"5,000 at Dedication of Ukrainian Church." *New York Times*, April 24, 1978, p. D9.

Fowler, Glenn. "A New Center for Moslems Here." *New York Times*, January 10, 1970, p. 33.

Frank, Sarah E. "Anglican Worship in French: Meet St. Esprit." *Episcopal New Yorker*, February–March 2001. Available at: dioceseny.org/eny/febmar01/stesprit.html.

Frantz, Douglas. "Scientology's Star Roster Enhances Image." *New York Times*, February 13, 1998, p. A1.

Frantz, Douglas, and Brett Pulley. "Harlem Church Is Outpost of Empire: House of Prayer Built Wide Holdings on Devotion to Sweet Daddy Grace." *New York Times*, December 17, 1995, p. 49.

French, Howard W. "Restoring Abyssinian Church's Stature." *New York Times*, February 27, 1988, p. 33.

Gelb, Arthur. "Actors Studio Moves." *New York Times*, February 20, 1955, sec. 2, p. 1.

Gibson, R. W. "A Modern Cathedral." *Architectural Record*, April–June 1892, p. 437.

Gilman, Susan. "The Glory of Historic Lower East Side Synagogue Is Born Again." *Jewish Week*, December 15, 1989, p. 7.

Giovannini, Joseph. "Living in a Former Church: Space, Drama and Tranquillity." *New York Times*, March 7, 1985, p. C1.

Glueck, Grace. "Hebrew Union's Temple Gets a New-Style Ark." *New York Times*, November 2, 1987, p. C16.

———. "642 Stones Will Soon Regain Form as an Egyptian Temple." *New York Times*, November 29, 1974, p. 41

Goldberg, Shari. "Vernacular Synagogue Architecture." *Common Bond* 16, no. 2 (2001): 2–4.

Goldberger, Paul. "A Rebirth of Imaginative Vision." *Faith & Form* 12, no. 1 (1978): 6–19

Goldfein, Josh. "The Secret History of the Sunshine Theater: Heritage Cinema." *Village Voice*, December 19–25, 2001. Available at: villagevoice.com/issues/0151/goldfein.php.

Goldin, Davidson. "Neighborhood Report / East Village: Practicing the Gospel in the Village." *New York Times*, December 11, 1994, sec. 13, p. 8.

Goldman, Ari L. "Catholic School Where Buddha Is Welcome." *New York Times*, February 16, 1991, p. 29.

———. "Church Is Shared Home of Jews and Methodists." *New York Times*, September 17, 1991, p. B5.

———. "Feeding the Soul: A Lunch with Religious Fervor." *New York Times*, January 13, 1988, p. B1.

———. "Homosexual Group Holds Its Final Mass." *New York Times*, March 9, 1987, p. B3.

———. "Neighborhood Report / West Side: Rabbi's Musical Spirit Endures." *New York Times*, March 26, 1995, sec. 13, p. 8.

———. "Pastor Confident of 'Miracle' to Help Rebuild Burned Church." *New York Times*, December 19, 1983, p. B1.

———. "St. Mark's, 'a Free Place,' Celebrates Its Rebuilding." *New York Times*, November 17, 1986, p. B3.

———. "Three Homes in 150 Years for a Reform Synagogue." *New York Times*, September 30, 1991, p. B8.

———. "Time 'Too Painful' to Remember." *New York Times*, November 10, 1988, p. A10.

Gonzalez, David. "The Glorious Mosaic." *New York Times*, December 5, 1993, sec. 13, p. 1.

Gonzalez, Juan. "Mormons Building Chapel and Support in N. Manhattan." *Daily News*, March 17, 2000, p. 14.

Goodman, George W. "Ground Broken for Islamic Center." *New York Times*, October 28, 1984, sec. 8, p. 6.

Goodnough, Abby. "Before the Wreckers Come, Lilies and Hymns of Hope: Beloved Manhattan Church Celebrates Last Mass." *New York Times*, April 13, 1998, p. B1.

Goodstein, Laurie. "The Imam: New York Cleric's Departure from Mosque Leaves Mystery." *New York Times*, October 23, 2001, p. 84.

Gray, Christopher. "Streetscapes / Annunciation Greek Orthodox Church: Country Ambiance in a Big-City Setting." *New York Times*, July 7, 1991, sec. 10, p. 5.

——. "Streetscapes / Broadway and 76th Street: A 1930 Church, with a Skyscraper Hotel on Top." *New York Times*, September 22, 2002, sec. 11, p. 7.

——. "Streetscapes / The Cathedral of St. John the Divine, Amsterdam Avenue Between 110th and 113th Streets: Much-Changed Century-Old Vision, Still Unfinished." *New York Times*, July 28, 2002, sec. 11, p. 7.

——. "Streetscapes / Catholic Apostolic Church: On West 57th Street, a Striking Victorian Sanctuary." *New York Times*, July 7, 1996, sec. 9, p. 5.

——. "Streetscapes / Church of the Heavenly Rest, Fifth Avenue and 90th Street: Restoring One of Manhattan's Magnificent Churches." *New York Times*, October 12, 1997, sec. 10, p. 5.

——. "Streetscapes / Church of the Holy Trinity: Soon They'll Hear the Tintinnabulation of the Bells." *New York Times*, June 25, 1995, sec. 9, p. 7.

——. "Streetscapes / The Church of St. Paul and St. Andrew: A Landmark with an Unwanted Status." *New York Times*, April 19, 1987, sec. 8, p. 12.

——. "Streetscapes / Congregation B'nai Jeshurun: Future Uncertain, a 1919 Synagogue Begins Repairs." *New York Times*, February 11, 1996, sec. 9, p. 7.

——. "Streetscapes / The 1893 Church of the Master: Reviving a Building Unused for 20 Years." *New York Times*, December 25, 1994, sec. 9, p. 5.

——. "Streetscapes / First Church of Christ, Scientist: A Grand Building Seeks to Protect Itself." *New York Times*, May 23, 1993, sec. 10, p. 9.

——. "Streetscapes / Harlem's Lafayette Theater: Jackhammering the Past." *New York Times*, November 11, 1990, sec. 10, p. 6.

——. "Streetscapes / The Immaculate Conception Church on East 14th: A Protestant Complex Converted to Catholicism." *New York Times*, July 26, 1998, sec. 11, p. 5.

——. "Streetscapes / The Judson Memorial Church: A Problem Solver Is Now Facing Its Own Problems." *New York Times*, April 29, 1990, sec. 10, p. 10.

——. "Streetscapes / The Leake & Watts Orphan Asylum: A Castoff in the Path of a Growing, Great Cathedral." *New York Times*, June 24, 1990, sec. 10, p. 6.

——. "Streetscapes / 141st Street and Convent Avenue: 1892 Church for a Congregation that Moved Uptown." *New York Times*, October 20, 2002, sec. 11, p. 7.

——. "Streetscapes / 161 West 93rd Street: A Building that Recalls the Days After Pearl Harbor." *New York Times*, September 30, 2001, sec. 11, p. 9.

——. "Streetscapes / Readers' Questions: A Converted Orphanage and a Stickley?" *New York Times*, December 6, 1992, sec. 10, p. 6.

——. "Streetscapes / The Regent Family Residence for the Homeless, Formerly the Broadway View, at 104th Street and Broadway: A Once-Grand

Hotel Gets a Socially Conscious Icon." *New York Times*, August 31, 2003, sec. 11, p. 7.

———. "Streetscapes / St. James' Church: A Metamorphosis Still in Progress." *New York Times*, October 20, 1991, sec. 10, p. 6.

———. "Streetscapes / St. Jean Baptiste Church: Restoration on Lexington Avenue." *New York Times*, December 30, 1990, sec. 10, p. 5.

———. "Streetscapes / St. Mary's Episcopal Church: A Demur on Designation, with a Decided Difference." *New York Times*, December 8, 1991, sec. 10, p. 5.

———. "Streetscapes / St. Michael's Episcopal Church: Restoration, and Perhaps a Striking Tiffany-Style Finish." *New York Times*, February 5, 1989, sec. 10, p. 12.

———. "Streetscapes / St. Paul the Apostle: Renewal and Change, Esthetic and Liturgical." *New York Times*, December 20, 1992, sec. 10, p. 5.

———. "Streetscapes / St. Peter's Episcopal Church: A Battle for Basic Survival." *New York Times*, December 9, 1990, sec. 10, p. 6.

———. "Streetscapes / St. Philip's Episcopal Church: After the Wooden Ceiling Came Tumbling Down." *New York Times*, January 21, 1996, sec. 9, p. 7.

———. "Streetscapes / St. Thomas More Roman Catholic Church: A Touch of the English Countryside in Manhattan." *New York Times*, April 2, 1989, sec. 10, p. 12.

———. "Streetscapes / St. Thomas the Apostle Church, 118th Street near St. Nicholas Avenue: A 'Wild Masterpiece' from 1907, in Neo-Gothic Style." *New York Times*, December 22, 2002, sec. 11, p. 7.

———. "Streetscapes / 67th Street Between Lexington and Third Avenues: 19th-Century Buildings that Still Make Statements." *New York Times*, May 3, 1998, sec. 11, p. 5.

———. "Streetscapes / Temple B'nai Israel: A Church Tackles Renovation." *New York Times*, September 17, 1995, sec. 9, p. 9.

———. "Streetscapes / Trinity Baptist Church: Repairs for a Study in Contrasts." *New York Times*, April 28, 1991, sec. 10, p. 6.

———. "Streetscapes / 12 West 129th Street: Changeling Resists Landmark Status." *New York Times*, July 14, 1991, sec. 10, p. 16.

———. "Streetscapes / West-Park Presbyterian: An 1890 West Side Church Fighting Landmark Status." *New York Times*, January 10, 1988, sec. 8, p. 11.

Greer, William R. "New St. Luke's Dedicated in Village." *New York Times*, November 17, 1985, p. 40.

Grimes, William. "Dorothy Maynor, 85, Soprano and Arts School Founder, Dies." *New York Times*, February 24, 1996, p. 12.

Gross, Jane. "A Talmudic Quandary for a Shul: Growth or Intimacy." *New York Times*, December 6, 1996, p. B1.

Gurock, Jeffrey S. "Synagogue Imperialism in New York City: The Case of Congregation Kehal Adath Jeshurun, 1909–1911." *Michael* 15 (2000): 95–108.

Gussow, Mel. "Nomadic New Dramatists End Trek." *New York Times*, November 26, 1969, p. 37.

Haddon, Rawson W. "St. John's Chapel, Varick Street, New York City." *Architectural Record*, May 1914, pp. 389–403.

"Harlem's Old Dutch Church." *New York Times*, January 28, 1894, p. 20.

Haynes, George E. "The Church and the Negro Spirit." *Survey Graphic*, March 1925, pp. 695–709.

Hays, Daniel, and Jere Hester. "Rudy to Rescue." *Daily News*, December 11, 1992, p. 2.

Heavenly Space: A Walking Tour of the Church of the Heavenly Rest [pamphlet]. New York: Church of the Heavenly Rest, n.d.

Hedstrom, O. G. "The New Bethel Ship John Wesley" [contribution certificate]. 1857.

Historical Places of Worship in Downtown Manhattan [pamphlet]. N.p.: n.d.

Hoffman, Henry B. "Transformation of New York Churches." *New-York Historical Society Quarterly Bulletin*, January 1938, pp. 3–27.

"Holmes Preaches in New Building." *New York Times*, September 27, 1948, p. 19.

Horsley, Carter B. "An Office Tower on Columns Designed for Church Facility." *New York Times*, April 8, 1974, p. 69.

Howe, Marvine. "Neighborhood Report / Midtown: The 'Miracle' at St. Malachy's." *New York Times*, November 7, 1993, sec. 13, p. 8.

Hu, Winnie. "No Landmark Status for St. John the Divine." *New York Times*, October 25, 2003, p. 4..

Hunter, Charlayne. "Muslim Center Blends Business, School and Mosque." *New York Times*, August 25, 1970, p. 39.

Huxtable, Ada Louise. "Architecture View / Recycling a Landmark for Today." *New York Times*, June 15, 1975, sec. 2, p. 29.

Imagine Greenwich Village Without Judson Memorial Church [pamphlet]. New York: Judson Memorial Church, 1990.

"Islam in New York: Growing Presence of Diverse Peoples United by Faith." *New York Times*, May 4, 1993, p. B12.

Jacobs, Andrew. "Confessions of Father Pete." *New York Times*, September 22, 1996, sec. 13, p. 1.

Jaynes, Gregory. "About New York / Shaky Scaffold and Waxy Paint: Saving a Mural." *New York Times*, July 30, 1988, p. 27.

Johnson, Thomas A. "Adam Clayton Powell, 63, Dies in Miami." *New York Times*, April 5, 1972, p. 1.

Kaufman, Michael T. "Puerto Rican Group Seizes Church in East Harlem in Demand for Space." *New York Times*, December 29, 1969, p. 26.

Kilgannon, Corey. "Harlem Journal / Generations Sound Off in a Brassy Gospel Jam." *New York Times*, July 9, 2001, p. B3.

Kirby, David. "St. John the Unfinished." *New York Times*, January 10, 1999, sec. 14, p. 1.

Kliment, Stephen A. "When Places of the Spirit Face Concrete Realities." *New York Times*, December 27, 1998, sec. 11, p. 1.

Knowles, Clayton. "U.S. Court Voids Act on Russian Church." *New York Times*, November 25, 1952, p. 31.

Kramer, Hilton. "Nevelsons Enhance Chapel." *New York Times*, December 14, 1977, p C24.

"Labor of Love Keeps Harlem Shul Alive." *New York Resident*, March 25, 2002, p. 19.

Lambert, Bruce. "The Rev. Paul Abels Dies at 54: Gay Pastor Led 'Peace' Church." *New York Times*, March 14, 1992, p. 12.

Lee, Denny. "Neighborhood Report / East Village: A Losing Battle to Save a Venerable but Dying Synagogue." *New York Times*, December 17, 2000, sec. 14, p. 8.

A Legacy of Liberation: The African Methodist Episcopal Zion Church [pamphlet]. Washington, D.C.: African Methodist Episcopal Zion Church, n.d.

Levine, Edward. "Neighborhood Report / Harlem–Morningside Heights: New Generation Affirms Life of a Synagogue." *New York Times*, November 1, 1998, sec. 14, p. 6.

Lewis, Paul. "Mosque Rising Is a First in New York." *New York Times*, September 26, 1988, p. B2.

Lii, Jane H. "Fatal Dispute Resolved, Block Shows New Life." *New York Times*, August 10, 1997, sec. 13, p. 5.

Lipsyte, Robert. "Coping / A Time to Heal, a Time to Move?" *New York Times*, May 17, 1998, sec. 14, p. 1.

"Lords Lose a Skirmish." *New York Times*, January 11, 1970, sec. 4, p. 3.

Lubasch, Arnold H. "Young Lords Give Food and Care at Seized Church." *New York Times*, December 30, 1969, p. 30.

Lyons, Richard D. "Postings / Condos and a Chapel: Site Sharing." *New York Times*, February 25, 1990, sec. 10, p. 1.

Madison Avenue Presbyterian Church, Architectural History and Current Rehabilitation [pamphlet]. New York: Madison Avenue Presbyterian Church, 1998.

"Man in the News / Controversial Priest: Ivan Illich." *New York Times*, January 23, 1969, p. 2.

"Manhattan Church to Build 23 Stories." *New York Times*, January 8, 1928, sec. 2, p. 2.

"Manning Forces Way into Church to Keep It Open to Negroes." *New York Times*, October 24, 1932, p. 1.

Marks, Alexandra. "Churches Try to Preserve Harlem's Character." *Christian Science Monitor*, November 20, 2000. Available at: csmonitor.com/dirable/2000/11/20/p2s2.htm.

Martin, Douglas. "About New York / In His Despair, Rabbi's Strength Revives Temple." *New York Times*, October 3, 1987, p. 29.

————. "Church's Comeback 'Like a Miracle.'" *New York Times*, April 24, 1994, p. 37.

————. "James R. Lawson, 84, Dies: Tamed the Mighty Carillon." *New York Times*, October 19, 2003, sec. 1, p. 44.

McFadden, Robert D. "Homeless Shelter in Church Is Upheld." *New York Times*, December 12, 1989, p. B3.

McKinley, Jesse. "Traditions Collide in a Chelsea Parish." *New York Times*, January 2, 1998, p. B3.

Mellins, Thomas. "The Bells of St. Martin's." *Cityscape News*, winter 1999. Available at: cityscapeinstitute.org/winter99.htm.

"Modern Gothic Bioshelter for Cathedral of St. John the Divine." *Architectural Record*, August 1991, p. 21.

Moore, Paul, Jr. "When a Former Church Becomes a Discotheque." *New York Times*, December 1, 1983, p. A26.

"Mount Neboh Temple." *American Architect*, October 31, 1917, pp. 334–335.

Muschamp, Herbert. "Architecture View / St. John the Divine: It Can't Go On. It Goes On." *New York Times*, December 20, 1992, sec. 2, p. 34.

Narvaez, Alfonso A. "Margaret Eddy, 63, Pastor and Educator in East Harlem Posts." *New York Times*, March 9, 1990, p. A20.

Navarro, Mireya. "In Many Churches, Icons Compete for Space: Multiple Shrines to Patron Saints Testify to a Rivalry of the Devout." *New York Times*, May 29, 2002, p. B1.

"New St. Andrew's Opens Sanctuary." *New York Times*, July 10, 1939, p. 8.

"Odyssey of an Apse." *New York Times Magazine*, May 28, 1961, p. 16.

"On E. 43d St., a Church Is Rising from Its Ashes." *New York Times*, October 20, 1996, sec. 9, p. 1.

"1,000 Lives May Be Lost in Burning of the Excursion Boat Gen. Slocum." *New York Times*, June 16, 1904, p. 1.

"Oust Architect Who Designed the Cathedral." *New York Times*, June 21, 1911, p. 1.

Pavlou, Effie. "Always on Sundays." *New York Newsday*, November 9, 1992, p. 21.

Phillips, McCandlish. "Church on 48th St. to House 2 Theaters." *New York Times*, November 29, 1968, p. 50.

————. "Egyptian Temple Is Delivered Here in 661 Crates." *New York Times*, August 22, 1968, p. 44.

Polgreen, Lydia. "Padlocking of a Church Brings Protest and Prayers." *New York Times*, September 1, 2003, p. B3.

"Postings / Lower East Side Parish: Home for a Homeless Church." *New York Times*, March 22, 1992, sec. 10, p. 1.

"Postings / Low-Income Units a Bonus: Grace Church Rebuilds." *New York Times*, July 28, 1991, sec. 10, p. 1.

"Postings / Rehabilitation in West Harlem: A New Church for Haitians." *New York Times*, August 2, 1992, sec. 10, p. 1.

Poust, Mary Anne. "Old and New: Sacred Heart of Jesus Parish Has Been a West Side Fixture for 125 Years." *Catholic New York Online.* Available at: cny.org/archive/ft/ft010302.htm.

"Predicts New Type of Church Building." *New York Times,* June 28, 1926, p. 20.

Price, C. Matlack. "The Chapel of the Intercession, New York City." *Architectural Record,* June 1914, pp. 527–543.

Purdum, Todd S. "Prayer and Praise Honor New Mayor." *New York Times,* January 1, 1990, p. 29.

Radomsky, Rosalie R. "Postings / $5 Million Renovation Begun at Serbian Orthodox Cathedral of St. Sava: For Landmark Manhattan Church, a Restoration." *New York Times,* April 19, 1998, sec. 11, p. 1.

——. "Postings / New Sanctuary to Hold 1,200 Worshipers: $4.5 Million Renovation for a Church in Harlem." *New York Times,* February 5, 1995, sec. 9, p. 1.

——. "Postings / A $600,000 Restoration-Renovation of a Church Interior: A New, Brighter, Palette at St. Jean Baptiste." *New York Times,* February 8, 1998, sec. 11, p. 1.

Ramirez, Anthony. "Making It Work / The Threatened Bells of St. Martin's." *New York Times,* June 7, 1998, sec. 14, p. 3.

Ratliff, Ben. "John G. Gensel, 80, the Pastor to New York's Jazz Community." *New York Times,* February 8, 1998, p. 42.

Rattner, Selma. "Renwick's Design for Grace Church: Religious Doctrine and the Gothic Revival." Master's thesis, Columbia University, 1977.

"Reformed Tipplers Open a Clubhouse." *New York Times,* December 24, 1944, p. 26.

"Religious News and Views / Flurry in Church Property Due to Railroad Development." *New York Times,* January 18, 1902, p. 10.

"Renovated Church Rededicated Here." *New York Times,* December 1, 1952, p. 26.

"Rev. Ike Welcomes You to the Church Under the Prayer Tower." *Miracles Right Now! Magazine,* no. 070599 (1999): 14.

Rice, Andrew. "Ministries at War." *New York Observer,* March 12, 2001, p. 29.

Riley, Clayton. "The Golden Gospel of Reverend Ike." *New York Times Magazine,* March 3, 1975, p. 12.

Robinson, Douglas. "Fugitive Priest Seized in Rectory." *New York Times,* April 22, 1970, p. 64.

Rothstein, Edward. "Amid Grandeur, a Subtle Palette." *New York Times,* April 29, 1993, p. C17.

Rothstein, Mervyn. "The Hellinger Theater Is Leased to a Church." *New York Times,* February 8, 1989, p. C20.

——. "Real Estate / Library Is Transformed into Synagogue's Home." *New York Times,* October 8, 1997, p. B6.

Rule, Sheila. "In Harlem, a Visitor Talks of Joy and Hope." *New York Times*, October 3, 1979, sec. 2, p. 6.

"Russian Prelate Dies of a Stroke." *New York Times*, March 18, 1934, p. 35.

St. Malachy's Catholic Church–The Actors' Chapel [pamphlet]. New York: St. Malachy's–The Actors' Chapel, n.d.

St. Vincent Ferrer, a Church for All Seasons [pamphlet]. New York: Church of St. Vincent Ferrer, n.d.

Saxon, Wolfgang. "John M. Corridan, 73, the 'Waterfront Priest.'" *New York Times*, July 3, 1984, p. B8.

———. "The Rev. John Howard Johnson, Religious and Civic Leader, 98." *New York Times*, May 25, 1995, p. B16.

———. "Thomas Kilgore Jr., 84: Led 2 Baptist Groups." *New York Times*, February 10, 1998, p. D22.

Schneider, Daniel B. "F.Y.I. / Out-of-the-Way Saint." *New York Times*, May 23, 1999, sec. 14, p. 2.

Schneider, Walter S., and Henry B. Herts. "The Temple B'nai Jeshurun." *Architecture*, January 1920, pp. 18–19.

Schuyler, Montgomery. "Recent Church Building in New York." *Architectural Record*, June 1903, pp. 509–534.

"Seeking Roots in New York." *Architectural Review*, March 1965.

Sellers, Michael. "Reclaiming the Sacred at St. Clement's." *Episcopal New Yorker*, October–November 2000. Available at: dioceseny.org/eny/oct-nov00/stclement.html.

September 11, 2001: In Memory, in Faith, in Hope [pamphlet]. New York: Greek Orthodox Archdiocese of America, 2002.

"Shaaray Tefila to Open Temple." *New York Times*, September 19, 1959, p. 48.

Shaman, Diana. "Chinatown Housing: Condo Project to Pay for a New Church." *New York Times*, January 18, 1991, p. A24.

Shenon, Philip. "A New Era for Historic St. Mark's in the Bowery." *New York Times*, September 26, 1983, p. B1.

A Short History of the Church of Saint Mary the Virgin, New York City [pamphlet]. New York: Church of Saint Mary the Virgin, 1997.

The Shrine of St. Elizabeth Ann Seton, Home of America's First Native Born Saint [pamphlet]. New York: Shrine of St. Elizabeth Ann Seton, n.d.

Siegal, Nina. "A Street's Baptismal Waters Touch Hundreds in East Harlem." *New York Times*, August 7, 2000, p. B5.

Simpson, A. B. "The Beginnings of the Work of the Alliance." *Communicate* 6, no. 3: 2–3.

Sloan, Julie L., and James L. Yarnall. "John La Farge and the Judson Memorial Church." *Antiques*, February 1998, pp. 300–309.

Smith, Richard T. W. "Fighters in the World's Battle for the Triumph of God's Kingdom on Earth." *Colored American Magazine*, December 3, 1907.

Sobler, Alix. "East Side Shuls Embark on Renovations." *Forward*, July 3, 1998, p. 9.

Solomon, Elias L. *The Story of Shaare Zedek* [pamphlet]. New York: Congregation Shaare Zedek, n.d.

Sontag, Deborah. "Canonizing a Slave: Saint or Uncle Tom?" *New York Times*, February 23, 1992, p. 1.

"Soon to Have a New Temple." *New York Times*, July 13, 1893, p. 9.

"Spellman Blesses New St. Andrew's." *New York Times*, December 1, 1939, p. 14.

Stein, Clarence S. "The Problem of the Temple and Its Solution." *Architectural Forum*, February 1930, pp. 155–168.

Steinfels, Peter. "For New York Muslims, a Soaring Dome Is Ready." *New York Times*, April 16, 1991, p. B1.

Stevens, Austin. "Old St. Nicholas Goes to Wrecker." *New York Times*, September 16, 1949, p. 29.

Taylor, Walter A. "A Criticism of the Riverside Church, New York." *American Architect*, June 1931, pp. 32–72.

"Temple Stone Laid by Ansche Chesed." *New York Times*, September 19, 1927, p. 17.

Thomas, Ned P. "Various Times and Sundry Places: Buildings Used by the LDS Church in Manhattan." *New York LDS Historian* 3, no. 1 (2000): 1–7.

"A Times Square Church Gathers Rave Reviews." *New York Times*, November 6, 1988, p. 46.

"Times Square Church Razed for Parking Lot." *New York Herald Tribune*, November 22, 1939.

"Topics of The Times / Churches Under a Cover." *New York Times*, July 6, 1926, p. 20.

Traub, James. "The Road to Mecca." *New York*, June 24, 1991, pp. 36–43.

"23-Story Church and Hotel Edifice for Broadway." *Real Estate Record and Builders Guide*, June 25, 1927, p. 7.

"$2,840,000 Edifice to Combine Church and Hotel." *Real Estate Record and Builders Guide*, February 11, 1928, p. 11.

"An Ultramodern Church Is Going Up in Harlem." *New York Times*, March 19, 1967, sec. 8, p.1.

Vecsey, George. "A Church Goes Co-op to Survive." *New York Times*, April 24, 1978, p. B1.

———. "Citicorp Towers over St. Peter's but the Church Is Not in Shadow." *New York Times*, October 16, 1977, p. 52.

———. "Norman Vincent Peale, Preacher of Gospel Optimism, Dies at 95." *New York Times*, December 26, 1993, p. 40.

"'Village' Church Rebuilding After Fire." *New York Times*, December 10, 1972, p. 63.

Wadler, Joyce. "At Historic Temple, a Joyous Revival." *New York Times*, September 10, 2001, p. B1.

Waggoner, Walter H. "Rabbi Mordecai Kaplan Dies: Leader of Reconstructionists." *New York Times*, November 9, 1983, p. B7.

Wakin, Daniel J. "Chapel and Refuge Struggles to Define Role." *New York Times*, November 28, 2002, p. B1.

——. "A Church's Fate, a Diocese's Plight: New York Catholics Reassess Where Parishes Should Be." *New York Times*, July 1, 2003, p. B1.

——. "Killed on 9/11, Fire Chaplain Becomes Larger than Life." *New York Times*, September 27, 2002, p. A1.

——. "Latino Church Greets Its New Home with a Procession of the Faithful." *New York Times*, April 14, 2003, p. F1.

——. "Memories Chiseled in a Cathedral's Stone." *New York Times*, February 23, 2001, p. A1.

——. "Modernization vs. Tradition as Egan Halts a Renovation." *New York Times*, March 30, 2002, p. B1.

——. "Mormons Plan a Temple Opposite Lincoln Center." *New York Times*, August 9, 2002, p. B3.

——. "Reprieve for Piece of Jewish Soul: Lower East Side Congregants Save Their Synagogue." *New York Times*, December 6, 2002, p. B1.

"Walker Urges Tolerance." *New York Times*, September 8, 1928, p. 8.

A Walking Tour of Saint Thomas Church [pamphlet]. New York: Saint Thomas Church, n.d.

Wicklein, John. "Churches Scored by a Developer." *New York Times*, November 22, 1962, p. 31.

Wile, Thomas. *A Brief History of the French Church of Saint-Esprit* [pamphlet]. New York: French Church du Saint-Esprit, n.d.

Williams, Lena. "Imam's Progress, Secular and Sacred: Guiding a Harlem Congregation Past Crises of Debt and Faith." *New York Times*, February 15, 1996, p. B1.

Williams, Monte. "Midtown Soup Kitchen Serves Its Last." *New York Times*, March 31, 2001, p. B3.

Witchel, Alex. "At Work With / Sharon Kleinbaum: 'Luckiest Rabbi in America' Holds Faith amid Hate." *New York Times*, May 5, 1993, p. C1.

Yardley, Jim. "Rabbi Promises to Rebuild Synagogue Damaged by Fire." *New York Times*, August 30, 1998, sec. 1, p. 29.

Selected Web Sites

All Souls Church	allsoulsnyc.org
Atlantic Division, Lutheran Church–Missouri Synod	ad-lcms.org
Bethel Gospel Assembly	bethelgospelassembly.org
B'nai Jeshurun, Congregation	bj.org
Catholic New York	cny.org
Childs Memorial Temple Church of God in Christ	members.aol.com/ cmtcogic/history.htm

Christ and St. Stephen's Church	csschurch.org
Christ the Savior Orthodox Church	oca.org
Civic Center Synagogue	civiccentersynagogue.org
Delancey, Iglesia Adventista	tagnet.org/spanish
del Séptimo Día	delancey
Eldridge Street Project	eldridgestreet.org
Emanu-El, Congregation	emanuelnyc.org
Episcopal New Yorker	dioceseny.org
Fifth Avenue Presbyterian Church	fapc.org
Fifth Avenue Synagogue	fifthavenuesynagogue.org
First Chinese Presbyterian Church	fcpc.org
First Presbyterian Church	firstpresnyc.org
Fourth Universalist Society	fourthuniversalist.org
Greater Refuge Temple	netministries.org
Harlem churches	harlemchurches.com
Holy Apostles, Church of the	holyapostlesnyc.org
Holy See	vatican.va
Holy Trinity, Archdiocesan	thecathedral.goarch.org
Cathedral of the	
Holy Trinity Church (Inwood)	holytrinityinwood.org
Incarnation, Church	churchoftheincarnation.
of the (Episcopal)	org
Kehilath Jacob, Congregation	carlebachshul.org
Lincoln Square Synagogue	lss.org
Little Church Around the Corner	littlechurch.org
/ Transfiguration, Church of the	
Macedonia, Iglesia Pentecostal	macedoniachurch.net
Madison Avenue	mapc.com
Presbyterian Church	
Manhattan Church of Christ	manhattanchurch.org
Marble Collegiate Church	marblechurch.org
Metropolitan Community	mccny.org
Church of New York	
New York Chinese Alliance Church	ycac.org
New York City Department	nyc.gov/html/dob
of Buildings / Building	/html/bis.html
Information System	
Or Zarua, Congregation	orzarua.org
Our Saviour's Atonement	nidial.com/~osa
Lutheran Church	
Pilgrim Cathedral of Harlem	pilgrimharlem.org
Place Matters	placematters.net
Primera Iglesia Bautista de	siervo.com/pibheny
Habla Española	

Ramakrishna-Vivekananda Center   ramakrishna.org

Resurrection, Church   resurrectionnyc.org
of the (Episcopal)

St. Cecilia, Church of   east-harlem.com/
    stcecili.htm

St. George Ukrainian   brama.com/stgeorge
Catholic Church

St. Ignatius of Antioch, Church of   saintignatiusnyc.org

St. Jean Baptiste Roman   sjbrcc.org
Catholic Church

St. John the Divine,   stjohndivine.org
Cathedral Church of

St. Mark's Church in-the-Bowery   saintmarkschurch.org

St. Michael's Episcopal Church   saintmichaelschurch.org

St. Peter's Church (Lutheran)   saintpeters.org

St. Sava Serbian   members.aol.
Orthodox Cathedral   com/saintsava

St. Thomas Church   saintthomaschurch.org

St. Thomas the Apostle Liberal   stthomaslcchurch.org
Catholic Church

Stephen Wise Free Synagogue   swfs.org

Trinity Presbyterian Church /   members.tripod.com/
Rauschenbusch Memorial   ~trinity.nyc
United Church of Christ

Washington Square United   wsumc.org
Methodist Church

West End Collegiate Church   westendchurch.org

Works Progress Administration   home.att.net
(WPA), Federal Writers' Project,   /~JGSNYCem/
Survey of State and Local   synagogues.htm
Historical Records (1939),
Church Records Jewish—
Synagogue

Zen Studies Society   daibosatsu.org

Respondents to October 2002 Questionnaire

Adas Yisroel Anshe Mezeritz, Congregation

All Saints Church (Roman Catholic)

Amor, Poder y Gracia, Iglesia de Dios Pentecostal

Annunciation, Greek Orthodox Church of the

Beth Israel West Side Jewish Center

Buen Vecino, Primera Iglesia Evangélica Presbiteriana el

Christ Temple of the Apostolic Faith

Christ the Savior Orthodox Church
Crucifixion, Church of the
East End Temple
East Fifty-fifth Conservative Synagogue
First Alliance Church
First Corinthian Baptist Church
First Hungarian Reformed Church
Gospel Temple Church of America
Gustavus Adolphus, Evangelical Lutheran Church of
Hermosa, Iglesia Cristiana la
Incarnation, Church of the (Roman Catholic)
Macedonia, Iglesia Pentecostal
Manhattan Church of Christ
Mesivtha Tifereth Jerusalem
Metro Baptist Church
Monte Sion, Iglesia Cristiana
Mount Calvary Baptist Church
Mount Neboh Baptist Church
New Mount Zion Baptist Church
New York United Sabbath Day Adventist Church
Ohab Zedek, Congregation
Old Broadway Synagogue
Our Lady Queen of Angels, Church of
Our Lady Queen of Martyrs Church
Park Avenue Christian Church
Ramakrishna-Vivekananda Center
Resurrection, Church of the (Roman Catholic)
Rock Church
St. Aloysius, Church of
St. Andrew's Episcopal Church
St. Brigid, Church of
St. James Presbyterian Church
SS. Kiril and Methodi Bulgarian Eastern Orthodox Diocesan Cathedral
St. Mark the Evangelist, Church of
St. Mark's United Methodist Church
St. Nicholas of Myra Orthodox Church
St. Thomas the Apostle, Church of
Salem United Methodist Church
Second St. John Baptist Church
Tercera Iglesia Cristiana (Discípulos de Cristo)
Third Church of Christ, Scientist
Upper Madison Avenue United Methodist Church
Washington Heights, Iglesia Pentecostal de
Washington Square United Methodist Church

ARCHITECTURE AND BUILDING
Books and Bound Volumes

Adams, Michael Henry, with photographs by Paul Rocheleau. *Harlem, Lost and Found: An Architectural and Social History, 1765–1915*. New York: Monacelli, 2002.

Alpern, Andrew. *The New York Apartment Houses of Rosario Candela and James Carpenter*. New York: Acanthus, 2001.

Alpern, Andrew, and Seymour Durst. *Holdouts!* New York: McGraw-Hill, 1984.

Atlas of the Borough of Manhattan, City of New York. Philadelphia: Bromley, 1921.

Blake, Peter, ed. *An American Synagogue for Today and Tomorrow*. New York: Union of American Hebrew Congregations, 1954.

Burnham, Alan, ed. *New York Landmarks: A Study and Index of Architecturally Notable Structures in Greater New York*. Middletown, Conn.: Wesleyan University Press, 1963.

Chase, W. Parker. *New York: The Wonder City*. New York: Wonder City, 1931.

Cram, Ralph Adams, ed. *American Church Building of Today*. New York: Architectural, 1929.

Diamonstein, Barbaralee. *The Landmarks of New York III*. New York: Abrams, 1998.

Dolkart, Andrew S. *Guide to New York City Landmarks*. 2d ed. New York: Wiley, 1998.

——. *Morningside Heights: A History of Its Architecture and Development*. New York: Columbia University Press, 1998.

Dolkart, Andrew S., and Gretchen S. Sorin. *Touring Historic Harlem: Four Walks in Northern Manhattan*. New York: New York Landmarks Conservancy, 1997.

Dripps, Matthew. *Plan of New York, from the Battery to Spuyten Duyvil Creek*. New York, 1867.

Dunlap, David W. *On Broadway: A Journey Uptown over Time*. New York: Rizzoli, 1990.

Early, James. *Romanticism and American Architecture*. New York: Barnes, 1965.

Editors of *Architectural Record*. *Religious Buildings*. New York: McGraw-Hill, 1979.

Francis, Dennis Steadman. *Architects in Practice, New York City, 1840–1900*. New York: Committee for the Preservation of Architectural Records, 1980.

Gayle, Margot, and Michele Cohen. *The Art Commission and the Municipal Art Society Guide to Manhattan's Outdoor Sculpture*. New York: Prentice Hall, 1988.

Goldberger, Paul. *The City Observed: New York, a Guide to the Architecture of Manhattan*. New York: Random House, 1979.

Goldstone, Harmon H., and Martha Dalrymple. *History Preserved: A Guide to New York City Landmarks and Historic Districts.* New York: Simon and Schuster, 1974.

Gray, Christopher. *Changing New York: The Architectural Scene.* New York: Dover, 1992.

Hall, Ben M. *The Best Remaining Seats: The Story of the Golden Age of the Movie Palace.* New York: Bramhall House, 1961.

Hamlin, Talbot. *Greek Revival Architecture in America: Being an Account of Important Trends in American Architecture and American Life Prior to the War Between the States.* New York: Oxford University Press, 1944.

The Heritage of New York: Historic-Landmark Plaques of the New York Community Trust. New York: Fordham University Press, 1970.

A History of Real Estate, Building and Architecture in New York City. Reprint. New York: Arno, 1967

Huxtable, Ada Louise. *Classic New York: Georgian Gentility to Greek Elegance.* Garden City, N.Y.: Doubleday, 1964.

The Investors' Map of Manhattan. New York: Rafalsky, 1910.

Landau, Sarah Bradford. *Edward T. and William A. Potter: American Victorian Architects.* New York: Garland, 1979.

Levy, Florence N. *Art in New York: A Guide to Things Worth Seeing.* New York: Municipal Art Society, 1935.

Lowe, David Garrard. *Stanford White's New York.* New York: Doubleday, 1992.

Manhattan Land Book. New York: Bromley, 1934.

Manhattan Land Book of the City of New York. New York: Bromley, 1970.

Miniature Atlas of the Borough of Manhattan in One Volume. New York: Hyde, 1912.

Newton, Roger Hale. *Town & Davis Architects: Pioneers in American Revivalist Architecture, 1812–1870.* New York: Columbia University Press, 1942.

Pierson, William H., Jr. *American Buildings and Their Architects.* Vol. 2, *Technology and the Picturesque.* New York: Oxford University Press, 1978.

Reynolds, Donald Marton. *The Architecture of New York City, Histories and Views of Important Structures, Sites and Symbols.* New York: Macmillan, 1984.

Robinson, Cervin, and Rosemarie Haag Bletter. *Skyscraper Style: Art Deco, New York.* New York: Oxford University Press, 1975.

Robson, John William, ed. *A Guide to Columbia University, with Some Account of Its History and Traditions.* New York: Columbia University Press, 1937.

Rorimer, James J. *The Cloisters.* 3d ed. New York: Metropolitan Museum of Art, 1963.

Ruttenbaum, Steven. *Mansions in the Clouds: The Skyscraping Palazzi of Emery Roth.* New York: Balsam, 1986.

Sanborn Manhattan Land Book of the City of New York. Weehawken, N.J.: First American Real Estate Solutions, 1999.

Schuyler, Montgomery. *American Architecture, and Other Writings.* Edited by William H. Jordy and Ralph Coe. Vol. 1. Cambridge, Mass.: Belknap, 1961.

Shanor, Rebecca Read. *The City that Never Was: Two Hundred Years of Fantastic and Fascinating Plans that Might Have Changed the Face of New York City.* New York: Viking, 1988.

Silver, Nathan. *Lost New York.* Boston: Houghton Mifflin, 1967.

Smith, G. E. Kidder. *The Architecture of the United States.* Vol. 1, *New England and the Mid-Atlantic States.* Garden City, N.Y.: Anchor, 1981.

Stern, Robert A. M., Gregory Gilmartin, and John Massengale. *New York 1900: Metropolitan Architecture and Urbanism, 1890–1915.* New York: Rizzoli, 1983.

Stern, Robert A. M., Gregory Gilmartin, and Thomas Mellins. *New York 1930: Architecture and Urbanism Between the Two World Wars.* New York: Rizzoli, 1987.

Stern, Robert A. M., Thomas Mellins, and David Fishman. *New York 1880: Architecture and Urbanism in the Gilded Age.* New York: Monacelli, 1999.

——. *New York 1960: Architecture and Urbanism Between the Second World War and the Bicentennial.* New York: Monacelli, 1995.

Tucci, Douglass Shand. *Ralph Adams Cram: American Medievalist.* Boston: Boston Public Library, 1975.

Upjohn, Everard M. *Richard Upjohn: Architect and Churchman.* New York: Columbia University Press, 1939.

Ward, James. *Architects in Practice, New York City, 1900–1940.* New York: Committee for the Preservation of Architectural Records, 1989.

White, Norval, and Elliot Willensky. *AIA Guide to New York City.* 4th ed. New York: Crown, 2000.

Willensky, Elliot, and Norval White. *AIA Guide to New York City.* 3d ed. New York: Harcourt Brace Jovanovich, 1988.

Wischnitzer, Rachel. *Synagogue Architecture in the United States: History and Interpretation.* Philadelphia: Jewish Publication Society of America, 1955.

Withey, Henry F., and Elsie Rathburn Withey. *Biographical Dictionary of American Architects (Deceased).* Los Angeles: Hennessey & Ingalls, 1970.

Periodicals, Reports, and Pamphlets

"Bertram G. Goodhue Dies Suddenly at 55." *New York Times,* April 24, 1924, p. 19.

Cram, Ralph Adams. "A Note on Architectural Style." *Architectural Review,* September 1905, pp. 181–183.

De Vries, Susan. "Kehila Kedosha Janina" [National Register of Historic Places Registration Form], July 15, 1999.

Eidlitz, Leopold. "The Vicissitudes of Architecture." *Architectural Record*, April–June 1892, p. 476.

New York City Landmarks Preservation Commission. "Abyssinian Baptist Church and Community House." Designation report LP-1851, July 13, 1993.

———. "Actors Studio." Designation report LP-1814, February 19, 1991.

———. "Anshe Slonim Synagogue." Designation report LP-1440, February 10, 1987.

———. "Audubon Terrace Historic District." Designation report LP-1001, January 9, 1979.

———. "Chelsea Historic District." Designation report LP-0666, September 15, 1970.

———. "Church of St. Ignatius Loyola." Designation report LP-0431, March 4, 1969.

———. "Church of St. Paul and St. Andrew." Designation report LP-1126, November 24, 1981.

———. "Church of St. Vincent Ferrer." Designation report LP-0416, February 28, 1967.

———. "Church of the Incarnation and Parish House." Designation report LP-1046, September 11, 1979.

———. "Eldridge Street Synagogue." Designation report LP-1107, July 8, 1980.

———. "The Free Church of Saint Mary-the-Virgin." Designation report LP-1562, December 19, 1989.

———. "Friends Meeting House and Friends Seminary." Designation report LP-0241, December 9, 1969.

———. "Gramercy Park Historic District." Designation report LP-0251, September 20, 1966.

———. "Greenwich Village Historic District." Designation report LP-0489, 2 vols., April 29, 1969.

———. "Hamilton Heights Historic District." Designation report LP-0872, November 26, 1974.

———. "Landmarks Commission Designates Riverside Church and Two Other Manhattan Buildings." News release, May 16, 2000.

———. "Landmarks Commission Designates Two Harlem Churches as N.Y.C. Landmarks." News release, March 8, 1994.

———. "Manhattan Survey." June 20, 1986.

———. "Mark Hellinger Theater." Designation report LP-1339, November 17, 1987.

———. "Metropolitan Baptist Church." Designation report LP-1134, February 3, 1981.

——. "Mother African Methodist Episcopal Zion Church." Designation report LP-1849, July 13, 1993.

——. "Mount Morris Park Historic District." Designation report LP-0452, November 3, 1971.

——. "Mt. Neboh Synagogue." Designation report LP-1272, February 9, 1982.

——. "New York Society for Ethical Culture." Designation report LP-0831, July 23, 1974.

——. "Old St. Patrick's Cathedral." Designation report LP-0187, June 21, 1966.

——. "Our Lady of Lourdes Roman Catholic Church." Designation report LP-0892, July 22, 1975.

——. "Park East Synagogue." Designation report LP-1056, January 29, 1980.

——. "Saint Cecilia's Church." Designation report LP-0933, September 14, 1976.

——. "Saint Marks-in-the-Bowery." Designation report LP-0229, April 19, 1966.

——. "St. Bartholomew's Church and Community House." Designation report LP-0275, March 16, 1967.

——. "St. Mark's Historic District. Designation report LP-0250, January 14, 1969.

——. "St. Michael's Chapel of Old St. Patrick's Cathedral." Designation report LP-0961, July 12, 1977.

——. "St. Nicholas Russian Orthodox Cathedral." Designation report LP-0834, December 18, 1973.

——. "St. Philip's Protestant Episcopal Church." Designation report LP-1846, July 13, 1993.

——. "Stuyvesant Square Historic District." Designation report LP-0893, September 23, 1975.

——. "The Synod of Bishops of the Russian Orthodox Church Outside of Russia." Designation report LP-0438, January 14, 1969.

——. "Towers Nursing Home." Designation report LP-0938, August 17, 1976.

——. "Treadwell Farm Historic District." Designation report LP-0536, December 13, 1967.

——. "Trinity School and the Former St. Agnes Parish House." Designation report LP-1659, August 1, 1989.

——. "Upper East Side Historic District." Designation report LP-1051, May 19, 1981.

——. "Upper West Side/Central Park West Historic District." Designation report LP-1647, April 24, 1990.

"Notable Group of Artistic Buildings." *New York Times*, January 28, 1910, sec. 10, p. 12.

Schuyler, Montgomery. "The Old 'Greek Revival'—Part IV." *American Architect*, May 3, 1911, pp. 163–168.

———. "The Romanesque Revival in New York." *Architectural Record*, July–September 1891, pp. 7–38.

———. "The Works of Messrs. Barney and Chapman." *Architectural Record*, September 1904, pp. 207–296.

———. "The Works of R. H. Robertson." *Architectural Record*, October–December 1896, pp. 184–219.

West, Edward. "Architectural Revivalism." *Faith & Form* 15 (1980): 22–25.

HISTORY AND DESCRIPTION

Anbinder, Tyler. *Five Points: The 19th-Century New York City Neighborhood that Invented Tap Dance, Stole Elections, and Became the World's Most Notorious Slum*. New York: Free Press, 2001.

Anderson, Jervis. *This Was Harlem: A Cultural Portrait, 1900–1950*. New York: Farrar, Straus and Giroux, 1982

Appletons' Dictionary of New York and Its Vicinity. New York: Appleton, 1888.

Appleton's Dictionary of New York and Its Vicinity. New York: Appleton, 1902.

Asia Society. *Asia in New York City: A Cultural Travel Guide*. Emeryville, Calif.: Avalon, 2000.

Belden, E. Porter. *New-York: Past, Present and Future*. New York: Putnam, 1849.

Bendiner, Elmer. *The Bowery Man*. New York: Nelson, 1961.

Bercovici, Konrad. *Around the World in New York*. New York: Century, 1924.

Blunt, Edmund M. *Blunt's Stranger's Guide to the City of New-York*. New York: Blunt, 1817.

Brown, Henry Collins, ed. *Valentine's Manual of Old New York, 1920*. New York: Valentine's Manual, 1919.

———. *Valentine's Manual of Old New York, 1921*. New York: Valentine's Manual, 1920.

———. *Valentine's Manual of Old New York, 1922*. New York: Valentine's Manual, 1921.

———. *Valentine's Manual of Old New York, 1925*. New York: Museum of the City of New York, 1924.

———. *Valentine's Manual of Old New York, 1926*. New York: Valentine's Manual, 1925.

———. *Valentine's Manual of the City of New York for 1916-17*. New York: Valentine, 1916.

———. *Valentine's Manual of the City of New York, 1917-18*. New York: Old Colony, 1917.

Browne, Junius Henri. *The Great Metropolis, a Mirror of New York*. Hartford, Conn.: American, 1868.

Burrows, Edwin G., and Mike Wallace. *Gotham: A History of New York City to 1898.* New York: Oxford University Press, 1999.

Casey, William Van Etten, and Philip Nobile, eds. *The Berrigans.* New York: Praeger, 1971.

Cross, Wilbur, and Ann Novotny. *White House Weddings.* New York: McKay, 1967.

Dakin, James H., and Theodore S. Fay. *Views in New-York and Its Environs: From Accurate, Characteristic and Picturesque Drawings, Taken on the Spot, Expressly for This Work.* London: Rich, 1831.

Davidson, Bruce. *East 100th Street.* Los Angeles: St. Ann's, 2003.

Delaney, Edmund T. *New York's Greenwich Village.* Barre, Mass.: Barre, 1968.

——. *New York's Turtle Bay, Old and New.* Barre, Mass.: Barre, 1965.

Diehl, Lorraine B. *The Late, Great Pennsylvania Station.* New York: American Heritage, 1985.

Disturnell, John. *New York as It Was and as It Is: Giving an Account of the City from Its Settlement to the Present Time.* New York: Van Nostrand, 1876.

Dodson, Howard, Christopher Moore, and Roberta Yancy. *The Black New Yorkers: The Schomburg Illustrated Chronology.* New York: Wiley, 2000.

Donoghue, Terry. *An Event on Mercer Street: A Brief History of the YMCA of the City of New York.* New York: Privately printed, 1951.

East Harlem Historical Association. *Rediscovering East Harlem* [illustrated and annotated map]. New York: Union Settlement Association, 1999.

Federal Writers' Project. *New York City Guide.* American Guide Series. New York: Random House, 1939. [More commonly known as the *WPA Guide*]

Fleischman, Harry. *Norman Thomas, a Biography: 1884–1968.* New York: Norton, 1964.

Garmey, Stephen. *Gramercy Park: An Illustrated History of a New York Neighborhood.* New York: Rutledge/Balsam, 1984.

The Great Metropolis, or Guide to New-York. Vol. 4, *1848.* New York: Doggett, 1847.

Haley, Alex, and Malcolm X. *The Autobiography of Malcolm X.* New York: Ballantine, 1992.

Hart, Harold H. *Hart's Guide to New York City.* New York: Hart, 1964.

Hemstreet, Charles. *Nooks and Corners of Old New York.* New York: Scribner, 1899.

Henderson, Mary C. *The City and the Theatre: New York Playhouses from Bowling Green to Times Square.* Clifton, N.J.: White, 1973.

Hone, Philip. *The Diary of Philip Hone, 1828–1851.* Edited by Allan Nevins. 2 vols. New York: Dodd, Mead, 1927.

Hurewitz, Daniel. *Stepping Out: Nine Walks Through New York City's Gay and Lesbian Past.* New York: Holt, 1997.

Ingersoll, Ernest. *Rand, McNally & Co.'s Handy Guide to New York City.* 21st ed. Chicago: Rand, McNally, 1907.

Israelowitz, Oscar. *The Lower East Side Guide.* 3d ed. New York: Israelowitz, 1988.

Jackson, Kenneth T., ed. *The Encyclopedia of New York City.* New Haven, Conn.: Yale University Press, 1995.

Johnson, James Weldon. *Black Manhattan.* Reprint. New York: Da Capo, 1991.

King, Moses. *King's Handbook of New York City: An Outline History and Description of the American Metropolis.* 2d ed. Boston: King, 1893.

Kouwenhoven, John A. *The Columbia Historical Portrait of New York: An Essay in Graphic History.* Garden City, N.Y.: Doubleday, 1953.

The Ladies' Guide and City Directory for Shopping, Travel, Amusements, etc., in the City of New York. New York: Putnam, 1885

Lee, Henry J. *The Brooklyn Daily Eagle Almanac 1925.* New York: Brooklyn Daily Eagle, 1925.

Leeds, Mark. *Passport's Guide to Ethnic New York: A Complete Guide to the Many Faces and Cultures of New York.* Lincolnwood, Ill.: Passport, 1991.

Limmer, Ruth. *Six Heritage Tours of the Lower East Side.* New York: New York University Press, 1997.

Little, Stuart W. *Off-Broadway: The Prophetic Theater.* New York: Coward, McCann & Geoghegan, 1972.

Macoy, Robert. *How to See New York and Its Environs, 1776–1876: A Complete Guide and Hand-book of Useful Information, Collected from the Latest Reliable Sources.* New York: Macoy, 1876.

McManus, Edgar J. *A History of Negro Slavery in New York.* Syracuse, N.Y.: Syracuse University Press, 1966.

Miller, James. *Miller's New York as It Is, or Stranger's Guide-Book to the Cities of New York, Brooklyn and Adjacent Places.* New York: Miller, 1866.

Moscow, Henry. *The Street Book: An Encyclopedia of Manhattan's Street Names and Their Origins.* New York: Hagstrom, 1978.

Mott, Hopper Striker. *The New York of Yesterday: A Descriptive Narrative of Old Bloomingdale.* New York: Putnam, 1908.

Ottley, Roi, and William Weatherby, eds. *The Negro in New York: An Informal Social History.* New York: New York Public Library, 1967.

A Picture of New-York in 1851: With a Short Account of Places in Its Vicinity: Designed as a Guide to Citizens and Strangers, with Numerous Engravings and a Map of the City. New York: Francis, 1851.

Pierce, Carl Horton. *New Harlem Past and Present: The Story of Amazing Civic Wrong, Now at Last to Be Righted.* New York: New Harlem, 1903.

Powell, Adam Clayton, Jr. *Adam by Adam.* New York: Dial, 1971.

Reynolds, John J., and Thomas D. Houchin. *A Directory for Spanish-Speaking New York/Directorio Hispano Para Nueva York.* New York: Quadrangle, 1971.

Richmond, J. F. *New-York and Its Institutions, 1609–1872: A Library of Information, Pertaining to the Great Metropolis, Past and Present.* New York: Treat, 1871.

Rider, Fremont, ed. *Rider's New York City: A Guide-Book for Travelers.* 2d ed. New York: Holt, 1923.

Rosenzweig, Roy, and Elizabeth Blackmar. *The Park and the People: A History of Central Park.* Ithaca, N.Y.: Cornell University Press, 1992.

Seidler, Murray B. *Norman Thomas, Respectable Rebel.* Syracuse, N.Y.: Syracuse University Press, 1967.

Shopsin, William C., and Mosette Glaser Broderick. *The Villard Houses: Life Story of a Landmark.* New York: Viking, 1980.

Sloane, Eric, and Edward Anthony. *Mr. Daniels and the Grange.* New York: Funk & Wagnalls, 1968.

Smith, Alfred E. *Up to Now.* New York: Viking, 1929.

Smith, Matthew Hale. *Sunshine and Shadow in New York.* Hartford, Conn.: Burr, 1869.

Stokes, I. N. Phelps. *The Iconography of Manhattan Island, 1498–1909: Compiled from Original Sources and Illustrated by Photo-Intaglio Reproductions of Important Maps, Plans, Views, and Documents in Public and Private Collections.* 6 vols. New York: Dodd, 1915–1928.

Strong, George Templeton. *The Diary of George Templeton Strong.* Edited by Allan Nevins and Milton Halsey Thomas. 4 vols. New York: Macmillan, 1952.

The Sun's Guide to New York: Replies to Questions Asked Every Day by the Guests and Citizens of the American Metropolis. Jersey City, N.J.: Jersey City Printing, 1892.

Tieck, William A. *Riverdale, Kingsbridge, Spuyten Duyvil: A Historical Epitome of the Northwest Bronx.* New York: Tieck, 1968.

Valentine, D. T. *Manual of the Corporation of the City of New-York, 1861.* New York: The Council, 1861.

——. *Manual of the Corporation of the City of New-York, 1865.* New York: The Council, 1865.

Wakefield, Dan. *New York in the Fifties.* Boston: Houghton Mifflin, 1992.

Walling, H. F. *The City of New York: A Complete Guide, with Descriptive Sketches of Objects and Places of Interest.* New York: Taintor, 1867.

Willis-Braithwaite, Deborah, and Rodger C. Birt. *VanDerZee: Photographer, 1886–1983.* New York: Abrams, 1993.

Wise, Stephen. *Challenging Years: The Autobiography of Stephen Wise.* New York: Putnam, 1949.

Wolfe, Gerard R. *New York, A Guide to the Metropolis: Walking Tours of Architecture and History.* 2d ed. New York: McGraw-Hill, 1994.

Wright, Carol von Pressentin. *Blue Guide: New York.* 2d ed. New York: Norton, 1991.

Zagat Survey 1997 New York City Restaurants. New York: Zagat Survey, 1996.

Zeisloft, E. Idell, ed. *The New Metropolis: Memorable Events of Three Centuries, 1600–1900.* New York: Appleton, 1899.

CREDITS AND PERMISSIONS

Photographs not otherwise credited are by the author.

HISTORICAL IMAGES

Benjamin Q. Force, *The History of the Charter Church of New York Method-ism, Eighteenth Street, 1835-1885* (New York: Phillips & Hunt, 1885): 60 [G44].

Booklet Showing Some Phases of the Work of the New York City Mission and Tract Society (New York: New York City Mission and Tract Society, n.d.): 54 [F55].

Brick Church Memorial, Containing the Discourses Delivered by Dr. Spring on the Closing of the Old Church in Beekman St., and the Opening of the New Church on Murray Hill (New York: Dodd, 1861): 31 [A1].

Christopher Gray: 253 [E21].

D. T. Valentine, *Manual of the Corporation of the City of New-York for 1858* (New York: The Council, 1858): 125 [A49].

D. T. Valentine, *Manual of the Corporation of the City of New-York, 1865* (New York: The Council, 1865): 88 [A35].

David Clarkson, *History of the Church of Zion and St. Timothy of New York, 1797-1894* (New York: Putnam, 1894): 230 [K39].

Gabriel P. Disosway, *The Earliest Churches of New York and Its Vicinity* (New York: Gregory, 1865): 36 [A9]; 118 [A20]; 159 [A11]; 183 [A14]; 229 [B62]; 264 [A44].

In This Place: A Centennial History of All Angels' Church in the Diocese of New York (New York: All Angels' Church, 1959) (Courtesy of the Rev. Milind Sojwal and Paul Johnson): 8 [M28].

James Grant Wilson, ed., *The Memorial History of the City of New-York, from Its First Settlement to the Year 1892*, vol. 1 (New York: New-York History Company, 1892): 224 [E35].

John F. Richmond, *New-York and Its Institutions, 1609-1872: A Library of Information, Pertaining to the Great Metropolis* (New York: Treat, 1872): 33 [H1]; 73 [J52]; 145 [A39].

John Gilmary Shea, *The Catholic Churches of New York City, with Sketches of Their History and Lives of the Present Pastors* (New York: Goulding, 1878): 13 [Q1]; 65 [H49]; 110 [F3]; 147 [F32]; 196 [J32]; 196 [F16]; 204 [E2]; 208 [N24]; 218 [J20]; 220 [N14]; 238 [R53]; 245 [E92]; 249 [G35]; 250 [L25].

Montgomery Schuyler, "The Works of R. H. Robertson," *Architectural Record*, October–December 1896 (Courtesy of Christopher Gray): 186 [K2].

Moses King, *King's Handbook of New York City: An Outline History and Description of the American Metropolis* (Boston: King, 1893): 34 [B10]; 134 [H15]; 172 [L9]; 185 [L33]; 186 [H25]; 195 [E70]; 255 [D18]; 259 [I33]; 266 [E42].

New York City Municipal Archives / "Tax" Department Photographs: 8 [F51]; 81 [V27]; 198 [G3]; 199 [K26].

"New-York Church Architecture," *Putnam's Monthly*, September 1853: 48 [E48]; 177 [E12].

New-York Historical Society: 6 [I50]; 12 [H54]; 12 [I6]; 14 [B18]; 21 [N46]; 28 [K13]; 28 [K14]; 29 [L27]; 48 [H6]; 55 [J37]; 61 [R43 *above*]; 62 [B33]; 62 [J39]; 103 [J48]; 103 [J49]; 106 [V17]; 112 [U8]; 194 [J41]; 232 [J25]; 243 [G33]; 260 [A45]; 262 [B29]; 270 [R27]; 272 [R28]; 278 [B25].

New-York Historical Society / Album File, New York Churches: 52 [S5]; 91 [R50]; 135 [L6]; 174 [P27]; 176 [P3]; 192 [H61]; 193 [E89]; 240 [K30].

New-York Historical Society / Album File, Thomas F. DeVoe Scrapbook: 29 [G11]; 140 [B58]; 143 [E24]; 237 [H42]; 254 [C51 *below*].

New-York Historical Society / Geographic File: 6 [E46]; 7 [H17]; 11 [L21]; 12 [B4]; 13 [E19]; 15 [C49]; 17 [E56]; 18 [I18]; 18 [H26]; 20 [E37]; 24 [E72]; 24 [G31]; 26 [A27]; 29 [E73]; 31 [N13]; 37 [K35]; 38 [B24]; 39 [L47]; 41 [G40]; 41 [G38]; 42 [B40]; 42 [H3]; 43 [J30]; 44 [L40]; 48 [E86]; 51 [H5]; 56 [H29]; 61 [R43 *below*]; 64 [L29]; 65 [H9]; 67 [C50]; 71 [B59]; 73 [B13]; 76 [A13]; 76 [A38]; 77 [J2]; 81 [B61]; 81 [J36]; 86 [X2]; 88 [E13]; 96 [J34]; 97 [H65]; 105 [H45]; 118 [A19]; 130 [J14]; 136 [H37]; 139 [S30]; 139 [Q25]; 144 [D4]; 145 [E59]; 148 [T22]; 160 [G34]; 173 [N17]; 181 [N32]; 184 [J33]; 184 [Q36]; 190 [R14]; 191 [E39 *above*]; 191 [E39 *below*]; 192 [E84]; 194 [E60]; 198 [E67]; 202 [B37]; 202 [H46]; 202 [H30]; 203 [L38]; 205 [H12]; 208 [J51]; 210 [L14]; 210 [L10]; 212 [I14]; 212 [N44]; 213 [R12]; 214 [D8]; 216 [O3 *both*]; 223 [I42]; 226 [H2]; 227 [C13]; 229 [Q2]; 231 [O22]; 233 [A26 *above*]; 239 [E10]; 241 [G43]; 241 [J35]; 242 [A2]; 242 [B43]; 242 [E76]; 246 [E74]; 247 [J8]; 254 [C51 *above*]; 256 [B19]; 257 [I51]; 258 [E23]; 263 [D1]; 264 [J55]; 265 [B7]; 266 [K33]; 272 [B8]; 277 [A32]; 278 [M6]; 284 [I21]; 285 [E66 *above*]; 287 [E32]; 291 [U16]; 293 [E81]; 293 [J46].

New-York Historical Society / George P. Hall & Son Photograph Collection: 74 [I22]; 211 [L8].

New-York Historical Society / Herman N. Liberman Photograph Collection: 15 [F35]; 22 [C7]; 30 [F17]; 46 [R42]; 63 [F22]; 67 [L36]; 85 [Q61]; 90 [O17]; 126 [I43]; 126 [E63]; 126 [F26]; 146 [C12]; 151 [M33]; 156 [E64]; 159 [V29]; 189 [B17]; 200 [G27]; 206 [E49]; 218 [J4]; 228 [E15]; 233 [I20]; 241 [J10]; 244 [H39]; 258 [O1]; 267 [J15]; 280 [F11]; 294 [Q10].

New-York Historical Society / Robert L. Bracklow Photograph Collection: 9 [M29]; 18 [I38]; 31 [J54]; 32 [H41]; 33 [K41]; 38 [I44]; 39 [K42]; 43 [K5]; 77 [E25]; 89 [I4]; 128 [E16]; 136 [H38]; 153 [W9]; 190 [B49]; 228 [I32]; 256 [O29]; 261 [H53]; 264 [G15]; 272 [G7]; 278 [I52]; 293 [I30].

Richard T. W. Smith, "Fighters in the World's Battle for the Triumph of God's Kingdom on Earth," *Colored American Magazine*, December 3, 1907 (Courtesy of the Rev. Dr. Charles A. Curtis): 152 [I9].

St. James' Church (Courtesy of Christopher Gray): 210 [L11].

Thomas De Witt, *A Discourse Delivered in the North Reformed Dutch Church (Collegiate) in the City of New-York* (New York: Board of Publication of the Reformed Protestant Dutch Church, 1857): 124 [A48].

W. Parker Chase, *New York: The Wonder City* (New York: Wonder City, 1931) (Courtesy of Barbara Cohen): 33 [V35].

INDEX

First Baptist Church of Harlem, 150
First Chinese Baptist Church, **73**
First Chinese Presbyterian Church, 74
First Christian Church of the Valley, 74
First Church of Christ, Scientist, 11, **74–75**, 80, 255
First Church of the Christian and Missionary Alliance, 73
First Church of the Disciples of Christ, 153
First Church of the Evangelical Association, **75**
First Collegiate Church of Harlem, 61, 64
First Colored Presbyterian Church (African Church), 29, 262
First Congregation Galiz Duckler Mogen Abraham, 22
First Congregational Church, 12
First Corinthian Baptist Church, 69, **75**
First German Baptist Church, 273
First German Baptist Church of Harlem, 16
First German Methodist Episcopal Church, 59, 274
First German Presbyterian Church, 15
First German Reformed Church, 72–73
First Hungarian Congregation Ohab Zedek, 162
First Hungarian Reformed Church, **75**, 227
First Mariners Methodist Episcopal Church, 67
First Methodist Protestant Church, 22
First Moravian Church, **76**, 134
First National City Bank, 241
First Presbyterian Church, 31, 63, **76–77**, 136, 184, 196, 256, 287
First Reformed Episcopal Church, 18, **77**
First Reformed Presbyterian Church, 62–63, **77**
First Roumanian-American Congregation (Congregation Shaarey Shamoyim), **78**
First Russian Baptist Church, **78**
First Sharon Baptist Church, **78–79**
First Spanish Baptist Church of Manhattan (Primera Iglesia Bautista Hispana de Manhattan), **176**
First Spanish Church, 34

First Spanish United Methodist Church (Primera Iglesia Metodista Unida Hispana), 156, **176**
First Spanish-Speaking Baptist Church of New York (Primera Iglesia Bautista de Habla Española de Nueva York), 150, **175**
First Swedish Baptist Church, 276
First Swedish Pentecostal Church, 185
First Ukrainian Assembly of God, **79**
First Union Presbyterian Church, 31, 172
First United Presbyterian Church, 264
First United Presbyterian Church of Harlem, 78
First Universalist Society, 297
First Waldensian Church, 123, 162, 163
First Wesleyan Chapel, 144
Fish, Hamilton, 58
Fish, Nicholas, 225
Fisher, Donald D., 82
Fitzgerald, E. G., 250
Five Points Mission, 42
Flagg, Ernest, 223, 225
Fleischer, Herbert, 267
Fleming, Daniel J., 116
Fletcher, Benjamin, 125
Floating Bethel Church, 26
Floating Church for Seamen, 254
Floating Church of Our Saviour, 254
Florence and Sol Shenk Synagogue, 84
Fontaine, Joan, 131
Forbes, James Alexander, Jr., 184
Forbin-Janson, comte de, 249
Ford, Butler & Oliver, 130
Fordham University Church (Bronx), 236
Fort Amsterdam, 124, 181
Fort George, Iglesia Presbiteriana, **79**
Fort Tryon Jewish Center, **79**
Fort Washington, Iglesia Adventista del Séptimo Dia, 37, **80**
Fort Washington Baptist Church, 245
Fort Washington Collegiate Church, 52, **80**, 140, 145, 292
Fort Washington Heights, Iglesia Presbiteriana, **80**
Fort Washington Presbyterian Church, 80
Fort Washington Synagogue, 176, 177
Forty-eighth Street Collegiate Church, **232**

Spring Street Presbyterian Church, **264,** 265

Springer, Jabez, 59

Springsteen & Goldhammer, 105

Stanley, Henry W., 172

Stanton Street Reformed Dutch Church, 245

Stanton Street Synagogue (Congregation B'nai Jacob Anshei Brzezan), **28–29**

Starkweather & Gibbs, 90

Steckler, Benjamin, 263

Steel Cathedral (Wright), 225

Stein, Clarence, 62

Stein, Cohen & Roth, 66

Steinback, Gustave, 28, 164, 169

Steinberg, Milton, 173

Steinmann & Cain, 249

Stelze, Charles L., 128

Stephanopoulos, George, 103

Stephanopoulos, Robert G., 103

Stephen Wise Free Synagogue, 146, 153, **265**

Stetson, Augusta Emma, 74, 255

Steuben, Friedrich Wilhelm von, 72

Stewart, A. T., 48, 164

Stilwell, William, 118

Stitt, Jesse W., 288

Stivale, William, 77, 103

Stohlmann, Carl F. E., 154

Stokes, Caroline Phelps, 238

Stokes, Isaac Newton Phelps, 238

Stokes, Olivia Egleston Phelps, 238

Stolzman, Henry, 292

Stoughton & Stoughton, 91, 138

Strangers, Church of the, 37, 256, **266**

Strasberg, Lee, 292

Streeton, George H., 93, 198, 200, 203

Strong, George Templeton, 244

Stroud, James, 77

Strzelecki, John H., 245

Stubbins, Hugh, 241

Studio 54, 226

Stuyvesant, Peter, 224

Stuyvesant Square, 58, 228

Stuyvesant Town, 44, 58, 107

Subud (Susila Budhi Dharma), 82

Subud Chelsea Center, 82

Sullivan Street Methodist Episcopal Church, 24, 192, 291

Sulzberger, Cyrus L., 270

Sung Tak Buddhist Association, 46, **266–267**

Sunshine Cinema (German Evangelical Mission Church), **84**

Sutton, Charles M., 157

Sutton Place Synagogue (Congregation Beth Hamedrash Hachodosh Talmud Torah), 163, **267**

Swamp, Church in the, 135

Swamp Church, 135, 229, 262

Swanke Hayden Connell, 71, 113

Swedenborg, Emanuel, 156

Swedenborgian (New) Church, 156

Swedish Bethesda Evangelical Church, **267**

Swedish Immanuel Congregational Church, 89

Swedish Methodist church, 130

Swedish Mission (St. Bartholomew's Church), 194

Swedish Seamen's Church, **267**

Sweet Daddy Grace (C. M. Grace), 124, 285

Swords into Plowshares (Marans), 49

Synagogue Rescue Project, 66

synagogues. See Jewish congregations

Synagogues of New York's Lower East Side (Wolfe), 46

Tachau, William, 270, 296

Tafel, Edgar, 54, 63, 77, 104, 214, 287

Taft, William Howard, 30

Taft Church, 287

Takamine, Jokichi, 32

Talman, Caroline, 247

Talmud Torah Adereth El, Congregation, **270**

Talmud Torah Anshei Marovi, Chevra (Old Broadway Synagogue), **162**

Tammany Hall, 136

Tandy, Vertner Woodson, 70, 91, 243, 284, 287

Taras Shevchenko Place, 206

Taylor, L. S., 128